Neil Young
FAQ

Series Editor: Robert Rodriguez

Neil Young FAQ

Everything Left to Know About the Iconic and Mercurial Rocker

Glen Boyd

Backbeat
Books

An Imprint of Hal Leonard Corporation

Published in 2012 by Backbeat Books
An Imprint of Hal Leonard Corporation
7777 West Bluemound Road
Milwaukee, WI 53213

Trade Book Division Editorial Offices
33 Plymouth St., Montclair, NJ 07042

The FAQ series was conceived by Robert Rodriguez and developed with Stuart Shea.

Book design by Snow Creative Services

Printed in the United States of America

Library of Congress Cataloging-in-Publication Data

Boyd, Glen.
   Neil Young FAQ : everything left to know about the iconic and mercurial rocker / Glen Boyd.
      p. cm.
   Includes bibliographical references and index.
   ISBN 978-1-61713-037-3
   1. Young, Neil, 1945– 2. Rock musicians–Miscellanea. I. Title. II. Title: Niel Young frequently asked questions.
   ML420.Y75B69 2012
   782.42166092—dc23
   [B]
                                                        2011047487

www.backbeatbooks.com

This book is lovingly dedicated to Dorothea "Miss Moo" Mootafes, who recognized and encouraged my writing talent even as I likely put several gray hairs on her head. Putting up with my antics back then alone qualifies Miss Moo for sainthood. The fact that she somehow saw a potential writer in an otherwise hell-raising teenager obsessed with rock 'n' roll was probably the first event in my young life that eventually made a book like this possible.

So, Miss Moo, this is for you.

I'd also like to dedicate this to my grandma, Theresa "Nana" Guyll, who took me to my first Neil Young concert (actually it was a CSN&Y show) as a thirteen-year-old boy. God bless you, Nana, and I hope that they have earplugs in heaven.

Contents

Foreword

For many of us, Neil Young's music has provided the soundtrack to our lives for almost as long as we can remember.

I can't say exactly when Young's music began to seep deep into my consciousness. But looking back on it now some forty years on, I can still vividly recall the exact moment when the spark of Young's music first began to flicker and burn. It all began on the morning of May 5, 1970.

The day before, on a college campus in Kent, Ohio, four students had been killed by the National Guard while protesting against the Vietnam War.

I was in the third grade at the time and couldn't really comprehend much about the world events swirling about us. As I walked into class that day, my third-grade teacher was deeply troubled and shaking her head as she stared at the front page of the day's paper.

"This is awful," she declared as she gestured toward the large photo across the top of the page. As I focused on the photo, I wasn't sure what I was looking at. It seemed to be a dead person on the ground, with a girl crying while kneeling before the body—her arms flung wide open and what appeared to be blood streaming down the pavement.

I had never seen a picture of a dead person.

"This is awful. Printing a picture like this on the front page . . . where children can see it?," the teacher intoned as my nine-year-old eyes stared, puzzled by the image.

Unknown to me at the time, immediately after the Kent State shooting (sometimes referred to as the "Kent Massacre") on May 4, 1970, Neil Young composed the song "Ohio" after looking at photos appearing in *Life* magazine and then taking a walk in the woods. Crosby, Stills, Nash, and Young went into the studio and recorded the song, which was released to radio stations shortly after the killings. Soon, the lyrics "Four dead in Ohio" became an anthem for a generation. In some parts of the country, the song was banned from playlists because of its "antiwar" and "anti-Nixon" sentiments.

Some years later, it would become widely known that "Ohio" referred to the Kent State shootings, with the lyrics "Four dead in Ohio" evoking that Pulitzer-winning image I had inadvertently seen as a young boy. But what really struck me was how the teacher had been most concerned about the printing of the photo in a family newspaper, rather than the events surrounding that tragic day in U.S. history.

David Crosby once said that Young calling Nixon's name out in the "Ohio" lyrics was "the bravest thing I ever heard." Crosby noted that at the time, it seemed like those who stood up to Nixon, like those at Kent State, were shot. "Neil Young did not seem scared at all," Crosby said.

And it is Neil Young's fearlessness to sing truth to power that I have come to admire most. Which is not to diminish my love in following his concerts, collecting his music, blogging about him, and perhaps most importantly, the camaraderie shared with fellow fans. My life is filled with these fond memories of Young's music, as I go on my very own journey through the past.

Like back to Woodstock in August 1969. No, I wasn't actually there on that culturally historic weekend on a farm in upstate New York. But my best friend's sister had the triple-disc album of the *Woodstock* film soundtrack, and I used to listen to it on her Dad's old hi-fi stereo—much to his dismay.

Or back to our very first album—Crosby, Stills, Nash, and Young's 1971 live double album *4 Way Street*. The between-song concert banter and camaraderie among the four struck me at once as clever, passionate, and humorous.

Or maybe it was back when AM top forty radio was playing "Heart of Gold" in 1972. I had never been "from Hollywood to Redwood," of course. But a drive up the California coastal highway sounded kind of cool while growing up far away on the other side of the country by the Atlantic Ocean.

Or possibly it was my first giant, outdoor stadium Crosby, Stills, Nash, and Young concert—on a blazing hot day in the summer of 1974. I was only thirteen years old at the time, but looking back, that day seems to have made quite an impression on me. Were all of those peace and love folks really the "hippies" that my parents feared so much?

But what is it about Neil Young and his music that so many miss that we fans seem to see and hear and feel?

In the parlance of our times, it's complicated to say what exactly drew us to Young's music. It seems more than just the warm, heartfelt, enigmatic, poetic lyrics. More than just the strange and often haunting vocal phrasings. More than just the gentle, folkie acoustic side, contrasted by the equally raging, wailing electric side.

The passion among Young's diehard fans—sometimes known as "Rusties"—is really what makes following his music such a joy and pleasure.

Rarely will you find as diverse a group of fans so united in their appreciation and celebration of an artist. Of course, Young is not just any artist but one of the most influential singer-songwriters ever to emerge from North America. Combining the lyrical complexity of Bob Dylan's songwriting and the emotional drama of a Bruce Springsteen concert, Young is truly one of last remaining giants of the twentieth century to still be as relevant and compelling today as he was forty years ago.

Full disclosure here. When author (and fellow music blogger) Glen Boyd asked me to help out on this book by suggesting some topic sections, proof chapters, and fact check them as he churned them out, as well as provide some materials, I was a bit hesitant. Not that I thought a *Neil Young FAQ* was a bad idea or anything. It was just thinking about the daunting task of trying to catalog the virtually uncategorizable Neil Young.

But I can say after watching Boyd's vision to comprehensively document Young's forty-plus-year career come together—all the while juggling all of the other challenges that come with following this rock-'n'-roll scene on a daily basis—*Neil Young FAQ* will hopefully be an essential reference book in your own music library. And just maybe it will provide some clues to unlocking the mysteries of Young's vast canon of work over some five decades and counting.

I've enjoyed working with Glen Boyd and all the other wonderful fans around the world who recognize, respect, and celebrate Neil Young's music. It is this global fan community that makes this all possible and such an honor to be part of.

Still hiding behind hay bales,

Thrasher
Publisher/Editor
Neil Young News Blog
http://NeilYoungNews.ThrashersWheat.org
March 2012

Acknowledgments

First and foremost to Robert Rodriguez, who somewhat amazingly found me and my work online at *Blogcritics*, and decided that he actually wanted to work with me anyway. Robert helped me immensely by guiding me through the process of pitching this project to Hal Leonard and has also remained an invaluable resource since signing on the dotted line. He is also author of his own two excellent books in this very series, *Fab Four FAQ* and *Fab Four FAQ 2.0*. Thanks, Robert!

There is also no way I could have completed this without the invaluable assistance of a guy I still know only by the name of Thrasher after all these years.

Thrasher runs what is for my money the best Internet resource bar none for all things Neil Young at his site Thrasher's Wheat (a.k.a. Neil Young News). You'll find him at http://neilyoungnews.thrasherswheat.org/.

This guy is an absolute fountain of information when it comes to Neil Young and a hell of a nice guy, too (at least for someone I've never actually met face to face and whose Christian name I have yet to learn). He was also an essential resource for this book—particularly in regard to some of the more obscure facts you'll find within these pages. There may well have been a *Neil Young FAQ* without Thrasher, but it definitely wouldn't have been anywhere near as "Neil-phyte worthy."

Donald Gibson, my good friend, fellow music editor and co-conspirator at *Blogcritics* magazine also deserves my gratitude for serving as my unofficial editor for this project. Donald graciously loaned me his expert eyes not only to spot any errors I might have missed, but was also exactly the honest, objective, no-bullshit sounding board I needed. So thank you, Donald.

Since *Neil Young FAQ* also contains numerous unique pictures and images—many of which are seen here for the first time ever—it goes without saying that the photographers and private collectors who contributed them need to be acknowledged and thanked.

Foremost amongst these would be Jeff Allen, who provided our beautiful cover shot, which Allen snapped as a teen who was fortunate enough to be in the studio audience during CSN&Y's TV taping for ABC's *Music Scene* in 1969. This amazing photo of Neil Young in full shred mode, along with a few others seen in the book, has never been published nationally until now. You can view more of Jeff's great work at http://cacheagency.com/scripts/IF/if.cgi?direct=Contributors /Jeff_Allen.

In addition to Jeff Allen's photos, never-before-seen Neil Young photos were provided by Mary Andrews, Kim Reed, Constanze Metzner, Chris Greenwood,

Ed Boutlier, Marc Chamberlain, Tony Stack, and Donald Gibson (yes, him again). My sincere thanks to all of you for these amazing photos.

The numerous images of rare, obscure, and out-of-print Neil Young LPs, 45 picture sleeves, sheet music, and memorabilia that account for more than half of those seen in *Neil Young FAQ* all come from the private collection of a single Neil Young fan, one Tom Therme. So Tom, many thanks, and be sure to alert me first if and when you ever decide to put your fabulous collection up for auction on eBay or elsewhere. Consider this my dibs on first bid.

I'd also be remiss if I didn't acknowledge and thank the rest of the good folks at *Blogcritics* magazine. BC gave me an Internet platform to get my stuff out there at a time when a lot of folks had given me up for dead as a rock journalist—resulting in a journey that eventually led me to this very book.

So many thanks to Eric Olsen, Phillip Winn, Lisa McKay, Connie Phillips, and the rest of youse guys. Thanks for providing me the medium to launch my second act as a writer. They've also got some great, and mostly undiscovered writers there, including my good friends Greg Barbrick, Jordan Richardson, El Bicho, Kit O'Toole, and others (and if I forgot you, it's probably 'cause I didn't receive your check).

Check them out at http://blogcritics.org.

To wrap up the personal thanks, let's go with Mom and Dad, all the fine folks at Backbeat Books and Hal Leonard Performing Arts Publishing Group, and of course my Lord and Savior Jesus Christ (it may not be a Grammy, but it is my first book, after all).

Now without further adieu, and as Neil himself would say, "Let's roll."

Introduction

Everybody Knows This Is Neil

By any measure, Neil Young has had one of the most remarkable careers in the history of music. At sixty-seven years old, Young has not only outlived many of his contemporaries and those artists whose music first inspired him ("From Hank to Hendrix" as one of Neil's own songs puts it), but he has also pulled off the rather amazing trick of remaining as relevant and vital as he has ever been, well into his fifth decade of making music.

In fact, Young's music continues to influence subsequent generations of young rock bands and artists—a list including, but not limited to, Nirvana's Kurt Cobain, Pearl Jam's Eddie Vedder, Sonic Youth's Thurston Moore, Radiohead's Thom Yorke, and—well, you get the idea.

Not to take anything away from the other greats of his generation, but with the possible exceptions of Bruce Springsteen and Bob Dylan, Neil Young is probably the only major rock icon from his era who has steadfastly (and quite stubbornly, many would add), followed his artistic muse without compromise, and often to his commercial detriment.

Young also continues to crank out records at a rate that would kill most artists half his age (and quite possibly nearly did back in 2005, but we'll get to all that in due course). When you figure in his solo albums, the live albums, as well as his work with Buffalo Springfield and Crosby, Stills, Nash, and Young, there have been well over fifty albums over the course of his five-decade career—and many of these have been boxed sets and multiple-disc collections.

In 2009, Neil Young released no less than three new collections—including the massive, decades-in-the-making *Archives Vol. 1* boxed set. Ambitious even by Young's own very exacting standards, the multiple-disc set comes in CD, DVD, and Blu-ray versions, and chronicles Young's career up until 1972. At least two more volumes are planned, and the December 2009 release of *Dreamin' Man Live*, a live concert rendering of the classic *Harvest Moon* album, is an apparent warm-up to one of them. Somewhere in the midst of all this, Young found time to release an album of new material (*Fork in the Road*), and to tour (which he does nearly every year like clockwork).

If nothing else, Neil Young is "prolific," to say the least. Yet, as staggering as the sheer volume of his recorded output has been over the years and decades, the fact that through it all he has made this music strictly on his own artistic terms every step of the way is a rather astonishing feat in and of itself. This is what makes Neil Young an artist who is truly unique in all of music.

This same uncompromising approach to his art—some would call it a stubborn streak—has both earned Young the admiration of his peers and drawn the fire of folks like the record company suits charged with marketing his music to the masses.

Two quick cases in point:

Following the release of his first #1 album *Harvest* in 1972—the album has long since gone platinum many times over and remains a steady seller to this day—Young followed it up with a series of bleak, desolate, and downright depressing records that were the very antithesis of the folky, singer-songwriter pop that made *Harvest*, and particularly its single "Heart of Gold," such a huge hit.

On the liner notes for his three-disc retrospective *Decade*, Young famously described the albums *Time Fades Away, On the Beach,* and *Tonight's the Night* as a period when he "left the middle of the road, and headed towards the ditch"— hence earning these records the fans' nickname of "the Ditch Trilogy."

When these albums earned Young the respect of then emerging new wave artists like Devo—bands who were otherwise notorious (and often quite brutal) in their disdain of other so-called dinosaurs from the sixties—Neil responded with *Rust Never Sleeps* in 1979, an album whose title track embraces "the story of Johnny Rotten" with its famous lines of how "it's better to burn out than to fade away."

But this would be only one of many incidents in which the mercurial (that's a word associated with him quite a bit, by the way) Young would follow his artistic muse in such a way as to cause record executives to tear their hair out in frustration.

After signing with David Geffen's self-named new label in the eighties, Young then spent the better part of that decade making albums that veered wildly from the Devo-inspired synthesized new wave of *Trans* to the goofy rockabilly of *Everybody's Rockin* ("they wanted a rock album, so I gave them one," he once explained)—his record with makeshift greasers the Shocking Pinks.

Geffen eventually sued Young for breach of contract, citing of all things, the artist's failure to deliver any actual "Neil Young records." You just can't make this stuff up.

But if Young has made a career of confounding critics and fans alike by following his at times seemingly strange artistic whims, the bottom line is he always seems to find his way back home. He did it after the Ditch Trilogy in 1979 with *Rust Never Sleeps*, and he did it again after the Geffen years in the eighties with the album *Freedom* and its anthemic single "Rockin' in the Free World."

When all is said and done, the two things Young is best known for are the cranked to eleven, feedback-laden noise he makes with his trusty guitar Old Black on albums with his on-again, off-again band Crazy Horse like *Rust* and

Ragged Glory, and the quieter, more introspective acoustic folk-pop of albums like *Harvest* and its equally gorgeous nineties successor *Harvest Moon*. As different as these two styles are, together they form the cornerstone of Young's sound. The glue that binds them—and everything else that Neil Young does—is the songs.

With Young, it always comes down to the songs. And make no mistake, when it comes to writing great songs that stand the test of time, he has very few equals.

At sixty-seven, he also remains as prolific and relevant as ever. He continues to record new material and tour constantly—and the amps are for the most part still cranked as high as God will allow—even as he pursues such side-projects as the shepherding of his back catalog and legacy with the ongoing *Archives* series, and his passion for energy efficient, environmentally sound cars like his beloved LincVolt.

As 2010 dawned, Young spent the first few weeks of the New Year being honored on Grammy weekend as MusiCares' Person of the Year for his charitable work with organizations like Farm Aid and the Bridge School by the Recording Academy. He also found time to perform "Long May You Run" on Conan O'Brien's final night of NBC's *Tonight Show*. Jimmy Fallon also paid respect to Young's continuing relevance by doing a spot-on parody of Young performing *American Idol* reject Larry Platt's viral sensation "Pants on the Ground" on his late night show. Fallon repeated the Neil Young parody again with a hilarious song based on the fifteen minutes of YouTube fame enjoyed by the "double rainbow" guy.

Even when he is relatively inactive (at least by his own prolific standards), Neil Young's influence continues to be everywhere.

On September 28, 2010, Young released *Le Noise*, a new album recorded with producer Daniel Lanois (best known for his work with artists like U2 and Bob Dylan). As boldly experimental as ever, *Le Noise* finds a mostly solo Neil Young cranking up the electric guitar unaccompanied by a band, but rather aided only by the "sonics" of Lanois. Lanois = Le Noise. Get it?

Following the practice of testing new material on live audiences that he has utilized for years, Young first played several of *Le Noise's* songs—including "Love and War," "Hitchhiker," and "Peaceful Valley Boulevard" on his 2010 *Twisted Road* tour (where he also performed them solo on electric guitar).

On October 23, 2010, Young also reunited the Buffalo Springfield for their first shows together in over four decades. The occasion of the reunion was the annual benefit concerts for the Bridge School, which serves the needs of children with severe disabilities (Neil's children Zeke and Ben both have forms of cerebral palsy, and his wife Pegi sits on the Bridge School's board of directors).

For the two Bridge shows, original Springfield members Young, Stephen Stills and Richie Furay were joined by bassist Rick Rosas and drummer Joe Vitale (replacing the late Bruce Palmer and Dewey Martin).

The second of a planned trilogy of concert films with director Jonathan Demme, called *Trunk Show*, also came out in 2010. The third installment of the Young/Demme trilogy, *Neil Young Journeys*, was filmed during the *Twisted Road* tour, and is expected in theatres through Sony Classics sometime in 2012. Young also continues to work on a planned second volume of his *Archives*, which will include the first official appearances of the "lost albums" *Homegrown, Chrome Dreams, Toast,* and *Oceanside, Countryside.* What other rock icon from the original sixties generation can you think of who maintains that type of pace today?

Quickly now . . . Jagger? McCartney? Nope. Didn't think so.

Neil Young FAQ is not intended as the definitive work on the artist (Jimmy McDonough has already accomplished that with his semiofficial biography *Shakey*), but rather as a reference guide that takes the reader through his recorded work album by album. I am also very proud to have my humble efforts here associated with a fine publishing house like Hal Leonard, and with a great series like the FAQ books.

My hope here is that this book both offers up the sort of facts known by few but the most devoted fans and serves as an introduction for the uninitiated Neil-phyte. In researching this book, I found myself coming across so many little known facts that I had either forgotten, or never knew in the first place, that in many ways it was as much a process of rediscovering this remarkably gifted artist as it was anything else.

I'd also be lying if I didn't say that listening to all those great albums again—not to mention the one thousand or so rarities and concert recordings I've got stored on my hard drive—was a blast. My hope is that in reading this, you will have much the same experience. It's definitely been a labor of love, and one that I hope you will enjoy reading as much as I did spending the many very late nights I did in writing it.

And forgive me if in between all the geeky facts here, I also occasionally offer my own personal insights into things like the many Neil Young concerts I've seen (my first was as a thirteen-year-old boy in 1970 accompanied by my grandma—God rest her soul), or how you'll learn why I'm most likely feeling depressed when I put on the album *On the Beach.*

Neil's just been that kind of a friend to me that way over the years. Mercurial and methodical, enduring and infuriating—everybody knows this is Neil.

Glen Boyd
December 2010

Neil Young
FAQ

I Am a Child

From Canada to California

There's Something Happening Here

For most of those who know and love Neil Young, this story begins in Los Angeles, California, in the mid-sixties with Buffalo Springfield, and most importantly with Young's often volatile relationship with Stephen Stills—the lifelong friend, rival, and all-around musical foil who would become one of, if not the most important person in Young's life.

If there were ever two people on this earth who might as well have been separated at birth, it is Young and Stills. Like two sides of the same coin, these two men have shared the sort of love/hate relationship throughout the decades that is truly the stuff of legend.

It is the sort of kinship that comes about as close to being a sibling rivalry as these things can—at least without the benefit (or the obstacle, depending on your viewpoint) of actual shared blood. It also comes complete with just about all of the elements you might suspect in such a strange but mutually beneficial partnership.

Yet there is no doubt that these two extraordinary musicians also share the sort of mutual, primarily musical bond that can only be described as a type of brotherly love. Although the dynamic of the Young/Stills relationship goes beyond the merely musical, there is also no denying the fireworks that occur between them when sharing a concert stage or in the recording studio together.

One only need listen to the electric sides on the live Crosby, Stills, Nash, and Young recording *4-Way Street*—and in particular the extended jams on the tracks "Carry On" and "Southern Man" for confirmation of this. Although somewhat rarer, bootleg recordings of CSN&Y's live version of Young's "Down by the River" only serve as further evidence. On the latter, Stills and Young feed off of each other's energy, stretching the already rather lengthy song often to well over twenty minutes in concert.

Perhaps as a by-product of their decades-long musical rivalry, Young and Stills trade off their lead guitar solos like two madmen possessed when sharing a stage, and the results are more often than not positively explosive. This was certainly evident during their early years playing together in Buffalo Springfield, and would become even more pronounced in CSN&Y.

Neil Young photographed during the 1969 television taping with Crosby, Stills, Nash, and Young for ABC-TV's *Music Scene* with David Steinberg. CSN&Y's "Down by the River" was a high point of the national, prime-time telecast.   *Photo by Jeff Allen*

Even without Stills by his side, though, Young himself has long been known to get into a hypnotic sort of state onstage—his "zone," if you will—particularly when the amps are cranked to eleven with Crazy Horse. This same zone that Neil Young often gets into when the Horse is having a particularly great night, and when he's peeling the paint from arena ceilings with Old Black—his trademark black 1953 Gibson Les Paul guitar—has in fact been one of the major stories within the stories that make up his legend.

But when playing with Stills—who is one of the only musicians the notoriously lone wolf Young is able to feed off of in this way—this zone has been known at times to blast off into different dimensions and universes altogether.

Needless to say, the Young/Stills relationship will be a theme that recurs very often in this book.

Anyway, we'll get to more on Young and Stills in due course. But before Neil Young ever met Stephen Stills, and before there ever even was a Buffalo Springfield, a CSN&Y, or a Crazy Horse, Young was this slightly weird kid who grew up in Canada.

There Is a Town in North Ontario

Neil Percival Young was born on November 12, 1945, in Toronto to his parents Scott and Edna "Rassy" Young (formerly Ragland). The Young family (which also included Neil's older brother Bob) eventually settled in the small town of Omemee, which Neil Young would later immortalize in the song "Helpless" from Crosby, Stills, Nash, and Young's classic *Déjà Vu* album.

Young expressed an interest in music at an early age (his first guitar was a plastic ukulele bought by his parents). But like many kids growing up in the fifties, he fell truly in love with rock 'n' roll after hearing it on one of those transistor radios that were as much a part of the teenage experience back then as texting, Facebook, and the Internet are now. In Young's case, these strange-sounding transmissions—which must have seemed like nothing less than personal communications from God himself—came through local Canadian station CHUM.

Since this book is not intended so much as a biography as a guide to Neil Young's music, we're not going to spend a whole lot of time on his childhood here.

But by most accounts, when it became apparent that his interest in music was more than just a youthful phase, Rassy was the more supportive of his two parents (who divorced after Scott began a relationship with fellow journalist Astrid Mead, who eventually became his second wife).

Although Scott Young—a journalist, writer, and sports broadcaster of some note himself—may have been the paternal source that Neil's formidable writing talent actually sprang from, he was the one who most say wanted to see his son pursue a more traditional career path. It should, however, be noted that Scott

Young later became a very big fan of his son's work, even going so far as to write about it extensively in his own book, *Neil and Me*.

The Squires: Sultans of Surf

Scott Young's marriage to Astrid Mead also produced a daughter, Neil Young's half-sister Astrid (who, like Neil, is also a professional singer-songwriter). Neil Young also has four other half-sisters from his father's two subsequent marriages following the split with Rassy—Deidre, Maggie, Caitlin, and Erin. When his parents split, Neil ended up with his more supportive Mom (at the time), and with her son in tow, Rassy ended up moving her half of the divided family to Winnipeg.

In Winnipeg, Young soon began to make a name for himself in the local music scene with a series of bands with names like the Jades, the Esquires, the Classics, and eventually the band he would make his first record with, the Squires.

He also paid close attention to the other bands on the local scene—and particularly to one called Chad Allen and the Expressions, which featured a hot young guitarist named Randy Bachman.

Bachman, who would later go on to his own commercial success with the Guess Who and Bachman-Turner Overdrive (BTO), was one of Young's earliest influences as a guitarist, and he soon found himself trying to emulate the vibrato- and tremolo-based guitar sound Bachman specialized in with the Expressions, which of course had itself been heavily borrowed from people like Link Wray and the Shadows.

That sound is readily apparent when you listen to the lone Squires single "The Sultan" and its flip side "Aurora," where Neil's guitar borrows equally from the echo-heavy sounds of both Wray's hit "Rumble" and the instrumental surf-rock records of the period by bands like the Telstars and the Ventures.

The single, which was overseen by then mentor Toronto DJ Bob Bradburn and released on the indie V Records imprint, is a far cry from the sort of feedback-laden, heavy guitar assaults Neil Young fans would later come to know and love on songs like "Cortez the Killer" and "Like a Hurricane." Other Squires tracks like "I Wonder," "Mustang," "I'll Love You Forever," and "(I'm a Man) and I Can't Cry" have since surfaced on the massive *Archives Vol. 1* boxed set.

But even now you can still hear the earliest hints of just where Neil Young would eventually carry that part of his trademark sound on that single. Fortunately, Neil Young (an artist who has meticulously shepherded the documenting of his career in a way that very few other musicians of his stature have) has immortalized his early work with the Squires for posterity on the *Archives* set.

Mortimer Hearseburg

One of the more famous Neil Young stories from his early days is how he traveled from his native Canada across two countries in search of fame and fortune, eventually winding up in Los Angeles, where, in his own words, he was going to become a rock star.

Although this account has been retold many times in countless stories and variations over the years, the one constant with these tales is that the trips that eventually got him there were by and large made in a pair of vintage hearse-mobiles.

The first of these, a 1948 Buick Roadmaster Hearse that he nicknamed "Mortimer Hearseburg" (or Mort or Morty for short), served as a combination of reliable transport vehicle (for a while anyway), occasional home, and unique rock-'n'-roll prop for Neil Young and the various incarnations of his early bands—at least before the transmission fell out on one famous and fateful road trip. The second, a 1953 Pontiac hearse called—what else?—Mort II, would be the vehicle that finally got Neil Young to Southern California.

By Young's own reasoning, the hearse was a perfect transport vehicle for the traveling musician he had by this time become, with the rollers in back ideal not only for rolling out coffins containing dead people but for the guitars, drums, and amplifiers plied in the trade of working rock musicians as well.

So it was on one such road trip, while driving one such hearse, that he would fatefully end up meeting Stephen Stills for the first time, in what was to become one of the most important events of Neil Young's life up to this point.

That first meeting took place in Fort William, Ontario, and Young bonded instantly with the young guitarist from Texas (who he once described as the funniest person he had ever met). Young would later travel to New York (by way of Toronto), attracted by the burgeoning folk music scene there (which he had by this time become quite enamored with), but also in the hopes of hooking up once again with this Stills guy. To Young, Stills wasn't just a fellow musical misfit and kindred soul—he was also Young's potential ticket to becoming the rock star he had so long had dreamed of.

Back in the Old Folkie Days

Neil Young's introduction to folk music had come largely by way of Canadian folk artists like Ian and Sylvia Tyson (whose song "Four Strong Winds" has been described by Young himself as "the greatest song I've ever heard"). Neil Young himself eventually would record his own version of the song for his *Comes a Time* album.

Young would also meet a then struggling folk artist named Joan Anderson during the same period in one of Toronto's folkie coffeehouses. Anderson would eventually become better known to the world as the brilliant (and iconic in her own right) artist Joni Mitchell.

The two would, of course, cross paths again many times over the years, traveling in the same social circle of musicians and assorted other freaks populating Southern California's Laurel and Topanga Canyon hippie communities, as well as sharing management (Elliot Roberts), record labels (Warner Brothers), and numerous concert stages.

In an interesting side note, Young and Mitchell had another thing in common besides music. Both had been afflicted with polio during childhood, producing later effects in adulthood that last to this day. In Young's case, polio was responsible for his hunched-over posture (which becomes even more pronounced due to his considerable height and lanky frame). With Mitchell, on the other hand, it affected her fingers, leading to the bizarre guitar tunings heard on many of her recordings.

When Young had first met Stephen Stills in Fort William, he was already experimenting with an early hybrid of rock and folk styles with a group of Canadian musical cronies playing under a variety of band names that seemed to change even more rapidly than the musical winds of the times themselves.

Stills, who was performing in town with the Company (an offshoot of his earlier New Christy Minstrels–styled vocal group the Au Go-Go Singers), was notably impressed with the "rock-folk" stylings of Young's group. But most of all, Stills was impressed with Neil Young himself.

Young's idea was to do something like a combination of the rock and folk styles—something that drew both consternation and awe at the time when he turned traditional folk songs like "My Darling Clementine," "Tom Dooley," and "She'll Be Comin' 'Round the Mountain" on their ear with his own electrified rock arrangements. It was also during this period that Young wrote what would become two of his signature songs in "Sugar Mountain" and "Nowadays Clancy Can't Even Sing."

Neil Young and the Squires had by this time become the de facto house band at Smitty's Pancake House in Fort William, playing under their new moniker of the High Flying Birds, and it was also there that they came across Ray Dee (a.k.a. Ray Delantinsky), who became a mentor for the group and also produced recordings like "I'll Love You Forever" for them.

"He was the original David Briggs," Young told biographer Jimmy McDonough, in comparing Dee to the producer who would later play such a major role in his career.

But even then, Young was nothing if not a restless vagabond soul, and before long he felt the need to move on. Leaving trusted friends and bandmates like Ray Dee, Ken Koblun, and Bob Clark behind (this would become one of his trademarks over the years), Young packed up Mortimer the Hearse and headed to Toronto, with the longer-term goal of a reunion with his new best friend Stephen Stills in New York. Back at Smitty's Pancake House, a sign on the marquee simply read "The Birds Have Flown."

Reprise Records 2004 reissue single of "The Loner" from Neil
Young's self-titled debut album.   *Courtesy of Tom Therme collection*

During this period, Young stayed at his father's house in Toronto, and
he eventually summoned musical accomplices Koblun and Clark to join him
there—although the Squires' reunion would be a short-lived one.

The music scene in Toronto was equally divided between the roughneck
crowd who favored the rawer blend of blues, rock, and country played by bands
like Ronnie Hawkins and the Hawks (who, sans Hawkins, would later back
Bob Dylan and become stars in their own right as the Band), and the more
willowy-sounding acoustic folk music of artists like Gordon Lightfoot and Ian
and Sylvia favored by the more bohemian, beatnik sort of crowd that frequented
the coffeehouses.

It was during this time that Neil Young cut several folk-influenced sides with
longtime friend and musical accomplice Comrie Smith. With little else but
a reel-to-reel recorder, Young's "Dylan kit" of a guitar and a harmonica, and
Smith's banjo, the makeshift duo recorded six Neil Young songs and a cover of
"High Heel Sneakers" in the attic of their old school, Lawrence Park.

The early Young originals include "Casting Me Away from You," and "There
Goes My Babe," a pair of folkie-sounding duets that may or may not have been
influenced by artists like Ian and Sylvia, as well as the more raucous-sounding,
R&B-influenced "Hello Lonely Woman." All three surviving recordings can now
be heard on the *Archives Vol. 1* boxed set.

The New York meeting with Stills never happened, but Young did meet and hook up with Stills's friend Richie Furay there—another then struggling musician with whom he would eventually make history by forming the Buffalo Springfield along with Stills and Bruce Palmer. Furay ended up following Stills to Los Angeles, with Neil and Bruce Palmer not far behind them.

The Loner Meets the Super Freak

Prior to that, however, a series of events that began with Young carrying his guitar and amp down a Toronto street one day (this is actually a recurring theme in the Neil Young story) ended with what in retrospect has to be considered one of the strangest musical pairings in rock-'n'-roll history.

Bassist Bruce Palmer, who was already playing in a band called the Mynah Birds (led by a brash young African American musician who fancied himself the next Mick Jagger named Ricky James Matthews), needed a guitarist for the band and asked Young to join.

The Mynah Birds also had a deal with Motown Records—which was a pretty big deal at the time since Motown was the preeminent soul music label of its day, and signing a mostly white rock-'n'-roll band (save for Matthews) was pretty much unheard of. To this day, there are those who continue to claim that the

Foreign (and likely bootleg) pressing on "Oscar Records" of Neil Young's eponymous debut album.   *Courtesy of Tom Therme collection*

Mynah Birds was the first "white rock band" signed to Berry Gordy's Motown Records, although the band Rare Earth may have a semi-legitimate beef with the rock history books on that point.

Matthews would later go on to superstardom as Rick James, the "punk-funk" pioneer with the trademark braids who would sell millions with hits such as "Super Freak" in the eighties, and even get a second act in the nineties when rapper MC Hammer remade the song as a rap smash called "You Can't Touch This."

Before James eventually crashed and burned in one of rock 'n' roll's most notorious stories of sex, drugs, and rock-'n'-roll excess, he also wrote songs and produced records for a variety of artists including Teena Marie, the Mary Jane Girls, and even comedian Eddie Murphy's singing debut (anyone remember "Party All the Time"?). Sadly, just before his death, James was reduced to a punchline for cocaine abuse courtesy of a brutal but dead-on portrayal/parody by comedian Dave Chappelle.

The Mynah Birds—with Young—did record some songs for Motown, including the song "Little Girl Go," which was co-written by none other than Neil Young himself and Ricky James Matthews. But once it was discovered that the future "Super Freak" was in fact an AWOL fugitive from the American navy, nothing further came of it.

But in retrospect, can you imagine the possibilities of what might have been? A few different twists and turns back then, and we might have just seen the world's first ever folk-rock-punk-funk supergroup—fronted by Neil Young and Rick James no less.

You just can't make this stuff up.

Hello, Broken Arrow

Buffalo Springfield

Perhaps even weirder than the idea of a band with both Rick James and Neil Young in it, though, is the thought of Stephen Stills as a member of the sixties made-for-TV band the Monkees.

Before forming Buffalo Springfield with Neil Young, Stills actually once famously auditioned for that job, but lost out on the opportunity to join Davy, Micky, Peter, and Mike on the weekly television show about the adventures of a rock band clearly patterned after the Beatles (well, except for the minor detail that for the most part the Monkees didn't write their own songs or play their own instruments).

Fortunately, Stills had a date with destiny awaiting him that would happen not long after that failed audition during a traffic jam on one of Los Angeles busiest streets. This is also another one of those stories from the "truth is stranger than fiction" file that has become legendary in the years and decades since it actually took place.

Flying on the Ground Is Wrong

By 1966, Neil Young and Bruce Palmer had finally made it to L.A. after making the cross-country trip in Neil's latest hearse-mobile (the lovingly dubbed "Mort II"). As the pair found themselves stuck in traffic one day on Hollywood's world-famous Sunset Boulevard, Stills and Richie Furay (who were stuck in the same traffic jam going the opposite direction) drove right by them when Furay spotted the hearse. And just like that, the Buffalo Springfield (the name was taken from a Buffalo Springfield steamroller) was born, and the rest as they say, is rock-'n'-roll history.

Although Buffalo Springfield had a relatively short run—producing just three albums between 1966 and 1968—their influence in the decades since is undeniable, and it continues to resonate today. They probably didn't realize it at the time, but what Buffalo Springfield did during its brief history as a band was to pretty much provide the blueprint for the folk- and country-influenced Southern California rock sound of such latter-day practitioners as the Eagles and Jackson Browne and more modern-day Midwestern alt-country acolytes like the Jayhawks and Wilco.

Buffalo Springfield Concert Poster with opening act Count Five (of "Psychotic Reaction" one-hit wonder fame).

Courtesy Noah Fleisher/Heritage Auctions

Along with the Byrds (who the band often gigged with back in those days), Buffalo Springfield is the band most associated with the folk-rock boom of the mid-sixties. But where the Byrds were mainly known for covering Bob Dylan tunes, and for the jangly-sounding twelve-string electric guitar of leader Roger McGuinn (which would later prove to be a big influence on bands ranging from Tom Petty and the Heartbreakers to R.E.M.), Buffalo Springfield was actually thought by many to be the "folkier"-sounding of the two groups.

Whatever the case, it didn't take long for the band—which by this time had been completed with the addition of veteran session drummer Dewey Martin (the only member of the band who would become a contestant on TV's *The Dating Game*)—to begin to make a quick name for themselves in the L.A. music scene. They also soon developed a reputation as a formidable live act, which allowed them to score prime gigs opening for both the Byrds and the Rolling Stones, and even got them an extended residency at Hollywood's premier rock showcase club, the Whisky A Go-Go, before they had even released their first album.

However, with three songwriters in Furay, Stills, and Young, and with the latter two having particularly headstrong personalities (not to mention the oil-and-water chemistry between them), it didn't take long for the egos involved to clash over what essentially amounted to leadership and creative control of

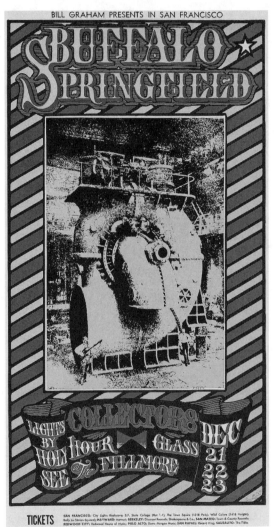

Early Buffalo Springfield concert poster from Bill Graham's Fillmore Auditorium in San Francisco. The opening act Hour Glass included a young Duane Allman, later of the Allman Brothers Band.

Courtesy Noah Fleisher/Heritage Auctions

the band. The clashes between Young and Stills—each of whom could make a legitimate claim at the time of Buffalo Springfield being "his band"—were particularly volatile and the beginning of what would become one of rock's most enduring and legendary love-hate relationships.

Young and Stills's personal and professional feuding began early on, when the band's first single had its A-side switched from Stills's "Go and Say Goodbye" to Young's "Nowadays Clancy Can't Even Sing." The two would continue to have numerous dustups over everything from Young's vocals to how to divide songwriting duties. Band managers Charlie Greene and Brian Stone did nothing to discourage the arguments, figuring that egging on the competition over the "Neil songs" versus the "Stephen songs" might spark the two writers to shoot for ever-greater creative heights. Whether this exercise yielded any positive results or not, there was little doubt it left at least one delicate artist's ego in a semifractured state.

Young's vocals had become a particularly contentious point within the group, with Richie Furay handling the vocals on many of Young's early songs, much to the latter's dismay. By most accounts, the way Stills saw it was that Young's role in the band was as lead guitarist, while the vocal duties would be split between Stills and Furay. Young, on the other hand, wanted to be able to sing his own songs.

The lack of confidence in Young's vocals was shared not only by the band members but also by their management team and the record label—with Stills being perhaps the most vocal critic of Young's strange "shaky" voice. This affected him deeply, and probably was one of the biggest contributing factors to the frustration he felt within Buffalo Springfield. It would eventually lead him to quit the band on numerous occasions.

This internal feuding would reach one of many boiling points when Young would walk out of the band on the eve of an important national television appearance on the *Tonight Show* with Johnny Carson.

Although landing the Carson show would have to have been considered prime exposure for a then up-and-coming band like the Buffalo Springfield, Young found playing a show like this somewhat beneath his own loftier artistic pretensions (he would later similarly object to CSN&Y playing the Tom Jones TV show, although unlike with Carson, in this case Young finally relented).

Young also missed playing the potentially star-making Monterey Pop Festival with his Buffalo Springfield bandmates as a result of walking out on them. Buffalo Springfield still performed at the festival, with David Crosby filling in for Young on guitar and vocals in something of a preview of things to come.

In no-showing Carson (not to mention Monterey) and essentially quitting the band, Young established what would become a career-long pattern of simply getting up and walking away from both his bands and his friends without a second thought, whenever any given situation wasn't to his liking. Everyone from CSN&Y to Crazy Horse has long since become resigned to the fact that in dealing with a mercurial personality like Neil Young, this just comes with the territory.

Hey, What's That Sound?

Although when looking back on the Buffalo Springfield's recorded output today, it mostly holds up pretty well, there was also a consensus at the time amongst both fans and the band members themselves that they were never quite able to duplicate the spark of their live shows on record. Where the group's live approach of three hot guitarists backed by the funkier-sounding rhythm section of Palmer and Martin was considered quite a novel one at the time, Buffalo Springfield's albums were plagued by poor production, despite the overall strength of the group's songwriting.

The band's 1966 self-titled debut album is a particularly sore spot even today. Produced by then managers Charlie Greene and Brian Stone (a classic pair of Hollywood hucksters if ever there was one), the album suffers from both a poor mix and even poorer separation that sounds like rechanneled stereo (because it largely was).

The album does, however, show early signs of the great songwriters that both Stills and Young would more fully develop into later. In particular, Young's "Burned"—a song that might have inadvertently been about the frustrations he was already feeling within the band—remains a strong piece of his overall catalog today and is an early example of the introspective, emotional songwriting that would characterize so much of his latter work as a solo artist.

Stills's "For What It's Worth" (which was added to the album later, after the single release became a major hit) is, of course, nothing less than an all-time rock-'n'-roll classic, one of the single greatest musical snapshots of that volatile time.

To this day, "FWIW's" signature chorus of "Stop! Hey what's that sound? Everybody look what's goin' down" conjures up visions of the sixties antiwar and civil rights protest movements in a way that very few other songs from the period do. Interestingly, it was written rather quickly after Stills read about the closing of a teen club and the subsequent riot that happened as a result. Whatever the circumstance, "FWIW" was a monumental songwriting achievement for Stills—and one that would prove to be the first of many.

Maybe the Beach Boys Have Got You Down

Young's first, rather abrupt departure from Buffalo Springfield didn't last long, and by the time he returned for 1967's *Buffalo Springfield Again* album, his growth as a songwriter had become palpable. Perhaps the brief vacation did him some good, because with new songs like "Expecting to Fly" and "Broken Arrow," Young was also showing a bolder willingness to experiment. If nothing else, the new songs were certainly not lacking ambition.

Produced by Jack Nitzsche, who had been involved with some of the legendary Phil Spector's "Wall of Sound" releases, both songs are essentially Young solo

Original album jacket for Buffalo Springfield's unreleased album
Stampede.   *Courtesy Noah Fleisher/Heritage Auctions*

efforts that bring a considerable degree of that same sort of Spector-esque sweep
into the mix.

"Expecting to Fly" is definitely the lusher-sounding of the two, with Young
turning in a somewhat uncharacteristically lilting vocal that still manages to work
within the swirling strings of Nitzsche's production.

"Broken Arrow," on the other hand, has often been criticized for having
a rather ostentatious sort of cinematic scope and ambition that some
would tell you may exceed the song's actual reach. However, despite the fact
that it sounds just a bit dated now (with its stop and start breaks to incorporate
goofy sound effects like a heartbeat and a loungey-sounding jazz band), the
song actually holds up pretty well. Its haunting refrain of "hello, broken arrow"
may have also been somewhat prophetic as far as the eventual fate of Buffalo
Springfield was concerned.

At a time when rock musicians were constantly trying to one-up each
other on their recordings, it's also highly likely that Young's new songs were
at least partially influenced by Brian Wilson's landmark recordings with the
Beach Boys like *Pet Sounds* and "Good Vibrations," not to mention the Beatles'
masterpiece *Sgt. Pepper's Lonely Hearts Club Band.*

At any rate, the song definitely has its share of fans in today's music community, as evidenced by Wilco's spot-on version at 2010's Grammy ceremony honoring Neil Young as MusiCares Person of the year (for his charitable efforts on behalf of Farm Aid and the Bridge School, among others).

Well Hello, Mr. Soul

But perhaps the most notable Neil Young contribution to *Buffalo Springfield Again* is "Mr. Soul." One of his earliest rockers and still one of his best, the song has also drawn criticism due to its close resemblance to the Rolling Stones hit "Satisfaction." On this song (which is also repeated in the first few seconds of "Broken Arrow"), Young cuts loose with both a very strong, confident-sounding vocal and some pretty ripping guitar. The song also shows his continuing growth as a lyricist, with its raucous party-rock sound serving as a strange backdrop for lines like "stick around while the clown who is sick does the trick of disaster" (a reference to Young's ongoing struggle with epileptic seizures, which often occurred while he was performing onstage).

With "Mr. Soul," Neil Young also set to music and lyrics what has since become one of his longer-running, better-known catchphrases about people who, as he has so often put it over the years, have got "soul."

In interviews, Young has often referred to people like manager Elliot Roberts and his on-again, off-again bandmates in Crazy Horse as having soul. He even makes this observation about Richard Nixon, of all people, in the song "Campaigner" with the line "Even Richard Nixon has got soul." Coming from Neil Young, being told you "have soul" has got to be considered high praise indeed.

I Held My Breath with My Eyes Closed

By the time of Buffalo Springfield's third and final album, 1968's *Last Time Around*, the band largely existed in name only. Young was already looking ahead to making his first solo album, and Stills would soon join ex-Byrds guitarist David Crosby and ex-Hollies member Graham Nash to form one of rock's first bona fide supergroups with Crosby, Stills, and Nash.

Richie Furay would also go on to experience success—although to a much lesser extent—with his own critically lauded but modest-selling country rock group Pogo (who later changed their name to Poco after a legal dispute with the creators of the comic strip *Pogo*).

Bruce Palmer, once considered the musical rock of the band, but whose drug abuse (and frequent busts for the same) had long since caught up to him, was out as bassist, and Jim Messina (who would later go on to success in the seventies as the non-Kenny Loggins half of seventies soft rock duo Loggins and Messina) was in as both bassist and producer. The aptly titled *Last Time Around* would prove to be Buffalo Springfield's swan song.

Since for all intents and purposes, Buffalo Springfield was already history by the time the album was released, much of what is heard there is the product of a splintered band recording as individual solo artists (much as the Beatles would do not long afterwards as they began to drift apart on the *White Album*).

Young's contributions to *Last Time Around* are of particular significance, however. In fact, "On the Way Home" and "I Am a Child" both remain staples of his live shows today, particularly when he is performing as a solo acoustic act.

The former is also one of Neil Young's loveliest songs, with its wistful lyrics "when the dream came, I held my breath with my eyes closed/I went insane like a smoke ring day, when the wind blows" filled with the sort of longing and regret that would become a signature of much of Young's latter-day songbook.

Although Young doesn't sing the song on the *Last Time Around* album (Richie Furay takes Young's vocal duties—as he so often did back then), there is a wonderful version of Young performing the song solo on CSN&Y's live *4-Way Street* album. "I Am a Child" has likewise become one of Young's earlier songwriting achievements that has stood the test of time.

3

A Dreamer of Pictures

Latter-Day Remembrances, Compilations, Anthologies, and Boxed Sets

A lthough Neil Young was all by accounts frustrated very early on by his arrangement with Buffalo Springfield during the band's brief run in the mid-sixties—he was, after all, both the first member of the band to leave and the guy who did so the most often—he has revisited that band's catalog numerous times in the decades since.

Young has in fact gone back to the Buffalo Springfield time and time again, both in song ("Buffalo Springfield Again" from his 2000 album *Silver and Gold*) and with a rather staggering number of hits collections, anthologies, and compilations—many of which have come in the form of multiple-disc boxed sets.

The earliest attempts by the band's label Atco Records to repackage Buffalo Springfield's hits suffer from many of the same problems that record company repackages so often do.

In fairness to the folks at Atco/Atlantic, though, and particularly to founder Ahmet Ertegun, there have been few record labels, then or now, that look after the recorded legacy of their artists with the sort of loving care as that great label did back then and continues to do so now. But there are fewer artists still who have meticulously, even somewhat jealously, shepherded their artistic legacy the way that Young has.

Not surprisingly, Young has gone to great lengths to right whatever wrongs the earlier, primarily record label–driven Buffalo Springfield anthologies and hit collections might have posed—most notably on 2001's Buffalo Springfield box set and on the first volume of the *Archives* series. What follows is a brief overview of these compilations.

Buffalo Springfield Retrospective (1969)
Atco Records

Peak Billboard Chart Position: #42
As greatest hits collections go, this is actually a pretty decent one, and serves as a more than adequate introduction for anyone in search of a brief, but mostly complete snapshot of Buffalo Springfield's short but historic career.

Nothing fancy here, just a quick overview that hits on just about all of Buffalo Springfield's high points musically—from Stills's folk-rock protest classic "For What It's Worth," through Neil Young's near hits like "Mr. Soul," "Nowadays Clancy Can't Even Sing," "On the Way Home," and "I Am a Child," and on to his later, more artistically ambitious songs with the group like "Expecting to Fly" and "Broken Arrow."

As a quick introduction to Buffalo Springfield—and particularly one that was probably more the product of the marketing department at the record company than the artists themselves—you really could do a whole lot worse than *Retrospective*.

Buffalo Springfield (Two-Record Set Anthology) (1973)
Atco Records

Peak Billboard Chart Position: Unknown
Basically an expanded double album version of the *Retrospective* hits collection, this two-record "anthology" set mostly reprises the former package, while going somewhat deeper into album cuts like "A Child's Claim to Fame" and "Pay The Price."

I may be somewhat in the minority here amongst the band's fans, but as a brief overview of Buffalo Springfield's career (that also makes for a hell of a great mix tape, by the way), I actually prefer the briefer but tighter and more compactly packaged *Retrospective*.

Neil Young Decade (1977)
Reprise Records

Peak Billboard Chart Position: #43
Originally released as a three-album retrospective of Young's career up to the point of its original 1977 release, *Decade* was also the catalyst for the massive *Archives* project that would so preoccupy him over the next several decades.

Japanese pressing of the 45 for "Sugar Mountain."

Courtesy of Tom Therme collection

To many Neil Young fanatics and purists, *Decade* is often regarded as a disappointment due to the fact that it doesn't contain anywhere near the number of rarities many had expected to find. But as a career retrospective (up to that point anyway), they just don't get much better than this. The rarities, though few in number, include some real doozies.

Sandwiched in between the obvious Buffalo Springfield ("Mr. Soul, "Broken Arrow," "Expecting to Fly," etc.), CSN&Y ("Helpless," "Ohio"), and Neil Young solo tracks ("Cowgirl in the Sand," "Down by the River," "Heart of Gold," "Southern Man," etc.) that you'd expect to find on a collection like this, are rarities like "Down to the Wire" (rumored to have been part of a lost Buffalo Springfield album called *Stampede*). *Decade* also includes a pair of tracks from Young's mythical, never-released "sequel" to *Harvest* called *Homegrown* ("Star of Bethlehem," "Deep Forbidden Lake").

Although it was considered somewhat flawed by the Neil-phytes at the time of its release, *Decade* holds up quite well as the sort of career retrospective for fans who have neither the patience, the time, nor the geekish sort of scholarly wherewithal to delve into the massive listening or viewing experience that came later on with Neil Young's *Archives*.

Crosby, Stills, and Nash (Boxed Set) (1991)
Atlantic Records

Peak Billboard Chart Position: #109

Although this four-disc boxed set contains only a handful of contributions from Neil Young, it is otherwise a very good representation of the collected works to that point of the group that—outside of Buffalo Springfield and Crazy Horse anyway—played the most important role in the artistic and commercial development of Young's own career.

As the story goes, Young originally gave his blessing to the project, essentially telling the rest of the group they could freely pick whatever songs of his they wished to use. From there, the story gets somewhat murkier as (depending on which version you choose to believe) the plug on his participation was rather abruptly—but also quite typically for Young—pulled by either Elliot Roberts or Young himself.

What is probably most likely is that while Young was beginning his own process of combing the vaults and compiling material for his own *Archives* project, he wanted to save his best work for the massive retrospective series he was then only just beginning to put on the drawing board. So, in typical Neil Young fashion, he then dispatched Roberts to handle the dirty work of delivering the bad news to CS&N (a task that is known to have ended up pissing off Graham Nash most notably).

So although a few CSN&Y songs made the final cut, only a very small handful of them ("Helpless," "Ohio") are actual Neil Young compositions, and unlike the other members, none of Young's solo work is represented at all. From a purely marketing standpoint, the other obvious sticking point is that this retrospective boxed set is billed as being the collected work to that point of Crosby, Stills, and Nash, where you have to figure that a CSN&Y box might have helped move a few thousand extra units.

Buffalo Springfield Box Set (2001)
Atco/Elektra/Rhino Records

Peak Billboard Chart Position: #194

Now this is more like it . . . or is it?

You'd think that for a band that only released three albums during its very short but influential career, this kind of extensive trip through the vaults of unreleased recordings is not exactly something that is all that warranted.

But Stills and Young did exactly that in 2001, filling this lavishly packaged box with loads of unreleased remixes, band demos, and otherwise rare recordings that pretty much put the final exclamation point on Buffalo Springfield's recorded output in the form of a more properly complete anthology document.

Much like Young's own *Archives* series, this one is largely a gift for the hard-core fans—because few others would honestly have the sort of dedication to sit through all of it.

But for those who do, *Box Set* is one hell of a history lesson, and there are some real gems to be found here as well (such as alternate mixes of Neil Young songs like "On the Way Home" and original demos for stuff like "Flying on the Ground Is Wrong").

On a more historical note, *Box Set* also served as the launch point for the 1999 CSN&Y reunion album *Looking Forward*.

As the story goes, when Stills and Young were working in the studio together on this project, Stills played some of the tracks that CSN were working on at the time, and Young was impressed enough to sign on, freely offering up songs he was working on for his own *Silver and Gold* album project to the band.

Young was said to be likewise impressed that his on-again, off-again band-mates in CSN&Y had divorced themselves from their relationship with long-time label Atlantic Records, and were planning on releasing their new album themselves.

Single release of "Southern Man," as taken from the three-LP anthology *Decade*.   *Courtesy of Tom Therme collection*

Neil Young Archives Vol. I (2009)
Reprise Records

Peak Billboard Chart Position: #102

As if you couldn't already go diving deeply enough into the vaults of unreleased material by Buffalo Springfield and by Neil Young himself, this massive first volume of Young's long-planned *Archives* series provides all the satisfaction any self-respecting fan could possibly ever want or need . . . well, up through the year 1972 anyway (future volumes of the series are already in the works).

Spread out over eight CDs or ten DVD or Blu-ray discs (depending on your preference), there is much to like about this set, but also much to criticize.

In the negative column, you have the fact that much of the material has already been previously released—including the complete Neil Young concert performances from Massey Hall (acoustic) and the Fillmore East (with Crazy Horse), both of which were issued as stand-alone releases quite some time prior to the arrival of the full *Archives*. On the other hand, the remastered sound quality is nothing short of stunning, and there are plenty of gems here that have never before seen the light of day (at least officially speaking), including rare tracks from Young's early days in Canada with the Squires and with Comrie Smith.

As for the Buffalo Springfield material included on the set, not a lot of new ground is covered, and what you get is pretty much what you would expect ("Broken Arrow," "Expecting to Fly," "Burned," "Mr. Soul," etc.). But there are also rarer tracks like "Kahuna Sunset," "Sell Out," and previously unreleased demos for songs like "Nowadays Clancy Can't Even Sing."

One of the most interesting tracks on *Archives* is an unreleased version of a song called "Down, Down, Down," where you can hear embryonic fragments for some of the ideas that would show up on later Neil Young songs like "Broken Arrow" and "Country Girl" being developed for the first time. Ideas for the latter track can also be heard in the Young solo track "Whiskey Boot Hill" on the *Archives* album.

For the stricter Buffalo Springfield purists out there, *Box Set* is probably the better bet. But for anyone who loves the music of Neil Young, there's little doubt that you could easily get lost for days on end with the *Archives* set.

4

Is This Place at Your Command?

Neil Young, Elliot Roberts, and David Briggs

He's the Perfect Arranger

It was around the time that Buffalo Springfield was rapidly disintegrating as a band that Neil Young first met Elliot Roberts, the man who would eventually guide his career through the decades as his manager. The two of them were introduced by Joni Mitchell (who was already a Roberts client), when Mitchell and Young were recording in the same building and Joni insisted that Roberts had to meet Young, who according to Mitchell was "the funniest guy I know besides you."

Upon meeting, Young and Roberts famously clicked to such a degree that Young even invited him to come live with him in the guest house of his Laurel Canyon home. However, Roberts's first attempt at managing Young's career (while he was still with Buffalo Springfield) wasn't nearly so fortuitous, and ended with Young famously firing him.

As the story goes, Young had taken ill (between the pressures he was feeling within the band at the time and his ongoing epileptic condition, his fragile health issues were an ongoing concern back then) at a hotel while on the road with Buffalo Springfield. When he summoned Roberts for the purposes of locating a doctor, it was to no avail, because the man who would eventually go on to guide the business affairs of Neil Young for decades to come was otherwise occupied shooting off some golf balls at a driving range located near the hotel.

Upon finally locating Roberts, Young informed his would-be manager that his services would no longer be required—even though the two were more or less living under the same roof at the time. One can only imagine the levels of discomfort that existed between them in regard to that arrangement, particularly on Roberts's end.

Still, Roberts, who at the time coveted the opportunity to manage the Buffalo Springfield—even as the group was falling apart—as a prize that was definitely worth fighting for, refused to give up.

In another of Roberts's later bids to manage the Springfield, Young successfully (and by some accounts rather venomously) argued against it in the subsequently heated meetings between the band and their would-be new manager. Although Roberts has long since gained a well-earned reputation as one of the toughest negotiators in the music business, Young's arguments in that meeting were so forceful that they reportedly reduced the normally tough-as-nails Roberts to tears.

But once Young left the band (permanently this time) and the Buffalo Springfield had finally split up for good, he went straight back to Elliot Roberts and asked him to manage his solo career, explaining his earlier arguments against it away by saying that this had been his true motive all along. In the typical Neil Young vernacular, he later explained the decision to go after Roberts by saying that "Elliot's got soul." Roberts's own response upon learning of Young's ulterior motives in sandbagging him with Buffalo Springfield was that the tactic reminded him of his former mentor, David Geffen.

Later on, Young would prove to be a strong Roberts ally in the bidding war over the management of what was then recognized as the biggest prize in all of rock 'n' roll—the newly formed supergroup that had been dubbed the "American Beatles" by the rock press, Crosby, Stills and Nash—which Young himself had just joined (more on that in a later chapter of this book). Of course, Roberts's association at the time with rising music biz hotshot David Geffen—who showed up with Roberts when he made his pitch to the band—didn't exactly hurt his case either.

Born Elliot Rabinowitz, Roberts had been mentored by Geffen working in the mailroom at New York's William Morris Agency (where, among other things, Geffen taught Roberts the art of things like steaming open the company mail and using the secrets contained within to one's own personal advantage). Eventually, Roberts took on Native American folk singer Buffy Sainte-Marie as a client, who in turn introduced him to then up-and-coming artist Joni Mitchell.

Depending on who is telling the story, Roberts has been described as both one of the most honest men in the record industry and one of its biggest liars. As Young's longtime manager, Roberts has also often been as much a hired gun for the artist as he has been merely his advisor and confidant.

Truth be told, Elliot Roberts has probably spent as much time running interference and subsequently dodging bullets for the notoriously mercurial artist—with his often volatile nature and tendency to shift gears on a dime—as he has done anything else. More than anything, though, Roberts has been Neil Young's most trusted ally, with the biggest key to their long relationship probably being his ability to simply let Neil be Neil.

In addition to building an impressive roster of artists for their own Lookout Management company, Roberts and Geffen would eventually form Asylum Records, the Warner Brothers–distributed label that would become most singularly associated with the Southern California singer-songwriter boom of the early seventies. Asylum's artist roster was packed with the most successful names in the

tuesday
FEB. 27
8:P.M.
veterans
memorial
auditorium
DES MOINES
*
TICKETS
$450 $550 $650
ALL SEATS RESERVED
available at:
KENNY BUTTREY   DES MOINES
TIM DRUMMOND   *STEREO TOWN
BEN KEITH   (all 3 locations)
*DOTTY DUMPLINGS DOWERY
JACK NITZCHE   *DES MOINES MUSIC
*VETS MEMORIAL AUDITORIUM
(BOX OFFICE)
*ALL DES MOINES HI SCHOOLS
(INTER-CITY SCHOOL COUNCIL REPS)
AMES
presented by   *STEREO TOWN
Celebration   MAIL ORDER CHECK OR MONEY
Concerts   ORDER & SELF-ADDRESSED
STAMPED ENVELOPES PAYABLE TO:
VETS MEMORIAL TICKET OFFICE
833 FIFTH AVE, DES MOINES 50309
(allow 3 weeks)
©2005 HeritageGalleries.com

Concert poster from 1971 for Neil Young during the post-Crazy Horse "folk-pop" period (despite the earlier *Everybody Knows This Is Nowhere* cover art).

Courtesy Noah Fleisher/Heritage Auctions

genre such as Linda Ronstadt, Jackson Browne, and its biggest act, the Eagles.

With the help of producer Jack Nitzsche (who had already been talking up Young to Warner executives like Mo Ostin), Roberts also engineered the signing of Young as a solo artist to Warner Brothers imprint Reprise Records—the label he would call home for his entire career (with the exception of his tumultuous ten-year association with Geffen Records during the eighties).

Be on My Side, I'll Be on Your Side

It was during the same period the Buffalo Springfield was imploding, around 1967, that Young also first encountered David Briggs.

Like so many Neil Young stories, this one begins with the artist hitchhiking. When Briggs, who was barreling down the highway in an army personnel carrier vehicle, decided to pick up the wayward hitchhiker, a bond began between the two men that would last decades and produce nearly twenty albums, including some of the most noteworthy albums of Young's career. Like Stephen Stills before him, David Briggs would in fact become one of the most important figures in Young's artistic life, and the two men would likewise share the same sort of love/hate relationship that ultimately bonded them like brothers.

Sharing a love of cars and music, Young also found a true kindred lunatic in Briggs. It's no wonder that in much the same way he so often returns to work with his on-again, off-again garage-rock band Crazy Horse, Young likewise kept coming back to Briggs to produce his records.

It's also probably no accident that Briggs has produced most of Young's collaborations with the Horse. Briggs's approach to recording rock 'n' roll in fact shares much in common with the way that Crazy Horse plays it. In Jimmy McDonough's *Shakey*, Briggs tells the author that he could teach him everything he knows about making records in an hour. He then goes on to explain his recording philosophy of just putting everyone in the room and letting them bang it out—preferably with the shortest, most direct line from the musicians playing in the room to the machines capturing the music on tape as possible.

Claiming that all of the advances in recording technology have destroyed the music business, Briggs is a firm proponent that "less is more." One of his most famous quotes is that when it comes to rock 'n' roll, "the more you think, the more you stink."

Born in Casper, Wyoming, Manning Philander "David" Briggs was a rock-'n'-roll fan early on, as well as a frustrated musician who ended up making records for other artists once he determined he couldn't play very well. As a teenager, Briggs also had a taste for fast cars, and ran with a local car club/youth gang called the Vaccaros. After producing his first record (for comedian Murray

Original Reprise 45 for the #1 smash "Heart of Gold."
Courtesy of Tom Therme collection

Roman), Briggs ended up going to work for Bill Cosby's Tetragrammaton Records.

Although his own legacy as a producer has become inextricably tied to his work with Neil Young, Briggs has also produced albums for Spirit, Alice Cooper, Nick Cave, and others and has played on sessions for a number of notable artists. David Briggs passed away in 1995 following a battle with lung cancer.

Often referred to as the unofficial fifth member of Crazy Horse, Briggs also worked with a number of artists more closely associated with Neil Young—most notably guitarist, one-time Crazy Horse member, and subsequent Young sideman Nils Lofgren and his band Grin in the sixties and early seventies.

Briggs's long professional association Neil Young ended with 1994's *Sleeps with Angels* (although much of their work together can also be heard on the *Archives* box set). But it was on Young's self-titled 1968 debut solo album that their long-standing personal and artistic partnership would first bear fruit.

I've Been Waiting for You, and You've Been Coming to Me

Once he was free of the Buffalo Springfield, Young was likewise determined to free himself of the artistic constraints he had previously felt within that band, and to do things his own way as a solo artist this time around. By most accounts, he had also become something of a new man as a result of this newfound freedom.

In fact, he not only seemed much less frail and sickly than he had been in the past (the epileptic seizures that had often been brought on by the stressful conditions he felt within Buffalo Springfield had become far less frequent by then), but there also seemed to be a new air of strength and confidence about him.

Perhaps for the first time since his arrival in Los Angeles driving a refurbished Pontiac Hearse, Young seemed truly grounded. At long last, he seemed to be becoming not only his own artist, but his own man as well.

For his first album as a solo artist, Elliot Roberts had negotiated a unique contract with the Warner Brothers' label Reprise (whose flagship artist had been none other than Frank Sinatra). Under the terms Roberts negotiated on his behalf, Young took a much smaller upfront advance than the industry norm at the time in exchange for a higher royalty rate (or "points" in the record industry vernacular) later for his future recordings. Although this may have seemed an ill-advised move (Young was still solidly in the "starving artist" category at the time), it would later on prove to be a brilliant one on Roberts's part, and one that would produce lasting dividends and financial security for his artist.

Although the advance was smaller than the standard for other artists at the time, it was still significant enough for Young to make a down payment on a brand new home for himself in the notorious hippie community that was L.A.'s Topanga Canyon neighborhood.

Situated in the Santa Monica Mountains between L.A. and Malibu, the Topanga Canyon of the sixties was something of an idyllic artists'

Picture sleeve 45 of CSN&Y's Joni Mitchell cover "Woodstock" backed with Neil Young's "Helpless."   *Courtesy of Tom Therme collection*

enclave—actually a "hippie haven" would probably be a better term—populated by a bizarre mix of outlaw bikers, musicians, and other assorted long-hairs and counterculture types. Neil's newfound neighbors at the time included such notables as actor Dean Stockwell, a fellow music freak and an early and vocal fan of Young's—who would eventually introduce the artist to new-wavers Devo in the late seventies—inspiring both Young's *Human Highway* film and his groundbreaking *Rust Never Sleeps* album in the process.

The atmosphere in Topanga was likewise typical of the sixties counterculture. Drugs and music were the driving force of the day, and by this time Young had become an avid marijuana smoker himself, which some of those around him saw as a sign of his newfound confidence (Young had previously been regarded as something of a lightweight when it came to pot and other drugs—perhaps because of his other fragile health issues—even as nearly everyone else around him indulged themselves both freely and, according to most accounts, quite often).

With the impromptu jam sessions that were coming out of the Topanga scene on a near nightly basis—not to mention the rather abundant drugs and sex that came along with them—came the inevitable string of bizarre and colorful counterculture characters that would pass through this community.

At one such juncture, Young would even end up rubbing shoulders with future mass murderer Charles Manson. At that time an aspiring musician himself, Manson's path crossed Young's through a mutual acquaintance with Beach Boys drummer Dennis Wilson.

With "Squeaky" Fromme and the rest of the ever-present "Manson Girls" always in tow behind their charismatic guru in various combinations whenever he showed up in Topanga, Young was also fascinated by their eerie devotion to him. "They looked right through the rest of us," Young has since said of the odd meetings with the future architect of one of history's most infamous mass murder sprees.

Young was nonetheless actually impressed enough with Manson's music to talk him up to Warner Brothers executives like Mo Ostin. Young once described Manson to Ostin and the Warner brass as "similar to Dylan" and that "he just makes this stuff up as he goes." Young has since also remarked that Manson's ultimate rejection by the record industry was what his crime spree was really all about.

It was as part of this same odd community of hippies, bikers, and freaks in Topanga Canyon that Young would also meet his first wife, Susan Acevedo.

According to most accounts, Acevedo—whom he met at the Canyon Kitchen diner she ran—functioned as equal parts personal manager and surrogate mother figure. She has been described by some as a "Rassy" type figure (referring to Young's own mother)—strong-willed, organized to a fault, very protective of her loved ones, and of her husband in particular.

Young's first solo album, released as the year 1968 ended and 1969 began, was, in record-industry lingo, a "stiff."

Not that the self-titled album doesn't have its share of gems—tracks like "The Old Laughing Lady" and especially "The Loner" have certainly stood the test of time in the decades since the album's original release. But at the time it first came out, Young's solo debut just didn't quite set the rock music world on fire in the way its creators had probably hoped for.

Produced by David Briggs, with some help from Jack Nitzsche (who had also helped craft the symphonic layers of Young's latter-day Springfield songs "Expecting to Fly" and "Broken Arrow"), much of the album is recorded with that same multilayered approach. The album was also recorded using studio musicians like latter-day Springfield bandmate Jim Messina and guitarist Ry Cooder (who is said to have somewhat thumbed his nose at Neil Young as a musician).

"I should have just left it alone," Young has been quoted as saying in interviews in the years since, speaking of the album's many recording studio tweaks and overdubbed tracks. Young has also said that he is nonetheless thankful that he learned from the experience and has since gotten the tendency to "over-record" well out of his system—something that would become readily apparent on his very next album, recorded with his newly christened band Crazy Horse.

Another factor that almost certainly affected the poor sales showing of Young's solo debut is the album cover. A painting of Young by Topanga artist Ron Diehl, the bizarre portrait featured Young's face with the buildings of L.A. coming up across his chest on the bottom, set against a backdrop of flaming mountains.

Most notably, the album cover didn't even have Neil Young's name on it, at least not on the original jacket. This was corrected on a second pressing of the album—which also cleaned up some of the more excessively overdubbed tracks.

But the commercial damage had already been done.

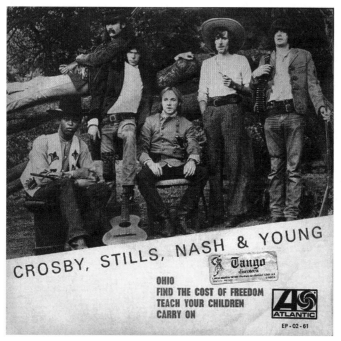

Rare four-track CSN&Y single combining tracks from *Déjà Vu* with the "Ohio" single.   *Courtesy of Tom Therme collection*

5

When I Saw Those Thrashers Rolling By

Neil Young and Crazy Horse

Neil Young has been quoted as saying, "If I played Crazy Horse tours every tour, I'd be dead."

Perhaps this at least partially helps explain his long-standing, on-again, off-again association with the group that has been described as "the third best garage band in the world" (by legendary concert promoter Bill Graham) and as "the American Rolling Stones" (by Young himself).

On the song "Thrasher" from his classic *Rust Never Sleeps* album (one of the many records Neil Young has made with Crazy Horse), some fans believe the song lyrics "So I got bored and left them there, they were just deadweight to me," refer to Neil Young's often contentious relationship with Crosby, Stills and Nash, and specifically to one of the many times he left that group over the years, usually over artistic differences. But in the very same song, when Young sings "When I saw those thrashers rolling by, looking more than two lanes wide, I was feelin' like my day had just begun," he could just as easily be referring to Crazy Horse.

"They're primitive, but they've got soul," Young has said of Crazy Horse. And when Neil Young says somebody "has got soul," it is high praise indeed.

Down in Hollywood, We Played So Good

Dating back to 1969's *Everybody Knows This Is Nowhere*, whenever Young wants to crank Old Black up to eleven and let it thrash, his band of choice has nearly always been none other than the mighty Horse. Although they sometimes have to wait years in between projects, Crazy Horse is also the band that has enjoyed the longest working relationship with the mercurial Young.

Twelve of the albums in Young's vast catalog—beginning with *Everybody Knows This Is Nowhere*, continuing through classics like *Rust Never Sleeps* and *Ragged Glory*, and ending with 2003's *Greendale*—are officially attributed to Neil Young and Crazy Horse. At least five others, including such albums as *Tonight's the Night*, *Zuma*, and *American Stars and Bars* prominently feature various members of the group. Although Crazy Horse are not officially billed on the album covers, it is common knowledge that the band are prominently featured on several cuts. These are, at least in part, Neil Young and Crazy Horse records.

How could albums that feature songs like "Tonight's the Night," "Like a Hurricane," and "Cortez the Killer" be anything but?

On a number of Young's other recordings, such as *Comes a Time* and *Are You Passionate?*, the Horse likewise played a significant role in their creation. But for various reasons their involvement was cut short.

In the case of the former, Young somewhat uncharacteristically uses Crazy Horse on the softer-sounding folk-rock songs of that album like "Lotta Love." The latter began as a Crazy Horse project but later took a left turn when he decided he wanted to pursue a more R&B feel and used members of Booker T. and the MGs and other studio musicians instead. Hey, nobody ever said working with Neil Young was easy.

One thing's for sure, when it comes to Crazy Horse there is no middle ground—you either love them or you hate them (David Crosby has been among the more vocal of the Horse's many detractors).

Full Moon and a Jumpin' Tune

When Neil Young first began playing with Crazy Horse in 1968, he didn't so much put together the group as he did steal them.

Crazy Horse actually began life as a vocal group based out of Columbus, Georgia, called Danny and the Memories (named after its then lead singer, future guitarist and ultimate rock-'n'-roll tragedy Danny Whitten).

Moving out west to San Francisco at the height of the hippie movement centered there, the band briefly changed its name to the Psyrcle and moved into a more psychedelic direction, releasing a record produced by Sly Stone (who was at the time a popular local DJ, prior to enjoying his own rock star success—and accompanying excess—with Sly and the Family Stone).

The group eventually wound up in Los Angeles, and by now had expanded to a seven-piece band featuring three guitarists, along with drums, bass, and an electric violinist. They called themselves the Rockets. Although Whitten was now playing guitar, it was his singing voice that seemed to draw the most attention. When Danny Hutton was first putting together his concept of a band fronted by three vocalists (who would later become very successful as the late sixties pop group Three Dog Night), Whitten was among the vocalists being considered for one of the three slots.

Young also became a fan of the Rockets, and began to join the group for informal jam sessions at their Laurel Canyon "Rockets Headquarters." At Whitten's invitation, Young also joined the band onstage during a gig at the Whisky A Go-Go, where his incendiary guitar work with Old Black blew everyone away and left original Rockets guitarist George Whitsell in the dust.

With Young already looking ahead to a more straightforward approach for his next record—following all of the overdubs and studio tinkering that had plagued his solo debut—he invited three members of the Rockets (Whitten, bassist Billy Talbot, and drummer Ralph Molina) to join him for a preliminary jam session in Topanga Canyon.

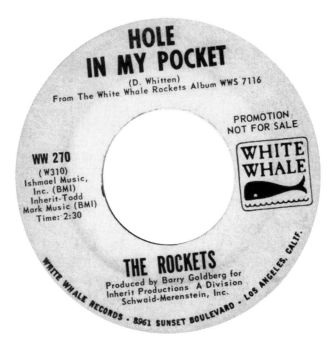

Original pre-Crazy Horse single by the Rockets on White Whale
Records (also home to the Turtles). "Hole in My Pocket" was written by Crazy Horse guitarist Danny Whitten, who later died a tragic
premature death the same day he was fired from the *Harvest* tour by
Neil Young.   *Courtesy of Tom Therme collection*

And that is the story of how Neil Young stole the Rockets in order to create
the longest-lasting and most durable of his many bands, Crazy Horse.

Has Your Band Begun to Rust?

While no one would ever accuse Crazy Horse of being virtuoso musicians—David
Crosby has summed up his opinion of the band on more than one occasion
by simply saying "they can't play"—there is little doubt that the sum of their
individual parts creates a more perfect whole. The Horse are capable of locking
into a very effective, if occasionally sloppy and loose groove whenever called
upon to do so, like no other band Neil Young was worked with. In short, they
fit Neil Young like a glove.

From "Down by the River" to "Cortez the Killer" to "Love and Only Love,"
Crazy Horse have also proven themselves time and time again to be the best
vehicle—perhaps the only vehicle, really—for those times when Young feels the
need to shred on those trademark extended, hypnotic guitar solos. Indeed, these
lengthy—and loud!—sonic explorations have become as much a signature of his
sound as the lusher-sounding folk-pop of albums like *Harvest*.

Nowhere, is this more apparent than on his second solo album—and his first with Crazy Horse—1969's *Everybody Knows This Is Nowhere.*

In sharp contrast to the tentativeness of his self-titled solo debut, this is the sound of an artist who has at long last found his true musical calling, and of a band responding to it by firing on all cylinders and locking into an absolutely magical groove throughout. With Crazy Horse behind him, Neil Young's second album was the first of what would be many truly great ones.

Purple Words on a Grey Background

The two centerpieces of *Everybody Knows This Is Nowhere* are also its two longest songs, "Down by the River" and "Cowgirl in the Sand."

With each of these songs, Neil established a template that would serve him quite well many times over in the years and decades to come. Both of these songs are more like sonic pictures, really. Clocking in at roughly nine and ten minutes long respectively, the songs show Neil Young and Crazy Horse turning the idea of the guitar solo as an instrumental break completely inside out.

In both instances, it is in fact Neil's vocals that serve as the brief breaks between the extended washes of guitar and feedback that dominate these two amazing songs. Both songs also marked the formal recorded introduction to the world of Old Black—the 1953 black Les Paul Neil Young purchased for fifty bucks from Jim Messina, and that has since become Neil's axe of choice when the job calls for that little extra something that is both dirty and loud.

Amazingly, both songs, along with the album's single "Cinnamon Girl," were written in a single day while Neil Young was sick and running a 103-degree fever. There has been ample speculation throughout the years over just who the subject of "Cinnamon Girl" was, with many stepping forward to claim credit for being the song's inspiration.

I Could Be Happy the Rest of My Life

One of the more credible stories we've come across can be found in a March 7, 2010, post on the Neil Young news site Thrasher's Wheat. In the article, an unidentified woman who was a high school student at the time in 1968 claims to have met the rock star in front of the Riverboat, a Toronto coffee house where Young was scheduled to play a gig that night. Spotting his guitar case, the then fifteen-year-old used an opening line about interviewing musicians to be her boyfriend. Young took the bait, replying "what's involved?"

Our "Cinnamon Girl" picks up the story from there:

> I said "You get to hang around with me for a couple of hours. I will ask you questions about dating and relationships and see if you pass. There will be kissing involved . . . are you a good kisser?"

Neil said "I guess so."

He seemed to be a little shy but amused by the situation. He didn't seem to be in any hurry to go anywhere and so the game started. When we were together that night, I asked Neil to write a happy song about me and he promised he would. My nickname at school was "The Cinnamon Girl."

The brief relationship ended when the "Cinnamon Girl" failed to meet Young at the Riverboat because she had taken sick. Interestingly, Young also became ill around this time, famously writing the songs "Down by the River," "Cowgirl in the Sand," and of course "Cinnamon Girl" in a single afternoon while nursing his fever. Coincidence? Not according to the alleged "Cinnamon Girl" herself:

"I think 'Cowgirl in the Sand' is also about me," she says today. "When we first met I was playing a crazy game with him, and he seemed amused by it. We talked about horseback riding, getting a farm one day, and the fact that I wouldn't tell him my age. I turned the conversation to the ages girls could wed in different provinces yet couldn't drink or vote. We spent the night in a park on the edge of a kid's sandbox talking about our lives, our dreams, and the urgency for him to get to California."

Reprise Records pressing of the Crazy Horse "solo" 45 "All Alone Now" written by original Crazy Horse member George Whitsell.

Courtesy of Tom Therme collection

The coincidences are intriguing. On his Thrasher's Wheat website, Young superfan Thrasher connects the dots this way: "Down by the River (boat)"; he shot his baby (broke up with his young girlfriend); a red head ("Cinnamon Girl"); who was a "Cowgirl (hippie) in the Sand (box at the park)."

Thrasher concludes this weaving of parallel lines with the simple observation: "you just never know." We tend to agree.

On "Cinnamon Girl," the tight, compact rocker that chugs along to a funky groove courtesy of Talbot and Molina, Young sings that he is "a dreamer of pictures." With *Everybody Knows This Is Nowhere*, he paints these sonic pictures with all the mastery of an artist who has truly perfected his craft.

The record-buying public likewise responded.

"Cinnamon Girl" became a modest hit as a single, and is also notable for its infamous guitar solo, which essentially is structured around the repetitive use of a single note. But it was mainly the FM progressive rock airplay of "Cowgirl in the Sand" and "Down by the River" that most helped *Everybody Knows This is Nowhere* become Neil Young's first hit on the Billboard albums chart, where it peaked at #34.

Buddy Miles, best known at the time as the drummer with both Mike Bloomfield's Electric Flag and Jimi Hendrix's Band of Gypsys, would also score a hit in 1970 with a cover of "Down by the River" on his own solo album *Them Changes*.

Sea of Madness

In the meantime, Stephen Stills, Young's former bandmate in Buffalo Springfield, had a hit of his own on his hands with the debut album from Crosby, Stills, and Nash, his newly formed supergroup with former Byrds member David Crosby and ex-Hollies member Graham Nash.

On the strength of songs like Stills's "Suite: Judy Blue Eyes" (his emotional outpouring of romantic emotion to his girlfriend, folksinger Judy Collins) and Nash's pop hit "Marrakesh Express," CSN's debut had become a megahit. The only problem was, Stills had produced and played nearly everything on the album (save for the vocals), and the "band" needed to tour the record.

Although Young was reluctant at first to sign on (and both Stills and Nash had their own doubts as well), Elliot Roberts (who was by now managing both Young and CSN) engineered a deal that amounted to the sort of offer Young simply couldn't refuse. Under the arrangement, Young would become a full one-fourth musical, creative, and financial partner in the newly christened Crosby, Stills, Nash, and Young, and he would be able to pursue his projects as a solo artist and with Crazy Horse at the same time.

Young's relationship with his new partners in the "American Beatles" would prove to have more than its share of ups and downs over the years—the schism between them became immediately and readily apparent by the time of the band's second gig at Woodstock, where Young refused to be filmed for CSN&Y's spot in the movie documenting the historic festival.

But at the time, the decision to complete CSN&Y was probably the right one for Young. With his own star already on the rise, Young's membership in America's hottest band at the time would pay its own dividends and eventually help launch him to superstardom, first breaking his 1970 album *After the Gold Rush* into Billboard's top ten and finally landing Young his first #1 album as a solo artist with *Harvest.*

The Needle and the Damage Done

Crazy Horse in the meantime would be put on the first of what would become several decades of holding patterns between Neil Young projects, where the band's services would only become required as needed.

Young did briefly use Crazy Horse on the early sessions for what became the *After the Gold Rush* album, but later ended up firing the band when, among other issues, it became apparent that guitarist Danny Whitten's drug problems were becoming an increasing liability. Neil Young and Crazy Horse had played a handful of concert dates in 1970 (including a great show at the Fillmore East,

Radio station promo single for "One Thing I Love" by Crazy Horse.
Courtesy of Tom Therme collection

which has since been captured for posterity on Neil Young's *Archives Vol. 1*). But eventually, Whitten's inability to hold it together became impossible to overlook when he began nodding out onstage right in the middle of the group's performances.

If Young's membership in CSN&Y had put any idea of Neil Young and Crazy Horse as a long-term proposition on hold—establishing a pattern that continues to this day—Whitten's drug problems only served to further complicate the situation. In the end, Whitten's condition worsened to such a degree that he was eventually fired altogether from Crazy Horse—the band he had created—by the rest of the group. About a year later, Whitten was found dead of a drug overdose after being fired from the guitar spot on the *Harvest* tour by Young earlier the same day.

Arguments can be—and have certainly been—made about the effect Whitten's death left on Young's own psyche over the years, as well as on his long-term, on-again, off-again relationship with the Horse. What is known for sure is that the lingering feelings of guilt over Whitten's death, along with other issues, played heavily enough on Young to cast a shadow of doom over what should have been the most triumphant tour of his career.

Instead, the *Harvest* tour found Young in an often surly mood both on- and offstage, while audiences who had come to hear the mellow folk-rock of his #1 megahit album were instead subjected to the darker, moodier new songs eventually documented on the live *Times Fade Away* album.

Guitarist Danny Whitten's heroin addiction and resulting death had left a deep enough mark on Young that his next several albums would take a sharp turn toward a darker new direction that Young himself has since described as "the ditch." Of the three albums that make up what fans now commonly refer to as the Ditch Trilogy, 1975's *Tonight's the Night* is the most direct response to the drug-related deaths of both Whitten and CSN&Y roadie Bruce Berry, who also became a casualty of drugs during the same period.

For their own part, the members of Crazy Horse seemed to have taken having their careers as Neil Young's band being put on hold mostly in stride over the years.

In 1971, they recruited young guitar prodigy Nils Lofgren (who also played on Young's *After the Gold Rush*) and producer Jack Nitzsche (doing double duty as the band's "fifth member" on keyboards) and released a "solo album" of their own without Young. Although the album sold poorly, it is notable for the inclusion of songs like "Dance, Dance, Dance" and "(Baby Let's Go) Downtown"—both of which would later prove to be significant entries in the Neil Young canon.

Whitten's guitar slot was eventually filled for good by Frank "Poncho" Sampedro, a guitarist Billy Talbot met in Mexico. In addition to Crazy Horse, Sampedro went on to play with several of Neil Young's bands, including the Bluenotes and the Restless.

6

Sleeps with Angels (Too Soon)

Departed Bandmates, Brothers in Arms, and Sisters in Song

W hat follows is a short list of musicians, collaborators, and otherwise significant supporting players who, over the course of Neil Young's long career, have played significant roles and who have since passed on.

This is not intended as a complete list by any means, but rather as a short overview of some of Young's most important musical partners in crime over the years, who were taken away far too soon and without whom many of his greatest artistic achievements would not have been possible.

Carrie Snodgress—Actress/Girlfriend

Although this chapter is primarily devoted to the artists and musicians who played significant roles in Young's career and who have since passed on, it would be a major omission not to include actress Carrie Snodgress on the list.

As far as I know, Carrie Snodgress has never sung or played a single note on a Neil Young album or performed with him onstage. But there is no question that she was a major influence on his songwriting—particularly during his most commercially successful period.

Several of the songs on Young's smash 1972 album *Harvest* were undeniably inspired by the actress he had fallen deeply in love with—most notably "Heart of Gold" and "A Man Needs a Maid."

At one point prior to the release of *Harvest,* Young had even taken to performing the two songs together as a suite (this can be heard on the *Archives Performance Series* release *Live at Massey Hall 1971*). A number of songs on subsequent releases were likewise inspired by his relationship with Snodgress, including "Motion Pictures" from *On the Beach* (which is even dedicated to her on the original album sleeve) and "New Mama" from *Tonight's the Night.*

In the song "A Man Needs a Maid," Young even describes how they met in lyrics like "I fell in love with the actress, she played a part that I could understand." After seeing Carrie Snodgress in the movie *Diary of a Mad Housewife* with roadie Guillermo Giachetti, Young dispatched him to arrange a meeting—which eventually took place in a hospital room where Young was nursing back problems.

After the two of them fell in love, Snodgress effectively turned her back on her then quite promising movie career (this was coming off of an Oscar nomination for her *Diary of a Mad Housewife* role) to take up permanent residence at Young's Broken Arrow ranch. Their son Zeke (who, like Neil's other son Ben with present wife Pegi, is afflicted with cerebral palsy) was born in September 1972.

After the two broke up, Snodgress eventually resumed her movie career, although it never quite regained the luster of her brief glory days as a Golden Globe winner and Academy Award nominee.

Carrie Snodgress died on April 1, 2004, at the age of fifty-seven of heart failure as she was awaiting a liver transplant.

Danny Whitten—Guitar, Vocals (Crazy Horse)

Danny Whitten was the brilliant but troubled guitarist, vocalist, and songwriter who (along with Neil Young himself) was responsible for the two-pronged guitar attack heard on "Down by the River" and "Cowgirl in the Sand" (from the classic *Everybody Knows This Is Nowhere* album—Neil Young's first recordings with Crazy Horse).

Although acknowledged by virtually everyone who has ever heard him as a brilliant musician with infinite rock-star potential—keyboardist and producer Jack Nitzsche once famously called him "the only black musician in Crazy Horse" in reference to his natural musical ability—some have also suggested that Whitten felt overshadowed by Neil Young in what had once been his own band, Crazy Horse.

But Whitten also had a darker side, which was most noticeably reflected in his heavy drug use. As early as 1970, his increasing addiction to heroin and other drugs had become an ongoing concern affecting both Young and the rest of Crazy Horse.

Things finally came to a head when, among other things, Whitten began nodding off during recording sessions and even onstage during the band's concerts. This led to Young eventually firing Whitten and the rest of Crazy Horse (save for drummer Ralph Molina) during the sessions for Young's third solo album *After the Gold Rush*.

Whitten was eventually asked to leave Crazy Horse altogether in 1972 by the rest of the band, who were by this time making albums on their own in addition to their higher-profile gig sometimes backing Neil Young. Whitten, the one-time leader of Crazy Horse, had become the band's biggest liability.

Danny Whitten died of a drug overdose in Los Angeles on November 18, 1972, shortly after being fired by Young earlier the very same day. Whitten was just twenty-nine years old.

Despite Whitten's drug problems, Young had decided to give him one final chance when he offered the guitarist a slot in the Stray Gators, the new band Young had assembled for a huge American arena tour booked to promote the 1972 #1 smash album *Harvest*. When the guitarist "wasn't cutting it" (as Young would later recall) during rehearsals for the tour, Whitten was given fifty dollars and a one-way plane ticket to L.A., and told to go back home. He was pronounced dead in Los Angeles later that night, apparently overdosing on a lethal cocktail of alcohol and Valium.

It's been said that upon receiving the news of Whitten's death, Neil Young blamed himself for some time afterwards. What's absolutely certain is that a significant number of his subsequent songs including "The Needle and the Damage Done" and those making up the album *Tonight's the Night* were at least partially inspired by Whitten's death (as well as another recent drug overdose casualty in the Neil Young camp, that of roadie Bruce Berry).

Of Whitten's own songs, the best known is probably "(Come On Baby Let's Go) Downtown," a song about scoring heroin he co-wrote with Neil Young, and that he eerily sings posthumously on the *Tonight's the Night* album. Another of Whitten's best-known songs, "I Don't Want to Talk About It," has been famously covered by Rod Stewart and others.

Bruce Berry—Roadie

Bruce Berry is probably best known today as the guy immortalized as the "working man who used to load that Ford Econoline," "sing a song in a shaky voice," and "sleep until the afternoon" on the title track from Neil Young's *Tonight's the Night* album.

He is also the very same guy his close friend Richard O'Connell found dead on June 7, 1973. Although the body was discovered by O'Connell on June 7, Berry had most likely died days three earlier on June 4—overdosing on a particularly lethal mixture of heroin and cocaine.

"'Cause people let me tell you, it sent a chill up and down my spine," Young sings on *Tonight's the Night*. "When I picked up the telephone, and heard that he'd died out on the mainline." The words sound as darkly chilling now as they must have felt when he first wrote them.

It was likely Berry's family connections with brothers Jan and Ken that got him the gig as a roadie with Crosby, Stills, Nash, and Young in the first place. Brother Jan was one-half of the chart-topping surf-rock duo Jan and Dean, while Ken owned and operated Studio Instrument Rentals, a very successful rehearsal space and gear shop favored by a number of the top Los Angeles–based rock bands of the day, including CSN&Y.

When Bruce began working with S.I.R. as a teenager, he also brought his pals McConnell and Guillermo Giachetti along for the ride. Before long, Berry was working on the road crew for CSN&Y, reaping all the usual benefits of drugs and girls you'd expect, while loading equipment in and out of the very same Ford

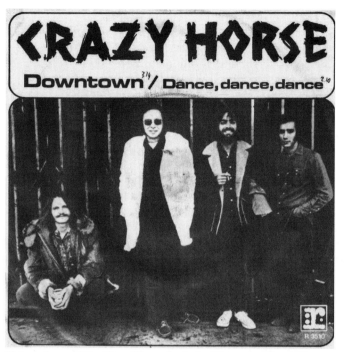

Picture sleeve of the Crazy Horse single for "Downtown" and "Dance, Dance, Dance." Crazy Horse founder Danny Whitten's life was tragically cut short by a drug overdose. *Courtesy of Tom Therme collection*

Econoline Van later made famous by the Neil Young song that prematurely eulogizes him.

As their confidence in the likable young man grew, Berry's duties eventually grew to include procuring drugs for some of the other musicians and roadies in the CSN&Y camp—which at one point got him into considerable trouble with Crosby and Nash when he showed up with cocaine at a 1973 CSN&Y band meeting in Hawaii.

It seemed that the meeting had at least been partially called for the distinct purpose of convincing Young that Stills's drug problems were reasonably under control, and that things would be just fine for an upcoming proposed CSN&Y tour. Crosby and Nash were said to have been furious when Berry crashed the botched "intervention" carrying his usual supply. Young himself decided afterwards that he wanted no part of it.

Even so, both Crosby and Stills continued to engage in drug-related activities with Berry, although the roadie was by most accounts actually introduced to heroin (somewhat ironically) by Young's partner in Crazy Horse, Danny Whitten. By the time Berry returned to America from an extended overseas stay with Stills in England, he was a full-fledged junkie—even going so far as to allegedly steal one of Crosby's guitars and sell it for drugs.

Berry's death by drug overdose, coming just months after Danny Whitten had likewise been taken by the "white lady," shook Neil Young to his core.

Not long afterwards, Young pulled out of the latest attempt at a projected new Crosby, Stills, Nash, and Young record—which no doubt considerably pissed off his CSN&Y bandmates—and instead devoted himself to making the album recorded at Ken Berry's Studio Instrument Rentals space that eventually emerged in 1975 as the dark, druggy masterpiece *Tonight's the Night.*

Comrie Smith—Rhythm Guitar, Banjo

Comrie Smith was Neil Young's grammar school buddy in Canada, as well as his one of his earliest musical accomplices. Long before he met the likes of Stephen Stills, or before there was ever a Buffalo Springfield, a CSN&Y, a Crazy Horse, or a Stray Gators, Young recorded some of his earliest original songs with his close friend Comrie Smith.

Like Young himself, Smith was heavily influenced by Canadian folk artists like Ian and Sylvia very early on, and the two budding young musicians soon bonded over this shared passion.

Together, Young and Smith cut several folk-influenced sides back in the early days using little else but a reel-to-reel recorder, Young's "Dylan kit" of a guitar and a harmonica, and Smith's banjo. They were recorded in the unlikely setting of an attic at their old school, Lawrence Park.

On these makeshift recordings, including such early original Neil Young originals as the folk-influenced "Casting Me Away from You," and "There Goes My Babe," as well as the more raucous-sounding, R&B-influenced rave-up "Hello Lonely Woman," one can already hear the two most recognizable elements in the duality of the Young sound we've come to know today. Even back then, Young was as comfortably adept at thoughtful, sensitive songwriting as he was at rocking the house (or, in this case, at least the school attic).

Fortunately, these early recordings with Comrie Smith survive today, and can be heard on Young's *Archives Vol. 1* boxed set. Smith passed away due to complications from heart failure on December 11, 2009. He was sixty-four years old.

Rufus Thibodeaux—Fiddle

Fiddle player Rufus Thibodeaux first began recording with Young on his *Comes a Time* album, but more notably was later part of the International Harvesters, the band Young assembled for his country-flavored album *Old Ways*. Thibodeaux can also be heard on Young's 1980 album *Hawks and Doves.*

Revered in Nashville as both a Cajun and country fiddler of the highest order, Thibodeaux's resume reads a who's who of country music legends—from Bob Wills and Jim Reeves to Lefty Frizell and George Jones. Along with musicians like Floyd Cramer and the late, great Chet Atkins, Thibodeaux was considered by most of his peers and fellow country music associates in Nashville and elsewhere as simply the very best at what he did.

Much like Ben Keith, Thibodeaux also became one of Neil Young's "go-to guys" during Young's occasional left turns away from harder rock and more toward folk- and country-influenced "singer-songwriter" records.

Rufus Thibodeaux died peacefully on August 12, 2005. Although he had been in declining health, due largely to complications from diabetes, Thibodeaux remained active, continuing to make music right up until the end of his life.

Jack Nitzsche—Keyboards, Producer

Although he is remembered today mostly for his work with Neil Young, Jack Nitzsche already had a pretty impressive resume as a composer, producer, and arranger before the two of them ever met. A true musical renaissance man, Nitzsche either wrote or co-wrote hits ranging from the Searchers' "Needles and Pins" to "Up Where We Belong" (from the film *An Officer and a Gentleman*).

Nitzsche also worked with Phil Spector, helping to craft the producer's legendary "Wall of Sound" on such landmark recordings as Ike and Tina Turner's "River Deep, Mountain High." He later helped develop the keyboard sound heard on such early Rolling Stones singles as "Paint It Black."

A naturally gifted keyboardist, Nitzsche was also a member of the legendary group of all-star L.A. session musicians known as the Wrecking Crew, along with people like drummer Hal Blaine, keyboardist Leon Russell, and guitarist Glenn Campbell—playing on numerous pop single hits by groups ranging from the Beach Boys to the Monkees during the sixties. Nitzsche has also either scored outright or contributed to the soundtracks for a very impressive number of films including *The Exorcist, Stand By Me,* and *One Flew Over the Cuckoo's Nest.*

Nitzsche's professional relationship with Young began when he produced the groundbreaking songs "Expecting to Fly" and "Broken Arrow" for Buffalo Springfield. Essentially Neil Young solo recordings, at the time both were still seen as a bold artistic step forward for the Springfield (particularly the former), and they continue to hold up very well today. From there, Nitzsche also co-produced Young's solo debut (with David Briggs), although the results there were far less spectacular.

Even so, Nitzsche maintained a long and often contentious relationship with Neil Young over the years, performing both with Crazy Horse and on the artist's more commercial albums such as *Harvest.*

Although Young has long since said that his brutal honesty was one of the qualities he admired most about Nitzsche, this was probably not always the case. The two of them have feuded both often and publicly, most famously in a 1974 interview with *Crawdaddy!* magazine, where among other things, Nitzsche criticized Young's lyrics ("His lyrics are so dumb and pretentious") and his guitar playing ("Everyone in the band was bored to death with those terrible guitar solos").

Nitzsche has also gone back and forth many times on the subject of Crazy Horse, calling them "the American Rolling Stones" in one breath and lambasting their musical limitations and lack of professionalism in the next ("Whatever clothes they woke up in, that's what they wear on stage").

Despite their often acrimonious relationship (Nitzsche even eventually took up with Young's former girlfriend, actress Carrie Snodgress), the two continued their on-again, off-again working relationship, striking gold together once again on Young's 1992 album *Harvest Moon*.

Jack Nitzsche passed away of a heart attack at the age of sixty-three on August 25, 2000.

Bruce Palmer—Bass (Buffalo Springfield, Trans Band)

Praised by both Neil Young and Stephen Stills as one of the best guitarists either man has ever had the pleasure to play with, Bruce Palmer would still never again fully reclaim the rock-star glory he had once briefly experienced as bassist for the Buffalo Springfield.

Replaced in that band after his drug problems began to catch up with him by Jim Messina during the group's final months, Palmer was briefly considered for the bass part in Crosby, Stills, Nash, and Young, only to be passed over in favor of the much younger Greg Reeves. In 1971, Palmer also released a solo album for Verve Records titled *The Cycle Is Complete*.

Years later, in 1982, Young once again tapped Palmer for the bass slot in the Trans Band, where he soon became a source of considerable frustration both to band members like Nils Lofgren and to Young himself. At one particularly volatile point, this even caused Young to come to blows with him during a heated band meeting in a hotel room. Although Young never actually fired him from the band, Palmer's alcohol abuse while on an already chaotic European tour plagued with technical problems nonetheless eventually cost him the gig.

As rumors of a Buffalo Springfield reunion tour continued to spring up every couple of years during the eighties, Palmer briefly attempted to put together his own version of a new Buffalo Springfield in 1986. But without the power of that band's two stars—Young and Stills—the new "Buffalo Springfield Revisited" died a predictable death.

Bruce Palmer and Neil Young first met when the latter joined the Mynah Birds, Palmer's band with a young Ricky "Rick James" Matthews (ironically it was James who later recommended Greg Reeves for the bass spot in CSN&Y, likely costing Palmer the gig). It was also Palmer who rode shotgun in Young's hearse when the two of them met up with Stills on that fateful day in a traffic jam on L.A.'s famous Sunset Boulevard—a legendary meeting that led to the formation of Buffalo Springfield.

Bruce Palmer, original bassist for the Buffalo Springfield, was found dead in Belleville, Ontario, Canada, on October 1, 2004, of a heart attack at the age of fifty-eight.

Dewey Martin—Drums (Buffalo Springfield)

Born Walter Milton Dwayne Midkiff, Dewey Martin completed the Buffalo Springfield lineup after being suggested to the band by Chris Hillman of the Byrds. Martin had previously been playing with the Dillards, a country rock band that had recently dismissed Martin after deciding to continue on without a drummer.

Prior to the Dillards, Palmer had played with the Northwest-based rock band Sir Walter Raleigh and the Coupons and had also done some work with fifties rock veterans Roy Orbison, Carl Perkins, and the Everly Brothers. As the oldest member of the band, Martin not only brought much-needed experience to the group, but as Young has since noted, "he was also one hell of a drummer."

Throughout the trials and tribulations of Buffalo Springfield's brief existence as a group, Martin stuck to the band like glue. Once they finally disbanded for good, Martin also attempted to carry on with the name, although he was eventually stopped from using it in a legal action filed by Young and Stills (Martin's "New Buffalo Springfield" was subsequently renamed Blue Mountain Eagle). Martin also signed on for Bruce Palmer's attempts to revive Buffalo Springfield during the eighties. Eventually, Martin retired from the music business and found work as an auto mechanic.

Dewey Martin was inducted into the Rock and Roll Hall of Fame in 1997 along with the other members of Buffalo Springfield—an event that Neil Young himself famously no-showed.

Buffalo Springfield drummer Dewey Martin died on February 1, 2009, in Van Nuys, California, of natural causes. He was sixty-eight years old.

Nicolette Larson—Vocals

During the seventies, Nicolette Larson earned a reputation as a great backup singer on albums by emerging "new country" artists like Emmylou Harris (*Luxury Liner*). She first became associated with Neil Young after mutual friend Linda Ronstadt recommended her as a backup vocalist for Young's *American Stars and Bars* album. Both Ronstadt and Larson would eventually be heard backing Young as "the Saddlebags" on the very same record.

Young, who by this time had also begun a brief romantic relationship with Larson, used her once again for his *Comes a Time* album, where Larson can be heard harmonizing with him on his cover of Ian and Sylvia's "Four Strong Winds," among other tracks.

Larson's strong showing on *Comes a Time* soon led to her own recording contract with Warner Brothers, which released her critically and commercially well-received 1978 solo debut album *Nicolette*.

Anchored by a strong cover version of Young's "Lotta Love" (also originally recorded for the *Comes a Time* album), the album earned raves from the likes of *Rolling Stone* magazine. However, despite showing such initial promise, the success of her debut album would never again be duplicated.

Larson continued to release solo albums over the years as well as sing backup vocals on albums by artists who mostly fell into the laid-back, seventies and eighties L.A. pop category of people like Christopher Cross and the Doobie Brothers.

Not surprisingly, Nicolette Larson eventually married Warner Brothers house producer Ted Templeman, who was the man behind the boards on many of these records. In 1992, Larson also musically reunited with Young to sing backup vocals on his *Harvest Moon* album.

Nicolette Larson, who is best remembered for her 1979 Neil Young–penned hit single "Lotta Love," died on December 16, 1997, from what was officially cited as complications from liver failure related to cerebral edema. She was just forty-five years old.

David Briggs—Producer

Long associated with some of Neil Young's most classic work—from *Everybody Knows This Is Nowhere* and *After the Gold Rush* to *Harvest* and *Rust Never Sleeps*—David Briggs was also the man behind the boards for some of Young's least commercially viable albums like *Re-ac-tor*, *Trans*, and *Old Ways*.

Perhaps most notably, Briggs was also the producer for Young's greatest work with Crazy Horse, where he harnessed the raw power of the Horse as perhaps no other producer could have. Briggs's final record with Young was 1994's *Sleeps with Angels*—another great but often overlooked work in the Neil Young canon.

Briggs and Young famously met when the former picked up the latter when he was hitchhiking, and soon developed a relationship that would result in Briggs getting a co-producer's credit on Young's self-titled debut solo album. From there, he went on to produce that album's classic follow-up *Everybody Knows This Is Nowhere*. Prior to their fateful meeting, Briggs had been working at Bill Cosby's Tetragrammaton Records label. He later produced records for a variety of artists including Alice Cooper, Spirit, Nils Lofgren, Grin, Blind Melon, Nick Cave, and others.

But it was Briggs work with Neil Young that became his true, lasting legacy as a producer. One of the more famous quotes attributed to Briggs came when he once answered the question about whether he produced Neil's albums, to which he replied "only the good ones." Another famous Briggs quote probably best sums up his approach to making records, and perhaps best explains why Neil has returned to him time and time again:

"When it comes to rock and roll," Briggs said, "the more you think, the more you stink."

It was this low-fi approach to recording—Briggs has also been quoted as saying he would just as soon eliminate studio gadgetry altogether and run a direct line from the instruments to the tape machines—that has perhaps most endeared him to Young (as well as a younger generation of musicians who likewise prefer Briggs's more basic technique).

Like Young himself, Briggs was a firm believer in capturing the immediacy of the moment, which meant he often had little use for returning later to what he considered a perfectly good track, only to muck it up with overdubs. This, of course, suited Neil Young just fine—particularly when it came to capturing the raw live sound of his work with Crazy Horse on albums like *Zuma* and *Ragged Glory.*

Another trademark of Briggs's work with Neil Young has been his occasional preference for sometimes strange recording locales over the more traditional confines of the recording studio. Much of *After the Gold Rush* was made in the cramped quarters of Young's home in Topanga Canyon at the time. For *Tonight's the Night,* the tequila-fueled sessions took place at the L.A. Studio Instrument Rentals rehearsal space owned by Ken Berry—where they simply knocked out a wall to accommodate the musical madness surrounding that particular landmark recording.

Briggs has also been known to express his opinions rather strongly, reflecting an honesty that also drew Young's respect (as an artist who has likewise become known for being rather opinionated himself).

Neil Young's longtime producer David Briggs passed away on November 26, 1995, following a battle with lung cancer. He was fifty-one years old.

By most accounts, Briggs's short life was one lived to the fullest. His fondness for "fast cars, beautiful women, Vegas trips, and insulting managers and lawyers" was noted by Neil Young biographer Jimmy McDonough in an obituary written for and published by the *Los Angeles Times.* David Briggs continues to be missed.

Larry "L.A." Johnson—Filmmaker, Videographer, Producer

Larry "L.A." Johnson first met Neil Young as a sound engineer on the legendary film document of the 1969 Woodstock festival (for which he also earned an Academy Award nomination for sound editing).

Although Young's reluctance to be filmed during CSN&Y's set that day has long since become the stuff of legend, something about Johnson must have hit a chord within Young, because the two of them have enjoyed a long, and by all accounts very satisfying, working relationship ever since.

Young recruited Johnson soon after *Woodstock* for his *Journey Through the Past* film. Young once again turned to Johnson to produce his experimental (and largely unseen) *Human Highway,* as well as the concert film for *Rust Never Sleeps.* In 1986, Johnson also directed a Neil Young pay-per-view concert with Crazy Horse called *Live from a Rusted Out Garage* that has been described by the few who have seen it as the best document of Neil and the Horse live ever captured on film.

Johnson is also credited as a producer for *Greendale* and *Living with War* albums, as well as the films that accompanied each of them. As head of Young's film production company Shakey Pictures, Johnson also oversaw Young's concert films ranging from *Year of the Horse* to *Red Rocks Live.*

Larry "L.A." Johnson, a filmmaker and producer long associated with Neil Young movie projects ranging from *Rust Never Sleeps* to *Greendale* to CSN&Y's *Déjà Vu Live,* died of a heart attack on January 21, 2010, at the age of sixty-three.

Ben Keith—Pedal Steel, Guitar, Piano, Multi-Instrumentalist (Stray Gators, Santa Monica Flyers, International Harvesters, and Others)

In addition to being Neil Young's pedal steel guitarist on albums like *Harvest* and *Harvest Moon* (which he also co-produced with Young), Ben Keith was the primary musical collaborator on a number of albums spread throughout Young's legendary career, including *Tonight's the Night, Time Fades Away, American Stars and Bars, Comes a Time, Prairie Wind,* and *Chrome Dreams II.* Keith also played pedal steel with a number of Young's touring bands including the Santa Monica Flyers, International Harvesters, and most notably the Stray Gators.

Ben Keith was first tapped in 1972 by Young to work with him on what would end up being Young's biggest-selling album, the worldwide #1 smash *Harvest.* After a chance meeting in Nashville, where he was taping a broadcast of the *Johnny Cash Show,* Young was introduced to Keith by bassist Tim Drummond.

Along with Drummond and drummer Kenny Buttrey, Young and Keith then formed the Stray Gators and began a concert tour to promote the *Harvest* album, which later carried over into shows featuring the newer, less radio-friendly songs eventually documented on the 1973 live album *Time Fades Away.*

Keith stayed on with Young for the dark masterpiece *Tonight's the Night* and remained a constant on his albums from that point forward. Eventually the Stray Gators officially re-formed for the *Harvest* "sequel," 1992's classic *Harvest Moon* album. At the time of his death, Keith had been staying at Young's California ranch and working on yet another new Neil Young album (2010's *Le Noise*) with producer Daniel Lanois.

In addition to his work with Young, Keith has worked with such artists as Todd Rundgren, Waylon Jennings, Linda Ronstadt, the Band, Ringo Starr, and Jewel (Keith produced her multiplatinum seller *Pieces of You*).

Early on in his career prior to his fateful meeting with Neil Young, Keith was well known as an ace Nashville session musician, playing on classic country tracks like Patsy Cline's "I Fall to Pieces." Just before his death, Keith had played on the *Foul Deeds* album by Young's wife Pegi and had completed a short West Coast club tour with the Pegi Young Band, supporting Bert Jansch.

Ben Keith, the multi-instrumentalist and producer best known for his work with Neil Young for nearly four decades, died as this book was being written on July 26, 2010, at the age of seventy-three.

As early reports of Keith's passing initially began surfacing on the Internet, there were few details about the nature or even the exact time of his death. However, director Jonathan Demme, who filmed both Young and Keith in the concert documentaries *Heart of Gold* and *Neil Young's Trunk Show,* confirmed that Keith died of a heart attack in a later report published by the *Los Angeles Times.*

Speaking about Keith in the same article, Demme called him "an elegant, beautiful dude, and obviously a genius. He could play every instrument. He was literally the bandleader on any of that stuff . . . Neil has all the confidence in the world, but with Ben onboard, there were no limits. Neil has a fair measure of the greatness of his music, but he knew he was even better when Ben was there."

Neil Young himself acknowledged Keith's passing onstage at a concert in Winnipeg during his *Twisted Road* tour. Dedicating the song "Old Man" to his friend and longtime collaborator, Young said "This is for Ben Keith. His spirit will live on. The Earth has taken him."

Kenny Buttrey—Drums

Aaron Kenneth "Kenny" Buttrey is best remembered as the drummer of note during Neil Young's transition from the smooth folk-pop of *Harvest* to the rougher-around-the-edges sound of his Ditch Trilogy records *Time Fades Away* and *Tonight's the Night.* Buttrey played on all three of these pivotal albums in the artistic development of Neil Young, as well as on the concert tours behind them.

Buttrey's name also comes up frequently as the guy whose grousing about money might have been a contributing factor (though not the only one) in Young's already foul mood during the tour for *Harvest*—a series of shows that eventually gave way to the abrupt, audience-confusing turn that characterized the latter part of the tour, as well as his next few records.

Even so, there was obviously something about Buttrey's skin work that Young liked, as the drummer was brought back for the "sequel" record *Harvest Moon* twenty years later, a re-creation that was, not coincidentally, also set in Buttrey's native Nashville.

Predictably, and somewhat humorously in retrospect, Buttrey bitched about the money for those sessions as well.

Born in Nashville in 1995, Buttrey also played on notable recordings by Bob Dylan (*Nashville Skyline, Blonde on Blonde, John Wesley Harding*) and Jimmy Buffet (his drums are heard on Buffet's signature tune "Margaritaville"), among numerous others.

Kenny Buttrey died of cancer in Nashville on September 12, 2004. His passing is noted on the inner sleeve liner notes of Young's 2005 *Prairie Wind* album (another *Harvest* rewind recorded in Nashville), alongside that of Young father Scott, who died during the same period.

You See Us Together Chasing the Moonlight

Neil Young's Bands

Crazy Horse—1969–Present

Neil Young (vocal, guitar), Danny Whitten (guitar, vocal), Billy Talbot (bass, vocal), Ralph Molina (drums, vocal), Frank "Poncho" Sampedro (guitar, keyboards) (1975–present).

The most durable of all Neil Young's bands, Crazy Horse's lineup has also featured on and off members like Jack Nitzsche and Nils Lofgren at various junctures—but otherwise has stayed relatively intact for four decades and counting.

They have also endured tragedy, the most notable of which was the heroin-related death of original guitarist Danny Whitten on November 18, 1972. Whitten's death occurred immediately after he had been given one last chance by Young to get clean of the drugs, which he subsequently failed to do, resulting in Young sacking him from a spot on the 1972 *Harvest* tour.

Whitten's death hit the other members of Crazy Horse hard, but perhaps had the most profound impact on the psyche of Neil Young himself (who felt at least partially responsible for the tragedy, and who would express this guilt over the course of a series songs found on his next several albums making up the infamous Ditch Trilogy).

Along with the passing of longtime Young/CSN&Y confidante and road crew warhorse Bruce Berry not long afterwards, this would particularly influence the songs found on Neil Young's very next album with Crazy Horse, 1975's *Tonight's the Night*.

For this album, Crazy Horse was completed with the addition of Frank "Poncho" Sampredo, a guitarist from Mexico who had came highly recommended by Billy Talbot. "Poncho," who has remained a member of the Horse ever since, has also performed double duty with several of Young's other bands including the Bluenotes and the Restless.

Throughout the years, Crazy Horse has become the band Neil Young most often turns to when he wants to crank the amps up to eleven and let the shit rip. For most (but not all) of Young's most paint-peeling, ear-splitting extended guitar jams, including classics like "Down by the River" and "Cortez the Killer" and albums ranging from *Everybody Knows This is Nowhere,* to *Zuma, Rust Never Sleeps,* and *Ragged Glory,* Young has called upon Crazy Horse in what has to be considered one of rock's strangest examples of a band that has endured for so long while being on a standby status as often as not.

Even so, Crazy Horse have not always been Young's first choice when he wants it loud.

A surprising number of his hardest-rocking albums have in fact been made without the Horse at all, including 1995's *Mirror Ball* (made with Seattle grunge slingers Pearl Jam) and 2006's infamous "folk-metal-protest" album *Living with War* (made with a more or less revived version of the Restless).

Although Crazy Horse will probably always be best known for the sloppy groove they provide when Neil wants to turn the amps up, they have also been Neil Young's go-to band for moodier-sounding records like 1994's *Sleeps with Angels* (an album that finds Young at his most preoccupied with issues like death—most notably the suicide of Nirvana's Kurt Cobain—and mortality since *Tonight's the Night*).

Crosby, Stills, Nash, and Young—1969–Present

Neil Young (vocal, guitar, organ), David Crosby (vocal, guitar), Stephen Stills (vocal, guitar, piano, organ), Graham Nash (vocal, guitar, organ), Gregory Reeves (bass), Dallas Taylor (drums), Calvin Samuels (bass), Johnny Barbata (drums), Joe Lala (piano), Russ Kunkel (drums).

Although they have officially only made five albums together as a band (and two of these are live recordings), Crosby, Stills, Nash, and Young also stand as the band Neil Young has played with the longest, outside of Crazy Horse.

Not that the relationship has always been an easy one—it's no accident that CSN&Y's albums have come decades apart from each other, and that up until the turn of the millennium they had only done two full-scale tours together (in 1970 and 1974). They have remained inactive as a complete unit in the recording studio since 1999's *Looking Forward* album, but have toured together more often in the past ten years than in the preceding three decades (most recently on 2006's *Freedom of Speech* juggernaut, which turned into more of a vehicle promoting Young's then current *Living with War* album).

In some respects, CSN&Y almost function as two separate entities—one being the Neil Young–dominated group and the other being the band featuring those other three guys.

From day one, it's been a strange relationship, but also one where Young is clearly calling the shots when he chooses to jump onboard. When he first joined the group (largely at the behest of Atlantic Records boss Ahmet Ertegun and Elliot Roberts, who managed both acts at the time), he only did so once it was agreed he would be a fully vested partner (the other members originally saw Young's role as more of a guest musician or sideman) with equal creative control and a full 25 percent of the financial stakes involved.

Since then, he has come and gone from the group on numerous occasions pretty much at his own will, often leaving abruptly on a moment's notice (or even with no notice at all) and returning only when he felt the moment and the conditions were absolutely right and most suited to his own artistic needs at the time.

As contentious as that relationship may sound—and the four principals involved have feuded both hard and often in public—there is also little doubt that these are four men who share a bond that borders on brotherly love. "It's fun to look around and see those guys," is how Young himself has described performing onstage with them.

Together, they have produced exactly one bona fide classic in 1970's *Déjà Vu*, of which Young's most noteworthy contributions are "Helpless" (his wistful song of yearning back to his earlier days in Canada) and the "Country Girl" suite (which recalls his more ambitious work with Buffalo Springfield like "Broken Arrow").

The Young-penned single "Ohio"—written in response to the National Guard shootings of four students at Kent State University during the height of Vietnam War protests in the Nixon era—also has to be considered one of the group's higher artistic watermarks.

During the peak of their popularity, CSN&Y also produced the live tour document *4-Way Street*, an album that still holds up remarkably well today—particularly during the mesmerizing guitar exchanges between Stills and Young on the extended versions of "Carry On" and Young's at the time still officially unrecorded "Southern Man."

On the *Déjà Vu* album, CSN&Y were completed with the rhythm section of bassist Greg Reeves (who came onboard at the recommendation of Young's former bandmate in the Mynah Birds Rick James) and drummer Dallas Taylor. But by the time of the tour documented on *4-Way Street*, both had been replaced by bassist Calvin Samuels and drummer Johnny Barbata.

On their next tour four years later in 1974, CSN&Y truly hit the big leagues by becoming the first rock band to play almost exclusively in sports stadiums— which they also mostly sold out.

As enormous and ambitious as this undertaking was—and it needs to be noted here that this was long before superstar rock stadium tours became the summer norm that they are today—the tour was also plagued by problems ranging from the four singers' blown-out voices to the sort of drug-fueled, rock-'n'-roll excess and ego you would pretty much expect. Even so, I have to confess that the four-hour, opening night set of the tour that I witnessed as a thirteen-year-old boy at the Seattle Center Coliseum was a show I'll never forget.

Although there were numerous attempts over the years to follow up the *Déjà Vu* album, it would be eighteen years before 1988's largely disappointing *American Dream*, and yet another decade before the equally tepid-sounding *Looking Forward*.

Sheet music for "Only Love Can Break Your Heart."
Courtesy of Tom Therme collection

The band have yet to make another studio record together, although there have been several of the high-priced reunion tours that every band from roughly the same era seems to be doing these days after following the lead of the Eagles' *Hell Freezes Over* tour.

The most recent of these tours has also produced another live CSN&Y album in the form of 2008's *Déjà Vu Live*—which also serves as the soundtrack to Young's "Shakey Pictures" film record of CSN&Y's 2006 *Freedom of Speech* tour. Rumors of a forthcoming live document of CSN&Y's 1974 stadium tour have also been fueled in 2010, based primarily on comments made in interviews with Graham Nash.

In the meantime, Crosby, Stills, and Nash continue to roll on as a trio, making albums on a sporadic basis but hitting the outdoor amphitheatres as a concert act every summer like clockwork. Another eventual tour featuring all four original members is almost certain to happen at some point, and another album has to likewise be considered a distinct, if not inevitable possibility.

The Stray Gators—1973–?

Neil Young (vocal, guitar, piano, harmonica), Ben Keith (pedal steel guitar), Jack Nitzsche (piano, vocal), Tim Drummond (bass), Kenny Buttrey (drums), Johnny Barbata (drums)

When Young began the sessions in Nashville for what would end up being his commercial breakthrough album *Harvest*, he drew from among the cream of that city's session veterans, including pedal steel guitarist Ben Keith, bassist Tim Drummond (who had also logged time on the road with James Brown), and drummer Kenny Buttrey.

Even though Keith and Drummond remained fixtures on Neil Young's albums for years and decades to come, the marriage between this group of seasoned Nashville cats and L.A. rocker Young (and especially his looser, one-take approach to recording) was anything but an ideal mix at first.

Buttrey in particular was dissatisfied with the arrangement, complaining first about the way Young made his records ("He hires some of the best musicians in the world, and then has them play as stupid as he possibly can"), and then later about how much the musicians were paid to play (or perhaps more appropriately weren't) on the tour behind *Harvest*.

Enlisting the support of the other hired help, Buttrey won the latter battle but was nonetheless eventually replaced by CSN&Y drummer Johnny Barbata in the band that had by now been dubbed the Stray Gators (after a reference to the stoned musicians Drummond encountered on the tour bus with Brown).

Filling out the Stray Gators for the shows (which began supporting the massive hit album *Harvest* but eventually carried over into concerts featuring the newer material that wound up being documented on *Time Fades Away)* was Crazy Horse holdover Jack Nitzsche on keyboards. Fellow Crazy Horse member Danny Whitten had also been invited to join but was subsequently fired by Young due to his ongoing drug problems, which ended up killing him in an overdose soon after.

By the time the Stray Gators hit the road in support of *Harvest*, Young had already grown bored with much of the material on the album, choosing instead to test out new material (in what became a long-standing pattern of frustrating concert audiences), while stubbornly, if perhaps selfishly following his own artistic muse.

The resulting live album from the tour, 1973's *Time Fades Away*, documents these shows, consisting entirely of new material and songs with darker lyrical themes than ever. The far less radio-friendly songs on *Time Fades Away* sound markedly different from the comparatively commercial-sounding So-Cal folk-pop of *Harvest*, represented as they are by the loose and lazy groove of the eight-minute "Last Dance" and the only slightly more accessible rough garage funk of "Don't Be Denied."

Coming after the worldwide #1 album *Harvest, Time Fades Away* proved to be a commercial stiff at the time, peaking at a dismal #22 on the Billboard albums chart.

Time Fades Away has today, however, gained a semimythical status amongst hardcore Neil Young followers, making up fully one-third (along with 1974's *On the Beach* and 1975's *Tonight's the Night*) of what many of these same fans now revere as the Ditch Trilogy.

As one of only two Neil Young albums (the other being the soundtrack to *Journey Through the Past*) that remains unavailable today as a commercial CD release (despite an ongoing petition effort spearheaded by the Neil Young fan site Thrasher's Wheat), *Time Fades Away* has also grown in status as something of a lost classic amongst the fans who prefer the rawer edges of Young's sound. Even so, by most accounts the album's rough recording isn't favored at all by Neil Young today (which most likely explains why it has never officially been reissued on CD).

Although the Stray Gators' only official shows together were those behind *Harvest* and the subsequently documented *Time Fades Away,* Young would reconvene the band two decades later for the *Harvest* "sequel" album, *Harvest Moon.*

Ben Keith and Tim Drummond were back (along with original drummer Kenny Buttrey). Spooner Oldham (who had become a fixture in Young's bands later on beginning with the International Harvesters) replaced Jack Nitzsche on keyboards (although Nitzsche is still credited with the arrangement on the *Harvest Moon* track "Such a Woman"). Once again, however, when it came time to take the shows out on tour, the Stray Gators were derailed by money issues (raised mainly by Drummond this time around), and Neil Young toured the album as a solo acoustic show.

Regardless of this, various combinations of the Keith/Drummond/Oldham lineup have long since become identified with the mellower folk-pop and country terrain Young has explored from time to time on albums ranging from *Comes a Time* and *Old Ways* to *Prairie Wind.* They may not always be the Stray Gators in actual name, but to fans around the world, they have rightfully come to be known as the closest thing to a full-time band for Neil Young, outside of Crazy Horse.

Sadly, Ben Keith—who, in addition to being the musical core of the group (and co-producer of *Harvest Moon* along with Young himself), also was a full-time member of Pegi Young's band—passed away on July 26, 2010, at the age of seventy-three.

The Santa Monica Flyers—1973

Neil Young (vocal, guitar, piano, harmonica), Ben Keith (pedal steel guitar, piano, vocal), Nils Lofgren (guitar, piano, accordion, vocal), Billy Talbot (bass, vocal), Ralph Molina (drums, vocal)

Although the album wouldn't actually be released for another two years, Young decided to take the bleak new songs of *Tonight's the Night*—an audio outpouring of raw emotion and grief inspired by the artist's reaction to the drug overdose deaths of his close associates Danny Whitten and Bruce Berry—and try them out before live audiences on the road almost immediately.

The songs had been recorded in a series of all-night, tequila-fueled sessions at Studio Instrument Rentals, the Los Angeles rehearsal space owned by Berry's brother Ken. Strange even by Neil Young standards, the *Tonight's the Night* shows—which usually began with Young welcoming his audience "to Miami Beach" (regardless of what city they were actually performing in)—commenced toward the end of 1973, barely four months after what began as the *Harvest* tour had ended with the ragged-sounding shows documented on 1973's *Time Fades Away*.

The band Young assembled for the tour, consisting of Ben Keith and guitarist Nils Lofgren, along with surviving Crazy Horse members Billy Talbot and Ralph Molina, played a total of thirty shows between August and November 1973, beginning with a string of dates at small venues in California and Canada. From there, the band headed to Europe, before finally coming back to America for a series of more club shows. The makeshift band was dubbed the Santa Monica Flyers.

In one of the many times over the course of his career that Young would be accused of committing career suicide, the shows consisted of the Santa Monica Flyers performing the as-yet unheard *Tonight's the Night* album in its entirety, played in sequential front to back order.

This even included the reprise of the title track at the show's end, which Young seemed to seize on as an opportunity to further confound the already frustrated audiences who had paid their hard-earned money to either see Neil Young sing the folk-pop songs of his hit album *Harvest*, or perhaps to hear some good old-fashioned blazing guitar jams from Young on Old Black.

When it came time to play "Tonight's the Night" for a second time at most of these concerts, Young would first tease his already frustrated audience by promising "something you've heard before" before launching into the same previously unheard song that had already opened most of the shows.

Taken together with the abrupt, artistic about-face heard on *Time Fades Away*, and following the smoother Southern California folk-pop of the megahit album *Harvest*, Young's apparent new artistic direction left even many of his most devoted fans scratching their heads in apparent bewilderment.

The tour was also poorly received by critics, some of whom also began to openly question Young's state of mind (rumors of him suffering his own addiction to heroin—which he has never once used—began to surface at about the same time). This would only be the first of many such premature pronouncements of his impending demise as a commercially viable artist.

Atlantic Records promo-only LP celebrating "Crosby, Stills, Nash, and Young month." Side one features solo tracks from Crosby, Stills, and Nash, while Neil Young (who was under contract to Reprise) is mysteriously absent. Neil appears on three tracks on side two as part of CSN&Y. *Courtesy of Tom Therme collection*

Stills-Young Band—1976

Neil Young (vocal, guitar, piano, harmonica), Stephen Stills (vocal, guitar, piano), Jerry Aiello (organ), George Perry (bass), Joe Lala (piano), Joe Vitale (drums)

Depending largely on who you talk to, *Long May You Run*, the lone album from the Stills-Young Band, was originally intended as one of the many aborted attempts over the years to record a second full-on Crosby, Stills, Nash, and Young studio album, or simply as an excuse for the two long-standing primary musical foils involved to flex their own muscles on more of the famous guitar duels they had long since made famous with both CSN&Y and the Buffalo Springfield.

The resulting album turned out to be neither, as David Crosby and Graham Nash's vocal contributions were unceremoniously removed (by Neil Young himself according to most accounts, although some say Stills may have had his own hand in the decision as well), and the blazing guitar interchanges many had hoped for and expected, for the most part never materialized.

The most memorable song from *Long May You Run* is probably the title track, a Neil Young–written folk-pop number inspired by "Mortimer," the hearse he once famously and fatefully traveled cross-country from Canada to L.A. in, and that he was driving when he met Stills in that legendary traffic jam on Sunset Boulevard. Young most recently performed the song on Conan O'Brien's final broadcast as host of the *Tonight Show* in 2010.

The Stills-Young Band also played eighteen shows together before Young abruptly left without warning. Traveling aboard a bus headed toward the next stop on the tour in Atlanta, Young instead instructed the driver to instead take him to Memphis where he caught a plane and went home. His only explanation came in the form of a cryptic note that was sent to Stills and the other band members. The message simply read, "Dear Stephen, funny how things that start spontaneously end that way. Eat A Peach, Neil."

Stills was forced to play out the remaining shows of the tour, at least the ones that weren't cancelled altogether, as a solo act.

In addition to on-again, off-again musical partners in crime Young and Stills, the short-lived Stills-Young Band was rounded out by members of Stills's touring outfit at the time, Mannasas.

The Ducks—1977

Neil Young (vocal, guitar), Bob Mosley (bass, vocal), Jeff Blackburn (guitar, vocal), Johnny Craviotto (drums)

Neil Young released two records in 1977. *American Stars and Bars* was made up of a combination of tracks that had been recorded for *Chrome Dreams* (another projected album that never actually materialized) as well as a handful of new songs recorded in a single day at his ranch with a cast of players including Ben Keith, members of Crazy Horse, and backup vocalists Linda Ronstadt and Nicolette Larson. Young also finally released his long-delayed three-record anthology set *Decade* in October of that year.

That summer, Young also played a handful of local club dates in Santa Cruz, California, with the Ducks, a group that also featured ex-Moby Grape bassist Bob Mosley, drummer Johnny Craviotto, and singer-songwriter/guitarist Jeff Blackburn. During their brief time together, the Ducks would regularly play gigs at local Santa Cruz venues like the Crossroads and the Catalyst for as little as a cover charge of three dollars—essentially becoming the town of Santa Cruz's best-kept little secret (at least until word eventually leaked out via the rock music press).

With the Ducks, Young found himself in the rare position of simply being one of the guys in the band. This was reflected in the band's set lists, which were equally divided between cover songs by artists ranging from Chuck Berry to Ian and Sylvia ("Four Strong Winds"), originals by Blackburn and Mosley, and a handful of Young's own tunes like Buffalo Springfield's "Mr. Soul" (Young famously claimed the Ducks' version was superior to the one by his original band) and early versions of "Comes a Time" and "My, My, Hey, Hey (Out of the Blue)"—which was actually co-written by Blackburn.

As word about them got out, the Ducks soon attracted a group of fans from outside the area who earned the nickname of "Duck Hunters." These fans would appear at the shows with duck whistles and boisterously holler out requests for Neil Young material during the songs by the less famous members of the group. While it isn't completely clear why Young eventually left the band (never to return)—and it's entirely probable that he never considered the Ducks anything more than a temporary diversion in the first place—this resulting, but of course inevitable, circus atmosphere probably was at least a contributing factor in his decision to do so.

Today, the Ducks are regarded as more of a footnote in Young's career than anything else. But for a heady, brief few months in the summer of 1977, it was actually possible to see international rock-'n'-roll super-star Neil Young for the same couple of bucks you might pay to see any other local bar band at the corner beer joint—at least if you happened to live in or around Santa Cruz.

Trans Band—1982–83

Neil Young (vocal, guitar, piano, vocoder), Ben Keith (pedal steel guitar, lap steel guitar, keyboards, vocal), Nils Lofgren (guitar, accordion, keyboards, vocal, vocoder), Joe Lala (piano), Bruce Palmer (bass), Larry Cragg (banjo), Ralph Molina (drums, vocal)

Of the numerous albums Neil Young has released over the course of his career that have confused and at times even angered his fans—and there have been just as many of these abrupt and often strange shifts in artistic direction as there have been the hits like *Harvest* and *Rust Never Sleeps*—perhaps the one that stands out as the most notoriously perplexing of them all was and still is 1982's *Trans*.

By the same token, this experimental, odd-sounding synthesizer- and vocoder-dominated album may also be among Young's least understood recordings.

At the time of its release, Young had just left Warner/Reprise Records after an association with the label that had lasted nearly two decades. Most agree that he was lured away from the Bunny at least in part by his own frustration with the lack of promotional efforts for his previous album, *Re-ac-tor*, but also by the creative freedom promised by his new label, Geffen Records.

When Geffen rejected his very first new album for the label—the so-called water album *Island in the Sun* (one of Neil's many unreleased recordings)—Young responded with the most abrupt shift in artistic direction of his entire career—at least up to that point.

Seen at the time by many of his older fans as a classic case of the artist sell-ing out to that era's synthesizer-driven "new wave" sound (popularized by such

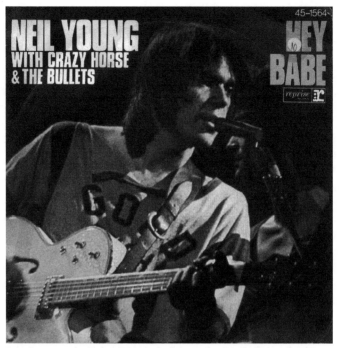

Reprise records 45 for "Hey Babe" featuring Neil Young with Crazy Horse and the Bullets.   *Courtesy of Tom Therme collection*

bands as the Human League and Soft Cell, and heavily favored by both MTV and the emergent "rock of the eighties" radio format of the time)—the cold electronically altered vocals and synthesizer-driven beats of *Trans* certainly must have been something of a shock.

What wasn't common knowledge back then, however, was that the emotional detachment and metronomic repetition of songs like "Transformer Man" were at least partially inspired by the heartbreaking condition of Young's youngest son, Ben, and how he was dealing with it as his father.

Like Young's older son, Zeke, Young suffered from cerebral palsy—only Ben's condition was far more severe, leaving him severely handicapped, particularly when it came to his ability to communicate. As a result, Ben's condition required nearly twenty-four-hour, round-the-clock attention from Young and his wife, Pegi. The parents also consulted with a number of different therapists, particularly with regard to Ben's communication issues.

True to his artistic vision as ever, Neil Young saw the more synthesizer-driven songs of *Trans* as a further expression of the push-button sort of technology he was then experiencing in his own personal life, both in the therapy used to treat his own son and in his efforts to communicate with him.

And in typical "fuck all" fashion, he stubbornly took this to its furthest extreme when he took the *Trans* album out on the road.

The "Trans Band" assembled for the tour combined some of Young's most reliable "go-to" musicians—guys like Ben Keith, Nils Lofgren, and Crazy Horse drummer Ralph Molina—with a number of names from his distant past including CSN&Y/Stills-Young Band keyboardist Joe Lala and original Buffalo Springfield bassist Bruce Palmer.

Palmer was a particularly interesting choice for the gig, given the newly "Trans-ized" version of "Mr. Soul" performed both on the album and at the shows. But he was eventually dismissed from the tour due to his excessive boozing.

The first shows of the tour, which took place in Europe, were by most accounts a total disaster.

One of the biggest problems was that Young's artistic vision for the shows probably far exceeded his actual reach. Looking back on the period now, it also probably represents one of his very few actual missteps in that regard.

The staging was also bigger than it had ever been before. The mountains of electronic equipment and technology required to pull it all off—including the synthesizers perhaps more suited to a prog-rock band like Emerson Lake and Palmer or Yes, as well as the backing tapes later favored by pop acts of the time like Michael Jackson and Madonna—had to seem rather off-putting to Young's core audience as well.

Mostly, though, the audience just didn't quite get the strange (at least by the standards he had set up to this point) new material Young chose to make the focus of these shows. A significant number of the European concerts were cancelled, and by the time the tour finally made it back to the States, the production values had been scaled down considerably. Neil also worked more of his crowd-pleasing hits back into the show, particularly with an opening acoustic set.

One of the more interesting factors introduced in the American shows of the *Trans* tour, though, was the use of something called "Trans TV."

Through the use of a roving camera, the audience was able to follow the action occurring backstage in between sets and even while the band was actually playing. A feed to the big overhead screens (which were just beginning to become standard practice with the biggest rock shows back then), provided an instant playback, and was hosted by emcee Dan Clear (in a role portrayed by actor Newell Alexander). In addition to the backstage and audience interaction, there was even a nightly interview with Young himself during the intermission, where he would critique how the evening had gone so far.

The only officially released document of the Trans Band in concert is a DVD recorded during the European tour called *Live Berlin*. Although somewhat rare and hard to find today, it provides a rare glimpse into one of the more bizarre chapters of Neil Young's concert performing career.

If nothing else, those wraparound shades will certainly take you back.

As for the *Trans* album itself, it actually holds up far better today than one might expect. Although it admittedly sounds somewhat dated now, in between the synthesized bleeps, blurs, and burps and the electronically altered vocals of songs like "Sample and Hold" and "Computer Cowboy," you can still hear brief flashes of the explosive guitar blasts Young is famous for.

Leftovers from the original *Island in the Sun* sessions that made the final cut like "Little Thing Called Love" and "Like an Inca" also stand up remarkably well.

The Shocking Pinks—1983

Neil Young (vocal, guitar, piano, harmonica), Ben Keith (guitar), Larry Byron (piano, trumpet, vocal), Anthony Crawford (marimba, tambourine, vocal), Rick Palombi (piano, vocal), Craig Hayes (baritone saxophone), Tim Drummond (bass), Karl T. Himmel (drums)

For Young's next record following *Trans*, the artist made another 360-degree turn and released *Everybody's Rockin'*, a slapdash rockabilly record whose ten songs clock in at about 25 minutes total, making it the shortest album of his career. As the story goes, Young had originally planned to follow *Trans* with *Old Ways*, a country album that Geffen subsequently rejected (a revamped version of *Old Ways* was later released after *Everybody's Rockin'*).

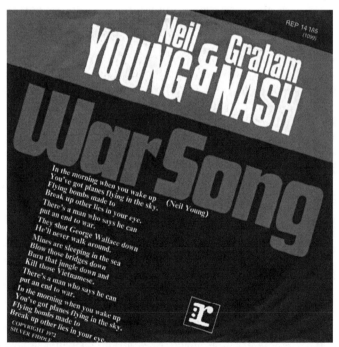

Neil Young and Graham Nash "solo single" "War Song." CSN&Y worked as a band, as solo performers, and in numerous combinations.

Courtesy of Tom Therme collection

When the label strongly suggested Neil instead needed to make a "rock-'n'-roll" record, Neil decided he would respond by literally giving them exactly what they asked for.

Whether or not Young took any of this seriously is open to conjecture. Either way, of all his various genre experiments in the so-called lost eighties, *Everybody's Rockin'* is easily among the most forgettable. To no one's surprise, the album was also a spectacular commercial flop, even by Young's newly established standards for alienating the fan base. Still, when he briefly toured the album with the Shocking Pinks, the group he assembled specifically for the project, he seemed to fully embrace the concept.

Adding a small horn section to the mix for the first time, the Shocking Pinks were a combination of longtime musical cronies like Ben Keith and Tim Drummond, along with new additions like sax player Craig Hayes, trumpet player Larry Byron, and multi-instrumentalist/vocalist Anthony Crawford. When the band took to the road, they not only played the part, but dressed for it as well—complete with loud fifties-style pink jackets and greased-back duck-billed hair.

If Young ever regarded the Shocking Pinks as anything more than a joke, he certainly wasn't letting on. To this day he has yet to reveal what possessed him to make the album.

Everybody's Rockin' has long since become something of the punchline in any serious discussion of Young's artistic output during those "lost eighties."

The International Harvesters—1984–85

Neil Young (vocal, guitar, harmonica), Ben Keith (pedal steel guitar), Anthony Crawford (guitar, banjo, fiddle, vocal), Rufus Thibodeaux (fiddle), Spooner Oldham (piano), Tim Drummond (bass), Karl T. Himmel (drums), Harold "Pig" Robbins (piano), Joe Allen (bass), Matraca Berg, Tracy Nelson (backup vocals)

Following the commercial flops of *Trans* and *Everybody's Rockin'*, Young continued his wildly genre-hopping ways with a newly revamped version of *Old Ways*, the country-influenced album that had already been rejected by his record label once before. If anything, the new version of the album represented an even more hardcore country direction than the original (which Young once described as something more like a "Harvest II").

Before long, he had booked another series of shows fronting yet another new band assembled for the tour, which had been dubbed the International Harvesters.

As with the album being supported, the International Harvesters' sound was pure country—eschewing big rock-'n'-roll guitars in favor of country fiddles and banjos. Many of the subsequent shows were also booked on the country circuit as Young performed alongside acts like Waylon Jennings and Willie Nelson at venues like the Grand Old Opry and at county fairs. The band also featured a number of seasoned Nashville pros alongside Young mainstays like Keith, Drummond, and Oldham.

Although his brief flirtation with straightforward country music only lasted about as long as his previous experiments with syntho-pop and rockabilly had before it, Young seemed more determined than ever to alienate his more traditional fan base. In published interviews at the time, he all but denounced his rock-'n'-roll past and also began to embrace the Republican politics of the Reagan era—quite possibly the ultimate sin coming from the former sixties hippie rocker who had once written about "tin soldiers and Nixon coming" in the song "Ohio."

By this time, the relationship between Young and his record label Geffen had also become more contentious than ever as the label filed a lawsuit against him citing his failure to deliver any commercial product—or what they described as more traditional-sounding "Neil Young albums."

One of the more notable developments that came out of the country period with the International Harvesters, however, was Young's friendship with Willie Nelson. This led to their partnership in the Farm Aid benefit concerts. Along with John Mellencamp (and later on, Dave Matthews), Young and Nelson have headlined the annual shows benefiting American family-owned farms ever since. Today, Young also sits on the board of directors of Nelson's Farm Aid foundation along with Mellencamp and Matthews.

The International Harvesters' live performances remain the greatest legacy of Young's short-lived country band, and many of these are documented on the live recording *A Treasure*, released nearly thirty years after the fact in June 2011 as part of his *Archives Performance Series*. The release unearths some of the better performances of the period (1984–1985), including a combination of rare, unreleased songs like "Grey Riders" as well as countrified remakes of Neil Young songs like "Southern Pacific." Young preceded this release with a goofy promotional video, which includes him rambling on about the inclusion of half-completed performances, and a particularly hilarious voiceover whenever he references the "Blu-ray" version of the album.

The Bluenotes/Ten Men Working—1987–88

Neil Young (vocal, guitar, harmonica), Ben Keith (alto saxophone), Larry Cragg (baritone saxophone), Steve Lawrence (tenor saxophone), Claude Cailliet (trombone), Tom Bray (trumpet), John Fumo (trumpet), Frank "Poncho" Sampedro (organ), Rick Rosas (bass), Chad Cromwell (drums)

Although Young's return to full-on commercial and critical prominence was still a year away, *This Note's for You* certainly seemed to be a huge step in the right direction at the time. The album was released by Reprise Records in 1988.

True enough, *This Note's for You* represented yet another genre experiment— this time around, Young was embracing the blues—and after a decade of similar artistic diversions, his once huge audience had shrunk considerably. The album peaked at a disappointing #61 on the charts.

But unlike most of his other eighties albums, radio seemed willing to give this one a chance. The title track—a brassy R&B number that blasted the willingness of rock-'n'-roll artists at the time to sell out their songs for use in product endorsements and commercials—became a minor hit. MTV, which had originally resisted playing the video (perhaps because the network itself was one of the primary targets of Young lyrical venom in the song), also eventually relented. The video was added to MTV's playlist after he took his "music or money" campaign to the network public. The video also eventually won the MTV Video Music Awards prize for video of the year.

But the real signs that Young was on the verge of a true return to his former greatness came in the form of his live shows with the Bluenotes, the nine-piece band he had assembled for both the album and its accompanying tour.

In typically over-the-top fashion, Young adopted a new persona for the concerts—a bluesman he dubbed with the moniker of "Shakey Deal." The concerts also featured a full six-piece horn section just as the album had, augmenting a core unit consisting of Rick "the Bass Player" Rosas, drummer Chad Cromwell, and Frank "Poncho" Sampedro from Crazy Horse on guitar.

Perhaps it was as a result of his nearly decade-long string of bad experiences with Geffen Records finally being put behind him (Young re-signed with Reprise for the album). But for the first time in nearly that long, he also really seemed to be enjoying playing again, and the concerts were by all accounts his best in years.

Most significant to fans was the reemergence of a Neil Young who was as willing to crank up the amps and get down and dirty with Old Black as he had been at anytime since the heyday of Crazy Horse.

Toward the latter part of this tour cycle, the Bluenotes morphed into a band renamed Ten Men Working (after a track from *This Note's for You* of the same name). It was on these latter shows that new songs like "Sixty to Zero (Crime in the City)" and "Ordinary People" began showing up in the sets.

Each of these became vehicles for the blazing, lengthy Neil Young guitar jams that fans had so longed for since what seemed like forever. They often stretch to up to twenty minutes in concert. Both tracks would also eventually show up on future Young albums. The former came just a year later (albeit in a much shorter and considerably turned-down version) on *Freedom*, while the latter wasn't officially released until two decades later on *Chrome Dreams II*.

These shows, documented on a number of bootleg recordings, have long since gone down as a legendary chapter in the Neil Young story. And the best was still to come . . .

Young and the Restless/The Restless/Lost Dogs—1989

Neil Young (vocal, guitar, piano, harmonica, banjo), Frank "Poncho" Sampedro (guitar, keyboards), Ben Keith (pedal steel guitar, dobro, vocal), Rick Rosas (bass), Chad Cromwell (drums)

Young's next move in 1989 was perhaps the most shocking of anything he had done in the preceding ten years. He made what the more litigiously minded folks at his previous label Geffen might call an actual Neil Young album.

For many long-weary fans, the 1989 album *Freedom* must have seemed to have arrived out of nowhere. Who knew that this once trailblazing artist who had spent the past ten years wandering through a seemingly endless series of genre experiments actually had a record this great still in him? But there was no denying it. *Freedom* was the best Neil Young album since *Rust Never Sleeps*.

Yet for those fans with the patience to continue patiently following Young closely, and who had witnessed the shows over the previous year leading up to this great record, it was already obvious that something rather big was coming.

Perhaps because he was feeling artistically emancipated from his experiences at Geffen (the album title *Freedom* is probably no coincidence), the shows Young played that year must have seemed like reunions with a long-lost friend who had

Lyrics to Neil Young's "Ohio" and Stephen Stills's "Find the Cost of Freedom" as seen on the sleeve of a rare CSN&Y 45 featuring two non-LP tracks.   *Courtesy of Tom Therme collection*

never really been away. What became obvious to anyone fortunate enough to see him throughout 1989 was that Neil Young—yes, *that* Neil Young—was clearly back.

For these shows, he ditched the horns and pared the Bluenotes/Ten Men Working lineup down to a raw core of Keith, Sampedro, Rosas, and Cromwell. Originally dubbed "Young and the Restless," this leaner and meaner lineup would eventually come to be known as simply the Restless.

Young's first attempt to capture the raw power of his newly pared-down band came with a never-released album called *Times Square*, recorded at New York's Hit Factory in 1988. By all accounts, this album featured some of the loudest, fiercest guitar shredding he had ever committed to tape up to that point. However, it was pulled by the artist himself due to what he perceived as a lack of anything close to a radio-friendly single.

Oddly enough, a five-song E.P. from the sessions survived and was issued in a run limited to five thousand copies in Japan called *Eldorado*. A highly coveted collector's item today, the *Eldorado* E.P. features earlier and much rawer versions of the songs that would eventually emerge on *Freedom* like "Don't Cry" and a paint-peeling cover of the standard "On Broadway," as well as the still officially unreleased B-side "Cocaine Eyes."

As the shows with the Restless progressed, a brilliant new song called "Rockin' in the Free World" was premiered in Seattle on February 21, 1989.

This anthemic rocker, which included lyrics critical of the senior George Bush's presidency like "we got a thousand points of lights for the homeless man, we got a kinder, gentler machine gun hand" (Young had by now apparently abandoned his brief flirtation with Republican politics), would become the centerpiece of the *Freedom* album, which was finally released that fall.

As was the case with "My, My, Hey, Hey (Out of the Blue)" ten years prior on the *Rust Never Sleeps* album, "Rockin' in the Free World" bookended *Freedom* with both acoustic and blasting, cranked- to-eleven electric versions.

Not only was Neil Young back—in *Freedom* he was back with the sort of instant classic fans believed he was capable of delivering at any point all along.

We Have All Been Here Before

A Brief History of Crosby, Stills, Nash (and Sometimes Young)

n theory, Crosby, Stills, Nash, and Young were perhaps one of the best million-dollar rock-'n'-roll ideas on paper ever, and during their all-too-brief original run together, they certainly made that amount of money many, many times over. But in reality, the supergroup that was being heralded as the "American Beatles" at the time (by legendary concert promoter Bill Graham, among others) was probably doomed from the very start.

As a trio, Crosby, Stills, and Nash already had a winning formula with their trademark three-part vocal harmonies and upgraded, mostly acoustic-based model of the folk-rock prototype popularized by such mid-sixties groups as the Mamas and Papas. They also had a multiplatinum smash debut album to back it up.

But when it came time to take the show on the road, they realized they would need a more ballsy rock guitarist to shake things up a bit onstage, provide "heavy rock cred," and otherwise add a much-needed extra edge to the mellower songs of their platinum-selling debut. After considering a variety of choices to fill the empty slot—ranging from Steve Winwood (who was already doing his own version of the supergroup thing with Eric Clapton in Blind Faith) to Jimi Hendrix (if one could even imagine that)—the name no one dared speak finally came up.

It's not totally clear who it was that first suggested Neil Young join the band. Conflicting reports over the years have credited everyone from Atlantic Records boss Ahmet Ertegun to Elliot Roberts to Stephen Stills. The financial advantages to both Ertegun and Roberts would certainly seem obvious—the resulting album sales produced by such a union had to have Ertegun seeing dollar signs, and Roberts likewise stood to gain monetarily as the manager for both acts.

If Stills had any hand in the decision, the motivations become much less clear however. Stills and Young's musical chemistry had certainly yielded its own considerable brand of musical fireworks within the Buffalo Springfield, especially onstage. But that same volatility and explosiveness had also bled over into their personal relationship in the band, greatly affecting how they functioned (or didn't) as a working unit. Stills and Young remained friends in spite of all this, of

Single "double-A side" release of CSN&Y's "Déjà Vu" and "Our House."

course. But it was no secret that their musical clashes were near legendary and that their shared experience in Buffalo Springfield had also ended rather badly.

Even more curious, though, was that Stills had to know that bringing Neil Young onboard would pose a serious threat to his leadership position in the band, which up to that point he had unquestionably controlled.

For their debut album, Stills had produced practically everything on it. He had also written many of the album's key songs (including its signature tune, "Suite: Judy Blue Eyes"), and played most of the instruments on the lion's share of the tracks as well.

David Crosby and Graham Nash's musical contributions to the record were largely limited to providing a few songs in addition to the harmonies that made the group an instant sensation. But by all accounts, CSN was primarily Stills's baby.

Regardless of whose idea it was to recruit Neil Young, the task of actually extending the invite ended up falling to his old friend and Buffalo Springfield bandmate Stephen Stills. Initially, both Crosby and Nash balked at the idea of having Young join the group at all. Even after they became convinced that he might provide the necessary spark they needed onstage, Crosby and Nash still saw Young's role as more that of a hired sideman playing lead guitar, rather than as a full member.

Meanwhile, Stills managed to sell Young on the idea with the promise of picking up their explosive onstage guitar duels right where they had left them off with Buffalo Springfield. The main sticking points left in the negotiations were over Young's role with the group—which both Young and manager Elliot Roberts insisted would be all or nothing. Either Young was in as a full one-fourth member in the partnership or he was out. He also insisted that he be able to continue his solo career and his partnership with his new band, Crazy Horse.

In the end, he got his way on both of these crucial points.

By the Time We Got to Woodstock

Among Crosby, Stills, Nash, and Young's earliest live performances were appearances at 1969's two biggest rock festivals, the legendary Woodstock gathering in upstate New York during the summer and later that year at the infamous Altamont disaster in Northern California.

One of the crazier stories about Woodstock happened when Young found himself stranded at an airport with Jimi Hendrix after a helicopter scheduled to transport them to the site failed to show up. As the story goes, high-powered showbiz lawyer Melvin Belli (who would later also play a key role in organizing the Altamont debacle) ended up stealing a pickup truck and driving Young and Hendrix to the concert.

Once Young actually arrived, he would also prove to be a thorn in the side of the camera crews filming the concert for what would eventually become the most famous documentary film of a rock concert ever made.

For CSN&Y's set, Young refused to be filmed and even went so far as to threaten any camera people who tried. Stills could have probably warned the filmmakers of Young's aversion to televised concerts, having been a firsthand witness to Young no-showing Buffalo Springfield appearances both on the *Tonight Show* with Johnny Carson and at the 1967 Monterey Pop Festival.

Either way, Young was not seen during the CSNY set in the original *Woodstock* film released by Warner Brothers the following year (there have since been subsequently updated versions where he can be seen if one looks hard enough).

At the infamous Altamont festival that took place in Northern California later that year, a combination of typically poor organization, ego, and possibly drugs resulted in what had to be the rather bizarre sight of CSNY making their way to the stage by coming through the crowd in a pickup truck. With Crosby and Stills shouting "Crosby, Stills, Nash, and Young comin' through" from the back of the truck, one can picture this in retrospect as an almost comedic moment.

Altamont has, of course, long been synonymous with the death of the six-ties rock-'n'-roll counterculture—a day surrounded in darkness and what the hippies of the day would probably call all-around "bad vibes." As famously captured on film in the brilliant documentary *Gimme Shelter*, the free concert once envisioned as a sort of "Woodstock West" and as the triumphant climax of the

Rolling Stones' reconquering of America in 1969, instead became the scene of everything from Jefferson Airplane member Marty Balin being assaulted onstage by Hells Angels while performing, to the murder of an audience member as the Stones looked on powerlessly.

Festival stories aside, CSN&Y did gain a well-earned reputation as a formidable live concert act during those early shows in 1969–70.

The four principal players were rounded out onstage by bassist Greg Reeves and drummer Dallas Taylor. Reeves came onboard at the recommendation of Neil Young's former Mynah Birds bandmate Rick James, after former Buffalo Springfield bassist Bruce Palmer was briefly tried out and subsequently turned away. Reeves, who besides being a wildly talented musician also had a bit of a reputation for such strange behavior as dressing up in voodoo gear, became a particular favorite of Young's. The young former Motown session bassist even ended up contributing to Young's third solo album, *After the Gold Rush*. However, Young was far less impressed with Taylor, often complaining that the drummer couldn't play his songs. According to most accounts, Taylor's short tenure in the band was eventually cut short due to drug problems, although his uneasy relationship with Young might have also played a role.

At their concerts, CSN&Y soon became known for the crowd-pleasing tactic of splitting the shows down the middle with an acoustic set favoring the mellower folk-rock harmonies of CSN's debut, and an often blistering electric set spotlighting the lead guitar duels between Stills and Young—which had become just as ferocious as Stills promised Young they would.

Crosby, Stills, Nash, and Young performing live in Memphis, Tennessee, circa 1973.

Photo by Mary Andrews

Still, internal dissension was already mounting, and when it was time to record the first album featuring all four members of rock's most celebrated supergroup, these tensions would become even more readily apparent.

Throwing Shadows on Our Eyes

When CSN&Y began the sessions for the album that would become *Déjà Vu* at Wally Heider's studio in San Francisco, the schism within the band was palpable.

On the one hand, Young was by now predictably asserting more control over the band that had once been ruled with an iron hand in the studio by Stephen Stills.

But there were also other factors threatening to unravel the already loose threads tying CSN&Y together. Several of the romantic relationships within the band members personal lives were simultaneously ending (Stills's with Judy Collins, Nash's with Joni Mitchell, and Crosby's with Christine Hinton—who had died in a head-on car accident).

Meanwhile, the ego problems were being further compounded by increasingly heavy drug use within the CSNY camp (as well as the inevitable paranoia that goes along with it), and by Crosby and Stills in particular. Casualties like roadie Bruce Berry were still a few years off, but the cracks were already showing.

For his part, Young recorded the basic tracks for his two major contributions to the *Déjà Vu* album—"Helpless" (a leftover from his sessions with Crazy Horse) and the "Country Girl" suite—mostly by himself. He also oversaw the studio overdubs (which included the harmonies committed to tape by the other members). Young did, however, participate in the full-band recordings of Crosby's "Almost Cut My Hair" (the second of his two songs paying homage to Robert F. Kennedy, following "Long Time Gone" from CSN's debut album) and a full-on electric cover of Joni Mitchell's "Woodstock."

When the album was finally released in March 1970, it became an immediate hit, shipping two million copies and topping the Billboard album chart. Even so, the division between two distinct camps—"CS&N" on the one hand and "Y" on the other—was becoming an increasingly pronounced one—particularly when Young publicly complained about the final mix of the album in the rock press (which Nash took particular offense to).

In the end, *Déjà Vu* would not only prove to be the definitive (if slightly flawed in some eyes) CSN&Y album—it would also be the only studio album released by Crosby, Stills, Nash, and Young for nearly two decades.

CSN&Y did take the *Déjà Vu* album out on the road during the spring and summer of 1970, however, complete with a new rhythm section. Crosby fired bassist Greg Reeves over musical disagreements (these may have also been related to Reeves's overall spaced-out personality), and drummer Dallas Taylor was likewise shown the door after his drug habit became a liability. Reeves and Taylor were replaced by Calvin "Fuzzy" Samuels, a bassist who had worked with Stills, and former Turtles drummer Johnny Barbata.

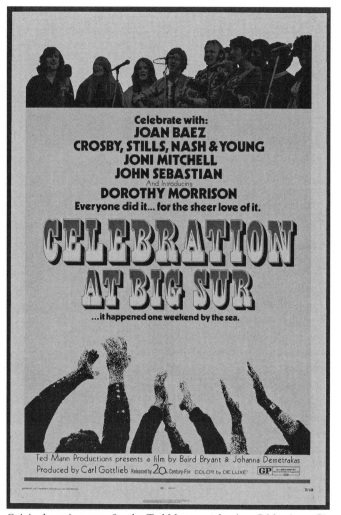

Original movie poster for the Ted Mann production *Celebration at Big Sur*, featuring folk-rock icons CSN&Y, Joni Mitchell, Joan Baez, and John Sebastian.   *Courtesy of Noah Fleisher/Heritage Auctions*

A live double album from the tour, *4-Way Street*, was released the following year. Young's contributions to the acoustic side of the original album include solo versions of "On the Way Home," "Cowgirl in the Sand," and "Don't Let It Bring You Down." But the electric set found on the second disc is where his fans will find the album's most significant fireworks.

These include the first appearance on a CSN&Y album of "Ohio," Young's blistering indictment of the killings of four students at Kent State University by National Guardsmen during a Vietnam War protest in May 1970. The song had previously been issued as a single earlier that year, peaking at #14 on the Billboard singles chart. But the studio version wouldn't appear on a CSN&Y album until *So Far*, the greatest hits collection hastily assembled by Atlantic in 1974 after CSN&Y failed to produce a new album to promote their huge stadium tour that same year.

The electric side of *4-Way Street* also marks the first appearance on record of Neil Young's "Southern Man," which is turned into a nearly fifteen-minute guitar extravaganza between Young and Stills here. The song as heard on *4-Way Street* bears little resemblance to the studio version that later turned up on Young's third solo album, *After the Gold Rush.*

By the time *4-Way Street* finally made it to CD release in the nineties, the inevitable "bonus tracks" also included a Young medley of "The Loner," "Cinnamon Girl," and "Down by the River."

Now My Name Is on the Line

For the next several years, Young remained a member of Crosby, Stills, Nash, and Young officially, but the relationship by and large existed in name only as Young devoted more and more of his creative energies to solo endeavors—which were by now beginning to catch fire commercially as well.

In 1972, he released *Harvest*, which became a smash hit, hitting #1 on Billboard, spawning the hit single "Heart of Gold," and going on to become the best-selling album of 1972. *Harvest* remains the best-selling album of Neil Young's career to date. Crosby, Stills, and Nash all contribute to the album at various points, mostly adding vocal harmonies. By this time, it had been two years since *Déjà Vu*, and the pressure to record a follow-up was mounting. There had also been some rumblings about a new tour.

In May and June 1973, Crosby, Stills, Nash, and Young convened in Hawaii to begin recording songs for a new album with the working title *Human Highway*, taken from a new Neil Young song of the same name. Stills's cocaine and alcohol abuse was becoming more of a concern by this time, particularly to Young (who refused to be around Stills when he was under the influence). The trip to the Hawaii locale had been intended as much as an effort to bring Stills under control as it was to record a new album.

Regardless, the sessions eventually ended up back at Young's Broken Arrow ranch in California, where even so, little progress toward an album was made. In Jimmy McDonough's *Shakey*, one of the biggest problems described about the sessions was getting all four members into the studio at the same time. Stills preferred to work late into the night and sleep most of the day, while Crosby and Nash preferred an earlier schedule so they could watch the televised drama of the Watergate hearings as it unfolded before a national viewing audience.

Although a few songs, including Young's "Human Highway" and "Sailboat Song," as well as Nash's "Prison Song" and Stills's "See the Changes," were recorded, the sessions proved to be a bust.

In his typical fashion, when the CSN&Y sessions weren't happening quickly enough for him, Young's attention soon turned back toward making another solo album—this time inspired by the drug-related deaths of CSN&Y roadie Bruce Berry and Crazy Horse guitarist Danny Whitten. The "rock-'n'-roll" record Young had in mind would eventually be released in 1975 as his dark masterpiece *Tonight's the Night.*

Winding Paths Through Tables and Glass

Crosby, Stills, Nash, and Young's 1974 "reunion" tour of America was at the time designed to be the biggest ever by a rock-'n'-roll band and the first to be played almost exclusively in outdoor sports stadiums.

Regardless of the fact that they had not released a new studio album since 1970, and despite the live *4-Way Street* album receiving mixed reviews (which still didn't stop it from becoming a platinum-selling chart-topper), demand was as high as ever for a new CSN&Y tour.

Even so, it had to take more than a few people by surprise when Young actually signed on for the trek. Booked by legendary concert promoter Bill Graham (who was fresh off of the success of booking Bob Dylan's 1974 comeback tour with the Band), the CSN&Y stadium tour was supposed to the biggest traveling rock-'n'-roll juggernaut ever. Yet the problems that had plagued Young's recent sold-out tour of American concert arenas behind the megahit album *Harvest* had to remain at least somewhat fresh in his own mind.

In that situation, he had still been somewhat in control—even to the point of eventually shelving the crowd-pleasing *Harvest* set lists in favor of the much rawer new songs that eventually surfaced on *Time Fades Away.* Dealing with the all-out craziness of a CSN&Y stadium tour, however, would take such seemingly trivial artistic concerns to an entirely new and unprecedented level.

For starters, there was no new album. Atlantic Records' solution to that problem was to release *So Far*, a hastily put-together greatest hits collection made up of material drawn from *Déjà Vu* and CSN's debut, as well as songs like Young's "Ohio" (making its first appearance on a CSN&Y album in the original studio version).

Fortunately, though, the old hits were good enough for audiences, and in this case, CSN&Y's near four-year absence from the concert stage had not only made the hearts of the fans grow fonder, but had also increased their legend.

The so-called Doom Tour began on July 9, 1974, with a four-hour, forty-song marathon set in Seattle.

The Neil Young fans in attendance that night particularly got their money's worth with a set list heavy on Young songs including, "Cowgirl in the Sand," "Long May You Run," "A Man Needs a Maid," "Don't Be Denied," and rarities like "Revolution Blues" (from Young's 1974 *On the Beach* album) and the unreleased "Love Art Blues."

For the remainder of the tour, however, things didn't go nearly as well.

Concert poster for the Oakland stop of CSN&Y's 1974 reunion "Doom
Tour." The shows were plagued by numerous problems but established
the early precedent for subsequent superstar rock stadium tours.

Courtesy of Noah Fleisher/Heritage Auctions

For one thing, the blowout in Seattle had the unfortunate side-effect of
resulting in a few blown-out voices amongst the principal performers. As the
ambitiously booked stadium tour rolled on, there were also logistical problems.
Although the biggest superstar rock-'n'-roll stadium tours today are all run like
a finely tuned machine, it was still a very new game back in 1974. Compounding
such now mundane tour issues as routing and catering was the fact that even
as late as 1974, the sixties hippie mentality of sex, drugs, and rock 'n' roll still
ruled the day.

To the credit of Bill Graham's organization, the sound system was still always top-notch, even if the star attractions weren't always in the best of shape or otherwise at the top of their own collective game.

In addition to having blown-out voices, the usual rock-'n'-roll excesses of the day also took an unfortunate, if all too predictable toll on some of the shows. Drugs were in abundant supply, and David Crosby has since been quoted as saying he did the entire tour with a beautiful woman (or more likely, a willing groupie) hanging off each of his arms.

And, of course, there were those legendary CSN&Y egos.

Bill Graham has recounted some hilarious but revealing stories such as how the Persian Rug had to be placed "just so" on the stage each night, as well as nightly battles over the order of each of the individual CSN&Y solo turns (Young always went on last, presumably because no one wanted to follow his set).

The personal divide between Young and his bandmates was also more pronounced than ever, with Young traveling separately from the rest of his bandmates as well as largely steering clear of the prevailing "sex, drugs, and rock-'n'-roll" party atmosphere once the show was over.

Amazingly, following all the madness surrounding the infamous reunion Doom Tour, Crosby, Stills, Nash, and Young still managed to record several new songs for a possible new album, including Young's "Long May You Run" and "Love Art Blues." However, once again Young himself brought an end to any possibility of a new CSN&Y record by simply walking away from the sessions without notice, as in the past leaving the others in the lurch.

A significant number of the shows from the 1974 Doom Tour were also recorded for a projected live album, which nonetheless failed to materialize after a general consensus was reached that what they had captured on tape just wasn't up to muster. However, in recent interviews Graham Nash has indicated a live document of the Doom Tour may just surface yet.

We've Been Through Some Things Together

The stars for another potential Crosby, Stills, Nash, and Young reunion album wouldn't properly realign themselves again until 1976, when Neil Young and Stephen Stills made what would turn out to be a one-shot album together as the Stills-Young Band.

What had begun as an informal project overseen by producer/engineer Tom Dowd soon blossomed into the album that would become *Long May You Run*, named for a Neil Young song dating back to at least 1974, and quite possibly further back than that.

The sessions for the Stills-Young Band album would nonetheless see long-standing tensions between Young and Stills resurface—mostly over their individual working habits (at one point, Young even called in Ahmet Ertegun to talk to Stills about this, and Stills's very next solo album ended up being released on Columbia rather than on his long-standing label Atlantic Records).

DAL FILM
"WOODSTOCK"

CROSBY, STILLS, NASH & YOUNG

SEA OF MADNESS
(IL MARE DELLE CATTIVERIE)

OHIO
(L'INVASIONE)

RI·FI MUSIC

Sheet music for CSN&Y's cover of Joni Mitchell's "Woodstock." During their appearance at the historic 1969 rock festival, Neil Young refused to be filmed for the proposed movie documenting the event.

Courtesy of Tom Therme collection

Despite this, there was eventually talk of the Stills-Young project morphing into a full-on CSN&Y reunion album.

Dropping their own recording project at the time, Crosby and Nash dutifully flew to Miami to add backing vocals to the album—only to have them subsequently wiped from the masters (presumably by, you guessed it, none other than Neil Young himself). Not surprisingly, Crosby and Nash weren't at all happy with this turn of events and said as much in an interview later published by *Crawdaddy!* magazine.

The Stills-Young Band ended up doing a brief tour together, which was just as suddenly cut short when Young abruptly pulled out—redirecting his separately driven tour bus away from the next stop in Atlanta and instead toward Nashville, Tennessee.

Stills played out the remaining shows—at least the ones that weren't cancelled altogether—as a solo act.

Revelations and Rumors Begin to Fly ... *American Dream*

By the time of the massive 1985 Live Aid benefit concert, Crosby, Stills, Nash, and Young's musical and cultural relevance was largely a thing of the past. Even so, big-time rock-'n'-roll reunions seemed to be the order of the day (although in all honesty, that day's most memorable performance was without a doubt the one turned in by then up-and-coming alt-rock band U2).

Still, Bob Geldof's benefit concert for African hunger relief had already pulled off the seemingly impossible reunions of bands like Led Zeppelin and Black Sabbath.

With the members of Crosby, Stills, Nash, and Young all present and doing their own individual sets earlier that day (Young was doing his country thing with the International Harvesters), the feeling had to be "why the hell not"?

Well, in retrospect, probably because CSN&Y were nowhere near ready to perform before an audience for the first time in over ten years—especially not one this massive (and also taking into account the internationally televised MTV feed).

As it turned out, the long-awaited CSN&Y reunion at Live Aid was a bust that might have been much more spectacular had anyone still cared. Their brief set, which was plagued by sound problems the whole way, included Young's "Only Love Can Break Your Heart" and a medley of "Daylight Again" and Stills's "Find the Cost of Freedom." The long-awaited CSN&Y reunion that took place at Live Aid—which up to that point had been so anticipated by the sixties generation—is mostly a footnote in rock history now, and is probably best left that way.

But it still wasn't the end of the line for CSN&Y. Not by a long shot.

The follow-up album to 1970 *Déjà Vu* finally came eighteen years later in 1988 with *American Dream*.

This album is largely the result of a promise by Neil Young to David Crosby, who had spent much of the eighties in and out of both jail and rehab as a result of what was by then a severe addiction to crack cocaine.

"Clean up your act," Young promised his old friend, "and we'll make another record." Crosby did. Young delivered.

The album itself is mostly forgettable, but is significant for the fact that the lines of personal and artistic communication had been reopened between Young and CSN—in a re-bonding of kindred musical spirits that would yield considerable dividends roughly ten years down the road.

Whatever one chooses to make of *American Dream* (and taken on purely artistic merits it's probably not going to be much), the long-standing logjam between Young and the rest of CSN was finally breached with this album once and for all. Even though Crosby had gotten himself free of drugs, there would still be no tour behind *American Dream,* as Stephen Stills's own substance abuse issues had yet to be sorted out.

Good to See You Again

Neil Young next crossed paths with Crosby, Stills, and Nash while working with Stills on the Buffalo Springfield boxed set in 1999. Stills played Young some demos from a then in progress CSN project, and apparently Young was impressed enough to offer up the pick of the litter of the songs he had written for his own solo project at the time, *Silver and Gold.*

The resulting CSN&Y album, 1999's *Looking Forward,* is every bit as forgettable as 1988's *American Dream.* But it is once again very significant, because it signaled some intriguing new possibilities for the two long-estranged parties.

Even if CSN&Y could no longer recreate the studio magic they once had, perhaps they could still do so on the concert stage.

This would indeed prove to be the case a few short years later.

Rare single release of CSN&Y non-LP tracks "Ohio" and "Find the Cost of Freedom." The 1970 Kent State shootings prompted a rush release from Atlantic Records of Neil Young's most famously political song.
Courtesy of Tom Therme collection

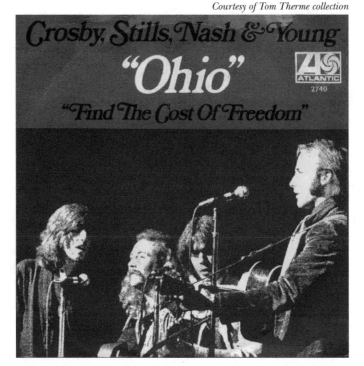

Let's Roll

Both of Crosby, Stills, Nash, and Young's two reunion tours after the dawn of the new millennium came about by most accounts at the behest of Neil Young himself.

The 2002 CSN&Y reunion tour came about as the result of Young's reaction to the American 9/11 terrorist attacks. He had just recorded the song "Let's Roll" for his album *Are You Passionate?* The song had been conceived as a reaction to reading about Todd Beamer, one of the passengers on the planes taken over by terrorists that day, who heroically tried to rally his fellow travelers in an effort to thwart the attack—uttering the now famous words "Let's roll" in doing so. This apparently struck a deep chord within Young.

The 2002 shows—though ridiculously overpriced—were largely seen as a spectacular return to artistic form by those who attended them—particularly during the extended guitar jams between Stills and Young on songs like Young's "Goin' Home."

Four years later however, Young would take a much different tack for CSN&Y's *Freedom of Speech* tour, rallying the troops in CSN&Y for a tour highlighting songs like 'Let's Impeach the President" from *Living with War*, which featured songs far more critical of President George W. Bush's post-9/11 policies in Iraq.

In these concerts—which are documented on the Shakey Films–produced documentary *Déjà Vu Live*—the audiences are much more politically polarized than at any other point in CSN&Y's entire career, very much reflecting the mood of the nation as a whole at the time. The shows themselves, however, found CSN&Y performing with a fire in their collective bellies not seen from the band since 1970.

The most curious thing about the 2002 and 2006 reunion shows, however, remains their high ticket prices, which, topping out at $300-plus in most markets, had to be a factor affecting those who have might otherwise have been the most receptive to the actual message of the incendiary new songs from Young's *Living with War* album.

An Open Letter to Neil Young

(Reprinted from an article originally published at *Blogcritics* magazine)

Dear Neil Young,

How's it going, buddy? It's your old pal Glen here. Oh, I know that you and I have never actually met, but I've always kind of viewed you as a dear old friend.

We actually go back a very long way. As early as I can remember—listening to your songs first with the Buffalo Springfield, then CSN&Y, and of course your solo work—your songs have always resonated with me on an emotional level like few artists I can think of.

In fact, I'd say that only Dylan and Springsteen really come close. I kind of like to think of the three of you guys as my own little "holy trinity" of artists whose music really "speaks" to me on a gut level.

For one thing, I've always admired your determination to follow your artistic muse wherever it may lead you. Not many artists would have followed a #1 smash album like *Harvest* with such artistically challenging releases as *Tonight's the Night* and *On the Beach*. But in the seventies you did exactly that, Neil. With records like that, you became the very definition of the term "artistic maverick."

Speaking of *On the Beach*, that record got me through some pretty rough times, Neil. To this day, I put that sucker on whenever I'm feeling depressed. It's very therapeutic listening.

So like all good friends should, I've also always stuck by you—which hasn't always been easy.

Remember the eighties?

Damn, some of that was awful stuff, Neil. I mean *Trans* has kinda grown on me over the years, but the Shocking Pinks? I understood, though, and I waited. It was that whole maverick artist thing, right? Anyway, I knew you'd eventually find your artistic center again.

Which you finally did in the early nineties with albums like *Freedom* and *Ragged Glory*.

Great stuff there, Neil.

Single release of "When You Dance" from *After the Gold Rush.*
Courtesy of Tom Therme collection

I also stood by you when you courageously released 2006's *Living with War*, an album that would've gotten you deported back to your native Canada if the pro-Bush righties had anything to say about it.

Hell, I even defended your honor right here on Blogcritics for months, when one such right-wing nut responded to my original review of that album by flaming the article with something like 500 angry messages about how releasing a record like that was somehow "anti-American."

Hey, what are friends for?

So, as you can imagine, I was really excited to hear about your new record *Chrome Dreams II* coming out on October 16.

I know a lot of this is old stuff that you've had lying around for awhile, and was originally supposed to be part of one of those mysterious "lost albums" that never got released of yours called *Chrome Dreams,*

But, as a longtime fan, how can you not get excited about an album that promises titles like the eighteen-minute "Ordinary People," or the eleven-minute "No Hidden Path?"

You know how I love the long ones, Neil.

I was also thrilled to hear that you'd be touring behind the record, and making a stop in my hometown in Seattle at the relatively intimate Wamu Theatre.

Which actually brings me to the real purpose of this letter, Neil. It's about those damned ticket prices. Quite frankly, they've got me a little concerned.

Don't get me wrong, Neil—I'll still be there.

I won't be making the trip to Oakland where I had planned to see Springsteen (whose tickets top out at $85, a fact you might wanna take note of), but I will be there—sitting dead center in the fourteenth row.

But holy freaking crap, Neil—$172 a pop after Ticketmaster gets their cut? That's not for a pair, that's for a single freaking ticket!

Look, I know that some of the other big tours like the Stones, the Police, and McCartney have gotten away with charging upwards of $300 a ticket.

But those are bigtime stadium rock-'n'-roll extravaganzas, Neil. Somebody's gotta pay for all those explosions and lasers. Somehow, I suspect we won't be seeing any of those at your show. At least I would hope not.

I also know that we are at least a couple of decades removed from the days when rock artists like Tom Petty would challenge the record companies over things like raising the list price of a vinyl LP to $8.98—but that was all a lot of idealistic, hippie bullshit, right?

I mean, weren't you the guy who once went to war with MTV over the video for "This Note's for You?" Weren't you the guy who decried things like corporate sponsorship of rock tours? Whatever happened to that guy, Neil?

Seriously, what happened?

I'm also a little concerned about some of the rumors I've heard about how *Chrome Dreams II* is going to be marketed. What's all this I hear about each copy featuring a different bonus track or something? How many copies of the CD do we need to buy to "collect them all," Neil?

I mean look, it's not like you need the money, right?

If I recall correctly, there was an interview you gave around the time *Living with War* came out, where you said you had made enough money where you didn't really care if the records sold or not, as long as you were able to play the music that you were feeling at the time.

So doesn't that rule also apply here?

Anyway, Neil, like I said before I've always stood by you, and I guess I'll stand by you now too.

I'm really looking forward to hearing the new album, and I can't wait for the concert—although at $172 a ticket, there better be one hell of a set list. How about the entire second side of *On the Beach* for starters? Sound good to you?

In closing, let me just say that I'd be less than a true friend if I didn't say I'm a bit concerned, and a bit disappointed.

Hoping this letter finds you well.

Your friend,

Glen Boyd

There Was a Band Playing in My Head, and I Felt Like Getting High

After the Gold Rush

O f all the songs in Neil Young's vast catalog, perhaps none have been as thoroughly and deeply analyzed as the title track of his third solo album, 1970's *After the Gold Rush.*

And why not?

On the surface, the song lyrics reference everything from knights in armor, peasants singing, and spaceships flying to lying in a burned-out basement, and, of course, Mother Nature herself on the run in the nineteen seventies (which has subsequently been updated in concert every decade since).

Among the more notable attempts to decipher this most famous of Young's many great songs is a lengthy article posted by a guy named Randy Schecter on the Neil Young fan site Thrasher's Wheat.

In his very well thought out post, Schecter makes the case (and quite convincingly I might add) for this song being nothing less than a doomsday prophecy of some distant apocalyptic future event involving UFOs, ecological catastrophe, and nuclear war.

It's heavy stuff, to be sure.

The thing is, Schecter makes a very good argument for this scenario of a biblical Armageddon, and the song lyrics—which are among the most vividly descriptive that Young has ever written—seem to back this up.

This would all be fine and dandy, of course. At least if that was what this particular song was actually written about.

The thing is, it most likely isn't about the aliens in spaceships rescuing us from a future doomsday or the visions swirling about Randy Schecter's keyboard at all. Rather, the lyrics of "After the Gold Rush" are most likely about the more personal apocalypse occurring in Young's own life at the time.

Like most everything else that exists in the Neil Young songwriting canon—from his most autobiographical songs like "Helpless," to songs that

Reprise Records promo 45 for "After the Gold Rush."

Courtesy of Tom Therme collection

more or less eulogize things like how "I watched the needle take another man"—
"After the Gold Rush" could be about any number of things. But it's just as likely
that what Neil was really singing about came from a place having more to do with
personal concerns than anything as apocalyptic as doomsday or as otherworldly
as being beamed aboard flying saucers from outer space.

Specifically, a decent case could be made that "After the Gold Rush" was
among the earliest of Neil Young's many antidrug songs.

Consider the lyrics coupling how "I felt like getting high" to how Neil was
"thinking about what a friend had said" and "hoping it was a lie," and the actual
sentiments of this song become crystal clear.

At the time *After the Gold Rush* was being recorded, Young found himself
faced with the difficult decision of having to fire Crazy Horse—his band of
choice at the time—even after he had already completed several sessions for
his impending new album, with what most will agree (warts and all) was his
greatest band.

The lines in this song about "a band playing in my head, and I felt like
getting High" are particularly telling when the condition of guitarist Danny
Whitten is taken into account.

Whitten, who by this time was deep in the throes of a severe addiction to
heroin, had in fact become a no longer ignorable liability to Neil Young and

Crazy Horse—the band that he cared the most deeply about on an artistic level (even as CSN&Y was still paying the bills at that point).

A short tour in 1970 produced some undoubtedly great shows (most notably the *Fillmore East* concerts eventually documented on the *Archives* boxed set).

But more often, Whitten had become so consumed by his increasing dependency on heroin and other drugs that he had even taken to passing out onstage in the middle of concerts (if you listen closely to the *Live at Fillmore East* album, you can even hear Neil Young admonishing him for this).

It is perhaps here that the line in "After the Gold Rush" that follows the part about the band playing in his head and feeling like getting high begins to make the most sense. "Thinking about what a friend had said, I was hoping it was a lie" is another of this song's key lines, and one that rings tragically true when read in this more personal context.

For Young, watching his friend—a great musician in his own right—waste away before his eyes had to be a most painful experience. But as is so often the case with addiction, this same pain often turns quickly to a deeper hurt and resentment.

"I sing the song because I love the man," he later went on to sing in "The Needle and the Damage Done." "I watched the needle take another man." The sadness heard in that song is equally mixed with a deep sense of hurt and betrayal. In many ways, "After the Gold Rush" was a precursor to the more direct lyrics about drug-related loss later heard on songs like "The Needle and the Damage Done" and on albums like *Tonight's the Night.*

In addition to the inner turmoil taking place within Crazy Horse, Young was also undergoing considerable upheaval in his personal life at the time the *After the Gold Rush* album was being recorded. His divorce from first wife Susan Acevedo, and his move away from Topanga Canyon, also took place the very same year.

Flying Mother Nature's Silver Seed to a New Home in the Sun

Still, there were some apocalyptic elements in the songs for Young's third solo album—at least initially. And his friends in the community of artistic types residing in Topanga Canyon were undeniably a big part of that—even as he himself was already eyeing his "new home in the sun."

At the time, actor/director Dennis Hopper—fresh from the unexpected success of 1969's *Easy Rider*—had been given the green light from Warner Brothers Pictures to develop his own film projects. As a result, Hopper and Neil Young's mutual friend Dean Stockwell developed a loose script for a projected film called—you guessed it!—"After the Gold Rush."

In the end, the album that eventually became Neil Young's *After the Gold Rush* really had little to do with Stockwell's original script for a projected film about an ecological disaster (something about a tidal wave hitting Southern California). But in retrospect one can certainly see where those original seeds may have been

One of the many vinyl pressings of "Southern Man" from Neil Young's third solo album *After the Gold Rush*. The song's controversial lyrics sparked a response from Lynyrd Skynyrd in the form of their own single "Sweet Home Alabama."   *Courtesy of Tom Therme collection*

sown (particularly in the title track—where perhaps Randy Schecter's detailed analysis posted on Thrasher's Wheat finally begins to make a little more sense after all).

As it ended up, *After the Gold Rush* became a far more personal statement from Young, and one that produced some of his most pointed songwriting to date. From this moment forward, Young's emergence—not just as one hell of a loud guitar player capable of making a big racket with Crazy Horse, but also as a highly sophisticated songwriter comparable to the true greats like Bob Dylan—would never be ignored again.

Of course, being the artistic iconoclast that he is, subsequent changes in Neil Young's artistic direction would only serve to further muddy these already murky waters, as future audiences would discover soon enough. The Ditch Trilogy and the wild genre hopping of the "lost eighties" were still some distance down the road. But by following the guitar-heavy *Everybody Knows This Is Nowhere* with the deliberately mellower singer-songwriter vibe of *After the Gold Rush*, Neil Young demonstrated that abruptly shifting musical gears—regardless of any commercial, critical, or even personal circumstance—came as naturally to him as breathing is to the rest of us.

By firing Crazy Horse (even though it turned out to be temporary), he showed he could be ruthless as well. Even though two of the songs from the original 1969 sessions with Danny Whitten and Crazy Horse survived to make the final record ("I Believe in You" and "Oh Lonesome Me"), and Whitten returned to add overdubs as the album neared completion, Young certainly proved he had no problem handing out pink slips if his own increasingly exacting standards weren't being met to the letter.

Sailing Heart Ships Through Broken Harbors

The majority of *After the Gold Rush* was recorded in a makeshift studio in the basement of Young's relatively modest home, establishing a pattern for making records in strange locales that would follow him throughout his career.

In some ways, the album has a flat sort of sound to it—particularly when compared to the dense and much thicker-sounding bursts of heavy guitar created by Neil Young and Crazy Horse on *Gold Rush's* predecessor, *Everybody Knows This Is Nowhere*. If the idea here was to create a "low-fi"-sounding album, in places the actual result is more like "no-fi," perhaps owing at least in part to the relatively cramped quarters where much of the music was made.

The space problem was solved soon enough, however, when Young purchased the several hundred acres of land near San Francisco that he renamed the "Broken Arrow Ranch" that same year. Broken Arrow remains home to Young and his family to this day. It has also been home to a number of other central figures in his life over the years, ranging from one-time girlfriend, actress Carrie Snodgress (and by some accounts, most of her family and friends as well) to chief musical co-conspirator Ben Keith, who lived at Broken Arrow up until his death in 2010.

The move would also signal the end of Young's first marriage to Susan Acevedo, which by that time had become a casualty of his increasing stardom and the constant parade of willing girls surrounding him that came along with it. As far as the possibility of Young actually being

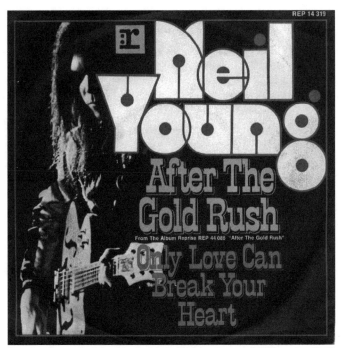

REP 14 319

Reprise Records "double-A side" single release of "After the Gold Rush" and "Only Love Can Break Your Heart."

Courtesy of Tom Therme collection

unfaithful, if it ever happened, the rock press and the tabloids never reported it. More likely, Susan probably just got sick of all the young girls throwing themselves at her husband. By all accounts, the divorce was an amicable one with Young settling for something in the neighborhood of $80,000.

For the sessions that made up the bulk of *After the Gold Rush*, he retained Ralph Molina from Crazy Horse as drummer and brought in CSN&Y bassist Greg Reeves as well as a young hotshot guitarist named Nils Lofgren.

As the story goes, Lofgren met Neil Young after sneaking backstage at a Washington, D.C., concert. After introducing himself, Young asked the kid if he had any songs, and after hearing several of them invited him out to Los Angeles. After walking the distance from the L.A. airport to Young's home in Topanga Canyon carrying his guitar on his back, Young signed him up to play on the album. But as was so often the case with Young, there was a catch.

He wanted Lofgren—the guitarist—to play the piano. The fact that Lofgren wasn't a piano player made no difference. Whether this was simply one of Young's more impulsive artistic whims, or just another example of the way he asserts total and complete control over every note played on his records (something that later drove the Stray Gators fairly crazy during the making of *Harvest*), Lofgren did as he was told and passed his audition by fire with flying colors.

Reprise Records promo pressing of Neil Young's *After the Gold Rush* LP.
Courtesy of Tom Therme collection

Young later explained away the decision simply by saying "I hate musicians who play licks." It was an explanation that would be repeated several more times over the years to justify the notorious control he exercises over the hired help. If there are any two clichés that sum up his approach to making records, they would probably come down to "more soul, less licks."

With his debut as a pianist (and yes, as a guitarist too) on *After the Gold Rush*, Lofgren began an on-and-off association with Neil Young that would last more than a decade. In addition to helping get Lofgren's own group Grin off the ground (with a David Briggs–produced debut album), Lofgren has also put in time with the lunatics in Crazy Horse and as a member of the infamous Trans Band in the early eighties.

These days, when Lofgren isn't recording solo albums and teaching guitar online, he serves as one of the three guitarists with Bruce Springsteen's E Street Band, which he joined as a full-time member in 1984.

I Heard Screamin' and Bullwhips Crackin'

Released in June 1970, *After the Gold Rush* became Neil Young's biggest hit up to that time, reaching the top ten of Billboard's albums chart, where it peaked at #8. The mellower sound of the album also effectively set the table for the worldwide #1 smash that would occur with its follow-up *Harvest.*

Although the album signaled an artistic shift to more of a singer-songwriter focus, the album also has its fair share of rockers, none of which would create a bigger fuss than "Southern Man."

In the five-and-a-half-minute version that appears on the album, "Southern Man" lacks some of the punch heard in the live versions on the CSN&Y tour that took place in the summer of that same year. In those shows, the song could often stretch out to nearly twenty minutes courtesy of the fiery guitar exchanges between Young and Stephen Stills.

A very good, but not quite great, example of this can be heard on CSN&Y's 1971 live album *4-Way Street.* By contrast, on the studio version, Young's guitar solos are still crisp and razor sharp, but they also seem to be over before they ever really get started. Perhaps owing to the much flatter sound of the album, they also lack much of the bite heard on concert stages that summer. A definitive version of "Southern Man" remains a major hole in Young's catalog.

The lyrics, however, stirred up the predictable controversy with southern fans, and particularly with the southern rock band Lynyrd Skynyrd. With its images of crosses burning, bullwhips cracking, and of course, those

Single picture sleeve 45 release of "Only Love Can Break Your Heart" from *After the Gold Rush.*   *Courtesy of Tom Therme collection*

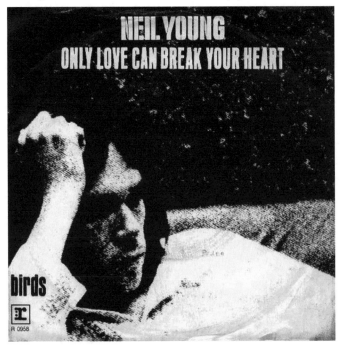

black men who are seen "comin' round," "Southern Man" may be one of the more naïve attempts at a political statement ever made by Young. For all of its good intentions, "Southern Man" is an even more confusing political statement when you consider it came the very same year as the much more direct, cutting-straight-to-the-bone lyrics heard in what is arguably his greatest "protest song" ever—CSN&Y's "Ohio."

Either way, the blunt, and perhaps somewhat misguided, lyrical bombs Young was hurling down on Dixie with "Southern Man" were certainly not lost on Lynyrd Skynyrd vocalist and lyricist Ronnie Van Zant (who was a big Neil Young fan himself, by the way).

Predictably, the good old boys in Lynyrd Skynyrd (if it wasn't them, it could just as easily have been the Allman Brothers) were quick to respond with exactly the southern pride you'd expect, releasing the single "Sweet Home Alabama." To this day, the song's most famous line remains, "Well I hope Neil Young will remember, southern man don't need him around anyhow."

Interestingly, Van Zant later wore a Neil Young *Tonight's the Night* T-shirt on the cover of Skynyrd's posthumously released *Street Survivors* album (three members of the group, including Van Zant, lost their lives in a plane crash just weeks prior to that album's release). An even more curious story handed down over the years says Van Zant was buried wearing the very same Neil Young T-shirt.

Find Someone Who's Turning and You Will Come Around

In addition to "Southern Man" and the title track, *After the Gold Rush's* other highlights include "When You Dance, I Can Really Love." In this rocker that finds Neil Young holding back on the guitar histrionics (well, relatively speaking anyway), Jack Nitzsche effectively steals the show from the star with a ripping performance on the piano (speaking of guys playing licks).

"Don't Let It Bring You Down" is an irresistibly mellow tune that is something of a precursor to the melancholic feel that would more fully manifest itself on *Harvest*. The song is also a textbook example of the lonesome-sounding, world-weary voice that is arguably the single most identifiable element of what most recognize as Neil Young's "sound" (if there even is such a thing).

"Only Love Can Break Your Heart" is likewise another, if slightly more light-weight exercise in the sort of singer-songwriter introspection so closely identified with its early seventies period, and for better or worse, with Neil Young himself. It also became a big radio hit, further setting the stage for the huge commercial breakthrough still to come with *Harvest*. Of the leftover 1969 sessions with Crazy Horse, "Oh, Lonesome Me" is also a standout—and here once again it's largely due to the achingly lonesome quality of Neil Young's voice.

In the final analysis, *After the Gold Rush* would have to be considered a major triumph if only for the very considerable merits of the title track alone—it's easily one of Young's greatest songs. From a commercial perspective, it's also fair

to say that it was a milestone in his career up to that point. As an overall artistic breakthrough, however, the arguments become a lot less convincing, particularly when the album is compared to such masterpieces as *Tonight's the Night, On the Beach, Rust Never Sleeps,* or even to latter-day albums like *Freedom, Harvest Moon,* and *Sleeps with Angels.*

That said, Neil Young's follow-up to *After the Gold Rush* blew the doors wide open, and nothing would ever again be the same.

I've Been to Hollywood, I've Been to Redwood

Harvest, Nashville, and the Stray Gators

For Neil Young, *Harvest* was the album that forever changed everything. Released in February 1972, the album was a complete blockbuster in every sense of the word. Both the album and its single "Heart of Gold" went straight to #1 on the Billboard charts, and the reaction was equally spectacular in Europe and much of the rest of the world. In America, it also ended up closing out 1972 as the top seller of the year. If Young was already a star, *Harvest* propelled him to the uppermost echelons of seventies rock royalty. The days of being mostly referred to as "the Young of CSN&Y" were over for good.

Nothing would ever be the same again, and to this day, *Harvest* remains the biggest-selling album of Neil Young's career.

I've Been to the Desert on a Horse with No Name

The success of *Harvest* also spawned imitators like the soft-rock trio America, who hit #1 that same year with "A Horse with No Name," a single powered by the lead vocals of a Neil Young soundalike that managed to fool many people (including Young's own father) into thinking it was actually Neil Young himself.

At one point, even Young's label Warner Brothers might have been hoodwinked, as some copies of *Harvest* were shipped to record stores with a sticker proclaiming "Includes the hit 'A Horse with No Name.'" When Elliot Roberts took on the soundalikes as a client for his Lookout Management company, Young's reaction was a predictably cranky one, as he complained, "Why do you need copy bands when you've got the original right here?"

Although most agree that Young previous three solo albums, as well as his work with Crosby, Stills, Nash, and Young, were clearly building toward a commercial breakthrough, the smash success of *Harvest* was something else entirely. By some accounts, Young himself was not altogether comfortable with it either. Producer Elliot Mazer has even recalled Young's reaction to hearing "Heart of Gold" played on top forty radio as one of being rather nonplussed by it all.

A decent argument could even be made that with the follow-up albums *Time Fades Away*, *On the Beach*, and *Tonight's the Night*, Young was actually sabotaging

Sheet music for "Old Man" from Neil Young's breakthrough album
Harvest. The song was one of several hits from the 1972 blockbuster.
Courtesy of Tom Therme collection

his success (or at least running as far away from it as he could). At the time,
more than one of his associates labeled the three albums making up the so-called
Ditch Trilogy as "career suicide" (an accusation that would also dog Young
during the eighties).

Even so, he has returned to the mellow country-rock of his most successful
record many times over the course of his career—probably most notably on the
early nineties *Harvest* "sequel" *Harvest Moon,* but also on albums as early as *Comes
a Time* and as recent as *Prairie Wind.*

I Fell in Love with the Actress

One thing for sure, is that some of *Harvest's* loveliest songs were directly inspired by the artist having fallen deeply and madly in love with the actress Carrie Snodgress. In the *Harvest* song "A Man Needs a Maid," in between lyrics that could be construed as sexist, but also as more honest, direct, and perhaps even oddly humorous ("Just someone to keep my house clean, Fix my meals and go away"), Young even describes in simple but accurate detail exactly how he fell in love with Snodgress ("I was watching a movie with a friend/I fell in love with the actress.").

The movie was *Diary of a Mad Housewife*, which garnered Snodgress two Golden Globe awards and an Oscar nomination. Young had gone to see the movie during a tour break from the solo shows he'd been doing in 1971, accompanied by roadie Guillermo Giachetti. Young was so smitten, he later dispatched Giachetti to set up a meeting with the actress. After a few dates (one of which took place in a hospital room where a bedridden Young was nursing severe—and ongoing—back problems), the two fell in love and began a live-in relationship.

With Snodgress taking up residence at the Broken Arrow Ranch (along with a large contingent of family and friends some insiders began referring to as "the Snodgress People"), the union eventually produced their son Zeke, born in September 1972.

Since both their stars were on a fast ascent at the time, you might think they had all the makings of a Hollywood power couple. But perhaps due to the still-lingering, antiestablishment hippie politics of the sixties, Snodgress in particular seemed to want no part of it. She effectively turned her back on a promising career as an actress, no-showing the Oscars after Young complained about having to wear a tux, to become Neil Young's lover, mother, and even occasional nurse (which, ironically, had been one of her earlier career choices). It would seem the man had found his maid.

Southern California Brings Me Down

A quick sidebar here to the whole "A Man Needs a Maid" story . . .

With the burgeoning women's liberation movement gathering a lot of steam back in the early seventies, the fact that Young's lyrics about needing a woman to "clean house, fix meals, and go away" never became a target for feminists is particularly remarkable. As his fan base grew exponentially with *Harvest*, one of the larger constituencies in this newly broader demographic was in fact young women, many of whom became smitten with Young's seemingly sensitive, romantic, and introspective lyrics.

Others just found the song either strikingly honest or more often just plain funny. In a particularly hilarious (and dead-on) Neil Young parody that came out around the same time called "Old Maid (Southern California Brings Me Down)," the National Lampoon comedy troupe sent the song up with hilarious lyrics like

"I need someone to live with me, to keep my bed warm, and sew patches on my jeans." In the song's four-minute running time, it likewise skewers a number of other Neil Young songs ranging from "Ohio" to "Alabama," nailing both Young's voice and distinctive guitar sound dead to rights in the process.

The song can be found on the now hard-to-find *National Lampoon's Goodbye Pop*. The album also features equally brutal send-ups of the popular reggae, progressive rock, and Philly soul sounds of the day, sandwiched in between bits that include a pre-*Saturday Night Live* Bill Murray portraying a typically laid-back, stoned seventies FM rock DJ. The album is definitely worth a listen, providing you can find a copy.

A Wheel in the Ditch and a Wheel on the Track

During 1970–71, Young played a series of concerts that saw him working in a solo acoustic format for the first time on an extended tour. The concerts were basically Young accompanying himself on guitar, piano, and harmonica and were played in small theatres and concert halls in America, Canada, and England (where he played at London's prestigious Royal Festival Hall).

Many of the songs that eventually wound up on *Harvest* were premiered at these shows, including songs that would go on to be considered Neil Young standards like "Old Man" and "The Needle and the Damage Done." Early versions of two of *Harvest's* key tracks, "A Man Needs a Maid" and "Heart of Gold," were being performed together as a medley at the time, as can now be heard on the *Archives Performance Series* release *Live at Massey Hall 1971.*

One of the best—if not *the* best—recorded documents of a Neil Young solo performance, producer David Briggs felt so strongly about the recording that he forcefully lobbied for Young to release it as his next record instead of the studio sessions that became *Harvest.* Briggs lost that battle in life, which led to a rift between artist and producer that lasted a few years ("he wouldn't listen," Briggs would later say about the experience). Years later, while reviewing material for the *Archives* project, Young finally did listen, and in 2007—some thirty-five years after the fact—Briggs finally got his wish.

Sadly, he was no longer alive to see it.

As it turned out, Young did end up going with the studio versions for his new songs, and as a result ended up with his biggest record ever.

Harvest was recorded in a total of four locations. Two tracks ("A Man Needs a Maid" and "There's a World") were recorded in England with the London Symphony Orchestra (with wildman Jack Nitzsche as arranger). "The Needle and the Damage Done" is taken from a live performance at UCLA's Royce Hall. The rest of the tracks were recorded either at "Broken Arrow Studio #2" (which was actually a converted barn on Neil's ranch, causing Nitzsche to later bitterly and hilariously complain about making an album in a bale of hay) or at Nashville's Quadrafonic Sound Studios.

In another humorous story related to the barn locale, Young had Elliot Mazer preview the *Harvest* album for his friends David Crosby and Graham Nash by placing one huge speaker on the porch at the main house at Broken Arrow, with the other stereo channel rigged up to the P.A. system in the barn. Crosby and Nash then sat in a rowboat on the pond between the two structures. When asked how the album sounded, Crosby and Nash would then yell things back to Mazer like "More barn!" or "More house!"

But it is the Nashville sessions that are really the heart and soul of the record. For the album, Neil began working with a group of Nashville-based studio musicians that included drummer Kenny Buttrey, bassist Tim Drummond, and multi-instrumentalist Ben Keith. The Stray Gators, as they came to be known, came from a variety of musical backgrounds ranging from Buttrey serving time in James Brown's touring bands (also the source of the Stray Gators name, which comes from a slang term that Brown's crew used for stoned musicians on the

Single picture sleeve 45 of "Old Man" from the *Harvest* album.

Courtesy of Tom Therme collection

tour bus) to Drummond playing on some of Bob Dylan's albums, to Keith's work with country artists like Patsy Cline.

The Stray Gators (in various combinations) have over the years served as the band Young returns to time and time again whenever his artistic muse turns toward more folk or country directions (or what some fans simply refer as his "Harvest" records).

Ben Keith in particular remained Young's chief musical accomplice right up until his death in 2010 (Keith was also staying at Young's Broken Arrow ranch at the time he passed). But the association didn't start out that way. Some of the Nashville veterans were initially taken aback by Neil's approach to making records, with Kenny Buttrey in particular complaining about Neil's controlling nature in the studio ("none of those drum parts are mine," Buttrey has said for the record about the *Harvest* sessions, "they were all Neil's").

Harvest-era double-A side single for "Old Man" and "The Needle and the Damage Done."
Courtesy of Tom Therme collection

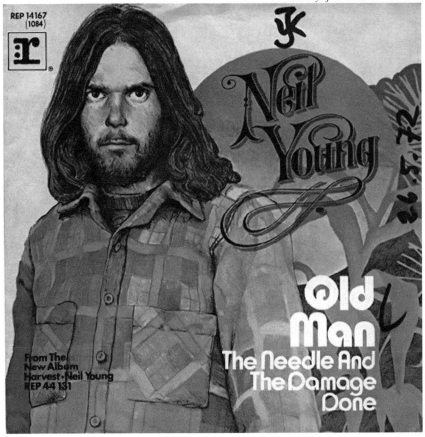

By some accounts, the musicians weren't even Young's first choice for *Harvest* and were only called in when the usual Nashville ringers weren't available for the spur-of-the-moment sessions.

Young had been in Nashville for a taping of the *Johnny Cash Show*, and had only arranged the sessions after being introduced to producer Elliot Mazer by his manager Elliot Roberts (the two Elliots were already longtime friends).

When Young said he wanted to record some new songs, Mazer hastily arranged the sessions at Quadrafonic Sound, bumping other sessions off the schedule in order to secure the slot for Young. With the Nashville sessions striking gold (particularly with the single "Heart of Gold"), an association with Mazer began, and he would go on to produce or co-produce a string of Young's albums from *Time Fades Away* and *Tonight's the Night*, right up through such "lost eighties" albums as *Old Ways* and *Everybody's Rockin'*.

Since they happened to be in town at the time (also for the *Johnny Cash Show*), Young was able to secure the services of two of the biggest names from the then commercially huge soft-rocking singer-songwriter genre—Linda Ronstadt and James Taylor—to sing backup vocals on several songs, most notably "Heart of Gold." Taylor also plays banjo on the album—reportedly for the first time ever, after being urged to pick up the instrument by Young.

For all of the control he is famous for exercising over his recordings, this is one of his more curious habits. Other examples of Young playing this bizarre game of musical chairs with the hired help include having guitarist Nils Lofgren play piano on the *After the Gold Rush* album and piano player Jack Nitzsche pick up a slide guitar on *Harvest*. Like Taylor, neither had ever played the instruments until Young asked them to.

For all of *Harvest's* success, though, Young himself was restless as ever when it came to following the muse, and just as soon as *Harvest* became a smash hit, he began to distance himself—some would even say run like hell—from it.

The Devil Fools with the Best-Laid Plan

Faced with his first headlining tour as a solo artist and newly anointed superstar, for Neil Young the pressure of playing sold-out sports arenas led to doubts that the *Harvest* material—which in fairness, probably was far better suited to a more intimate setting—would translate well in the sort of barns built more for things like NBA Basketball, the Ice Capades, and the occasional Rolling Stones concert.

There were troubles within the band as well. With all the big bucks now involved, some of the musicians—particularly Kenny Buttrey—complained about their paychecks (which ended up being adjusted upwards).

Young had also decided to give his old Crazy Horse running buddy Danny Whitten another chance by offering him a slot in the Stray Gators for the tour. As a result of a severe addiction to heroin, Whitten had fallen on hard times, first getting sacked by Neil during the *After the Gold Rush* sessions, and then finally being fired by the other members of Crazy Horse—the band he had created—altogether.

When it soon became apparent that Whitten—despite all personal assurances to the contrary—wasn't in any better shape during rehearsals for the *Harvest* tour, Young was again forced to dismiss him, handing him fifty dollars and a plane ticket back home to Los Angeles. Whitten was found dead of an overdose of alcohol and valium later that same day. While the final verdict on Whitten's death was accidental overdose, there are also some who believe that he might have committed suicide—including Jack Nitzsche.

In the years since, Nitzsche has related the story of receiving a strange phone call from Whitten the same day, where he asked "would you be there for me no matter what?" When Nitzsche replied that indeed he would, Whitten said "that's all I wanted to know." It may have been the last phone call Danny Whitten ever made.

It has been suggested that "The Needle and the Damage Done" was written about Whitten, although in doing research for this book it's a little hard to match his death with that exact timeline.

What is certain, though, is that Whitten's death had a profound impact on Neil Young personally and that it would also significantly influence the abrupt artistic turn away from "the middle of the road" and towards "the ditch" of his next three albums—and most notably on his masterpiece *Tonight's the Night* .

Over the course of what was supposed to be the *Harvest* tour, Young began focusing less on the crowd-pleasing

Sheet music for "Heart of Gold," the smash hit that propelled *Harvest* to become the biggest-selling album of 1972 and ultimately the biggest of Neil Young's career.
Courtesy of Tom Therme collection

favorites of that album and more on testing out his new, decidedly harder, edgier, and even abrasive songs. In the wake of the drug-related deaths of both Whitten and, later, roadie Bruce Berry, these rawer expressions of grief had also come to represent his world view at the time—depressing as it may have been.

These songs would eventually make up what may be the strangest follow-up to a multiplatinum smash album in all of rock-'n'-roll history, a live recording called *Time Fades Away*—the first of the infamous Ditch Trilogy.

Single release of "Heart of Gold" from *Harvest*.   *Courtesy of Tom Therme collection*

12

So I Headed for the Ditch

Time Fades Away, On the Beach, and *Tonight's the Night*—Neil Young's Ditch Trilogy

O n the liner notes of his 1977 triple-disc anthology release *Decade*, Neil Young famously writes about how the success of "Heart of Gold" and *Harvest* put him in the middle of the road, and how, after becoming bored with it all, he instead decided to head toward the ditch. In retrospect, it's rather doubtful that Young's then abrupt, and quite intentional, turn away from commercial success amounted to anything nearly that simple. But at the same time, and again in retrospect, it makes complete sense.

That famous quote has long since been repeated in virtually every major biography or serious critical analysis of Young's body of work. As a result, the three albums released between 1973 and 1975 have come to be known as the Ditch Trilogy (also referred to, though slightly less often, as the "Doom Trilogy").

Time Fades Away, On the Beach, and *Tonight's the Night*—though widely dismissed (and certainly misunderstood) by some fans, and even by some within his own camp at the time—have since come to occupy a rather hallowed place among Neil Young's most devoted followers.

In the case of *Time Fades Away*, the album has even become the rallying cry for a particularly rabid segment of that same fan base—some of whom have even petitioned for the album's reissue on the very popular Neil Young fan site Thrasher's Wheat. Despite their impassioned pleas, *Time Fades Away* (along with the soundtrack to Young's first Shakey Pictures film project *Journey Through the Past*) remains the only album in his vast catalog that has yet to see a reissue on CD.

In 2010, *Uncut* magazine listed *Time Fades Away* as its #1 choice on a list of the "50 Greatest Lost Albums." When put into the sort of hindsight that only comes after years and decades of watching Neil Young's miraculous growth as an artist, it's easy to see why the album has become such a preciously sought-after commodity. If there is such a thing as the precise recorded moment where Neil Young cemented his reputation as a maverick willing to follow the muse wherever it leads him—even if it means going over a cliff—*Time Fades Away* is it.

At the time of its original release in 1973, though, the album landed with a resounding commercial thud. Coming a year and change after the worldwide chart-topper that was *Harvest*, the album peaked at a comparatively dismal #22 on Billboard. The *Journey Through the Past* soundtrack, released a year earlier (and foolishly marketed by Warner Brothers—however briefly—as the "new" Neil Young album), did even worse, climbing no higher than #45 on the albums chart. It was truly the commercial stiff heard around the world.

Still, as abysmal as the sales of these albums was, it was amazing either of them even did that well—a fact probably owing more to Young's critical reputation at the time than anything else.

As many of the record company promotion guys charged with the unenviable task of pushing his strange, abrasive new music could—and indeed did—attest at the time, Young seemed hell-bent on committing career suicide back then.

But by some accounts, the rather down mood of the Ditch Trilogy albums was also reflective of the artist's depressed state at the time, coming on the heels of the deaths of Danny Whitten and Bruce Berry as they did. Even so, there is now no question that this period marked the beginning of an artistic watershed. To many, the Ditch Trilogy heralds the beginnings of what is arguably the most creatively fertile period of Neil Young's career. Beginning in 1973, and continuing on through most of the seventies, the already prolific Young went on something of a record-making tear—shelving as many potentially great projects (such as the mythical "lost albums" *Homegrown* and *Chrome Dreams*) as were actually released.

Though *Time Fades Away* remains one of those mysteriously missing pieces of the overall puzzle that is Young's catalog as it is seen today (particularly among his younger fans), it also has yet to gain the hallowed stature afforded the now more universally recognized critical masterpieces *On the Beach* and especially *Tonight's the Night*.

(Just as a quick personal sidebar here, as much as I love *Tonight's the Night*, I'd actually have to place *On the Beach* a bit higher on a personal favorites list.)

For his own part, Young himself seems to be in no hurry to rewrite history with a CD reissue of *Time Fades Away* either. Along with *Journey Through the Past*, that album stands alone as a rare missing link in his catalog that the artist himself appears quite content to have completely disowned. Of course, if there is anything to be learned in the case of an artist as prone to sudden, and sometimes seemingly illogical artistic whims as Neil Young (at least from a commercial perspective), it is that these sort of things can change—and often quite suddenly—at the drop of a dime.

The Businessmen Crowded Around, They Came to Hear the Golden Sound . . .

Regardless of his own feelings about it today, it remains a matter of historic record that *Time Fades Away* is the album where Neil Young began his long, dark, and some would say quite depressing journey down into "the ditch."

Misunderstood and even reviled by some of his biggest fans at the time, today *Time Fades Away* remains among the most confusing releases of his career. Young himself has gone on record as saying it is the least favorite of his albums (which probably accounts for its still unreleased status on CD). Sales were pretty much abysmal when it was first released in 1973, and the reviews weren't much better.

Yet, in what might be the ultimate case of absence making the heart grow fonder, the album has subsequently become the focus of an impassioned petition for its reissue by fans on Internet sites like Thrasher's Wheat. Critics have likewise seemed to come around to *Time Fades Away*, with *Uncut* magazine recently naming it as their #1 entry on a list of the fifty greatest lost albums ever.

Time Fades Away was recorded live in concert during what was supposed to be the triumphant tour behind the massive *Harvest* album, but instead became something of a disaster. Young's band for the tour, the Stray Gators, which included many of the same top-flight studio musicians used on *Harvest*, was largely in disarray. On the eve of the tour there were disputes among the musicians over things like salaries, and of course the nasty business of Danny Whitten's firing and subsequent death was still hanging over everyone like a dark cloud. Without Whitten to support him on vocals, Young's voice was also completely shot by the end of the tour, which led him to recruit David Crosby and Graham Nash as backup vocalists for some of the final dates.

Young himself was said to be miserable during the tour as well, between the terrible news about Whitten, the bickering amongst the band, and questions over how the mellow pop songs of *Harvest* could possibly translate to the rather ominous prospect of playing ninety sold-out shows in hockey arenas.

The performances on *Time Fades Away* reflect this chaos.

With Whitten's death still fresh on his mind, Young had taken to performing a series of new songs on the road that represented an abrupt shift from the feel-good country pop of *Harvest*. With songs like "Last Dance," "Don't Be Denied," and "Yonder Stands the Sinner" showing a darker lyrical side, the murkier rock sound of this new material likewise reflected the doom and gloom.

For those who doubt the claims of Neil Young being "the Godfather of Grunge" that would surface some two decades later, one only needs to point them toward *Time Fades Away*. Needless to say, audiences expecting to hear the hits like "Heart of Gold" or even "Cinnamon Girl" were not amused as Young shifted the focus of the shows toward the newer, more downbeat songs.

By the end of what became dubbed the *Time Fades Away* tour, these darker, never-before-heard songs accounted for as much as two-thirds of the show. When the bad vibes surrounding the tour failed to produce a new album during studio rehearsals, Young chose instead to release the live versions of the songs (since he had been recording all of the shows anyway).

If Crazy Horse has at times been compared to an American Rolling Stones, on *Time Fades Away* the boozy, sloppy sound of the Stray Gators could be likened to something more closely resembling Rod Stewart's work with the Faces, his notoriously ragged-sounding seventies outfit with Ronnie Wood (and remember, the Stray Gators were seasoned Nashville pros when Young first signed them up for *Harvest*).

On *Time Fades Away*, the Stray Gators sound every bit as tanked up as Rod Stewart's famous band of drunken rogues—but played at a much slower, more deliberately lazy and dirge-like tempo. If Roddy and Woody's boozy wailing on songs like "Had Me a Real Good Time" represented the party, the pre-Seattle grunge of *Time Fades Away* sounds more like the day-after hangover.

Completely oblivious to the wants of a live audience who just wanted to hear the damn hits, Young's performance on *Time Fades Away* can be seen more as a precursor to the direct and intentionally confrontational music that avant and punk-rockers like Lou Reed (on *Metal Machine Music*), Iggy Pop, and the Sex Pistols would later elevate to performance art, than as simple rock 'n' roll (despite the fact that the songs on this album in fact represent some of the simplest, most primal-sounding rock 'n' roll of Young's career).

The ragged quality of the performances on *Time Fades Away* is matched equally by the low-fi sound of the live recording itself. Tape hiss can be heard throughout the recording, which actually adds to its raw feel in a weird sort of way. Original vinyl copies were even stamped with a warning of sorts: "This Recording Was Mastered 16-Track/Direct to Disc (acetate) by Computer."

The album also produced at least one bona fide Neil Young classic in "Don't Be Denied." Written the day after Danny Whitten died, the song is really more of an autobiographical tune recalling Young's early days in Winnipeg, and is in many ways a more rocking successor to the CSN&Y song "Helpless."

"Last Dance" is another standout. Clocking in at nearly nine minutes, the song probably best demonstrates the sort of raucous, wheels-coming-off-the-wagon playing that so frustrated Young's audiences on that tour. His primal screaming of "no, no, no" over and over toward the end also represents the sort of naked, standing-over-the-cliff demonstration of raw emotion that wouldn't be a bit out of place on something like John Lennon's *Plastic Ono Band* album.

Like everyone else at the time it first came out in 1973, I didn't "get" *Time Fades Away* at all. In hindsight, though, Young's least favorite album has to be recognized as something of a great, lost classic—misunderstood at the time as it was.

Tonight's the Night Part I

Seven months after Danny Whitten's overdose, the Neil Young camp was rocked by another equally tragic, drug-related loss.

Sheet music for "Walk On" from *On the Beach*, one of the three albums comprising what would come to be known as Neil Young's mid-seventies "Ditch Trilogy."   *Courtesy of Tom Therme collection*

Bruce Berry's dead body was found on June 7, 1973. The former roadie for both Neil Young and CSN&Y had apparently been dead for several days after overdosing on a lethal cocktail of cocaine and heroin.

For those in CSN&Y's inner circle, though, Berry's drug problems were hardly a secret.

Although his official job title was listed as roadie, Berry was also the band's unofficial dealer, supplying drugs to a number of people in the CSN&Y camp, including Stephen Stills.

Not long before he was found dead, Berry in fact had particularly pissed off Crosby, Nash, and Young when he showed up with drugs at a band meeting in Hawaii that was really intended more as an intervention for Stills, in the hopes of getting the band back together for a reunion album and tour. The incident in fact effectively scuttled any dreams of a proposed tour (at least for the time being), when Young stated he wanted nothing to do with any of it and walked out of the meeting.

Even so, the deaths of Whitten and Berry—along with a recent drug deal gone bad that resulted in the murder of a drug dealer during a party at Young's old Topanga Canyon stomping grounds—had much of the inner circle understandably spooked, and probably none more so than Neil Young himself.

Not surprisingly, he responded in the most appropriate and perhaps only way he knew how. Putting yet another CSN&Y reunion project on hold (much to the chagrin of his bandmates), Young got in touch with his old pal David Briggs and said he wanted to make what he then described as "a rock-'n'-roll record."

Young and Briggs hadn't worked together since *Harvest*, as the result of a falling out over a disagreement with the product that was ultimately released. Briggs had wanted to release a live acoustic recording of the *Harvest* songs from 1971, rather than the studio version that ultimately came out. The recording was finally released three decades later as *Live at Massey Hall*, part of the massive *Archives* project.

In the end, the album that became *Tonight's the Night* was much more than a simple rock-'n'-roll record. Today it is recognized, and rightfully so, as Neil Young's first true masterpiece.

To record the album, Briggs and Young knocked out a wall with a sledgehammer at the Studio Instrument Rentals rehearsal space owned by Bruce Berry's brother Ken. From there, they ran some cable through the hole in the wall and converted it into a makeshift studio.

Young's idea was to let it all hang out and make a record as raw and unhinged-sounding as possible, warts and all. Recorded during round-the-clock sessions fueled by copious amounts of booze, the musicians—a combination of Crazy Horse players like Nils Lofgren, Jack Nitzsche, and Ralph Molina, Billy Talbot, and Stray Gators holdover Ben Keith—would spend the day getting more or less out of their minds on tequila and then running through the songs late into the night.

The result is a series of raggedly played songs that are more like glimpses into Neil Young's darkly troubled soul. Stark, raw, and ultimately beautiful, his vision of what he has since described many times as "audio verité" is captured with a breathtaking sort of minimalist beauty on *Tonight's the Night*.

Although the version of the album eventually released two years after it was recorded in 1975 was cleaned up considerably, the spirit of those original sessions—complete with botched cues and missed notes—remains largely intact. As a brutally honest artistic document of both its time and the altered states of consciousness of the players involved, *Tonight's the Night* is arguably unmatched in the entire history of rock 'n' roll. With songs that are about as far removed from the peace-and-love, California hippie sentiment of *Harvest* as it gets, Young had crafted his first genuine masterpiece.

But unlike other rock-'n'-roll masterpieces of the era made by people like the Beatles and Brian Wilson, for example, the beauty of *Tonight's the Night* lies not in any sort of studio-manufactured magic, but rather in its brilliant and raw nakedness. If there ever really was such a thing as a "one take, and that's a wrap" album, *Tonight's the Night* was it, particularly in its original, still unreleased version.

The album that ultimately surfaced in 1975 maintains much, but not all of the raw spirit of those original tequila-fueled sessions. Even so, Young still couldn't resist some last-minute tinkering.

No less than David Briggs himself has maintained that the original version of the album, untouched by overdubs and studio technology, most accurately captures the spirit of those all-night sessions fueled by a volatile combination of grief and Cuervo Gold. As a result, the original *Tonight's the Night* album—unhinged, unreleased, and believed to still exist somewhere on a cassette tape—represents something like the holy grail of all the many great lost Neil Young recordings amongst diehard fans.

Tonight's the Night begins and ends with the title track—a habit Young would continue to follow to great effect with future releases *Rust Never Sleeps* and *Freedom*.

Jack Nitzsche's boozy-sounding piano intro sounds like the sort of thing you might hear around last call at the piano bar from hell. This soon gives way to Neil's raggedly barking out the personal lyrics about how "Bruce Berry was a working man," and how he would "sing a song in a shaky voice," before finally cutting to the chase with the chilling line about how he "heard that he died out on the mainline." With its dark, personal, and quite frankly depressing, tone, it was clear that with *Tonight's the Night* Young was no longer content with merely dancing on the artistic edge, but rather had chosen to take his music to the edge of oblivion.

On the second version of the song that closes the album, Young pushes the emotional intensity even further. With a vocal that plays more like an anguished howl, he sounds like he is within seconds of becoming completely emotionally unglued. It is one of the more brutally honest examples of an artist completely baring his soul ever heard on a rock-'n'-roll record.

From there, songs like "Tired Eyes" (inspired by the murderous drug deal gone bad and resulting shootout in Topanga) continue his dark journey down into the drug-infested cesspool of post-hippie Los Angeles. Young doesn't so much sing lyrics like "was he a heavy doper" and the like, as he does mutter them in what amounts to a foggy whisper. In some ways, the song plays more like a long conversation Young is having with himself about the event ("Well he shot four men in a cocaine deal, And he left them lyin' in an open field"). If nothing else, he certainly keeps it real on this bleak and harrowing account of a real-life event that offers a rare look inside the darker, seedier underbelly of the Los Angeles hippie subculture. It's one of the very best tracks from *Tonight's the Night*.

Other songs, like "Roll Another Number," could be interpreted as a hypocritical endorsement of the druggy lifestyle that so tragically came home to bite Neil Young on the ass during the recording of *Tonight's the Night*. But once the album is heard in full, with the songs played in their proper sequence, there's no mistaking the antidrug—or at least antiheroin—sentiment of the overall record. One of the more eerie aspects of the final version of the album released in 1975 is the inclusion of a 1970 Crazy Horse live performance from the Fillmore East where Danny Whitten posthumously sings "Come On Baby, Let's Go Downtown" (a song that none too coincidentally is about scoring heroin).

The original version of *Tonight's the Night* said to be floating around somewhere out there on bootleg tapes and the like was by all accounts even rawer sounding, and includes several boozy-sounding raps in between the songs themselves (producer David Briggs has confirmed as much in interviews after the fact). These same strange, rambling raps would become a centerpiece of Young's shows as he took the songs from *Tonight's the Night* out on tour for a test run. But if audiences had been left confused by the *Time Fades Away* shows, they were in for a particularly rude awakening this time around.

Promotional LP pressing of *Time Fades Away*, the live recording of new songs that kicked off Neil Young's Ditch Trilogy. As of this writing, it remains unreleased on CD.   *Courtesy of Tom Therme collection*

Welcome to Miami Beach . . . Everything Is Cheaper Than It Looks

Although it would be two more years before *Tonight's the Night* was even released—in a considerably altered, and, at least according to folks like David Briggs, watered-down version from the original booze-fueled sessions laid down at S.I.R.—Young still wasted no time in taking his new songs out on the road.

For those fans still hoping for either "mellow Neil" or the religiously sha-manistic rock-'n'-roll experience of Neil Young with Crazy Horse, the *Tonight's the Night* tour would offer no respite.

If anything, Neil Young was more out there and weird on this tour than ever before. The stage was a strange display of everything from a collection of gawdy platform boots to props like a wooden Indian and a palm tree (which had clearly seen better days) plucked from S.I.R. Young himself was sporting a disheveled look, complete with long, stringy hair, a scruffy-looking half growth of beard, over-the-top Elvis shades, and the sort of cheap jacket you might find on the dollar rack at the Goodwill. This rather nightmarish-looking Young inspired comparisons to Charles Manson, the "hippie cult" mass murderer still fresh in the minds of anyone who followed the news of the day back then.

More than anything else, though, the *Tonight's the Night* shows were an exten-sion of the boozy atmosphere of the sessions for the album itself. More often than not, the band—who changed their name to the Santa Monica Flyers for the tour—was tanked on a combination of tequila and lord knows what else, and none more so than Young himself. In the many years that have passed since, he has referred to the shows from the *Tonight's the Night* tour as the closest thing to "performance art" he has ever done—and in retrospect that observation probably isn't far off the mark.

At the time, though, concertgoers mostly experienced an artist who seemed to be nothing if not zonked clean out of his freaking mind. Rumors began spreading during the tour that Young had developed a severe drug problem (he hadn't) or that he might even be dead (he wasn't).

Meanwhile, from an insider's perspective, everybody from band members like Ben Keith and Nils Lofgren to Young himself were having the time of their lives. Well, at least everyone except for perhaps Elliot Roberts, who was concerned enough about future commercial prospects for his flagship artist that post-show, back-of-the-bus pep talks became a nightly ritual during the tour.

Aside from his increasingly confrontational tone toward his audience—and in particular, their reluctance to indulge his artistic muse and just take in the new material without complaint—there were also things like the night Young bought a round of drinks for the entire house during a show at L.A.'s Roxy to consider. Later on that night, when he dared female audience members to come to the stage topless, his then girlfriend Carrie Snodgress took him up on it—which only served to further horrify an already nervous Elliot Roberts.

For opening acts on the tour ranging from the Eagles to Linda Ronstadt—both of whom were still riding the laid-back seventies L.A. singer-songwriter wave the *Harvest* album had helped establish—the shows had to seem equally strange. Critics, who by this time were already puzzled by recent artistically questionable decisions like the *Time Fades Away* tour and subsequent album, reacted to the shows with some of the worst reviews of Young's career up until that time.

Still, in spite of all of this, for Young every stop on the *Tonight's the Night* tour was just another night at the beach, or to be more specific, another night at Miami Beach.

For every show of the tour, he played the role of emcee, beginning each performance with the introduction "Welcome to Miami Beach, where everything is cheaper than it looks."

From there, he would run through the new, unheard songs for the dumb-struck audiences. Like the still unreleased album, the concerts both began and ended with the song "Tonight's the Night"—which also served as a launch point for boozy, borderline incoherent raps that almost always centered on the subject of Bruce Berry. Keep in mind that it is almost certain that 90 percent of the crowd had no idea who Bruce Berry even was.

By the time the song was played for a second time that evening, Young would often tease the crowd by saying "here's one you've heard before," which only served to further fuck with the expectations of concertgoers expecting to hear the hits like "Heart of Gold" or "Cinnamon Girl." What they got instead was an even more raggedly intense reprise of "Tonight's the Night" that could stretch to thirty minutes or longer. It was almost as if Young were purposefully trying to get the most negative reaction possible.

His raps about how Bruce Berry "put David Crosby's guitar into his arm" (a reference to how the addiction-ravaged Berry had once stolen Crosby's guitar and hawked it for junk) were undoubtedly lost on audiences who didn't know who Bruce Berry was, and could probably have cared less (particularly with regard to songs they had never heard before to begin with).

Still, Young remained undaunted. Not only was he unwilling to spare audiences who paid their money to hear the hits this latest of his increasingly frequent artistic indulgences—if anything, he seemed hell-bent on force-feeding them whatever the muse demanded, regardless of any critical or commercial fallout that might follow.

Hello, Waterface, Goodbye Waterface

As brutal as the notices in such normally supportive publications as *Rolling Stone* had been, one of the most scathing reviews of the *Tonight's the Night* shows came from Dutch critic Constant Meijers. Interestingly, when the *Tonight's the Night* album was finally released nearly two years later, Young reproduced Meijers's article, still written its original Dutch language, as part of the album artwork.

Another curiosity about the album art is a strange letter to someone named "Waterface" included on the sleeve.

In addition to more references to "Miami Beach," the letter contains the particularly cryptic line "Tell Waterface to put it in his lung and not in his vein," which is almost certainly a reference to the drug overdose deaths of Danny Whitten and Bruce Berry. Because of this, it has been speculated that the name "Waterface" could refer to Whitten, Berry, or even both of them.

During the seventies when vinyl was still the preferred format for long-form albums, messages from the artists etched into the inner groove of the vinyl (the blank space closest to the paper label) were also somewhat common. The unidentified "Waterface" appears on such an etching on *Tonight's the Night* as well, where one side reads "Hello Waterface" and the other reads "Goodbye Waterface."

The actual identity of "Waterface" has never been revealed and remains a mystery to this day.

Tonight's the Night Part 2

It would be two more years before *Tonight's the Night* would see the light of day. Even then, the album's eventual release came about only by way of a sort of happy accident. In between the time of the original 1973 S.I.R. sessions and the release of *Tonight's the Night* two years later, Neil Young completed two more albums and also reunited with Crosby, Stills, Nash, and Young for the 1974 stadium juggernaut that became known as the Doom Tour.

Of the two albums Young made in between, *Homegrown* was the return to the commercially viable, million-dollar mellow folk-pop sounds of *Harvest* that everyone from the label executives at Warner Brothers to Elliot Roberts had been salivating for. Not surprisingly, for anyone who really knows this story, it was shelved at the last minute by Young himself and never released. Many of the songs from *Homegrown* eventually surfaced on albums like *American Stars and Bars* and *Zuma*. Young himself has been quoted in interviews as saying that he put the brakes on releasing *Homegrown* because he felt that the songs—many of which were inspired by his then disintegrating relationship with Carrie Snodgress—hit a little too close to home on a personal level.

The album has since gone on to somewhat mythical status as one of several great lost albums in the Neil Young canon, and is widely believed to be the true sequel to *Harvest*. Rumors persist that the full album will finally see official release as part of the second volume of the *Archives* boxed set series.

The other album Young recorded during this period (and that actually was released in 1974) was *On the Beach*, which is even bleaker than *Tonight's the Night* and has gone on to be recognized as a high-water mark in the artist's catalog (even if it was seen as simply the latest of his commercial failures at the time).

Meanwhile, Young continued to tinker off and on with *Tonight's the Night* in the studio. At one point, the idea of making the album into a

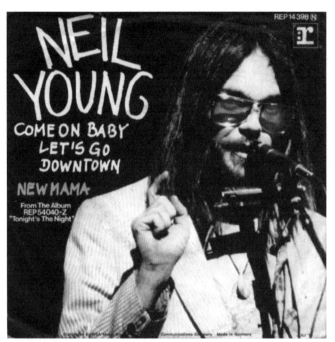

Single release for "Come On Baby, Let's Go Downtown," sung by Danny Whitten on the *Tonight's the Night* album. Whitten's death haunted the sessions for what later became known as the dark masterpiece of the Ditch Trilogy.   *Courtesy of Tom Therme collection*

Broadway musical production was even floated, strangely enough, by Elliot Roberts. As odd as that may sound now, at one point Roberts even enlisted Mel Frohman (who was married to Roberts's secretary) to work up a treatment for the purposed Broadway production about Bruce Berry set to Neil Young songs. The result was a musical based loosely on Berry's life and featuring songs from *Tonight's the Night*, which at one point was going to be called *From Roadie to Riches* but ultimately never saw the light of day.

In the end, after all of Young's endless tinkering with the original tapes, it was Rick Danko from the Band who can probably be credited with this bleak masterpiece finally seeing the light of day.

After Young played the reels for *Homegrown* for a group of people including Danko, as well as the Band's Richard Manuel and Crazy Horse's Ralph Molina in a room at L.A.'s Chateau Marmont hotel (also the site of John Belushi's death), the tapes for *Tonight's the Night*, which had apparently made it on the same reel, unexpectedly followed.

When Danko said "if you guys don't release this album, you're fucking crazy," Young listened. And although it must have broken the hearts of more than a few Warner Brothers executives who were instead expecting the *Harvest* sequel, the rest is history.

The World Is Turnin', I Hope It Don't Turn Away

On the Beach may be the most depressing-sounding record that Neil Young, or anyone else for that matter, has ever recorded. It is also a largely underappreciated masterpiece.

There are probably any number of factors contributing to the decidedly downbeat mood of the album, not the least of which is the fact that it was recorded as Neil Young's relationship with Carrie Snodgress was disintegrating (even though of the album's eight songs, only "Motion Pictures" appears to be directly about her).

But in the end, what probably contributed most to the down feel of *On the Beach* (and when it comes to this record, calling it merely laid back would be a considerable understatement) was the sort of home-cooked recipe you more likely might find in a cookbook written by Timothy Leary or Ken Kesey for something called "honey slides."

Where tequila had been the recreational intoxicant of choice during the making of *Tonight's the Night*, the sessions for what became *On the Beach* were fueled by the lethal concoction that came to be known to everyone surrounding the project as honey slides. But this particular mind-altering confection was just one facet of the overall craziness that Cajun wildman Rusty Kershaw brought to the table during the sessions for *On the Beach.*

If there was such a thing as a wild card during the making of the album, then Kershaw, brother of the legendary fiddler Doug Kershaw, was truly it.

Brought into Young's scene by Ben Keith, Kershaw came along with enough baggage to a fill a jumbo jet. Among his other antics, he ran up an exorbitant tab at the hotel during the *On the Beach* sessions on Young's dime that included wheeling in crates of wine and later badly damaging the room with wine stains and burnt cigarette holes in the carpet.

And then there were those honey slides. Kershaw's wife would cook up this potent combination of high-grade hashish and honey into little cakes that resembled cow pies, which the musicians would then eat. Even for a bunch of stoner veterans like Neil Young's crew, the honey slides packed one hell of a knockout punch. The honey slides would put them in a state somewhere between catatonic and just being rendered plain, out and out comatose. It was the perfect backdrop for a record that ambles along at the slow, lazy pace of *On the Beach.*

In addition to the lunatic Kershaw, Young assembled a colorful cast of characters for the making of *On the Beach* that included many of the usual suspects like Ben Keith, Tim Drummond, and Ralph Molina, as well as David Crosby and Levon Helm and Rick Danko from the Band.

Despite Kershaw's antics, the one thing that most impressed Young about him was the way he vibed off of his playing. Where Young was known for putting musicians through their paces by having them lay down tracks for songs they barely knew, Kershaw not only would record his parts for the album with little preparation, but actually thrive on this first-take environment.

For the sessions, many of Kershaw's contributions playing fiddle and slide guitar—particularly on songs like the epic "Ambulance Blues"—were recorded with him not having heard the song beforehand at all. Kershaw also insisted on being situated as close as possible to Young in the studio, for the sole purpose of being able to "vibe off of him."

Recorded mostly at Sunset Sound in Los Angeles (save for the tracks "For the Turnstiles" and "Walk On," which were recorded at Broken Arrow), *On the Beach* contains some of the most down, desolate, and depressing music of Young's entire recorded catalog—particularly on the three songs that make up the second side of the original vinyl album.

Yet, for all the doom and gloom of the album, there is also something strangely cathartic about it. It's as though Young is facing down some of the darkest demons lurking in his closet—even if he is probably only doing so on a subconscious level—and confronting them head-on. Experienced on this level, *On the Beach* feels at times like something more resembling an exorcism.

I Went to the Radio Interview, but I Ended Up Alone at the Microphone

The title track establishes the downer mood right out of the gate. In a voice that sounds so completely isolated and world-weary, it almost sounds like a part of him is channeling the ghost of Hank Williams doing "I'm So Lonesome I Could Cry," Young sings the lines "the world is turnin', I hope it don't turn away."

As the song continues to crawl along to one of the most downcast slow blues you are ever likely to hear, Young sounds so completely alone and withdrawn from the outside world you almost fear for his sanity. "I need a crowd of people, but I can't face them day to day," he sings in something closer to an anguished whisper in one line. "Though my problems are meaningless, that don't make them go away," he sings in another line with the sort of world-weariness dripping off of his voice that it sounds like he could go right over the edge at any moment.

Eventually, the song finds him at a radio interview where he "ended up alone at the microphone." It's the sort of strange and startling confession about celebrity that is even stranger coming from an artist like Neil Young—one who is not usually known for such revelations in his music.

If *Tonight's the Night* ever seemed like a downer of an album, when compared to *On the Beach* it sounds almost like goodtime party rock.

Though he has since claimed he didn't realize it at the time, the song "Motion Pictures" appears to be the first of many that Neil Young wrote during this period about his then crumbling relationship with Carrie Snodgress (the majority of these would be later recorded for the still unreleased *Homegrown* album). The closest thing to a tone of optimism you'll find here is in the line

"I'm deep inside myself, but I'll get out somehow," a lyric that eerily echoes the feeling of desolate isolation already expressed on the title track.

You're All Just Pissing in the Wind

On the album's centerpiece, the sprawling "Ambulance Blues," Young alternates between wistful remembrances from "back in the old folky days" where "the air was magic when we played" and rejecting such nostalgic feelings altogether ("it's easy to get buried in the past, when you try to make a good thing last').

Later on, he lashes out at his detractors ("so all you critics sit alone, you're no better than me, for what you've shown") and an unidentified man "who could tell so many lies, he had a different story for every set of eyes."

At the time, many thought this lyric might have been referring to then President Richard Nixon. *On the Beach* came out in 1974, the same year Nixon was forced to resign because of the Watergate scandal. The album jacket also famously makes reference to Watergate. In the front cover photo, Young is seen with his back turned to the camera, alone on a beach in white pants and a ridiculous bright yellow jacket, amidst a beach table and chairs with the fins of an older, fifties model car sticking up out of the sand. Lying underneath the table is a newspaper with the headline "Sen. Buckley Calls for Nixon to Resign."

By the time "Ambulance Blues" is over, Young concludes that "there ain't nothing like the friend, who can tell you you're just pissing in the wind" in what may go down as one of his most sublime lyrics ever. There have been numerous claims over the years that the song is really about his famously fractious relationship with Crosby, Stills, and Nash (a subject Young would later address more directly in the song "Thrasher" from *Rust Never Sleeps*). But the references to Nixon and others seems to be more of a statement on the generally pessimistic national mood of its post-Watergate times than anything else, at least when viewed in retrospect.

Interestingly, Young has gone on record as stating that he subconsciously stole the melody for "Ambulance Blues" from Scottish folk guitarist Bert Jansch (who he has also subsequently praised more than once as being the acoustic guitar equivalent of a virtuoso like Jimi Hendrix).

We Got Twenty-Five Rifles Just to Keep the Population Down

Of the few upbeat songs from *On the Beach*, "Walk On" is probably the best known, but "Revolution Blues" is without a doubt the most infamous. Inspired by hippie cult messiah and mass murderer Charles Manson, the song rather audaciously sets the Manson murder spree to a rock-'n'-roll beat with lines like "Well, I hear that Laurel Canyon is full of famous stars, But I hate them worse than lepers and I'll kill them in their cars."

David Crosby, who plays guitar on the track, was reportedly so horrified by the lyrics that he refused to play it with Young on CSN&Y's 1974 reunion tour. In another line, Young snarls "I hope you get the connection, 'cause I can't take the rejection." In the years since the song was released, he has stated in published interviews that he knew Manson as an acquaintance, and that his murderous rage may have come in part after his songs were rejected by all the record labels in town from Warner Brothers on down.

"Charlie didn't take rejection well," he has been quoted as saying. Young may be the only artist of his time who would have the balls to record a song about a pariah like Manson, particularly during a time when the Tate-LaBianca murders, and the dark ripple effect they had on much of the Hollywood entertainment subculture, was so fresh in people's minds.

The other standout track from *On the Beach* is "For the Turnstiles," which sounds for all the world like it could have been made somewhere on a front porch in the Mississippi Delta with Neil Young and Ben Keith's respective funky blues picking on the banjo and dobro.

The lyrics, which are said to be at least partially inspired by idle conversation with Carrie Snodgress as the song was being created, reference everything from seasick sailors and pimps with tailors, to great explorers and bush league batters—all wrapped around the central lines "You can really learn a lot that way."

As a piece of inspired songwriting, "For the Turnstiles" ranks right up there with Young's best. Some have also described it as his "Dylan song."

Tonight's the Night concert shirt.   *Courtesy of Tom Therme collection*

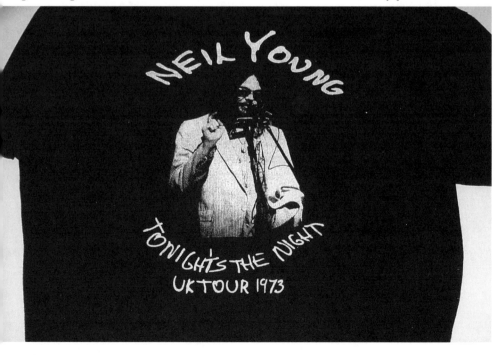

Citizen Kane Junior Blues

Although Young never embarked on a full solo tour to support *On the Beach*, many of the songs from the album were performed with Crosby, Stills, Nash, and Young during the reunion Doom Tour of 1974.

However, he did make a surprise appearance at New York's famous folk showcase club the Bottom Line on May 16, 1974. During this surprise appearance, he performed most of the still unreleased *On the Beach* album alone on an acoustic guitar before a stunned crowd that had come expecting to see only Ry Cooder and Leon Redbone (the scheduled headliners that night).

In addition to playing versions of still unheard songs from *On the Beach* like "Ambulance Blues," "For the Turnstiles," and "Motion Pictures" for the first time before a live audience, the crowd was also treated to other unreleased songs of the period like the hallucinatory, quasi-psychedelic "Pushed It Over the End" (which Young introduced as "Citizen Kane Junior Blues") and a beautifully rendered cover of "Greensleeves."

In between songs, an uncharacteristically relaxed and animated Young jokes with the audience about things like making the record with Kershaw, and of course, those "honey slides." In response to a request for "Southern Man" from the audience, he also relates a humorous story about why he stopped performing the song following a show at the Oakland Coliseum.

Fortunately, the Bottom Line show was widely bootlegged. Since this performance stands as the only known recorded document of Young doing the *On the Beach* material live, it is also an essential listen (provided, of course, that you can find it). As Neil Young bootlegs go, it's a definite keeper.

13

Why Do I Keep Fuckin' Up?

Neil Young's Biggest Commercial Flops

Over the course of his remarkable career, Neil Young has scored a number of big commercial breakthrough hits—none of which were bigger than 1972's worldwide #1 blockbuster, the classic album *Harvest*.

Even so, with a catalog that numbers somewhere in the neighborhood of fifty albums—particularly when you figure in his work with Buffalo Springfield and CSN&Y—it is, of course, inevitable that there would also be some commercial disappointments along the way.

These range from albums like *Tonight's the Night* and *On the Beach*—which, although they sold poorly at the time, have long since become recognized as classics—to out and out duds like his mid-eighties albums *Life* and *Landing on Water*. There are also the albums that came along after his creative and commercial resurgence in the nineties, like his latter-day work in that decade on the albums *Broken Arrow* and *Silver and Gold*.

When one goes back over the original sales figures and Billboard chart positions of Young's catalog, another thing that stands out are the relatively poor chart showings of his numerous live recordings.

Live Rust, released on the heels of the commercially and critically well-received *Rust Never Sleeps* album and film, remains Young's best-selling live album, peaking at #15 on the Billboard albums chart. But the more recent *Live at Massey Hall* album—a live recording from 1971 that wasn't officially released until 2007 as part of the *Archives Performance Series*—actually scored higher on the Billboard charts, peaking at #6.

Interestingly, the relatively strong performance of that album backs up the career-long trend of Young's mellower releases faring better commercially than his more rocking affairs with bands like Crazy Horse.

For example, a live recording with Crazy Horse made at Bill Graham's Fillmore East from 1970—long sought after by Neil Young fans and released a scant six months before *Live at Massey Hall* in 2006 (also as part of the *Archives Performance Series*)—topped out at a comparatively dismal #55 on the Billboard albums chart.

Even more surprising is the fact that the 1991 double live album *Weld* only climbed as high as #154. What is most amazing about this is that it happened despite the fact that *Weld* (and its extended triple-disc counterpart *Arc-Weld*) was recorded during the tour behind the critically lauded *Ragged Glory* album. Regardless of its relatively poor showing in stores, *Weld* is also regarded by many Neil Young fans as one of his best official live recordings. If nothing else, it's certainly his loudest.

Other live Neil Young albums have fared even worse, though—2000's *Road Rock*, recorded live at Colorado's Red Rocks Amphitheater, topped out at a totally embarrassing #169—and that's out of 200 reported positions on the Billboard albums chart. Ouch!

Another thing that stands out when looking back at Young's catalog history on the Billboard charts is the fact that many of the albums now considered among Neil Young's most seminal works also did a lot less well than you might think when they first came out.

Did you know, for example, that *Harvest Moon*, the highly anticipated, long-awaited "sequel" to *Harvest*, only made it to #16 on Billboard?

Equally hard to believe is just how well some of the albums that are commonly regarded now by some as Young's far lesser works actually performed from a chart standpoint at the time of their original release.

As hard as it may seem to believe now, albums like 1995's *Mirror Ball* (#5) made it higher on the charts than either 1979's *Rust Never Sleeps* (#8) or 1989's major comeback record *Freedom* (which only made it to #35, even with the inclusion of an all-time Neil Young classic like "Rockin' in the Free World").

Even an album as widely (if somewhat unfairly) dismissed as *Trans* managed to crack the top twenty with its original #19 showing.

What follows here is a quick look at a few of Neil Young's all-time biggest commercial flops.

Journey Through the Past—1972

Believe it or not, this double album collection was the follow-up to the #1 worldwide mega-smash *Harvest*. So you'd probably figure it would have at least cracked the top ten on Billboard, right?

Not so.

Even though it was mostly a somewhat thrown-together collection of odds and ends that was originally intended as the soundtrack to Young's first feature film—which in itself could also be seen as a largely thrown together affair—you'd at least think that the rub from *Harvest* would've given it some legs. Here again, this just wasn't to be.

The film—a mishmash of CSN&Y concert footage interspersed with home movies of Young with his various Topanga Canyon hippie neighbors and cronies—didn't impress the film divisions at either Warner or Universal (who actually fired Carrie Snodgress after viewing a scene from the film where the actress is seen smoking a joint).

But Warner nonetheless did, at least briefly, make the very ill-advised decision to market the soundtrack—which at best could be called the sort of collection of outtakes you might more commonly find on a bootleg—as an official Neil Young album. Needless to say, this strategy backfired in rather spectacular fashion.

The original double-disc vinyl album—and follow-up to *Harvest*—crashed and burned on the charts, stalling at #45.

Along with *Time Fades Away* (which didn't do much better with its peak Billboard chart position of #22), it remains one of only two Neil Young albums yet to see official release on compact disc—a situation that, based on Young's own comments about the albums, is unlikely to change anytime soon.

Hawks and Doves—1980

So, how do you follow up the amazing *Rust Never Sleeps*—an album that brought Neil Young back from the brink of commercial oblivion and established him as perhaps the only "dinosaur" from the original sixties rock era with any continuing artistic relevance in the 1980s era of punk rock and new wave?

In the case of Young, you follow it with *Hawks and Doves*, a largely forgettable album consisting of leftovers from unreleased albums like *Chrome Dreams* ("Captain Kennedy") and *Homegrown*, along with a handful of newer songs that reflected his increasing infatuation with country music at the time.

In many ways, *Hawks and Doves* is the predecessor to the full-blown country album that would come later on with 1985's *Old Ways*.

Even so, it was a very strange choice to follow up *Rust Never Sleeps* with—an album that not only reenergized Young's original classic rock fan base, but also endeared him to an entirely new generation of punk-rock and new wave fans reared on the Ramones, Patti Smith, Television, the Clash, and the Sex Pistols.

Rust Never Sleeps was a top ten hit—Young's first since *Harvest*—peaking at #8 on Billboard. By contrast, the highest that *Hawks and Doves*, his very next album, ever rose on the charts was a comparatively dismal #30.

Everybody's Rockin'—1983

As much as many critics like to single out the infamous 1982 techno experiment *Trans* as the point where Neil Young "lost it" and kicked off the commercial disaster of his "lost decade" in the eighties, this album actually didn't perform as poorly in the marketplace as you might expect.

Although it could very well have been due in large part to the curiosity factor (Holy crap! Neil's gone techno!), *Trans* actually managed to crack the Billboard top twenty anyway, peaking at a hardly earth-shattering, but still somewhat respectable #19 on the charts. The 1983 follow-up, however—the goofy Shocking Pinks rockabilly experiment *Everybody's Rockin'*—didn't fare nearly as well.

It climbed no higher than #46—an abysmal chart position for an artist of Young's then iconic stature.

Why Geffen even chose to release the album at all—especially during a period when they had rejected far more "traditional" Neil Young projects like *Island in the Sun* or even the original version of the country album *Old Ways*—remains something of a mystery.

As one legendary story goes, even Young himself made the album out of something more like spite than anything representing a genuine artistic vision (or as the artist himself has said "they wanted a rock-'n'-roll album, so I gave them one").

Clocking in at a scant twenty-eight minutes, if there is any such thing as a legitimate throwaway in the Neil Young catalog, *Everybody's Rockin'* is certainly that record.

Old Ways—1985

By the time *Old Ways* was released in 1985 (in a much more glossed over studio revamping of the original version recorded a few years earlier), Young's career was already well into a dramatic commercial meltdown.

In between making bizarre statements rejecting the rock-'n'-roll audience that had made him a millionaire, and embracing the hard-line, right-wing stance of Ronald Reagan (as far removed as possible from the hippie politics of songs like "Ohio" that had so endeared him to the more radicalized leftovers of the sixties generation), Young certainly was not doing himself any favors commercially.

Although his "country album" *Old Ways* is in some respects a fairly decent, if spotty record—in places it even recalls the cozy warmth of *Harvest*—by this time, the damage to his natural commercial base had pretty much been done.

The country audience—despite the support of heavyweights like Willie Nelson, Waylon Jennings, and Kris Kristofferson—never fully embraced him as a credible artist, and the original rock audience shrugged their shoulders indifferently or simply moved on altogether.

As much as the country fan base of pre-red state rednecks could respect such old lefty outlaws as Waylon and Willie, there was still enough of the more divisive elements of the leftover antiestablishment sixties sentiment to make one thing perfectly clear—you can never trust a hippie.

Especially one like Neil Young.

For as many new fans as he made playing the state fairs of the country circuit with the International Harvesters—and newly born-again Republican political endorsements aside—Young was still viewed with distrust in some quarters of the country establishment. After all, this was still the same damned hippie who wrote "Southern Man," right?

One sheet for Neil Young's experimental film *Journey Through the Past*. A two-disc soundtrack album, marketed by Reprise as the follow-up to the platinum blockbuster *Harvest*, proved to be a colossal stiff with the record-buying public.

Courtesy Noah Fleisher/Heritage Auctions

Old Ways was a colossal flop, peaking at #75 on Billboard. The one good thing that did come out of the *Old Ways* period, though, was Young's association with Willie Nelson and his Farm Aid organization—a partnership that lasts to this day.

Life—1987

By the mid-eighties, Young was still slowly finding his way back toward his more familiar and natural artistic identity. But it would still be another couple of years before he made it all the way back with his miraculous 1989 comeback record, *Freedom.*

In the meantime, records like 1987's *Life* and its 1986 predecessor *Landing on Water* served as a bridge between the "lost eighties" and the magnificent return to creative form that was still to come in the nineties. After experimenting with synthesizers, rockabilly, and country, he finally seemed to be ready to make that actual "Neil Young album" both the record label and his fan base so desperately wanted.

Of course, it goes without saying that when it comes to Neil Young, nothing ever comes so easy.

Vinyl promo pressing for the *Journey Through the Past* soundtrack album.   *Courtesy of Tom Therme collection*

Although *Life* reunited Young with both Crazy Horse and David Briggs, and was originally intended as a live album of new songs (much like the classic *Rust Never Sleeps*), the album was subsequently watered down by excessive studio overdubs, much as its predecessor *Landing on Water* had been.

Neil Young was particularly obsessed with getting the same sort of big drum sound popularized by then very much in vogue eighties producers like Hugh Padgham (XTC, the Police) and Steve Lillywhite (U2), as well as drummers like Phil Collins. In the eighties, and especially when it came to drums, bigger was better—or so the idea went.

You can almost excuse his artistic confusion and apparent attempts to please a record label (Geffen) that he found himself increasingly at odds with at the time. What is far less excusable, however, is all of the excessive studio tinkering. In the end, "Lifeless" may have actually been a better title for this album.

If all Young wanted was for Crazy Horse to sound exactly like the studio pros he had recently hired for *Landing on Water*, one has to wonder why he didn't just go out and get ace drummer Steve Jordan and producer Danny Kortchmar on his speed dial.

Still, *Life* is not a terrible album by any means. It's just not a great, or particularly memorable one. Despite the presence of decent songs like "Prisoners of Rock 'n' Roll," the biggest problem with *Life* is that it contains so little of it.

There is no good reason why an album reuniting Young with his greatest band (and arguably his best producer) should have come out sounding so ultimately flat. Yet by all accounts, the dull sound of *Life* was not the product of an outside producer or the record company imposing its will on an unwilling artist, but rather that of Neil Young himself.

"Inca Queen," for example, falls right into the tradition of Young's many "Indian songs" like "Cortez the Killer" and "Pocahontas." Heard today, the song plays like a companion piece to "Like an Inca" from *Trans* (one of that album's few non-techno-driven songs). One of the brighter spots on *Life*, it is still buried by dreadfully flat mixing.

Not surprisingly, both *Landing on Water* and *Life* were met with a collective yawn from the record-buying public. *Life* in particular was a huge commercial disappointment, stalling at #75 on Billboard. These days, it can be had at bargain basement prices either on eBay or in the cutout and used-CD bins at the few brick-and-mortar record stores still left out there.

Broken Arrow—1996

After making a string of great albums—including *Ragged Glory*, *Harvest Moon*, and *Sleeps with Angels*—following his 1989 comeback with *Freedom*, Young fell into something of another commercial black hole toward the end of the nineties.

Although the slump was nowhere near as severe as the one he experienced in the "lost eighties," there was still a feeling among some observers that for whatever reason, Young had at least briefly lost his way again with both 1996's

Broken Arrow and 2000's *Silver and Gold*. In fairness, in the case of the latter album, he had also consigned some of that record's best songs to the likewise artistically disappointing and commercially underperforming CSN&Y reunion album *Looking Forward*.

Young would again pick up the pace soon enough with albums like *Greendale*, *Prairie Wind*, and *Living with War*. But *Broken Arrow* in particular, while not without its moments, seems to represent a stopgap, at least when measured against his more major nineties work like *Ragged Glory* and *Sleeps with Angels*.

It's not an awful album by any stretch. But it's also not one of his particularly stronger efforts either. Following the #9 showing of 1994's *Sleeps with Angels* and 1995's *Mirror Ball* album with Pearl Jam (Young's first top five album since the #1 showing of *Harvest*), *Broken Arrow* barely cracked the top fifty, peaking at #31.

Hey, Ho, Away We Go, We're on the Road to Never

Neil Young's Most Underrated Albums

Now that we've dealt with Neil Young's most noteworthy commercial flops, it's only fair that we address the subject of his most underrated albums.

We all know the recognized classics. You've got the mega-hits like *Harvest* and *Rust Never Sleeps*. You've got the critically acclaimed masterpieces like *Tonight's the Night* (that didn't as well commercially at first, but that the record-buying public finally caught up to years after the fact). And then you have those albums that fall into that category just underneath these. Records like *After the Gold Rush, Everybody Knows This Is Nowhere,* and *Harvest Moon* that all sold relatively well, received great reviews, and have their share of classic tracks, but still fall just short of being recognized, at least with any universal sort of consensus, as Neil Young classics. *After the Gold Rush,* in particular, is an album that inspires much debate amongst fans. Many revere it as a masterpiece, while others have complained about its flat sound.

The following list deals with none of these, but is rather about those albums that for whatever reason have become permanently lodged in the cracks. In some cases, they represent great Neil Young albums that may have been initially judged somewhat unfairly or have otherwise just been misunderstood or plain overlooked. In any case, this list is purely subjective. In other words, welcome to my world.

Trans—1982

Trans is arguably the least understood album in Neil Young's entire body of work. What is now known about it (but wasn't at the time), is that the album was largely the product of an artist who was both keeping very serious details of his private life—specifically the inner turmoil surrounding a family emergency involving his youngest son Ben—away not only from the public, but even from some of his closest associates.

Like Young's oldest son Zeke (with actress Carrie Snodgress), Ben was born with cerebral palsy. But in Ben's case, it was far more serious. In addition to the cerebral palsy condition, Ben (his son with wife Pegi) was born both quadriplegic and nonoral (meaning he was unable to communicate).

The result of all this was Young's withdrawal from performing onstage (although he continued to record) for about four years—a period that began after the *Rust Never Sleeps* shows and continued right up through the tour behind *Trans*—as he and Pegi concentrated their energies on trying to make their son better.

This involved a series of therapy programs, including sessions that could consume up to eighteen hours a day, as well as trying to find a way that would enable Ben to communicate. All of this took place very quietly, without any type of publicity, and in fact was known only to a handful of Neil and Pegi's closest associates, relatives and friends.

Trans is an album largely about that experience.

On the one hand, Young has said that the album (as well as others from the same period like *Re-ac-tor*) came about as a result of him completely closing himself off to the pain he felt as a father, because of his son's condition. On the other hand, songs like "Transformer Man," "Computer Age," "We R in Control," and "Sample and Hold"—with their synthesized whirrs, clicks, and beeps—are in some ways musical expressions of Young's own desperate search for a medium that might allow his son to be able to communicate with his parents and the rest of the outside world.

Young himself has said that he wrote "Transformer Man" specifically for Ben. Perhaps its eerie, ghost-in-the-machine-sounding vocoder effects were something he hoped his son might be able to connect with. "Sample and Hold" was also inspired by his son, or more specifically about a desire for Ben to be able to play with the model trains Young had so enjoyed himself as a boy—a passion that he had also just recently rediscovered as an adult.

To the record-buying public, these lyrical references to a personal tragedy they knew nothing of probably seemed somewhat obscure, and understandably so. To the fans of the eighties new wave bands like Human League and Flock of Seagulls that dominated MTV and new wave radio playlists at the time, it might have seemed that the old dinosaur was simply trying to get a piece of the action. Young's classic rock fan base, on the other hand, probably didn't get it at all, and if anything might have seen *Trans* as a sellout to the trendy new wave of the day.

Here again, although both of these fan perspectives seem somewhat short-sighted and perhaps even a bit elitist now (coming from opposite ends of the eighties musical divide as they did), they are also understandable in retrospect. Basically, Young had confused his audience.

Again.

Looking back on *Trans* now, the album actually holds up much better than you might think. Hearing songs like "Transformer Man" and "Computer Cowboy" today (and with the benefit of hindsight), there is a strangely lonesome and even heartbreaking quality about them (check out the "come-a-tie-yi-yippie yays" on the latter). The eerie, otherworldly yelps of Young's electronically treated voice set these songs apart from much of the other commercial techno-pop of the eighties. His snarling guitar also breaks through the mix on "Sample and Hold," even if it is in far shorter staccato bursts than usual.

Of the three non-techno tracks on *Trans* (which actually came from sessions for a separate, aborted album project called *Island in the Sun*), "Like an Inca" is also a standout. The recording suffers from a bit too much studio sheen—especially considering it's for a Neil Young album. But despite the gloss, the lyrics of "Inca" fall right into the beautiful imagery of other of Young's Indian-themed songs like "Cortez the Killer" and "Pocahontas." The chorus line "I wish I was an Aztec, or a runner from Peru, I would build such beautiful buildings, to house the chosen few, like an Inca from Peru" actually comes from a much earlier song, "Like an Inca (Hitchhiker)." But other than the chorus line and the title, the two songs actually share very little in common. The earlier song was eventually released as "Hitchhiker" on Neil Young's 2010 album *Le Noise*.

In one sense, you could almost call the album title *Trans* a shorter way of saying "transitional"—since for so many the album marked such an abrupt change in direction for Young. Actually, make that a series of changes in direction that would last for nearly the rest of the eighties. It was also his first album for his new label, Geffen Records, and the beginning of an acrimonious association that is more noteworthy for its contentiousness and legal wrangling than for any of the actual music that came out of it.

One other thing that should be noted in any discussion of *Trans*, though, is that perhaps more than any other record since *Tonight's the Night*, this was a case of Young stubbornly following his artistic muse regardless of any commercial consequences (which proved to be quite lasting and considerable in this case).

A very convincing argument could also be made that of the remaining rock artists from the sixties generation still making commercially viable music during the musically polarized eighties—and you can start by referencing Paul McCartney, the Rolling Stones, and Bob Dylan—not one of them made an artistic move anywhere near as boldly different as Neil Young did with *Trans*.

In retrospect, *Trans* holds up much better than you might think. As a period piece, there are songs on the record that would more than hold their own on an eighties mix tape with other bands from the era like Simple Minds and Human League. Knowing what we know about the album now, its often harsh appraisal from fans—both then and now—seems more like a classic case of the book being unfairly judged by its cover rather than by the actual contents within.

Mirror Ball—1995

Mirror Ball, Neil Young's 1995 album with Pearl Jam—along with its companion, the Pearl Jam E.P. *Merkin Ball*—is, pound for pound, the most ferociously beautiful, cacophonous noise that Young made with anybody during the nineties—and that includes the much ballyhooed *Ragged Glory* reunion album with Crazy Horse. In short, *Mirror Ball* is an album where Young and PJ crank up the amps, and for fifty-five minutes of ear-shattering bliss, proceed to blow the doors down.

In 1994, Pearl Jam already had a well-earned reputation, not only as one of the main groups behind the Seattle grunge sound sweeping rock at the time, but also as a world-class live rock-'n'-roll band. But who knew that these grungy Seattle boys would prove to be one of Neil Young's best backing bands ever? Well okay, maybe anyone who has ever heard the way that PJ backed him doing "Rockin' in the Free World" on MTV's *Video Music Awards* a year prior. He and Pearl Jam fit each other like a hand to a glove.

Not only did *Mirror Ball* prove to be a classic case of the Punks meeting the Godfather—Pearl Jam were already diehard Neil Young fans—but these two forces that seemed to come from such opposite places complemented each other as though they had been playing together for years. *Mirror Ball* (and PJ's *Merkin Ball*) was made over two separate sessions of two days each at Seattle's Bad Animals studio (built by the Wilson sisters of Heart fame), with producer Brendan O'Brien. Most of the songs were reportedly first takes—a fact that becomes more than evident when hearing the primal immediacy of the finished product.

Don't get me wrong here, because I love Crazy Horse as much as anyone. But where Crazy Horse is a band whose greatest function has always been to lay down a solid, funky (if slightly sloppy) groove—which, at its best, serves more as a launchpad for Young's soaring guitar—Pearl Jam function more like a finely tuned machine. If Crazy Horse's role was the launchpad, PJ function more like the engine itself.

On songs like "Peace and Love" and "Throw Your Hatred Down," his lead guitar snarls and screeches over the deep, bass-heavy rhythmic din created by PJ's then monster drummer Jack Irons and bassist Jeff Ament. Guitarists Stone Gossard and Mike McCready likewise lay down a positively audacious and ferocious groove, inspiring Young to new heights of hallucinogenic flight.

Although this is a rare case of his lyrics taking a backseat—as if they could cut through the din made by Pearl Jam anyway—there is also an undeniably nostalgic look back toward the sixties hippie era here on songs like "Peace and Love." Both "Downtown" and "Throw Your Hatred Down" contain references to musical icons of the sixties period like John Lennon and Jimi Hendrix (and their peacenik political sentiments). In the song "Big Green Country," Young even sneaks in some of his trademark Indian lyrics ("With folded arms the chief stood watching/painted braves slipped down the hill").

There's probably not a chance in hell you will ever hear "Big Green Country" or "Peace and Love" played on classic rock radio (despite the album's #5 showing on Billboard). This is one of the biggest reasons I place *Mirror Ball* in the category of Young's most underrated albums ever. With all due respect to *Ragged Glory, Mirror Ball* is easily his most rocking album of the nineties. A decent argument could even be made that the album stands out as some of the most cacophonously beautiful noise of his entire career.

Pearl Jam's companion E.P. *Merkin Ball* features the same lineup, except Young sticks to guitar, while Eddie Vedder takes over the vocal chores. Since Sony—Pearl Jam's label at the time—refused to allow their golden cows to lend their name to the Warner-distributed Neil Young album, the band issued *Merkin Ball* as kind of a bonus E.P., complementing the original. Besides the similar titles, both albums also share album covers that look very much alike, and are even printed on the same plain brown cardboard. *Merkin Ball* also features one of Young's best guitar performances to come from the sessions, on the song "I Got Id." (fans may also recognize this song as "I Got Shit"). Eddie V's got the vocal covered here, but there is no mistaking the menacing snarl of Young and Old Black.

Sadly, the combination of Neil Young and PJ didn't produce an extended American tour, although there were some scattered dates played mostly in Europe. When he and Pearl Jam played one such "secret" club gig in Seattle back when *Mirror Ball* was released, I thought I had an "in" with my then drinking buddy Kim Thayil from Soundgarden. No such luck (unfortunately), and I have to admit I've never completely forgiven Kim for that.

American Stars and Bars—1977

Exactly why this album has been as overlooked as it has is something I've never been able to completely figure out.

It could be because it came out during one of the most prolific periods of Neil Young's career, sandwiched as it was between albums like *Zuma* and *Comes a Time* (which, come to think of it, are both fairly underrated albums in their own right).

It also can't be stated enough that the career-spanning, three-disc *Decade* anthology set (and precursor to the *Archives*) came within a mere six months of *American Stars and Bars*. Or perhaps it is because so many of Young's most hardcore fans actually prefer the unreleased *Chrome Dreams* album that shares so many of the same songs found on *American Stars and Bars*.

Because *Chrome Dreams* is readily available to anyone who wants it as a bootleg online—and because of the song sequencing of the album, with early versions of such later seventies titles as "Pocahontas"—it could almost be seen as a late seventies "Neil Young's Greatest hits" album of sorts.

Either way, and for whatever reason, *American Stars and Bars* is a Neil Young album that often gets lost in the much greater scheme of such an amazing, all-encompassing catalog. Considering that the album contains two of Young's all-time greatest songs in "Will to Love" and "Like a Hurricane," its relatively underrated status is even more astonishing.

On some levels, *American Stars and Bars* can be seen as something of a precursor to Young's later foray into country music on albums like *Old Ways*. The

neil young

Side One
WILL TO LOVE 7:11

Side Two
CORTEZ THE KILLER (LIVE) 9:12

"Y'MEAN ALL THIS BOOTLEG STUFF? IT DOESN'T BOTHER ME. MORE POWER TO THEM - THEY CAN SELL 'EM IN THE PARKING LOT. I DON'T GIVE A SHIT. I HAVE NOTHING AGAINST BOOTLEGS - I THINK THAT FOR AN ARTIST LIKE ME, THEY'RE ESSENTIAL. THERE'S JUST NO WAY THAT THE RECORD COMPANY'S GONNA ACCEPT AS MANY RECORDS AS I WOULD LIKE TO GIVE THEM." -NEIL YOUNG

COMPILED BY PAUL NICKERSON AND FRANCIS ENGLEHARDT
For Slow To Speak / S.F.C

PROMOTIONAL COPY. NOT FOR SALE

'WILL TO LOVE' TAKEN FROM THE ALBUM AMERICAN STARS 'N BARS (MSK 2261)
'CORTEZ THE KILLER' TAKEN FROM THE ALBUM LIVE IN SAN FRANCISCO (80101)
© 1977 REPRISE RECORDS INC. FOR THE U.S. MADE IN THE U.S.A ALL RIGHTS RESERVED.
THE THING ABOUT MY MUSIC IS, THERE REALLY IS NO POINT.

Rare, promo-only single featuring "Cortez the Killer" from *Zuma* and "Will to Love" from *American Stars and Bars*.   *Courtesy of Tom Therme collection*

laid-back feel of songs like "The Old Country Waltz" and "Star of Bethlehem"—with their fiddles, Emmylou Harris backing vocals, and Ben Keith's pedal steel—stand out in such marked contrast to the blazing guitar heard on "Hurricane" that it's almost like listening to two completely different albums in one.

Which, in a sense, gives *American Stars and Bars* much of its admittedly schizophrenic feel. The divide between "Hurricane" and "Bethlehem" in particular is so palpable it is as though they could have come from two completely separate artists.

At least, that is one way of looking at it.

Another way, however, is to approach the album as a random sampling of everything that makes Young the brilliantly gifted, stylistically broad artist that he is. More than anything else, though, *American Stars and Bars* rates as a great Neil Young album for the inclusion of "Will to Love" and "Like a Hurricane" alone.

Amongst a catalog that includes some of the greatest extended electric guitar solos ever recorded, "Like a Hurricane" may just be the greatest of them all. The song's soaring guitar breaks are some of the most fluidly melodic that Young has ever committed to a record, even as they take off ever higher into a dreamlike, hypnotic sort of upper stratosphere. The guitar solos here, even when compared to such classics as "Cortez the Killer," "Down by the River," and "Cowgirl in the

Sand," are simply on another level altogether—a perfect melding of melody, distortion, and counterpoint.

"Will to Love" is an equally stunning song. Recorded in front of a crackling fire (which can be clearly heard throughout the recording) over an erased tape, the song's meandering vocal performance complements the lyrics equating a spawning ocean fish ("I'm a harpoon dodger, and I can't, won't be tamed") with the unquenchable "will to love" ("Never lose the will/It's like something from up above"). The vivid lyrical imagery woven here is approached only by his Indian songs like "Pocahontas" and "Like an Inca." It is, simply, an absolutely masterful piece of songwriting.

If only for the inclusion of these two songs, *American Stars and Bars* ranks as a classic Neil Young record.

Sleeps with Angels—1994

Young's intimate relationship with both cutting-edge punk rock and drug-related death are a matter of record.

His connection with and influence on punk-rockers—from Johnny Rotten and Devo to Sonic Youth and Pearl Jam—has been documented both often and in quite considerable detail. Likewise, Young's uncomfortably intimate relationship with the casualties of drug abuse has often struck far too close to home—as is most notably documented on the album *Tonight's the Night*.

Sleeps with Angels is the album where these two themes came most completely together. Largely inspired by the suicide of Nirvana's tragically heroin-addicted frontman Kurt Cobain (who quoted Neil Young's "it's better to burn out than to fade away" line about Johnny Rotten from "My, My, Hey, Hey" in his suicide note), *Sleeps with Angels* is in many ways the sequel to Young's dark masterpiece *Tonight's the Night*.

If nothing else, it is certainly the bridge between the druggy, booze-fueled hippie haze that permeates songs like *Tonight's the Night's* "Tired Eyes" and the older, much wiser observer of songs like the latter album's centerpiece "Change Your Mind."

Where the songs on *Tonight's the Night* have more of a raggedly unrehearsed feel to them, songs like "Drive By," "Prime of Life," and especially "Change Your Mind" have a much more deliberately haunting quality.

The latter is also yet another tremendous vehicle for the sort of atmospheric guitar soloing that Young is simply unmatched at once he gets into that particular zone. Yet, unlike other great Neil Young "guitar songs" like "Cortez" and "Hurricane," for example, there is an undeniably doomier air of darkness and foreboding here.

Young stretches the solos out here as much, if not more, as he has ever done on previous recordings. But where such previous excursions have seemed more like dreamscapes, the feel here is more like waking from a dark nightmare. This point is driven even further home on a fantastic, largely acoustic live version of the song found on the five-disc bootleg anthology *A Perfect Echo*. Here, Young stretches the already lengthy song to nearly twenty minutes, in a deliberately slower and quieter version that places a much greater emphasis on the emotional impact of his powerful lyrics about Cobain. It stands as one of his single most spellbinding live performances.

Sleeps with Angels, underrated as it is, is also one of Neil Young's greatest latter-day albums.

On the Beach—1974

Of the three albums that make up the Ditch Trilogy, *On the Beach* is probably the most overlooked.

This is actually somewhat easy to understand, considering the album preceded the more universally acclaimed *Tonight's the Night* by a year, as well as the fact that *Times Fades Away* has developed something of a mythical status itself over the years, mainly because it has never been officially reissued on compact disc (and if Young is to be taken at his word, probably never will).

So, when it comes to the Ditch Trilogy—the dark and depressing trio of albums recorded in the wake of the drug-related deaths of Danny Whitten and Bruce Berry—you have to call *On the Beach* at least slightly underrated. It is also one of the finest albums in Young's catalog. The songs range from the slightly off-kilter "Vampire Blues" to the more overtly macabre "Revolution Blues"— about the infamous Charles Manson cult murders. Young had once made Manson's casual acquaintance.

Like a lot of Neil Young albums, *On the Beach* also feels like two records contained within a single disc. In addition to the previously mentioned two songs, the first side is a bit all over the map stylistically. You've got the lazy rocker "Walk On" kicking things off, followed by the mellower "See the Sky About to Rain" and "For the Turnstiles"—which comes about as close to Neil Young wearing his Dylan and Joni Mitchell influences proudly on his sleeve as it gets.

With the wildly shifting styles on the first side of *On the Beach*, it would be easy to accuse the album of lacking a certain unifying theme. Yet, for all of its stylistic jumps, the five songs on side one hang together quite well as a unified whole.

Side two is something else altogether.

Taken together, the three long pieces that make up the side (back before the CD era when the vinyl albums of the day actually had two of them) —"On the Beach," "Motion Pictures," and "Ambulance Blues"—might very well make up the single greatest album side Young has ever recorded. If nothing else, they certainly comprise some of the loneliest, desolate, and most depressing-sounding music of his entire career.

It has often been suggested that the laid-back feel of *On the Beach*—and especially side two—was a direct product of the "honey slides" that Cajun wildman Rusty Kershaw introduced into the mix at the sessions for the album. Cooked up by Kershaw's wife, "honey slides" were a potent combination of honey and hashish that became the recreational drug of choice during the sessions. Those who were there have described them as packing a powerful punch capable of rendering the user borderline comatose.

Whether or not the honey slides were the culprit, side two of *On the Beach* is much more than merely laid back. These three songs are stripped down to such a nakedly emotional core, it almost feels like the listener is getting a glimpse into the darkest recesses of Neil Young's soul.

Tonight's the Night may be an album that name checks people like Bruce Berry, and one in which Danny Whitten's posthumous performance of "(Come On Baby Let's Go) Downtown" brings the message home. But for all its brutal honesty, *Tonight's the Night's* loose garage rock feel makes the album seem more like a boozy-sounding wake than the actual funeral.

The second side of *On the Beach,* on the other hand, feels more like a case of the artist laying his emotions out there naked for all the world to see. Although Young rarely tips his hand on such a personal level in his songs, *On the Beach's* second side has just that sort of feel, whether that was his intention or not. As starkly minimal as the songs are, there is also a dark, austere beauty about them.

The down mood is established early on with the title track, which finds Young showing up to a radio interview where he ends up alone at the microphone. By the time the side and the album itself ends with "Ambulance Blues," he manages to lash out at everyone from critics who "sit alone, you're no better than me, for what you've shown" to an unidentified man (who some say could be President Richard Nixon) who "could tell so many lies, he had a different story for every set of eyes."

In the end, he comes to the conclusion that "there ain't nothing like the friend, who can tell you you're just pissing in the wind."

At the time of its release, *On the Beach* wasn't a big seller. In the years since, it has come to be recognized—as part of the Ditch Trilogy—as one of Young's most significant releases. Even so, it gets nowhere near the reverential sort of treatment afforded *Tonight's the Night,* and for that reason alone has to be considered one of his most underrated albums.

It is certainly one of his best.

Sooner or Later It All Gets Real

Zuma, The Stills-Young Band, and the Return of the Horse

When Neil Young finally emerged from the dark early seventies period that gave birth to the Ditch Trilogy, he did so with a vengeance.

The remainder of the seventies would in fact mark one of the most prolific, creatively fertile periods of his career. Young went on something of a recording tear during this period, making a series of albums that melded themselves one into another in a way that seemed more like the product of a no-stop, five-year recording session than a series of individual projects.

In addition to four new Neil Young solo albums, a collaboration with his old bandmate Stephen Stills, a three-album retrospective set, and a double live album with Crazy Horse, this insanely prolific period also produced at least three albums that were never officially released at all.

See the Colors Floating in the Sky

Homegrown, an album said to be in the commercial folk-pop vein of Young's megahit *Harvest,* was shelved in favor of the rawer-sounding *Tonight's the Night* (and reportedly after The Band's Rick Danko urged Young to "go with the rawer one" after hearing the two albums back to back during a stoned get-together in a Hollywood hotel room). In subsequent interviews, Young has also said that the very personal nature of *Homegrown's* songs—many of which were written in the aftermath of his breakup with Carrie Snodgress and deal directly with that very subject—cut a little too close to the bone for him to put out there for the entire world to see.

Chrome Dreams was likewise cast aside by Young at the last minute in favor of *American Stars and Bars,* an album that features many of the same songs intended for *Chrome Dreams,* as well as several more country-flavored tunes cut with backing vocals by both Emmylou Harris and a duo featuring Linda Ronstadt and Nicolette Larson dubbed the Saddlebags. In the case of both of these albums, many of the songs were eventually parceled out to other Neil Young projects ranging from *American Stars and Bars* and *Decade* to *Rust Never Sleeps* and *Hawks and Doves.*

The third unreleased album made during this rush of creative productivity was an acoustic version of the songs that eventually were released in full-band format on the album *Comes a Time.* When Young played the original solo acoustic version of the album for label executives, they suggested he try recording the same songs with other musicians. In a rare example of the artist letting the label influence his creative direction, Young agreed.

The unreleased acoustic album, *Oceanside, Countryside,* is reportedly going to finally see the light of day as part of Young's ongoing *Archives* series, as are both the *Homegrown* and *Chrome Dreams* albums.

I Saw You in My Nightmares, but I'll See You in My Dreams

In addition to the rush of creative activity, there were also significant changes in Young's personal life. His relationship with Carrie Snodgress, which had been on the rocks for some time, finally came to an end when he dispatched his famously overbearing mother Rassy to vacate Snodgress and her things from the Broken Arrow Ranch. Young himself was also spending less time at Broken Arrow, and

Foreign LP pressing of Neil Young's *Zuma.*

Courtesy of Tom Therme collection

had rented a place in Malibu that soon became a hangout for friends, musicians, and other assorted cronies.

Among the wildest and craziest of the bunch was Frank "Poncho" Sampedro, a hard-drinking and drugging, skirt-chasing rogue who, even at a mere five feet eight inches tall, still cast a larger-than-life figure to any and all who came to know him.

A guitarist who at least partially taught himself to play by spending hours learning every note of Neil Young and Danny Whitten's parts on *Everybody Knows This Is Nowhere*, Sampedro was in many ways the ideal choice to fill Whitten's spot in Crazy Horse. What Sampedro may have lacked in musical chops was more than compensated for by his balls—which were big enough to stand up to Neil Young (earning him instant respect from the mercurial rock star).

Sampedro also possessed the magnetic, firecracker type of personality that endeared him first to Billy Talbot and eventually to Ralph Molina (who was skeptical at first about Sampedro joining the Horse).

Looking for the New World in That Palace in the Sun

Sampedro's entry into the Horse came by way of a trip to Mexico he made with Talbot, where the two of them ending up jamming together on a beach. By the time Young summoned Crazy Horse for a recording session in Chicago, Talbot brought along Sampedro and more or less initiated him as the newest member of the group.

When the Chicago sessions didn't turn out as well as expected, Sampedro shocked the other members of Crazy Horse by going directly to Young himself and offering to leave the band (after blaming himself for the botched recordings). Young responded by saying that he thought the new guitarist had a future both with the Horse and indeed with Young himself. Sampedro has been closely associated not only with Crazy Horse, but with many of Young's other projects and bands ever since.

Frank "Poncho" Sampedro made his official debut as the new guy in Crazy Horse on *Zuma*, the 1975 album that also marked Neil Young's return to a harder rock sound more in the vein of *Everybody Knows This Is Nowhere*.

Much like that album's "Down by the River" and "Cowgirl in the Sand," *Zuma's* two centerpieces are also vehicles that serve as a launchpad for the extended Neil Young guitar solos many fans thought he had abandoned altogether somewhere in between *After the Gold Rush* and *Harvest*. For these long-suffering fans, "Danger Bird" and especially "Cortez the Killer" represented a stunning return to ear-shredding, feedback-laden form.

The latter is also one of the many songs Young was writing at the time displaying an increasing lyrical fascination with Indian cultures (another of Neil's notable Indian songs, "Pocahontas," was recorded around the same time for the aborted *Chrome Dreams* album, but later finally surfaced on *Rust Never Sleeps*).

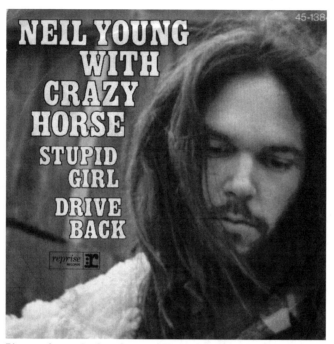

Picture sleeve single release of "Stupid Girl" backed with "Drive
Back" from *Zuma*. "Stupid Girl" is a Neil Young original and should
not be confused with the Rolling Stones song of the same name.

Courtesy of Tom Therme collection

However, not everyone was entirely pleased with Young's lyrical romanticiz-
ing of the Aztec culture on "Cortez."

In Spain, where Hernando Cortez is revered as the hero who conquered
the Aztec Empire of Mexico for the Spaniards, the seventies regime of General
Franco (yes, the same Franco Chevy Chase used to make fun of on *Saturday Night
Live*) ordered the song banned. Certain historians of Aztec culture have also
taken issue with Young's romantic depiction of the ancient Aztecs in lyrics like
"hate was just a legend, and war was never known" as being wildly inaccurate.

"Cortez the Killer" nonetheless has taken a much-deserved place as one of
Neil Young's signature rock songs, and it remains a perennial concert favorite
to this day.

Zuma's other guitar showcase of note, "Danger Bird," hasn't had quite the
same legs as "Cortez," but is nonetheless an equally stunning, if somewhat more
underrated contender for a Neil Young and Old Black hall of fame.

Some of the lyrics could also be interpreted as a metaphor for his split with
Carrie Snodgress. In the song, the danger bird makes curious references to how
"you've been with another man" (one of the final straws that broke the back of
Neil Young's relationship with Snodgress was when he found the actress cavort-
ing naked on a sailboat with an unsavory mutual acquaintance with the odd

nickname of "Captain Crunch"). Another key line in "Danger Bird" somewhat cryptically says, "I lied to keep it kind when I left you behind."

Elsewhere on the album, Young's lyrics making reference to women in general (and possibly Snodgress in particular) are far less subtle.

On the song "Barstool Blues," he sings, "He trusted in a woman and on her he made his bets/Once there was a friend of mine who died a thousand deaths." "Pardon My Heart" contains lines that likewise may be telling, such as, "It's a sad communication with little reason to believe/When one isn't giving and one pretends to receive."

And, of course, any song with a title like "Stupid Girl" (no relation to the Rolling Stones song) really requires no further explanation.

With Trunks of Memories Still to Come

With Young back playing with the Horse again, you'd think the natural next order of business would be a barnstorming tour of America. But since this is Neil Young we are talking about here, there simply wasn't going to be anything natural at all about his next move.

After playing a handful of warm-up dates at small venues in California, Young took the Horse across the pond for triumphant arena tours of Japan and

Picture sleeve for "Lookin' for a Love" features the *Zuma* artwork.
Courtesy of Tom Therme collection

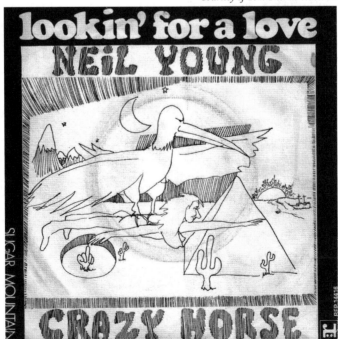

Europe. But rather than bring his favorite, and newly revitalized band back home to play American arenas, he made an abrupt about-face and left his Crazy Horse bandmates in the lurch once again. This time around, the Horse were left behind in order for Young to reunite with Stephen Stills for what became the ill-fated Stills-Young Band album and tour.

The sessions for the Stills-Young Band album *Long May You Run* in Miami should have been a wake-up call to Young, when Stills would often arrive at odd late-night hours and apparently on his own schedule. This ran completely opposite of Young's punctual work ethic, where the artist would arrive on time or early for the sessions. After Young complained to Atlantic Records head honcho Ahmet Ertegun about this, Stills was given a "talking to" about it, and perhaps not coincidentally his next album would end up being released on another label.

At one point, David Crosby and Graham Nash were also called in to add backing vocals to the record, sparking rumors of a possible full-on CSN&Y reunion album. But in the end (and depending on who you talk to), either Stills or Young wiped the backing vocals clean from the masters—which left both Crosby and especially Nash absolutely livid. The normally classy Englishman would in fact take his anger very public, airing the dirty laundry in interviews with rock publications like *Rolling Stone*.

With or without the other half of CSN&Y, the resulting album was largely a dud anyway, sparking only one minor hit, the Young-written title track, a loving ode to his lamented hearse Mort.

But if the album was a disappointment, the tour itself was a disaster.

With Stills being in a particularly surly mood most of the time, and often berating the road crew with little cause, Young finally decided he'd seen enough. After playing only a handful of dates, he abruptly bolted the tour, leaving Stills holding the bag on the remaining shows and leaving his longtime friend with the now famous "Eat A Peach" note.

The note read "Dear Stephen, funny how some things that start spontaneously end that way. Eat A Peach, Neil." Whether or not one of rock's most famous breakup notes was inspired by the Allman Brothers album of the same name (or vice versa) is anyone's guess.

16

Dancing on the Night from Star to Star

Chrome Dreams, American Stars and Bars, the Ducks, Decade, and Comes a Time

For the next several years, Neil Young went on something of a creative tear.

During this unprecedented flurry of near nonstop recording activity, he rejected nearly as much of his finished work as he ultimately released.

There were solo recordings made by no one but himself "alone at the microphone," as well as sessions with Crazy Horse, and with trusted partners in musical crime like Ben Keith, Spooner Oldham, and Tim Drummond. There were recordings made in locales ranging from Indigo Studios and Broken Arrow in California, to Nashville and at Triad Studios in Miami.

This wave of creative activity was so intense, it soon became little more than a blur to many of the participating musicians, who had to do all they could just to keep up with the seemingly endless string of songs pouring out like water from Neil Young's brain.

Still, many of these same players, such as Crazy Horse's Frank "Poncho" Sampedro, for example, were often unaware which record would feature the tracks they had worked on, or if they would even end up being released at all.

In Jimmy McDonough's *Shakey*, Sampedro recalls this period:

"We just played and recorded," the Crazy Horse guitarist says. "Every once in a while Neil would say 'Hey man, I sent in a record,' and I remember it shocking us. I said 'Oh Yeah? What was on it?'"

Some of the best music produced during this period came from the mostly solo acoustic sessions made over the course of several weeks during occurrences of the full moon showing itself at Indigo Studios in Malibu, California.

The sheer number of great songs committed to tape during this time—songs like "Powderfinger," "Pocahontas," and "Will to Love" that have long since gone down as classics in the Neil Young canon—was nothing short of mind blowing.

For those who were there, Young's songwriting and recording process has been described with such colorful adjectives as the "demon taking control" of him. For those who witnessed the sessions, it was as though he was magically grabbing all of these great new songs from somewhere out of thin air. Recording during the full moon has long since become standard operating procedure whenever Neil Young makes records.

Of course, there were also concerts during this period.

Among them were a series of shows in California where Neil Young and Crazy Horse would essentially just show up at a small club and proceed to blow the roof off of the joint.

There was also a 1976 tour of Japan. One of these shows, which took place at the Nippon Budokan Hall on March 11, has become legendary among fans. Although there were mistakes such as blown vocal cues and the like, and at least two of the musicians—Sampedro and Billy Talbot—were flying high on acid, the Horse were said to have scaled new heights of garage rock nirvana that night.

The show was both filmed and recorded, but as has so often been the case with many of these mythically great, lost Neil Young performances, no film or album ever came of it. However, rumors of an eventual release of the Nippon Budokan show—most likely as part of the *Archives Performance Series*—continue to make the rounds at websites and amongst the Neil Young fan network. One can only hope.

You Put the Load Right on Me

Perhaps the best known of his concert performances during this period was his appearance as part of *The Last Waltz*, the extravagant and elegant farewell gala at Bill Graham's Winterland Ballroom in San Francisco, organized as a swan song to the career of the Band.

Performing alongside an all-star lineup of rock royalty that included the likes of Dylan, Clapton, Joni Mitchell, Van Morrison, and a somewhat out of place Neil Diamond (whose *Beautiful Noise* album had just been produced by the Band's Robbie Robertson), Young's performance of "Helpless" is probably not among the highlights of the Martin Scorsese film document of the legendary event.

A lesser-known fact about the film is that there was a close-up shot of Young during the performance where an enormous rock of cocaine could be seen dangling precariously from out of his nose. Although both Scorsese and Robertson lobbied Young and Elliot Roberts hard to keep the offending footage in the film—citing, among other things, its rock-'n'-roll immediacy in their arguments—it was mercifully removed from the final cut.

The Ducks

During the summer of 1977, Neil Young also performed a handful of shows with a short-lived band he assembled along with Moby Grape bassist Bob Mosley and guitarist Jeff Blackburn (who Young knew from the Springfield era) called the

"LOTTA LOVE"

Single release of the title track from *Comes a Time*. Neil Young was so disappointed with the album's sound that he famously bought back 200,000 copies of the initial pressing and shot bullet holes through them.   *Courtesy of Tom Therme collection*

Ducks. Blackburn also shares a writing credit with Young on the latter's "Hey, Hey, My, My (Out of the Blue)" from the classic *Rust Never Sleeps* album.

The makeshift group mostly played small, unannounced gigs at bars in Santa Cruz, California, like the Crossroads and the Catalyst, performing a mix of older rock covers, along with a small handful of originals—the most noteworthy of which was a Neil Young instrumental called "Windward Passage." The cover charge to see Young playing with the Ducks at these tiny dives was usually around three bucks. But the Ducks were not so much another Neil Young project as a case of the rock superstar simply slumming with a bunch of other guys as just another member of the band.

Although the Ducks were supposed to be Santa Cruz's best-kept little rock-'n'-roll secret, word inevitably leaked out (mentions of the gigs in magazines like *Rolling Stone* probably didn't help), and before long, the small but rabidly devoted group of fans known as the "Duck Hunters" had plenty of unwanted company at the gigs. Shortly after the beach house he was renting in Santa Cruz was broken into and several guitars and other items were stolen, Young bolted the scene without so much as a warning.

Through Nets, By Hooks, and Hungry Bears

The Indigo sessions produced an astonishing array of great new original Neil Young songs, including those that eventually made their way to albums that were still to come, like *Rust Never Sleeps* ("Pocahontas," "Sedan Delivery," and "Powderfinger") to *Decade* ("Campaigner").

The bulk of these were at one point compiled for an album scheduled for release called *Chrome Dreams*.

Although this album has, at least to this date, never officially been released, it has since seen fairly wide distribution amongst fans as a bootleg. Most who have heard the recordings agree that it could have been one of Neil Young's finest albums.

With songs like "Pocahontas" and "Campaigner" placed right alongside barn burners such as "Like a Hurricane," the unreleased *Chrome Dreams* album actually flows far better as a whole than does *American Stars and Bars*, which ended up being released in its place.

For anyone in doubt of this, just do a quick Google search for "Chrome Dreams.rar" on the Internet, download the album and listen to it, and I can pretty much guarantee that any lingering questions about it will be answered convincingly.

Even so, it's hard to imagine hearing a classic album like *Rust Never Sleeps* now without the inclusion of such key songs as "Pocahontas" and "Powderfinger." In the case of the latter, however, the rawer, more stripped-down take heard on the *Chrome Dreams* bootleg is in many ways the more powerful version of the song.

American Stars and Bars combines songs from the Indigo sessions—and in particular the amazing three-song punch of "Star of Bethlehem," "Will to Love," and "Like a Hurricane" that kicks off side two of the album—with the more country-flavored songs made with Crazy Horse, Ben Keith, and backup vocalists Linda Ronstadt and Nicolette Larson (with whom Young would enjoy a brief romantic fling) at Young's Broken Arrow ranch in April 1977.

American Stars and Bars lacks the more cohesive feel of *Chrome Dreams*—the album really feels more like two unfinished halves than a complete whole. But the second side of this album ranks right up there with some of the most amazing sides of Neil Young's career.

Sandwiched in between the tranquil, almost sanguine-sounding "Star of Bethlehem" and the frenzied, over-the-top electric guitar harmonics of Old Black on "Like a Hurricane," "Will to Love" is really the centerpiece of this remarkable series of songs. It also stands out as one of the most beautiful songs Young has ever recorded, and certainly as one of his most unique.

Recorded over a discarded cassette tape of a Stills-Young Band recording, and complete with Young's fireplace cracking loudly in the background throughout, "Will to Love" has a dreamy, atmospheric quality that is only further amplified by the lyrics equating the lonely journey of a fish swimming (or perhaps spawning) his way upstream to the impossible yearning and loneliness associated with the "Will to Love."

The song has a beautifully haunting, impossibly detached sound to it, and is quite possibly the nearest Young has ever come to the sort of ambient New Age soundscapes made back then by people like Brian Eno and Tangerine Dream (with the possible exception of his unreleased and unheard "New Age" album *Meadow Dusk*). "Will to Love," to this day, stands as one of Young's greatest recorded achievements.

The haunting ambience of "Will to Love" segues effortlessly into the electrified harmonic blast of "Like a Hurricane," a song that legend has it came to Young after spotting a beautiful girl in the "crowded hazy bar" quoted in the lyrics. But even more than the lyrics of the unrequited love that comes at closing time after last call (and that serve as such a perfect complement to "Will to Love" immediately before it), "Like a Hurricane" is a showcase for what is arguably Young's greatest recorded electric guitar solo ever.

Rich with piercing notes that "dance upon the night from star to star" and that reach higher into the upper harmonic stratosphere, "Like a Hurricane" is the sort of song that should be part and parcel of any course in Rock-'n'-Roll Guitar 101. Along with "Cortez the Killer," it is one of Young's signature guitar solos, and is again, arguably one of the single best rock guitar songs ever made.

Even Richard Nixon Has Got Soul

Young's next move was the release of the expansive three-disc set anthology *Decade*.

Although his more devoted fans have long since gone on record with their vociferous bitching about the lack of unreleased goodies and extras included on the original set—their wish lists for these same rarities would be granted some three decades later with the first volume of the *Archives* series—*Decade* holds up remarkably well even today as a summation of Neil Young's career up to that point.

To this day, along with albums like *Harvest* and *Rust Never Sleeps*, *Decade* remains one of the strongest, most consistent sellers of Young's entire catalog.

Perhaps most importantly, what *Decade* did at the time of its original October 1977 release was to firmly establish Young as a major artist with marquee value on a par with the likes of Bob Dylan. Dylan's own career-spanning retrospective, *Biograph*, which came a few years later in the early eighties, in fact followed the template set by *Decade* to the letter in many ways.

As a retrospective set covering Young's career up to that point, *Decade* does in fact hit on all of the major points, even while throwing in a few rarities like "Campaigner" (from the aborted *Chrome Dreams* album), which is best known for the famous line "even Richard Nixon has got soul.". One of his best-known songs, "Sugar Mountain," also makes its first official appearance on a Neil Young album with *Decade*.

Beyond the inclusion of its few select rarities, *Decade* covers the high points of Young's career up until its 1977 release very well. The lack of any depth covering the Ditch Trilogy—where are the deeper cuts from *Time Fades Away* and *On the Beach* anyway?—represents the only really glaring major omission.

Outside of this, *Decade* hits on all the major points from his work with Buffalo Springfield ("On the Way Home," "Expecting to Fly," "Broken Arrow," "Mr. Soul") and CSN&Y ("Ohio," "Helpless") all the way through to "Love Is a Rose" (which became a hit for Linda Ronstadt) and "Long May You Run." In the case of the latter, it also provided a much-needed way to get that particular song without having to buy the actual album (sorry, Stephen).

The Springfield and CSN&Y tracks are all there (well at least mostly—just where the heck is "Country Girl" anyway?), as are the best of Young's recordings as a solo artist, from "Cowgirl in the Sand" and "Down by the River" to "Cortez," "Tonight's the Night," and "Like a Hurricane."

As career retrospectives go, I'd rank *Decade* as one of the better ones, and the sort of album I'd point anyone toward who was looking for a worthy introduction to the early career of Neil Young.

This Old World Keeps Spinning Round

Comes a Time is a particularly strange standout amongst the ranks of Young's latter seventies releases.

At the time of its 1978 release, it was his biggest commercial success since *Harvest*—having outsold all of his albums from that point forward. Over the longer haul, however, it has maintained nowhere near the staying power with hardcore fans that originally lesser-selling albums like *On the Beach* and *Tonight's the Night* have enjoyed.

Originally recorded as a solo acoustic album at Miami's Triad Studios, when Neil Young played the original *Comes a Time* for label executives at Warner Brothers, they responded by telling him to try out the same songs again with a band. In a rare show of willingness to let the label dictate his artistic vision, Young agreed and gathered up a crew of the usual suspects like Ben Keith and Tim Drummond, along with newcomers Karl Himmel, Spooner Oldham, and Rufus Thibodeaux. Of these musicians, the great R&B songwriter and keyboard player Spooner Oldham in particular would play a significant role on many of Young's future recordings (as would drummer Karl Himmel and fiddler Rufus Thibodeaux, although to a lesser degree).

Perhaps as a joke playing on the southern geography of the sessions, Young dubbed the loose aggregation the Gone with the Wind Orchestra.

The resulting sessions were reconvened in Nashville, site of Young's biggest hit, *Harvest*, and, not surprisingly, the resulting *Comes a Time* album shares much of that album's smooth folk-pop feel.

Among the many things that stand out most about *Comes a Time* is the fact that the album has a studio sheen not seen on a Neil Young album since *Harvest.*

Many of the tracks are overdubbed, which is kind of strange since he has histori-cally favored a rawer, less produced sound on his records. It also stands in sharp contrast to the way the songs had originally been recorded in Miami, for the acoustic version of the album that was never released.

There has been some loose talk of late about finally putting out this lost album, called *Oceanside, Countryside,* as part of the next volume in the *Archives* series.

The biggest difference on *Comes a Time,* however, was Nicolette Larson, whose backing vocals were by now taking on much more prominence than they had on *American Stars and Bars.* Her presence is felt all over the *Comes a Time* album, on tracks like "Goin' Back," a beautiful cover version of Ian and Sylvia Tyson's "Four Strong Winds" (the same song Young has called the greatest he has ever heard), and of course "Lotta Love," one of the album's two tracks cut with an uncharacteristically laid back-sounding Crazy Horse (the other being "Look Out for my Love"). "Lotta Love" would also be a surprise top ten hit for Larson as a solo artist.

Ben Keith in particular has been unwavering in his praise for Larson's work on *Comes a Time.* In Jimmy McDonough's *Shakey,* Keith says she "tracked him per-fect" and calls her "the best harmony singer I've ever heard." *Comes a Time* also

Japanese pressing of Reprise Records 45 "Lookin' for a Love."

Courtesy of Tom Therme collection

roughly coincides with Young's brief romantic relationship with Larson, which ended shortly before he met and married Pegi Morton.

With the exception of "Motorcycle Mama," a raunchy but equally goofy send-up about biker babes that sounds somewhat out of place on this album, *Comes a Time* mines much of the same familiar-sounding folk-pop terrain.

Lyrically, the songs seemed to indicate that Young was also moving on from the sometimes bitter tone of the songs that came in the wake of his split from Carrie Snodgress. Nearly every song on *Comes a Time* approaches the subject of love in a warm and fuzzy way that is about as far a cry from songs like *Zuma's* "Stupid Girl" as it gets. "Already Gone," a warm, loving tribute to his son Zeke, and the aforementioned "Motorcycle Mama" are really the only songs on *Comes a Time* that don't fall into this category.

Now, My Name Is on the Line

A humorous footnote to the *Comes a Time* story is the fact that Neil Young himself bought back two hundred thousand copies of the album when a recording flaw was discovered. As the story is told by his father Scott Young in his book *Neil and Me*, Neil actually shot bullet holes into every copy of the record, rendering them unplayable.

Remember that this was also right around the same time that the Bee Gees' colossal flop remake of the Beatles' *Sgt. Pepper* was the subject of industry jokes that it had gone platinum in returns. In the case of the first pressing of *Comes a Time*, the reality wasn't too far off from the punchline of that particularly inside music industry joke.

Another important development in the evolution of rock music at the time of the release of *Comes a Time* was the growing rise of punk rock.

Although it would be several more years before the influence of bands like the Ramones, the Clash, and the Sex Pistols would translate into an actual impact in the commercial marketplace, the changing direction of rock 'n' roll was something that was not lost on Neil Young. Punk rock in general, and the Sex Pistols in particular, would in fact play a major role in the direction of Neil Young's very next record.

17

More to the Picture Than Meets the Eye

Human Highway, Rust Never Sleeps, and the Punk-Rock Connection

The end of the seventies marked one of the stranger, more polarized periods in the history of rock 'n' roll.

FM Rock radio stations, once the place for the most progressive, artistically challenging, and experimental music—the kind of stuff that the more traditional, top forty formats wouldn't touch with a ten-foot microphone—had become about as sterile and sanitized by strictly controlled playlists and formats (which were often determined by consultants and demographic research) as their much more conservative counterparts on the AM dial.

The end result of this was a steady and ultimately mind-numbing stream of highly formulaic, softer-leaning rock created by bands with a slick, recording studio-produced sheen like the Doobie Brothers, Fleetwood Mac, the Eagles, and Steely Dan.

Occasionally, the FM rock stations would break these up with older hard-rock cuts by bands like Led Zeppelin and the Who. But even in those cases, they stuck mostly to the familiar, overplayed hits like "Stairway to Heaven" and "Won't Get Fooled Again."

Meanwhile, even in the hard-rock arena, the only hope for new artists getting their records played was by likewise watering down their sound to fit the increasingly tight playlists of FM rock radio formats. This subsequently gave rise to a newer wave of formula rock bands like Boston, Styx, Foreigner, and Journey.

Of these bands, Boston made the biggest splash, with their self-titled debut album selling a mind-boggling seven million copies.

But it was Journey that had the longest legs.

Consisting of ex-Santana and Frank Zappa alumni such as one-time teenaged guitar prodigy Neal Schon and monster drummer Aynsley Dunbar, and fronted by a high-pitched vocalist named Steve Perry—Journey's credentials as a group of amazing musicians were never in question. But the fact that they cashed it all in for a ride to the top that lasted well into the eighties (and continued long after the other formula rockers of their day had bitten the dust, careerwise) ended up costing them both their artistic credibility and any hopes for critical respect.

Meanwhile, the record business itself was in the best shape it had ever been. Multiplatinum blockbusters like Fleetwood Mac's *Rumours*, the Eagles' *Hotel California,* and the aforementioned debut from Boston had all but assured that. The concert business was also booming. Tours by the old warhorses like the Stones, Zeppelin, and the Who were selling out stadiums, even as the increasingly theatrical stage shows of groups like Kiss, Queen, and Aerosmith were bringing bigger, bolder, and better lighting, staging, and production values to the shows themselves.

The question nearly everyone in the music business was collectively asking themselves privately by the end of the seventies, though, was a simple one:

If everything was going so damn great, why were so many of the music critics wondering aloud where rock's originally cutting edge had gone? And exactly when and how did the audience for this music become so damned polarized?

"The kids," as so many jaded music promoters referred to their bread and butter back then, were clearly looking elsewhere for their music. That much was painfully clear.

As much as bands like Journey, Boston, and the Eagles continued to sell truckloads of albums, and Kiss and Led Zeppelin continued to sell out arenas and stadiums, rock fans were becoming split into a set of opposing camps, with the battle lines being drawn based on little more than genre preference. Rock 'n' roll had become divided against itself like no other time since the post-Elvis, pre-Beatles era of pop crooners and white-bread teen idols like Fabian and Pat Boone.

As everyone seemed to be collectively searching for the next big thing all at once, some of these fans found their refuge in disco—which had become kind of a catchphrase describing a music genre encompassing everything from the tight, gritty funk sounds of Earth Wind and Fire to the slickly produced, albeit considerably sped up, R&B-based rhythms of Nile Rodgers and Chic and the white bread Euro-pop of Abba.

Once the Bee Gees took their somewhat sanitized version of studio-enhanced pop-disco hits into the stratosphere with their blockbuster, multimillion-selling soundtrack to *Saturday Night Fever,* the street sounds of disco moved out of the black and gay clubs and into the American mainstream.

This in turn prompted an immediate backlash of "Disco Sucks" fashion gear and record burnings, often sponsored or promoted by FM rock stations. The racist and homophobic undertones of these "demonstrations" were so thin as to be virtually transparent.

A few other disgruntled rock fans—okay, make that more than a few—turned to the progressive rock of synthesizer-driven bands like Genesis, Yes, and Pink Floyd—groups that specialized in a fusion of rock, jazz, and classical sounds, as well as extended solos that could take up entire sides of an album. The prog-rockers often made for a curious fan base, divided as it was between the stoners who enjoyed the way the spacier elements of prog could enhance a good bong hit, and the nerdy types who enjoyed the pseudo-intellectualism of rock music that incorporated literary influences from J. R. R. Tolkien to Greek mythology in the lyrics.

But the one force that was driving the divisions among musical genre lines more than any other—including disco—was punk rock.

This Is the Story of Johnny Rotten

Punk rock in the seventies was the sort of phenomenon that could only happen in a musical climate that was starved for artistic change the way that rock 'n' roll was as the decade lumbered to a close.

Punk was the rallying cry—more like an explosion, really—of an entire generation of rock fans who had watched their heroes grow into bloated shadows of their former artistic selves, and who had stood by as the resulting excesses of money and success had seen the distance between audience and performer grow into something more like a continental divide.

The promise of a cultural, political, and societal revolution once represented by the sixties rock generation had largely become silenced. Not only was the music's original cutting edge long gone, it seemed that yesterday's culture-bending radicals had in fact turned into today's musical conservatives.

In its seventies infancy, punk sought to bring rock's initial immediacy back to the streets on a gutteral, visceral level. By bringing together elements of music, politics, and a weird sense of anti-fashion, along with plenty of prerequisite attitude, punk was by its very nature the kind of collective "fuck you" directed toward the established order of things not seen in rock 'n' roll since the mid- to late sixties.

Only this time, the enemy was no longer the over-thirty generation. In this case, the enemy was the rock music establishment itself.

Although punk had considerable roots in the Detroit garage rock of bands like Iggy and the Stooges and the more politically charged MC5, the seventies punk rock scenes were centered primarily in New York and London. In New York, a particularly energized scene emerged in clubs like CBGB's and Max's Kansas City, and was centered around bands like the Ramones, the New York Dolls, Television, and the Talking Heads, as well as artists like Patti Smith and Richard Hell.

Where Patti Smith, Television, and the Talking Heads represented more the leftover school of avant-garde experimentalists like Lou Reed, it was the fast, young, loud, and snotty minimalist rock of bands like the Dolls and the Ramones that first caught fire across the pond in England.

Applying the same fuck-you attitude of the Ramones to a harsher, more direct message fueled by a crippled economy and the conservative political climate in the U.K., bands like the Clash and the Sex Pistols soon brought their own elements of revolution into the mix. Although the Clash were undoubtedly the most overtly political of these bands, it was the Sex Pistols, fronted by the snarling but undeniably charismatic Johnny Rotten (Lydon) who took it the most over the top with singles like "Anarchy in the U.K." and "God Save the Queen" (because, after all, "she ain't no human being").

Although none of these bands sold squat in America—at least not initially—the buzz and the curiosity factor surrounding punk was still significant enough to create a cult following of fans that could guarantee a group like the Ramones, for instance, a decent house at a 700–1,000 seat club in just about any major city in America.

Put them on a punk rock triple bill with, say, the Talking Heads and Blondie, and you might even sell out a three thousand-seat theatre or auditorium. Imagine that.

Meanwhile, there was still enough lingering curiosity about the punks within the mainstream arena that even a more traditionally based classic rock-'n'-roll band like Tom Petty and the Heartbreakers could draw attention simply by adopting a little punk attitude (or in the case of Petty, by putting him in a black leather jacket on the cover of the Heartbreakers' debut album).

Another way of breaking a band like Tom Petty and the Heartbreakers was to book it on one of those punk-rock triple bills. The very first time I saw the group was at just such a punk show, where they opened for the Ramones in Seattle.

The record companies also took notice, and did little to discourage any punk connections with then breaking new artists like Elvis Costello, Nick Lowe, and Graham Parker—who, although they shared some of the same rawer, back-to-basics minimalist aesthetics of the punks, could hardly be lumped into the same category.

This subgenre of punk eventually morphed into "new wave" and a whole slew of new bands wearing skinny ties.

But that's another story . . .

It's Better to Burn Out Than It Is to Rust

Lying somewhere in the middle of all of this musical polarization was one Neil Percival Young.

Although he had certainly carved out his own well-earned reputation as an uncompromising artistic maverick and all-around iconoclast during the earlier half of the seventies with albums like *Tonight's the Night* and *On the Beach*, the commercial success of his latest album *Comes a Time* had put Young squarely back in the middle of the road.

In offering up the song "Lotta Love" to his then girlfriend Nicolette Larson (who went on to have a typically disco-driven late seventies hit with a very slick-sounding studio production and eventually married its producer, Ted Templeman), Young had even joked that he was giving her his "Fleetwood Mac" song.

Sheet music for "Hey, Hey, My, My (Into the Black)" from Neil Young and Crazy Horse's landmark album *Rust Never Sleeps*.   *Courtesy of Tom Therme collection*

For his own part, Young was also settling down from some of the wilder, druggier, skirt-chasing ways of his early career.

Following his split with Larson, he married Pegi Morton, who he had gotten to know as a waitress in a diner near his ranch in 1977. Their son Ben (who, it was later discovered, suffered from an even more severe form of the cerebral palsy that afflicted his older brother Zeke), was born the next year.

What was clear, though, was that Young had taken notice of the bigger picture of the musical marketplace, including what was happening with the punks.

Although the emergence of MTV—along with the rise of albums like Michael Jackson's *Thriller* and Prince's *1999*, the cultural ascendance of hip hop, and the brief, early eighties success of punk rock bands like the Clash—would soon bring a thankful end to the musical and racial divisions that still existed in the late seventies, the reality of a musically charged, polarized climate in rock 'n' roll was still very real at the time.

What made Neil Young stand out—and indeed, largely alone—from many of his fellow rock "dinosaurs" (as the punks liked to call them) was his tacit endorsement of the same punks who had infuriated so many of his peers from the sixties and seventies rock era.

Rather than speaking out against the rising tide of the new punk rock guard in the same condescending and dismissive tones as so many of his fellow Woodstock-era rockers—including his own bandmates in CSN&Y—did back then, Neil Young chose instead to embrace them. As much as it may have seemed a strange decision at the time, it was one that would pay considerable commercial and artistic dividends down the road.

As later comments in the eighties defending his syntho-pop album *Trans* have long since demonstrated—comments where he cited bands like the Human League and A Flock of Seagulls in making his arguments—it is entirely possible that Young was nowhere near as plugged into the new music scene as he may have liked the rest of the music world to believe.

However, and to this day, he still mostly stood alone among his dinosaur rock peers at the time in his ringing endorsement of punk rock, fostering a rare connection with (and influence on) newer, younger rockers that has continued well into the nineties and beyond with bands like Nirvana, Sonic Youth, Radiohead, and Pearl Jam (who Neil eventually even made a record with).

It's no coincidence that Young would eventually be labeled "the Godfather of Grunge" in the nineties.

More importantly, he put his money where his mouth was with his next couple of projects.

Out of the Blue and into the Black

Neil Young's early endorsement of, and brief association with, the experimental new wave band Devo is one of the more curious choices of his entire career.

If Young was looking to make a commercially motivated and calculated connection with the emerging punk-rock and new wave movements, there was certainly no shortage of bands that might have been better choices for allowing the aging rock veteran to voice his allegiance to the new revolution.

But, of course, as he has so adamantly and repeatedly demonstrated over the years, Young has never been one to opt for the most obvious choice.

His introduction to Devo came by way of his pal Dean Stockwell, who had been passed a tape of the Akron, Ohio- based proto-punkers by his friend Toni

Basil (who was then still a few years away from her one-hit wonder status with the early eighties new wave and MTV staple "Oh, Mickey (You're So Fine)."

Basil's passing of the tape to Stockwell completed a chain of events that had seen Devo's demo tape pass through the hands of David Bowie and Iggy Pop, among others.

If nothing else, Devo was a band of true weirdos, even going by the oddball standards of seventies punk. But they were also a strikingly original band of weirdos.

Fronted by art-school types Mark Mothersbaugh and Jerry Casale, Devo's specialty was a brand of minimalist, robotic, pre-new wave rock with an accent on herky-jerky rhythms and lyrics spouting their strangely existential punk philosophy of "devolution."

The band would routinely dress in the sort of matching hats and yellow jumpsuits that could be readily purchased at the nearest K-Mart, and that often gave them more the appearance of a haz-mat team than a traditional rock-'n'-roll band. Donning these makeshift outfits, they would also perform original songs like "Mongoloid" and "Are We Not Men? (We Are Devo)" alongside such covers as their deconstructed take on the Rolling Stones' "(I Can't Get No) Satisfaction"—all the while jerking about the stage in a kind of robotic unison.

What wasn't there to like, right?

Mothersbaugh also adopted numerous bizarre stage personas—the most notorious of which was "Booji Boy," a full-grown baby, complete with the over-sized, presumably poopy diapers to match.

I Got Lost on the Human Highway

If Devo were something of an acquired taste, they were one that Neil Young "got" instantly.

For their part of the bargain, Devo got both a professional management contract with Elliot Roberts's Lookout Management, and a record deal with Warner Brothers. Young, on the other hand, was given the opportunity to mostly be made fun of by Devo's audiences (such as when crowd members shouted "Real Dung" at him after he showed up for one of their more infamous surprise shows together at San Francisco's Mabuhay Gardens).

Devo did nothing to discourage this kind of abuse, of course, and for his own part, Young good-naturedly accepted it for the joke it largely was. In the long run, though, his association with Devo produced something of far greater value.

If the pairing of Devo and Neil Young seemed an unlikely one, the common ground they found can probably best be summed up as a meeting of two genuinely oddball sets of minds. So, when Young recruited the self-proclaimed "devolutionists" to play nuclear waste workers for his truly weird film project *Human Highway*, the pairing was as natural as the sum of these two equally combustible elements could be. Promotional materials for the film proudly declared that "It's so bad, it's going to be huge."

In retrospect, *Human Highway*—a self-described "nuclear comedy" that also features a cast including Stockwell, Dennis Hopper (at the height of his substance abusing craziness), Sally Kirkland, and Russ Tamblyn—is one of those bizarre experimental messes that only someone with money to burn like Neil Young could have gotten away with.

With such a colorful cast of characters, it is, of course, needless to say that considerable wackiness ensued during the making of the film.

In one particularly notable incident, Kirkland was apparently stabbed by a knife-wielding Hopper, which prompted a lawsuit by the actress against, among others, Hopper and Neil Young. For his part, Hopper claimed it was an accident that occurred while he was "in character" for his role as "Cracker," a cook at the same diner where Kirkland played a down-and-out waitress. Her eventual lawsuit (which she lost) was finally heard in 1985, at right around the same time Young was fighting another battle for his artistic life against David Geffen. Neil Young spent a lot of time in court that year.

There is good reason that *Human Highway* went from a limited theatrical release to cut-out oblivion in near record time. Nowadays, provided you can even find an original copy, of course, it's a much-coveted collector's item.

The film, which is said to have evolved from an earlier, even weirder and more off-the-wall film project called "The Tree That Went to Outer Space," loosely revolves around some sort of future apocalyptic nuclear event. The loose story is intertwined with footage of Young and his friends in private moments, playing music and generally getting wasted out of their minds. The film had no script to speak of and was subsequently seen by virtually no one.

In the scenes with any actual dialog, Young played two characters: a mechanic named Lionel Switch (an obvious reference to the electric toy trains he had loved since his childhood, and the company he eventually ended up buying into), and a drug-addled rock star named Frankie Fontaine (who, it is claimed by some, was inspired by David Crosby).

But in what is probably the most memorable scene in *Human Highway*, Young and Devo bash out a ridiculously long (and loud) version of "Hey, Hey, My, My (Into the Black)," a song Neil had co-written with his old bandmate in the Ducks, Jeff Blackburn. In providing vocals to the song, Mothersbaugh, adopting his ridiculously over-the-top Boogi Boy persona, sings—or, more like incoherently shouts—the lyrics to the song from an oversized crib, injecting a line of his own that would greatly inspire Young's very next project.

The line was "Rust Never Sleeps."

What Young did with this single line—inspired by Devo's art school days working on an ad campaign for something called rustoleum, and then adopted by the band as a tongue-in-cheek part of their "devolutionist" philosophy on the corrosive nature of humanity—was to run with it in a way that would play a pivotal role in producing one of his greatest albums.

When Young brought the song back to Crazy Horse—the band he would later tour and record it with—he made a particular point of playing back the loud, unhinged version of it that he had committed to tape with Devo, and asking them to recreate it.

Members of Crazy Horse have long since been quoted as saying that they learned to play, and perhaps even overplay, their asses off on the song.

It's Better to Burn Out

Rust Never Sleeps, the album borne out of this period and released by Warner Brothers in June 1979, is, hands down, one of Neil Young's greatest records.

But even more than that, it is the album that forever bridged the seemingly unfathomable generation gap that had existed up to that time between the punks of the late seventies and early eighties, and the classic rock of the hippies that preceded them. In Neil Young, the punks had found an unlikely link between past, present, and future. He would remain an unwavering supporter of, and influence on, younger bands for years to come as a direct result.

Comprised of live recordings that Young made both solo and with Crazy Horse during 1978, and later augmented with studio overdubs (mainly with the vocals), the centerpiece of *Rust* is also what became its unofficial title track.

The two versions of the song "Hey, Hey, My, My", that bookend the album include an acoustic opening take with just Young on guitar and harmonica, and a full-on electric assault with Crazy Horse at the end. The latter version rocks with a ferociousness that is nothing short of louder than God.

As much as this song is the centerpiece of what is undeniably one of Young's greatest albums, and as much as it has taken a well-deserved position as an all-time rock-'n'-roll classic, there is not so much as a single clunker in the seven songs on the album that separate both "My, My, Hey, Hey (Out of the Blue)" and "Hey, Hey, My, My (Into the Black)."

But it is this song that really sets the tone for the entire record (as well as the entire *Rust Never Sleeps* concept and tour that produced it).

Right from the get-go, and with the tragic death of Elvis Presley still fresh in many people's minds in 1979, Young spins a tale that takes Devo's devolutionist philosophy of "Rust Never Sleeps" one step further to equate the King's sad end with the struggle for aging musicians like himself to maintain a sometimes tenuous grip on their own artistic relevance in the wake of their own creeping mortality. In other words, "It's better to burn out than to fade away."

"The King is gone, but he's not forgotten," Young sings in one of this song's most memorable lines. "This is the story of Johnny Rotten."

In equating these two unlikely antiheroes—the bloated "king of rock 'n' roll" who had so recently died facedown near the crapper, and the snarling punk-rock brat who relished nothing more than spitting in the face of everything so-called dinosaur rock represented in 1978—Neil had perfectly connected the dots between them. In one of the more brutally honest statements on the nature of rock-'n'-roll mortality ever written, he also turned the mirror

Japanese pressing of *Rust Never Sleeps*.   *Courtesy of Tom Therme collection*

directly back upon himself as an aging artist striving to remain relevant during these rapidly shifting times, even while questioning the point of doing so at all.

He may not have known it back then, but it was one of Young's boldest artistic statements to date, and one that time has since proven to be one of his most enduring ever. Coming from an artist as historically guarded as Neil Young, the song was also a milestone on a number of levels. First and foremost, it represented an uncompromisingly honest peek into the looking glass of an artist already eyeing his own place in history.

"It's better to burn out than to fade away," he sings. In light of the subsequent deaths (inflicted by gun or otherwise) of artists ranging from John Lennon to Kurt Cobain, these words have an almost prophetic ring to them.

At the time, however, Young's referencing of Johnny Rotten, the snotty lead singer of the punk-rock upstart Sex Pistols, at all—and in the same line as the late, great king of rock 'n' roll, no less—was considered truly shocking.

Sandwiched in between the alternating versions of "My, My, Hey, Hey" on the album are some of Neil Young's greatest songs.

The fact that *Rust Never Sleeps* is largely a live album consisting of new material is of little consequence. Other artists of the period—most notably Jackson Browne with *Running on Empty*—had also done this. But no one had done it quite like Neil Young did with *Rust*.

In the years since its original release, the album has also gone down, along with *Harvest*, as one of his most consistent catalog sellers. There are numerous other great songs on *Rust* that could be rightfully singled out for praise as among his best.

"Pocahontas" comes most immediately to mind here. One of the best of his many great Indian-themed songs, this one revolves around an imagined meeting between Young, Marlon Brando (the legendary actor was at the time particularly well known for his support of Native American issues), and Pocahontas herself, sitting around a campfire. In the song, Young fantasizes about sleeping with Pocahontas, "to find out how she felt."

In earlier versions (the song was first recorded as part of the mythically aborted *Chrome Dreams* album), Young and Brando are joined at the campfire by then infamous Nixon crony and Watergate conspirator John Ehrlichman.

"Thrasher" is another standout, if for nothing else, its blasting of Young's former bandmates in CSN&Y. Outside of the Beatles, Young's on-again, off-again, love-hate relationship with Crosby, Stills, and Nash is one of the most storied in all of rock 'n' roll, and at the time of *Rust Never Sleeps*, you have to assume that things were not particularly rosy amongst the parties involved.

In lines like "So I got bored and left them there, they were just dead weight to me, better down the road without that load," Young seems quite content to leave his pals in CSN&Y behind for good. The song continues, "But me I'm not stopping there, Got my own row left to hoe, Just another line in the field of time," just before offering what seems to be a final twist of the knife with a reference to "dinosaurs in shrines." This may or may not be Young's way of equating his former bandmates with the derogatory term Johnny Rotten and the rest of the punks routinely used to dismiss members of the older rock generation back then.

Young and his CSN&Y bandmates would eventually reconcile (again), of course.

In fact, they would go on to record a pair of largely forgettable reunion albums, and then go out on a pair of much more noteworthy tours (particularly in the case of the post-9/11 *Freedom of Speech* tour behind Young's anti-Bush album *Living with War*).

We'll have much more on that later on in the book.

But speaking of tours . . .

Rock 'n' Roll Will Never Die

The one-month concert trek that originally spawned the *Rust Never Sleeps* album, was first conceived as a series of shows with Crazy Horse designed to promote the mellower, more commercially accessible *Comes a Time* release.

Soon enough, however, it ballooned into something else entirely—spawning not only the *Rust Never Sleeps* album, but a subsequent double live release and concert film as well.

No one is exactly sure what Young was thinking at the time of what became the *Rust Never Sleeps* tour (as if anyone ever does). But the wheels turning in his head seemed to include everything from visions of giant-sized amplifiers and hooded, red-eyed, pint-sized roadies (that looked like something straight out of the Ewok characters from *Star Wars)*, to a determination to boldly go where no man's eardrums had gone before.

Somehow, it not only all worked, but also went on to create one of the more pivotal concert tours in rock-'n'-roll history.

What is clear today is that this one month's worth of shows—culminating in the October 22, 1978, performance captured for posterity on the *Rust Never Sleeps* concert film and *Live Rust* double concert album)—constitute some of the loudest, most abrasive-sounding rock 'n' roll Neil Young and Crazy Horse have ever played. It has long since gone down as one of those "you had to be there" moments, and the stuff of legend for Young's most devoted fans. Much of the San Francisco Cow Palace performance can also be heard on the original *Rust Never Sleeps* album (albeit in overdubbed versions) of the original new songs that were debuted on the tour.

To this day, roadies and others associated with this tour recall personal memories of chaos, mayhem, and hearing loss.

The *Live Rust* album is today regarded by many fans as Young's best live release ever, and as one of the best live rock albums of all time (although some fans will tell you that the nineties release *Arc-Weld* trumps it, at least in terms of sheer overall volume). Interestingly, the only song from *Comes a Time*, the commercial folk-pop album the tour was originally designed to promote, represented is Young's self-described "Fleetwood Mac" number, "Lotta Love."

Even more revealing, though, is the filmed document of the tour, shot primarily at the Cow Palace show in San Francisco.

This footage is largely grainy by today's high-definition, Blu-ray standards, but reveals an artist at the top of his game. From the oversized mikes and amplifiers and the hooded, *Star Wars*–inspired "road-eyes" (as well as characters like Briggs playing Dr. Decibel) onstage, all the way through to the taped Woodstock stage announcements bridging the gaps between sets, and the "Rust-O-Vision" 3-D glasses worn by the audience, it was clear that Neil Young was taking his game to new and unprecedented levels. Unfortunately, this was a very brief artistic high that wasn't going to last.

Get Off of That Couch, Turn Off That MTV

Neil Young's Live Recordings

When a musician has been making music as long as Neil Young has, it isn't at all surprising that this same artist would have a veritable ton of officially released live recordings—with even more of them available on bootlegs.

What is surprising in Neil Young's case, however, is just how many of these recordings are now long out-of-print collector's items.

This applies in particular to Young's filmed performances, including a number of very good concerts released during the eighties and nineties on VHS tape that, for whatever reason, have yet to make the transition to DVD. If you go to sites like Amazon or eBay, many of these are surprisingly easy to find. But in a lot of cases they will also cost you a small fortune.

Year of the Horse—Jim Jarmusch's mid-nineties film documentary on Crazy Horse—for example, commands prices in the seventy to eighty-dollar range (and for a VHS tape, no less). Others, such as the surprisingly good 1983 *Trans* tour document *Live in Berlin*, can often be had at bargain basement prices of around fifteen dollars for a DVD copy.

With such a wide variety of live recordings—coming from nearly every phase of Young's long career—to choose from, it also shouldn't surprise anyone that the actual performance quality varies widely from disc to disc. For every classic like a *Live Rust* or a *Weld*, you'll also find slightly more tepid-sounding outings like *Red Rocks Live* (or, for that matter, *Year of the Horse*, collector's prices notwithstanding).

In recent years, Young's raiding of the vaults for the *Archives* project has also resulted in the release of some rare concerts long sought after by fans, as part of the *Archives Performance Series*. These recordings include a legendary 1970 show with Crazy Horse at New York's Fillmore East and the acoustic 1971 performance from Massey Hall that David Briggs once said he wanted to put out instead of *Harvest*.

What follows is a rundown of Young's officially released live albums. Although they were both recorded in a live setting, we have omitted the albums *Time Fades Away* and *Rust Never Sleeps* from this list, both because they are considered more part of his catalog of original music and because both are covered at considerable length elsewhere in this book.

CSN&Y 4-Way Street (1971/CD)

Neil Young's first official live release was this double album set recorded with CSN&Y on the 1970 tour behind *Déjà Vu.*

Although this album often gets shit on both by critics and by certain segments of Young's hardcore fan base, it is still noteworthy mainly for the two extended jams with Stephen Stills on the songs "Carry On" and "Southern Man."

It is also the first appearance on an album for the latter, which would later become one of the key tracks from Young's third solo album, the classic *After the Gold Rush.* The live version is also radically different from the one found on *Gold Rush*, as it serves as a vehicle for some fiery-sounding, if occasionally a bit all over the place, guitar interplay between Stills and Young.

Although I may be in the minority among Neil Young fans on this, I actually prefer the live version found here to the studio recording for this very reason.

Live Rust/Rust Never Sleeps (1979/CD/DVD)

Neil Young's first official live album with Crazy Horse is today widely recognized as a classic by fans, and rightly so. Recorded during a tour that audiences, the musicians involved, and members of the road crew will tell you is remembered as much for its sheer, ear-splitting volume as anything else, there are still plenty of memorable moments to be found on *Live Rust.*

The way that "Cortez the Killer" shifts into a reggae groove toward the end is certainly one of these, as are the blistering solos heard on "Hurricane" and "Hey, Hey, My, My." Many of the songs from *Rust Never Sleeps* that show up on this double-disc are also the exact same takes used on the original *Rust* album, but without any of the overdubs and studio tinkering—so you actually get the more direct, as-it-happened sort of experience here.

As the first officially released live document from Neil Young and Crazy Horse—recorded as it was during one of Neil's most legendary tours—*Live Rust* more than lives up to its status as a classic.

Neil Young in Berlin (1983/VHS/DVD)

Young's European tour behind the infamous album *Trans* was originally conceived to be the mother of all rock concerts. After he had seen one of the Rolling Stones' stadium extravaganzas during their 1981 *Tattoo You* tour, he decided he wanted to up the ante for his own upcoming shows, and hired Woodstock veteran Chip Monck to stage a similarly humongous production for his European trek.

But by most accounts, the tour instead turned into something of a disaster. Bassist Bruce Palmer, Young's former bandmate in Buffalo Springfield, was fired (and later rehired) due to his excessive drinking; the audiences were mostly indifferent to the vocoders and synths of the new material from *Trans*; and the exotic staging was both impractical and a huge factor in the tour losing buckets of money (by the time the *Trans* tour made it back to the U.S., the production was scaled down considerably).

Still, watching this now hard-to-find DVD today, you'd never know that the *Trans* shows were considered such a bust at the time.

Although much of the audience does sit there on their hands, all stony-faced during songs like "Computer Age" and "Transformer Man" (a few crowd close-ups on this DVD reveal some mouths wide open in apparent shock at what they were witnessing), they also come alive again when Young and Nils Lofgren crank up the guitars during a positively blistering version of "Sample and Hold."

For all of the talk over the years about how Young sprang his shocking new musical direction on an audience just wanting to hear the older hits, the set list here is also a lot more varied than you might expect. You get everything from folkie Neil ("Old Man," "The Needle and the Damage Done") to the full-on rockers ("Cinnamon Girl," "Hey, Hey, My My").

What makes *Live in Berlin* such a keeper more than anything else, though, is seeing Young and Lofgren all decked out in ridiculous eighties rock star hair and gear. The result makes them look like something straight out of an eighties Jefferson Starship video.

Lofgren in particular, draped as he is in nearly as many scarves as Aerosmith's Steven Tyler, plays this role to the hilt, too—striking nearly every clichéd rock guitar pose he can steal from the playbook of his hero Keith Richards.

For Young's part, his wrap-around sunglasses and skinny tie are cut straight from the era of early eighties new wave. At one particularly hilarious point in the video, his tie becomes tangled up in his guitar during the otherwise incendiary solo on "Like a Hurricane," until he finally just tosses it over his shoulder like one of those Aerosmith scarves. This DVD is also noteworthy for containing the only released version of the rare track "Berlin."

Live from a Rusted Out Garage (1986/VHS/DVD)

Originally filmed by Larry "L.A." Johnson as a TV special broadcast on the premium cable channel Showtime, this hard-to-find video of a 1986 show at San Francisco's Cow Palace has been called the best document of a Crazy Horse show ever captured on film, and it's really hard to disagree. If nothing else, it is certainly among the goofiest.

Filmed at the same site as the infamous *Rust Never Sleeps* show from 1978, this performance brings back many of the same props from that concert film—the oversized microphones and amps and the goofy guys running around in white doctor's coats for starters—as well as some leftovers from the *Trans* tour (Dan Clear is back as your intermission emcee).

New additions include giant mechanical cockroaches and a stage redesigned to resemble a garage, where the "third best garage band in the world" (Crazy Horse) are trying to conduct band practice. The late comedian Sam Kinnison makes a particularly memorable guest appearance as the stereotypical neighbor pissed off by all of the noise. Needless to say, hilarity ensues.

In the midst of Kinnison's screaming and all of the other chaos occurring onstage, Young and Crazy Horse knock out a killer set, including some great guitar shredding by Young on songs like "Down by the River," "Like a Hurricane," and "Opera Star."

There are also some funny bits with Clear during the intermission as he encounters Kinnison and legendary concert promoter Bill Graham backstage, and shamelessly hawks T-shirts and other tour merchandise. One perhaps unintentional bit finds Young berating the other guys in Crazy Horse for sounding lousy—an ironic twist on the reality of much of this tour imitating art in a dramatically scripted scene for this video.

Although Young was by most accounts disappointed with Crazy Horse's performances for much of this tour, and both Ralph Molina and Billy Talbot were said to be fairly miserable as well, the band sounds great here. Reports to the contrary, everyone also seems to be smiling as the garage door comes down at the end. If you can find it, this really is a great Neil Young and Crazy Horse show, and the video quality is excellent.

Freedom/Rock at the Beach (1989/VHS/DVD)

First released as a VHS video to coincide with his 1989 "comeback" album *Freedom*, this concert features Young performing songs like "Crime in the City" from that album mixed in with classics like "Heart of Gold" and rarely played chestnuts like "For the Turnstiles." The VHS has been out of print for years, and sadly it has never been revived as a DVD release (if you are listening, this one is part of our wish list, Neil).

However, if you search for it on sites like Amazon, there is an apparent bootleg DVD from the *Freedom* era that may or may not be from the same source called *Rock at the Beach* available relatively cheaply.

The bad news here is that the video quality is said to be quite poor (although the same reader reviews all rated the sound as either very good or excellent). The good news is that this DVD, recorded live at the Jones Beach Theatre, Long Island, New York, features a version of "Down by the River" where Neil rips it up with none other than Bruce Springsteen.

I admit that I haven't actually seen this film myself. But between the guest shot by the Boss and the fact that the show I saw in Seattle during the *Freedom* period was the best Neil Young show I've ever witnessed (and indeed, one of the best rock concerts I've ever seen period), I've been more than tempted to risk ordering it.

Weld and Arc-Weld (1991/CD/VHS)

The biggest rub on *Weld* (which documents the Neil Young and Crazy Horse juggernaut in support of 1990's *Ragged Glory* album) over the years is that it duplicates so much of the same material already heard on *Live Rust*. This argument to me has always seemed to be more a case of perfectionist nitpickery amongst the hardcores than anything else. True, "Cortez," "Powderfinger," "Hurricane," and the rest are all here. But so are the two great Neil Young guitar showcases from *Ragged Glory*, "Love to Burn" and "Love and Only Love." Old Black gets a workout and then some with each of these in the blistering versions heard on *Weld*.

Weld is also an even louder recording than *Live Rust* was, as if that were even possible. The often notoriously sloppy-sounding Crazy Horse also seem to have been captured on one of their "on nights" here. *Weld* also marks the first appearance of the anthem "Rockin' in the Free World" on a live Neil Young album, and Young does a pretty blazing cover of Dylan's "Blowin' in the Wind" here as well.

If you like feedback, and if you can find it, the three-disc version that includes *Arc* is also worth seeking out. The *Arc* disc consists entirely of feedback recorded at the shows, and may just be the best practical joke a major rock artist has played on his public since Lou Reed's *Metal Machine Music*. My promotional copy of "Arc: The Single" remains one of the most prized possessions in my Neil Young collection to this day.

Equally hard to find are original VHS copies of the Shakey Pictures film document of the tour shot by Larry "L.A." Johnson, but bootleg DVD versions do exist and are worth seeking out. Besides capturing a particularly loud and over-the-top set from Young and the Horse, the numerous shots of various freaks in the crowd getting their groove on are particularly funny to watch today. The video also features the original David Briggs mixes of the concert (which are far superior to those found on the album).

Unplugged (1993/CD/VHS)

For the first half of this performance made for MTV's then wildly popular series of stripped-down "Unplugged" concert telecasts, Young offers up a fairly standard acoustic performance that is reflective of the early nineties *Harvest Moon* period when it was recorded.

As solo Neil Young concerts go, this one is certainly decent enough, covering most of the hits you'd want to hear in such a setting ("Pocahontas," "The Needle and the Damage Done," and a very bluesy, lower-key take on "Mr. Soul" being among them) as well as the expected new songs from Neil's then current *Harvest Moon* album.

Although the first half of *Unplugged* lacks any of the sort of surprises or risk taking (save for a really nice turn at the pipe organ on a gorgeous-sounding reworking of the song "Like a Hurricane"), heard on some of the other, more noteworthy entries in the series (Nirvana's *Unplugged* session for MTV springs most immediately to mind), Young does offer up a few of them for the second act.

Joined by a small band including longtime cronies Ben Keith, Tim Drummond, Spooner Oldham and Nils Lofgren at about the halfway point, Neil turns in an acoustic reworking of the *Trans* track "Transformer Man" that is really quite stunning. The quieter, more subtle arrangement heard here reveals that there was a beautiful song there all along, lying in wait underneath all of the synthesized vocoder effects heard on the original. Backing vocals by Lofgren, Nicolette Larson, and Young's sister Astrid are particularly effective here, just as they are on a letter-perfect version of "Harvest Moon" (which even finds guitar tech Larry Cragg getting into the act by pushing a broom across the floor in perfect time).

For the most part, *Unplugged* is definitely a keeper, although for a really great Neil Young acoustic show, you'll do much better with *Massey Hall* or, if *Harvest Moon* is your thing, the *Dreamin' Man Live* CD.

Neil Young and Crazy Horse: *Complex Sessions* (1994/VHS)

When I first spotted this on Amazon, I just about fell out of my chair. As rarities go, the *Complex Sessions* video E.P. would have to be considered among the rarest of the rare.

Filmed by Jonathan Demme (who would go on to direct Young's concert films *Heart of Gold* and *Trunk Show*), *Complex Sessions* features live-in-the-studio performances by Neil Young and Crazy Horse of four songs from the criminally underrated *Sleeps with Angels* album: "My Heart," "Prime of Life," "Change Your Mind," and perhaps to lighten things up a bit, "Piece of Crap."

The keeper here is, of course, "Change Your Mind," Young's haunting eulogy for Nirvana's Kurt Cobain that also features one of his greatest consciousness-expanding, psychedelic rock guitar excursions down the rabbit hole ever. The performance of "Change Your Mind" captured here is nothing short of spellbinding.

Even though it was on VHS, when I saw this on Amazon (at $7.50 no less), I ordered it immediately. Guess I'm gonna have to dust the mothballs off the old VCR.

Year of the Horse (1997/CD/VHS/DVD)

I'm not really sure why Jim Jarmusch's 1997 concert documentary on Neil Young and Crazy Horse is commanding the crazy prices it is on Amazon and elsewhere.

The concert footage from the film for the most part captures the Horse at just about their sloppiest ever (although the rare electric version of "Pocahontas" seen here is kind of cool), and it has probably been years since I pulled out the CD to give it a fresh spin.

The rest of the film is kind of a mishmash that digs up older footage of Young and Crazy Horse from long since aborted projects like "Muddy Track," as well as some funny bits (like when Young responds to a guy yelling "they all sound the same" from the crowd with the classic quip "it's all the same song").

The rarity of this film today makes it somewhat of a novelty, but I'd probably rank it right next to *Road Rock* as being among Young's least memorable live documents. One additional note here is that he provided the soundtrack to Jarmusch's film *Dead Man*, starring Johnny Depp, at right around the same time as this documentary.

Silver and Gold (1999/DVD)

Originally released on VHS as a complement to the *Silver and Gold* album, this is another acoustic performance that concentrates mainly on songs from that album like "Daddy Went Walkin'" and "Buffalo Springfield Again," as well as material from the forgettable CSN&Y reunion album *Looking Forward*, along with a generous smattering of other songs from Neil Young's catalog.

Although the real highlights here are few in number, they do include a rare performance of the song "Philadelphia" (Young's contribution to the soundtrack from the Jonathan Demme film of the same name), as well as a beautiful version of "Long May You Run" played on the pump organ. Overall, this is another very decent, if not quite essential acoustic Neil Young concert document.

Road Rock/Red Rocks Live (2000/CD/DVD)

If you like your Neil Young set lists heavy on slightly obscure or otherwise rarely played songs, this document of his 2000 concert tour may be exactly what you're looking for. The obscurities, mixed in with tracks from Young's then current *Silver and Gold* album, are in abundance here, including such rarely played gems as "Bad Fog of Loneliness," "Words (Between the Lines of Age)," "World on a String," "Walk On," and "Everybody Knows This Is Nowhere."

Despite the cool set list, however, the performances captured here contain very few fireworks. The one possible exception is a version of "Cowgirl in the Sand" where Young briefly soars in an exhilarating display of guitar pyro, that also seems to end prematurely, just as Old Black is beginning to reach its uppermost levels of flight velocity.

Part of the problem here may be with the band. For this tour, Young assembled an all-star lineup of pros ranging from Booker T. and the MGs bassist Donald "Duck" Dunn and veteran session drummer Jim Keltner, to longtime musical partners in crime like Ben Keith and Spooner Oldham.

But despite their heavy credentials, this group of seasoned vets never really seems to gel as a cohesive unit and often plays tentatively and just a bit too safe. With a band like Crazy Horse—sloppy as they can be—what you hear is often what you get, warts and all. Yet, for every missed note or botched part, there is also an undeniable soulfulness there, and the unpredictable spontaneity can often result in magic.

There is precious little of either to be found on *Road Rock* and *Red Rocks Live*. All too often, this feels like just another gig for these guys, with everybody simply playing their parts.

Heart of Gold (2006/DVD)

In terms of overall quality, Jonathan Demme's 2006 film documentary of Neil Young's shows at Nashville's historic Ryman Auditorium may be the single best document of a Neil Young concert to date. If nothing else, it is certainly the warmest.

Beautifully shot, much of *Heart of Gold* finds Young and a "band" that some-times numbers as many as forty musicians and singers, bathed in gorgeous pastel shades that only serve to enhance the overall quiet ambience of this film. *Heart of Gold* is a concert experience that conveys a sense of comfortable, fuzzy warmth that is only matched by the music itself.

The songs, mostly from Young's then most recent *Harvest* sequel, 2005's sadly overlooked *Prairie Wind*, are also some of the most personal of his career. Appropriately, they are often accompanied by stories ranging from how Young came to acquire Hank Williams's guitar to the pride of a father witnessing the blossoming of his daughter into a fully grown woman. There is also an underly-ing acknowledgment of Young's own mortality in this performance, as the artist had just recently lost his father, Scott Young, to Alzheimer's disease, and survived his own narrow brush with death, in the form of a 2005 brain aneurysm.

Despite the fact that it often seems there are nearly as many musicians on the stage as there are people in the audience, there is also a sense of reverence (perhaps owing to the legendary concert venue where the film was shot) and quiet understatement to the performances here.

Heart of Gold is the most elegantly sublime of all Neil Young's many concert performances documented on film.

CSNY *Déjà Vu Live* (2008/CD/DVD)

In sharp contrast to the warm and fuzzy feelings generated by *Prairie Wind* and *Heart of Gold*, Young's next project would go to the opposite extreme. *Living with War*, released in 2006, is his loudest, most cranked up-sounding record since 1995's *Mirror Ball* with Pearl Jam.

It is also his most pissed off.

Like a number of other artists of this period (the most notorious being the rather unlikely Dixie Chicks), Young chose to voice his own objections to President George W. Bush's policies in Iraq through his music. In Young's case, this objection came in the form of *Living with War*, a cranked up to eleven collection of songs that Young himself described at the time as his "folk-metal-protest" record.

While his decision to tour the record with CSN&Y (Crazy Horse would have seemed the likelier choice) was a somewhat curious one, the results as documented on the *Déjà Vu Live* CD and concert film are often surprisingly explosive.

Although the *Freedom of Speech* tour captured on *Déjà Vu Live* was billed as another CSN&Y reunion, the concert itself is more of a case of the other guys serving almost as Neil Young's backing band. Almost all of the songs here come from the *Living with War* album, along with a sampling of songs from the other guys in CSN with similarly political themes like Graham Nash's "Military Madness" and Stephen Stills's sixties protest anthem "For What It's Worth."

For a bunch of guys most often labeled as old, laid-back hippies, Crosby, Stills, and Nash also really rise to the challenge of the material. For the most part, the performances seen and heard here really do rock.

But what makes *Déjà Vu Live* such a fascinating concert film is the stuff that happens in between sets and mostly offstage, once the concert is over. With much of the country polarized across political lines at the time, you see people in the audience who came to hear the hits like "Suite Judy Blue Eyes" and "Helpless" booing the band and extending middle-finger salutes during the more heavily anti-Bush songs.

One guy is even seen leaving the concert saying he'll never listen to a CSN&Y record again because of the band's vociferous objections to Bush and to the Iraq war.

Apparently, this guy had never heard of songs like "Ohio."

Sugar Mountain—Live at Canterbury House (Recorded in 1968, Released in 2008/CD/DVD-A)

The first entry in the *Archives Performance Series* is this acoustic concert recorded in 1968 at the rather unlikely location of a church in Ann Arbor, Michigan. In between projects at the time—Buffalo Springfield had just split up, and Young's first solo album was still a few months away—Young was also said to be quite unsure of himself as a performer when this show took place.

Right up until the time of the concert (which to everyone's surprise had sold out), Young was reportedly so nervous about performing and about how he would be received, he had to be gingerly talked into going out there by manager Elliot Roberts. Once he was finally relaxed enough to perform, the concert that then unfolded (and is subsequently documented here) was one that in many ways provided the blueprint for all of his solo shows in the many years of his long career to follow.

In between songs, Young delivers the folksy, homespun sort of raps that pepper his acoustic concerts to this day. One of the most off the wall heard here concerns "Classical Gas," the instrumental hit made famous by Mason Williams.

It's also a revelation to hear a song like "Broken Arrow"—which on record is a sprawling and ambitious epic psychedelic suite in the *Sgt. Pepper* or *Pet Sounds* vein—stripped down to its raw core, revealing that a strikingly beautiful song, minus all of the studio gimmickry, was right there all along.

Among the other highlights on *Canterbury House* are "Sugar Mountain" (the very same version that first appeared on the anthology album *Decade* and as the original B-side to the "Cinnamon Girl" single), and early versions of songs like "I've Been Waiting for You" and "Winterlong."

As a period piece capturing a future legend who was still very much in the process of discovering his own voice at the time, *Live at Canterbury House 1968* is an essential listen for hardcore fans and a fascinating snapshot in time for the rest of us.

Live at the Fillmore East (Recorded in 1970, Released in 2006/CD/DVD-A)

With the release of this legendary performance from Bill Graham's equally legendary New York City music venue the Fillmore East, the hunger amongst Neil Young's biggest fans for a full concert from the Crazy Horse period featuring the brilliant late guitarist Danny Whitten was finally satisfied . . . sort of.

While there has been some grumbling among these same fans over what songs actually did (or didn't) make the final cut ("What? No Cinnamon Girl?"), as well as some complaints over the somewhat short length of this CD, there is really very little to bitch about on *Live at the Fillmore East*.

Fans who have long salivated to hear the wonderful guitar interplay between Young and Whitten in a live concert setting should be more than satisfied with the goods delivered here—particularly on the lengthy guitar showcases "Cowgirl in the Sand" (which convincingly tops the studio version from *Everybody Knows This Is Nowhere*) and "Down by the River." Together, it is these two songs that make up the centerpiece of *Live at the Fillmore East*.

It's also really cool to finally hear Whitten's "(Come On Baby Let's Go) Downtown" in its proper context (the live version here is also the same one heard on *Tonight's the Night*). An early version of the oddball track "Wonderin'" that eventually showed up decades later on Neil Young's goofball eighties rockabilly album *Everybody's Rockin'* probably comes the closest thing to being the lone clunker here.

For those who can afford the high-end equipment needed to support it, the high-resolution mixes heard on the DVD are also a real treat. Crank this baby up, and the next-door neighbors will swear you've got a live band playing in your living room.

Live at Massey Hall 1971 (Recorded in 1971, Released in 2007/ CD/DVD-A)

Live at Massey Hall 1971 is yet another of those legendary Neil Young concert performances long rumored to exist locked up in a vault somewhere, without ever seeing the light of day until now.

Its release in 2007, so many years after the fact, comes only by way of Neil's tireless trolling of his own unreleased catalog for the *Archives* project. Albums like this one serve as a reminder of why we as fans can only thank both God and Neil Young that the artist has so meticulously (and obsessively) recorded and cataloged nearly everything he has ever done the way that he has. That said, a big part of the fun in watching the *Archives* project finally come together after years and decades of waiting, has been the slow but steady recent trickle of legendary performances such as this one.

First off, it needs to be said that this is easily the best of all Neil Young's many recorded and officially released live acoustic performances.

What makes this one so special, though, is that it is for all intents and purposes the precursor to Young's career-making album *Harvest*. Here, he is heard trying out his then brand new, never-before-heard music—songs that he later become famous for like "Old Man" and "The Needle and the Damage Done"— for the very first time.

The songs are also not always heard the same way as they would come to be known when released in their final, finished form. Two of *Harvest's* most famous songs, "Heart of Gold" and "A Man Needs a Maid," for example, are presented here as a single piece—in the form of a medley called "A Man Needs a Maid/ Heart of Gold Suite."

The performances heard on this and several other songs that eventually became parts of *Harvest* are so powerful they led producer David Briggs to lobby Young long and hard for releasing this concert as his new album, rather than the studio recordings that came out instead. Even after *Harvest* became the monster hit and commercial breakthrough it was, it has been said that Briggs continued to feel—strongly—that they had gone the wrong way.

In addition to the *Harvest* material, *Live at Massey Hall* also features stripped-down versions of Young's two guitar showcases from *Everybody Knows This Is Nowhere*, "Down by the River" and "Cowgirl in the Sand," as well as acoustic takes on singles like "Ohio" and "On the Way Home."

If you had to choose just one solo Neil Young acoustic concert to add to your own collection, this would be the one to own.

Dreamin' Man Live '92 (Recorded in 1992, Released in 2009/CD)

Dreamin' Man Live '92 is a collection of live performances of the songs that eventually made up the final track listing for the classic 1992 album *Harvest Moon*.

Since the performances are all taken from shows recorded before the album actually came out, this is not so much a fully realized concert album as it is a document of the artist trying out his then new material on a live audience (much as he had once done for *Harvest* at Massey Hall).

For those already familiar with *Harvest Moon*, one of the first things you'll notice about *Dreamin' Man Live '92* is the difference in the sequencing. The only songs that maintain their positions on *Harvest Moon* here are the title track (#4) and "Old King" (#8).

The songs also feature much smaller arrangements. Stripped of any studio sheen—not to mention the backing of Ben Keith and the rest of the Stray Gators—all that's left are Young's voice, guitar, and the occasional piano and harmonica. This is definitely bare-bones Neil Young.

In the case of "Harvest Moon," what this means is that you may find yourself missing those breezy-sounding cymbal brushes, lush backing vocals, and especially that lonesome pedal steel that lend so much to the song's lyrical imagery of a gorgeous summer night under wide-open, starlit skies. To his credit, Young still manages to nail the electric guitar part on his acoustic, though.

The backing vocals are likewise missed on songs like "Unknown Legend," and especially on "War of Man." However, in the case of the latter, the lack of any backing choir vocals only serves to better bring out the lonesome cry of Young's guitar and voice. What once sounded so lush on *Harvest Moon* seems far better suited to a more desolate-sounding album like *On the Beach* here. Played alone at the piano, "Such a Woman" takes on an almost hymnlike quality. "Natural Beauty" is likewise another track that sounds more powerful in a stripped-down arrangement for solo voice and guitar.

Although *Dreamin' Man Live '92* will never be mistaken as a replacement for the original *Harvest Moon*, these early, embryonic versions of its songs make for a very worthy companion piece to that classic album.

Neil Young *Trunk Show* (2010 Theatrical Release/DVD/Blu-ray Release TBD)

As the second installment of a rumored trilogy of Neil Young concert films by award-winning director Jonathan Demme, *Trunk Show* is about as far removed from the warm intimacy of its predecessor *Heart of Gold* as—well, as a big rock show in a hockey arena is from a smaller performance in a theatre or club.

Compared to the mellow, folksy vibe of *Heart of Gold*, *Trunk Show* is all big arena rock bombast. The camera angles veer wildly from crowd shots (on what are presumably handhelds), to crystal-clear high-definition images of all the action occurring onstage. Recorded during a stop at Philadelphia's Tower Theatre during Young's *Chrome Dreams II* tour, *Trunk Show* features performances of songs from that album like "Spirit Road" and a searing fifteen-minute-plus version of "No Hidden Path" that, even at his sixty-two years of age, is just as ear-splitting and intense as anything the artist has recorded.

In addition to fan favorites "Like a Hurricane" and "Cinnamon Girl," *Trunk Show* also features live performances of rarely played songs like *On the Beach's* "Ambulance Blues" (yes!) and even the old Squires surf instrumental "The Sultan." He is backed in the film by a band including longtime cronies Ben Keith, Ralph Molina, and Rick "the Bass Player" Rosas.

A DVD/Blu-ray is planned, but no release date has yet been set.

Piece of Crap

Five Essential Neil Young Bootlegs

Although the idea of bootlegs—the unauthorized recordings made and released either by well-meaning fans with the best of intentions, or by sleazy promoters and former band associates who obtained the material through, for a lack of a better term, "stealing" it from the artist—is, on paper at least, an insulting affront to the way musicians actually earn their living, they have also become something of a necessary evil over the years.

This is not to say that we endorse bootlegging, or any other illegal activity that robs artists of their ability to pay the bills, purchase chrome-plated rims for the Bentley, or otherwise exercise artistic control over their own music.

We don't.

The other thing about bootlegs, though—at least this was true in the old days—is that you never really know what you might be getting.

Back then, bootleg albums, CDs, and even DVDs purchased at a brick-and-mortar retail store could be packaged in anything from a plain brown sleeve with the title crudely stamped over the front, to more ambitious jackets rivaling the best cover art of the official releases by the labels themselves.

The funny thing is, the ones with the worst covers often contained the best-sounding stuff, since the more lavish packages were often used to mask the dreadfully lousy audience recordings contained inside. Go figure, right?

So, as greedy music collectors all too often obsessed with getting every piece of their favorite artists' work they could get their grubby little hands on, these same fans soon learned a few key points about the art of collecting bootlegs.

When it comes to concert recordings, radio broadcasts and soundboard recordings are generally a good thing, while audience tapes are most often not (although there are some exceptions to this rule). Concert videos should be avoided altogether, since they will inevitably feature audience members blocking the view of the cameraman (or worse yet, blurry images taken from the overhead screens at a big stadium show).

With all of that having been said, bootlegs have also become something of a guilty pleasure over the years for the most obsessed music fans. How else is such a fan to obtain such legendary unreleased recordings as Neil Young's *Chrome Dreams* or Bruce Springsteen's *The Promise*, for example, without having to wait years or even decades for them to finally show up on the *Archives* or on the *Darkness on the Edge of Town* remastered box set?

Another thing that has taken the guilt out of collecting bootlegs for many of these fans is the fact that the digital age has made many of these recordings readily available for free by downloading them on the Internet.

It's a little easier to listen to a bootleg knowing that a disgruntled ex-roadie off somewhere in Bootlick, Montana, isn't snorting up a line of coke off the profits he made by stealing it from his former employer (who, in this case, also happens to be your favorite artist).

As an artist whose officially unreleased output over the years is particularly legendary for its unusually high number of great lost albums (*Homegrown, Chrome Dreams, Times Square,* and the list goes on) alone, Neil Young has to know that he is something of a magnet both for those who manufacture bootlegs and for the fans who either buy or download them.

Thanks to the wonders of modern technology and the Internet, most of these recordings—*Chrome Dreams* being the most obvious example—can be found fairly easily by those willing to undertake a diligent Google search.

What follows is a short list of some of the better ones.

Citizen Kane Junior Blues (Live at the Bottom Line, New York City, May 14, 1974)

Although it is regarded (at least by those in the know) as one of Neil Young's best albums, the songs from 1974's *On the Beach* have rarely been given a proper representation on the concert stage.

In this surprise appearance at New York's legendary folk and blues showcase club the Bottom Line, Young appeared at a show headlined by Ry Cooder and Leon Redbone and did a surprise set performing nearly every song from the then unreleased album.

In between stunning acoustic versions of such haunting songs from that album as "Motion Pictures," "Ambulance Blues" "Revolution Blues," "For the Turnstiles," and the title track, Young is also caught in an uncharacteristically animated mood, rattling off stories about everything from the honey slides that powered the sessions for *On the Beach,* to why he no longer performs the song "Southern Man" in concert (the latter coming in response to an audience request for the song).

In addition, Neil plays such still unreleased songs from the same period as the hallucinatory dirge "Pushed It Over the End" and a particularly stunning cover of "Greensleeves" (move over, Jimmy Page).

Topping things off here are some very nice-sounding takes on "Ohio," "Long May You Run," "Helpless," and "Flying on the Ground Is Wrong."

SET LIST
1. "Pushed It Over the End"
2. "Long May You Run"
3. "Greensleeves"

4. "Ambulance Blues"
5. "Helpless"
6. "Revolution Blues"
7. "On the Beach"
8. "Roll Another Number for the Road"
9. "Motion Pictures"
10. "Pardon My Heart"
11. "For the Turnstiles"
12. "Flying on the Ground Is Wrong"

Restless in Seattle: Neil Young and the Restless, Paramount Theatre, Seattle, Washington, February 21, 1989

This one holds particular significance for me not only because I was there, but also because of all the Neil Young concerts I have attended over the years, it is hands down the best of those I've witnessed. It is also one of the very best rock-'n'-roll concerts of the thousands I have ever seen, period.

What is of most interest to hardcore Neil-phytes, however, is the fact that this hard-to-find recording contains the world concert debut of Young's future anthem "Rockin' in the Free World."

Billed as an acoustic evening with Neil Young, the concert begins innocently enough with a nine-song acoustic set combining favorites like "Heart of Gold" with less often heard gems like "For the Turnstiles," "Silver and Gold," and "Days That Used to Be."

But it is the second set where the real fireworks happen. Here, Young and his lean and mean three-piece band the Restless proceed to blow the doors off of the grand old Seattle building with a positively blistering, and completely unexpected, electric set.

Although this extremely loud performance does include a few familiar songs like "Mr. Soul" and "Down by the River," the focus was mainly on new songs from a then unreleased album called *Eldorado*. Most of the same songs eventually were released on Young's comeback album *Freedom* later that same year, but not before surfacing on a limited-edition Japanese E.P. (five thousand copies pressed), also called *Eldorado*.

I can still remember my jaw dropping to the floor as I heard songs like "Don't Cry," "Eldorado," "Cocaine Eyes," and especially "Rockin' in the Free World" for the very first time, alongside more familiar songs like the aforementioned "Down by the River" and Neil's twisted take on the standard "On Broadway."

This bootleg of this show is a surprisingly good audience recording—especially given the sheer volume of this show—and is absolutely worth seeking out for the most devoted Neil Young fan.

It is also somewhat difficult to find, but copies do in fact exist. I finally located mine more than a decade later through the diligent efforts of my occasional pro-wrestling tag team partner, and extremely well-networked in the home taping community good buddy James "Wendall Rose" Tolin.

So, thanks again, Q-Tip!

SET LIST

Acoustic Set
1. "Comes a Time"
2. "Sugar Mountain"
3. "The Needle and the Damage Done"
4. "After the Gold Rush"
5. "For the Turnstiles"
6. "Silver and Gold"
7. "The Ways of Love"
8. "Days That Used to Be"
9. "Heart of Gold"

Second Set (with the Restless):
1. "Heavy Love"
2. "Don't Cry"
3. "Cocaine Eyes"
4. "Eldorado"
5. "Box Car"
6. "Mr. Soul"
7. "Cinnamon Girl"
8. "Rockin' in the Free World" (World Premiere)
9. "Bad Fog of Loneliness"
10. "Down by the River"
11. "Hey, Hey, My, My"
12. "On Broadway"
13. "Tonight's the Night"

Archives Be Damned 2000 (Five-CD Set/Studio Outtakes and Rarities)

In which one bootlegger asks the musical question, why wait around for the *Archives* when you can just make your own?

This is exactly what one enterprising bootlegger did with this amazing five-CD compilation of Neil Young rarities, drawing from both studio rehearsals and outtakes, as well as rarely heard live recordings.

To be sure, there is a lot of the sort of filler included here that makes one realize why Young never chose to officially release some of this stuff. But most of it is well worth wading through to get to such gems as the *Ragged Glory* era outtake "Born to Run" (an original Neil Young rocker not to be confused with

Bruce Springsteen's famous song of the same name), "Sweet Joni" (Young's sweet tribute to the lovely Ms. Mitchell), and the Spector-esque "Lady Wingshot."

Coming as it did nearly a decade in advance of the first official volume of Young's *Archives*, this set makes for a very fine companion piece to that set.

TRACK LIST

Disc One
 1. "Born to Run" (rehearsals 1990)
 2. "Forever Young" (San Francisco, November 3, 1991)
 3. "Bad Fog of Loneliness" (Studio, 1973)
 4. "It Might Have Been" (Cincinnati, February 25, 1970)
 5. "Everybody's Alone" (San Francisco, February 19, 1970)
 6. "War Song" (Studio, 1972)
 7. "Johnny" (NYC, October 1, 1983, played on the PA after the show)
 8. "Goodbye Dick" (Uniondale, NY, August 14, 1974)
 9. "Pushed It Over the End" (Chicago, August 27, 1974)
10. "Everything Is Broken" (Mountain View, CA, October 28, 1989)
11. "Ordinary People" (Wantagh, NY, August 27, 1988)
12. "Farmers' Song" (Bristow, VA, September 12, 1999)
13. "Berlin" (West Berlin, October 19, 1982)
14. "Nothing Is Perfect" (St. Paul, MN, October 1, 1985)
15. "Come Along and Say You Will" (Toronto, January 15, 1973)

Disc Two
 1. "If You Got Love" (Goteburg, Germany, October 8, 1982)
 2. "Sweet Joni" (Bakersfield, March 11, 1973)
 3. "There Goes My Babe" (Studio demo, 1966)
 4. "Dance, Dance, Dance" (London, February 23, 1971)
 5. "Soul of a Woman" (Dallas, July 15, 1983)
 6. "Your Love Is Good to Me" (Santa Cruz, CA, February 6, 1984 early)
 7. "Do You Wanna Dance?" (Dayton, OH, September 18, 1983)
 8. "Hello Lonely Woman" (Wantagh, NY, August 27, 1988)
 9. "Lady Wingshot" (Eureka, CA, February 18, 1989)
10. "Fool for Your Love" (Detroit, September 4, 1988)
11. "Aurora" (Single demo, July 23, 1963)
12. "Live to Ride" (Torhout, Belgium, July 3, 1993)
13. "Big Room" (Santa Cruz, CA, November 2, 1987 late)
14. "So Tired" (Santa Cruz, CA, February 7, 1984 late)
15. "Grey Riders" (St. Paul, MN, September 1, 1985)
16. "Rock, Rock, Rock" (Santa Cruz, CA, February 7, 1984 late)
17. "Bright Sunny Day" (Clarkston, MI, September 18, 1978)
18. "Leavin' the Top Forty Behind" (Studio, 1985)
19. "I Ain't Got the Blues" (Demo, November 1965)

Disc Three

1. "Love Hotel" (Birmingham, UK, September 24, 1982)
2. "Kansas" (Oakland, CA, March 20, 1999)
3. "Homefires" (Upper Darby, PA, March 24, 1992)
4. "Love Art Blues" (Seattle, July 9, 1974)
5. "Separate Ways" (Torhout, Belgium, July 3, 1993)
6. "Crime of the Heart" (Albuquerque, NM, October 25, 1988)
7. "Bad News" (Wantagh, NY, August 27, 1988)
8. "Stranger in Paradise" (Mountain View, CA, November 6, 1993)
9. "Run Around Babe" (Demo, November 1965)
10. "Find Another Shoulder" (Santa Cruz, CA, November 2, 1987)
11. "Your Love Again" (Outtake 1985)
12. "Guilty Train" (Boston November 22, 1976)
13. "Dog House" (Detroit September 4, 1988)
14. "Windward Passage" (Santa Cruz, CA, August 22, 1977)
15. "No One Seems to Know" (Santa Cruz, CA, January 5, 1983)
16. "Extra, Extra" (Demo, November 1965)
17. "Give Me Strength" (Chicago, November 15, 1976 late)
18. "Walking After Midnight" (NYC, April 19, 1988 late)

Disc Four

1. "Rainin' in Paradise" (Studio, 1982)
2. "Amber Jean" (Austin, TX, September 25, 1984)
3. "Hawaiian Sunrise" (Long Island, NY, September 8, 1974)
4. "One More Sign" (Studio, 1966)
5. "Winter Winds/Turbine" (Berkeley, CA, October 3, 1980)
6. "Hillbilly Band" (Costa Mesa, CA October 24, 1984)
7. "Modern World" (Santa Cruz, CA, May 19, 1997)
8. "Road of Plenty" (Minneapolis, October 17, 1986)
9. "Beautiful Bluebird" (Outtake, 1985)
10. "High Heels" (Santa Cruz, CA, November 2, 1987 late)
11. "I Shall Be Released" (Mountain View, CA, October 30, 1999)
12. "That's All Right" (Dallas, July 15, 1983)
13. "Sultan" (Single, July 23, 1963)
14. "The Rent Is Always Due" (Demo, Nov 1965)
15. "Hitchhiker" (Saratoga Springs, NY, June 29, 1992)
16. "Time Off for Good Behavior" (Outtake 1985)

Disc Five

1. "Sixty to Zero" (Toronto, August 19, 1988)
2. "Box Car" (Spokane, WA, February 23, 1989)
3. "Traces" (Studio, 1973)
4. "Sad Movies" (London, March 28, 1976)
5. "I'm Goin'" (Wantagh, NY, September 27, 1988)
6. "I Wonder Why" (Studio, 1986)

7. "Don't Pity Me, Babe" (Demo, 1965)
8. "Sittin' on the Dock of the Bay" (Santa Cruz, CA, June 13, 1993)
9. "Evening Coconut" (Springfield, MA, June 27, 1976)
10. "Fingers" (Austin, TX, September, 25, 1984)
11. "I Wonder" (Studio, Winnipeg, April 23, 1964?)
12. "Mediterranean" (Studio, mid-1970s)
13. "Greensleeves" (NYC, May 16, 1974)
14. "Dead Man, Acoustic Theme" (Promo, 1995)

Rock 'N Roll Cowboy: A Life on the Road 1966–1994 (Four-CD Live Compilation)

Although the sound quality on this collection of unreleased live recordings gathered from every phase of Neil Young's career varies quite wildly, the overall listening experience is both a satisfying one and a quick education on Neil Young's long concert career.

The highlights include everything from the Massey Hall medley of "A Man Needs a Maid/Heart of Gold" to rarities like "Sweet Joni," "Amber Jean," and "Lady Wingshot," to an acoustic version of the *Re-ac-tor* track "Shots" and such *Freedom* era standouts as an early version of "Eldorado ("Road of Plenty") and Young's blistering performance of "Rockin' in the Free World" from *Saturday Night Live.*

His 1974 performances of "Pardon My Heart" and "On the Beach" from the legendary surprise show at New York's Bottom Line are also here.

Low points include live performances of such eighties-era throwaways as "Kinda Fonda Wanda" from Young's brief rockabilly flirtation with the Shocking Pinks.

Track List

Disc 1 (1966–1973)
1. "Nowadays Clancy Can't Even Sing"
2. "Birds"
3. "Cowgirl in the Sand"
4. "Tell Me Why"
5. "Only Love Can Break Your Heart"
6. "Everybody's Alone"
7. "A Man Needs a Maid/Heart of Gold"
8. "Out on the Weekend"
9. "Love in Mind"
10. "Dance Dance Dance"
11. "Cripple Creek Ferry"
12. "L.A."
13. "Soldier"
14. "Harvest"

15. "Sweet Joni"
16. "Tonight's the Night"
17. "Tired Eyes"

Disc 2 (1974–1978)
 1. "Pardon My Heart"
 2. "On the Beach"
 3. "Traces"
 4. "Human Highway"
 5. "Love Art Blues"
 6. "Hawaiian Sunrise"
 7. "Like a Hurricane"
 8. "Stringman"
 9. "Evening Coconut"
10. "Long May You Run"
11. "Southern Man"
12. "Give Me Strength"
13. "Comes a Time"
14. "Sail Away"
15. "Lady Wingshot"
16. "Shots"
17. "Downtown"

Disc 3 (1982–1985)
 1. "If You Got Love"
 2. "Transformer Man"
 3. "My Boy"
 4. "Old Ways"
 5. "Kinda Fonda Wanda"
 6. "Gonna Rock Forever"
 7. "Touch the Night"
 8. "Amber Jean"
 9. "Let Your Fingers Do the Talking"
10. "Helpless"
11. "Down by the River"
12. "Interstate"
13. "Grey Riders"
14. "Nothing Is Perfect"
15. "Southern Pacific"

Disc 4 (1986–1994)
 1. "Mideast Vacation"
 2. "Road of Plenty (El Dorado)"
 3. "Computer Age"
 4. "Bad News"
 5. "Ordinary People"

6. "Rockin' in the Free World"
7. "Winterlong"
8. "Silver and Gold"
9. "Campaigner"
10. "Homefires"
11. "Only Love Can Break Your Heart"
12. "Mr. Soul"
13. "Separate Ways"
14. "Philadelphia"

A Perfect Echo, Vols. 1–4: Four-volume, Eight-disc Compilation of Live Soundboard Recordings

In a word, this is the freaking motherlode of all Neil Young bootleg recordings.

The highlights on this staggering, and very lovingly assembled collection of rarely heard live soundboard recordings from Young's long career could probably take up an entire book by themselves. But the ones I keep coming back to most often include an extremely rare live take of "Country Girl" with CSN&Y, and a rare version of the *On the Beach* track "Ambulance Blues" from the same group's Doom Tour of 1974.

Neither of these, however, hold a candle to the amazing, stripped-down performances from 1994 at the Shoreline Amphitheatre in Mountain View, California, of the *Sleeps with Angels* tracks "Prime of Life," "Drive By," and especially a spellbinding "Change Your Mind." On the latter, Young stretches the haunting tribute to Kurt Cobain out to nearly twenty minutes, and the quieter version captures a dark beauty only hinted at on the more psychedelically enhanced jamming of the album version with Crazy Horse.

Also notable is the inclusion of several soundboard-quality recordings from the legendary February 7, 1984, show with Crazy Horse at Santa Cruz's Catalyst Club. These recordings, including blistering takes on "Barstool Blues," "Tonight's the Night," and an earlier, much gnarlier version of "Touch the Night," were already on record as being part of one of the greatest lost Crazy Horse shows ever, by virtue of their inclusion on a widely circulated bootleg version going by the titles *Catalytic Reaction* or *Touch the Night*.

That boot on its own would certainly warrant inclusion on a list like this one—particularly if we expanded it to a top ten—but the recordings heard on *A Perfect Echo* are of much higher sound quality.

TRACK LIST

VOLUME 1—1967–1976

Disc 1—1967–1971
1. "Mr. Soul" (Buffalo Springfield – Hollywood, CA August 11, 1967)
2. "Birds" (CSNY – Los Angeles, CA, August 26, 1969)

3. "I've Loved Her So Long" (CSNY – Los Angeles, CA, August 26, 1969)
4. "Sea of Madness" (CSNY – Big Sur, CA, September 13, 1969)
5. "Helpless" (CSNY – Houston, December 18, 1969)
6. "Country Girl" (CSNY – Houston, December 18, 1969)
7. "Broken Arrow" (Cincinnati, OH, February 25, 1970)
8. "Come On Baby Let's Go Downtown" (New York, March 6, 1970)
9. "Everybody Knows This Is Nowhere" (New York, March 6, 1970)
10. "Winterlong" (New York, March 6, 1970)
11. "Cinnamon Girl" (New York, March 6, 1970)
12. "Cowgirl in the Sand" (New York, March 6, 1970)
13. "On the Way Home" (CSNY – Los Angeles, March 28, 1970)
14. "Tell Me Why" (CSNY – Los Angeles, June 28, 1970)
15. "Out on the Weekend" (London, February 23, 1971)
16. "Journey Through the Past" (London, February 23, 1971)
17. "Love in Mind" (London, February 23, 1971)

Disc 2—1974–1976
1. "Walk On" (CSNY – Westbury, NY, September 8, 1974)
2. "Ambulance Blues" (CSNY – Westbury, NY, September, 8, 1974)
3. "Lookin' for a Love" (San Francisco, March 23, 1975)
4. "No One Seems to Know" (Tokyo, March 10, 1976)
5. "Human Highway" (London, March 31, 1976)
6. "Cortez the Killer" (London, March 31, 1976)
7. "White Line" (Fort Worth, TX, November 10, 1976)
8. "Don't Cry No Tears" (Chicago, November 15, 1976)
9. "Peace of Mind" (Chicago, November 15, 1976)
10. "A Man Needs a Maid" (Chicago, November 15, 1976)
11. "Give Me Strength" (Chicago, November 15, 1976)
12. "Lotta Love" (Chicago, November 15, 1976)
13. "Like a Hurricane" (Chicago, November 15, 1976)
14. "Harvest" (Boston, November 22, 1976)
15. "Campaigner" (Boston, November 22, 1976)
16. "Here We Are in the Years" (Atlanta, November 24, 1976)
17. "The Losing End" (Atlanta, November 24-1976)

VOLUME 2—1978–1989

Disc 3—1978–1984
1. "Thrasher" (San Francisco, CA, October 22, 1978)
2. "Little Thing Called Love" (Berlin, October 19, 1982)
3. "Old Man" (Berlin, October 19, 1982)
4. "Transformer Man" (Berlin, October 19, 1982)
5. "Sample and Hold" (Berlin, October 19, 1982)
6. "Don't Be Denied" (Dayton, OH, September 18, 1983)
7. "Barstool Blues" (Santa Cruz, CA, February 7, 1984)

8. "Touch the Night" (Santa Cruz, CA, February 7, 1984)
9. "Tonight's the Night" (Santa Cruz, CA, February 7, 1984)
10. "Comes a Time" (Austin, TX, September 25, 1984)
11. "Southern Pacific" (Austin, TX, September 25, 1984)
12. "Down by the River" (Austin, TX, September 25, 1984)

Disc 4—1984–1989
1. "Heart of Gold" (Austin, TX, September 25, 1984)
2. "Flying on the Ground Is Wrong" (New Orleans, September 27, 1984)
3. "Road of Plenty" (Mansfield, MA, September 21, 1986)
4. "Hippie Dream" (Minneapolis, October 17, 1986)
5. "Prisoners of Rock 'n' Roll" (Minneapolis, October 17, 1986)
6. "When You Dance I Can Really Love" (Birmingham, England, June 2, 1987)
7. "See the Sky About to Rain" (Birmingham, England, June 2, 1987)
8. "Mideast Vacation" (Birmingham, England, June 2, 1987)
9. "Southern Man" (CSNY - Oakland, CA, December 4, 1988)
10. "For the Turnstiles" (Tulsa, OK, January 13, 1989)
11. "Sugar Mountain" (Tulsa, OK, January 13, 1989)
12. "Four Strong Winds" (Tulsa, OK, January 13, 1989)
13. "Cocaine Eyes" (Tulsa, OK, January 13, 1989)
14. "Like a Hurricane" (Tulsa, OK, January 13, 1989)
15. "Rockin' in the Free World" (New York, NY, September 30, 1989)

Volume 3—1989–1993

Disc 5—1989–1990
1. "Rockin' in the Free World" (Hamburg, Germany, December 8, 1989)
2. "Don't Let It Bring You Down" (Hamburg, Germany, December 8, 1989)
3. "After the Gold Rush" (Hamburg, Germany, December 8, 1989)
4. "Ohio" (Hamburg, Germany, December 8, 1989)
5. "Too Far Gone" (Amsterdam, December 10, 1989)
6. "Hangin' on a Limb" (Amsterdam, December 10, 1989)
7. "Crime in the City" (Amsterdam, December 10, 1989)
8. "Eldorado" (Amsterdam, December 10, 1989)
9. "Someday" (Amsterdam, December 10, 1989)
10. "My My Hey Hey" (Amsterdam, December 10, 1989)
11. "The Old Laughing Lady" (Paris, December 11, 1989)
12. "The Needle and the Damage Done" (Paris, December 11, 1989)
13. "No More" (Paris, December 11, 1989)
14. "Days That Used to Be" (Mountain View, CA, October 26, 1990)
15. "Mansion on the Hill" (Mountain View, CA, October 26, 1990)

Disc 6—1991–1993
1. "Love and Only Love" (Mountain View, CA, October 26, 1990)
2. "Forever Young" (San Francisco, November 3 1991)
3. "Harvest Moon" (Irving, TX, March 14, 1992)

4. "Unknown Legend" (Irving, TX, March 14, 1992)
5. "Dreamin' Man" (Chicago, November 17, 1992)
6. "You and Me" (Chicago, November 17, 1992)
7. "Natural Beauty" (Chicago, November 17, 1992)
8. "From Hank to Hendrix" (Ames, IA, April 24, 1993)
9. "Separate Ways" (Torhout, Belgium, July 3, 1993)
10. "Love to Burn" (Torhout, Belgium, July 3, 1993)
11. "Live to Ride" (Torhout, Belgium, July 3, 1993)
12. "All Along the Watchtower" (Torhout, Belgium, July 3, 1993)

VOLUME 4—1993–2001

Disc 7–1993–1998 Disc 8–1999–2001
1. "The Loner" (Torhout, Belgium, July 3, 1993)
2. "Country Home" (New Orleans, September 18, 1994)
3. "Prime of Life" (Mountain View, CA, October 2, 1994)
4. "Driveby" (Mountain View, CA, October 2, 1994)
5. "Train of Love" (Mountain View, CA, October 2, 1994)
6. "Change Your Mind" (Mountain View, CA, October 2, 1994)
7. "Big Time" (Werchter, Belgium, July 7, 1996)
8. "Hey Hey, My My" (Werchter, Belgium, July 7, 1996)
9. "Music Arcade" (Werchter, Belgium, July 7, 1996)
10. "Pocahontas" (George, WA, September 14, 1996)
11. "Throw Your Hatred Down" (Tinley Park, IL, October 3, 1998)

Disc 8—1999–2001
1. "Red Sun" (Austin, TX, May 29, 1999)
2. "Distant Camera" (Austin, TX, May 29, 1999)
3. "Philadelphia" (Austin, TX, May 29, 1999)
4. "Buffalo Springfield Again" (Austin, TX, May 29, 1999)
5. "Only Love Can Break Your Heart" (CSNY– Los Angeles, CA, February 18, 2000)
6. "Looking Forward" (CSNY– Atlanta, March 14, 2000)
7. "Out of Control" (CSNY– Atlanta, March 14, 2000)
8. "Slowpoke" (CSNY– Atlanta, March 14, 2000)
9. "Southern Man" (CSNY– Atlanta, March 14, 2000)
10. "Ohio" (CSNY– Atlanta, March 14, 2000)
11. "Long May You Run" (CSNY– Atlanta, March 14, 2000)
12. "Winterlong" (Morrison, CO, September 20, 2000)
13. "Bad Fog of Loneliness" (Morrison, CO, September 20, 2000)
14. "Words" (Morrison, CO, September 20, 2000)
15. "World on a String" (Morrison, CO, September 20, 2000)
16. "Powderfinger" (Rio de Janeiro, January 20, 2001)

A Kinder, Gentler Machine Gun Hand

Five Great Neil Young Concerts from Seattle, Washington

Crosby, Stills, Nash, and Young
July 9, 1974
Seattle Center Coliseum
Seattle, Washington

To borrow a line from Led Zeppelin, Crosby, Stills, Nash, and Young's 1974 reunion tour doesn't get a whole lotta love from the rock history books—in fact, by most accounts it was a complete disaster.

But opening night in Seattle was a freaking doozy! In a stunning four-hour, forty-song marathon blowout, CSN&Y played and sang their asses off—going the distance to such a degree, it's quite possible the rest of the tour suffered simply because they didn't have much left once that show was over.

Subsequent reviews from the tour indicate that at least a few members of CSN&Y, if not all four of them, had completely blown their voices out, but none of that was evident on opening night. Rock 'n' roll's four most famous harmonizing voices sounded as sweet as ever that night at the Coliseum.

For the fortunate 15,000 or so who witnessed it, what they got was quite a treat—especially for the Neil Young fans. The concert's many highlights included a full-band take on "Revolution Blues" (from Young's *On the Beach* album), as well as "Cowgirl in the Sand," "Long May You Run," "A Man Needs a Maid," "Don't Be Denied," and the unreleased "Love Art Blues."

The remainder of CSN&Y's 1974 reunion tour would be marred by everything from organizational problems and chaotic routing to the usual band member excesses and clashing egos. But on that first night in Seattle, CSN&Y lived up to all of the expectations and hype. It was a marathon run that went the distance and then some.

SET LIST

1. "Love the One You're With"
2. "Wooden Ships"
3. "Immigration Man"
4. "Cowgirl in the Sand"
5. "Change Partners"
6. "Traces"
7. "Grave Concern"
8. "Black Queen"
9. "Almost Cut My Hair"
10. "Ohio"
11. "Suite: Judy Blue Eyes"
12. "Helplessly Hoping"
13. "Blackbird"
14. "Human Highway"
15. "Prison Song"
16. "As I Come of Age"
17. "Carry Me"
18. "For Free"
19. "Guinnevere"
20. "Southbound Train"
21. "Another Sleep Song"
22. "Our House"
23. "4 + 20"
24. "Know You Got to Run"
25. "You Can't Catch Me/Word Game"
26. "Love Art Blues"
27. "Long May You Run"
28. "A Man Needs a Maid"
29. "Don't Be Denied"
30. "First Things First"
31. "Déjà Vu"
32. "My Angel"
33. "Pre-Road Downs"
34. "My Favorite Changes"
35. "Long Time Gone"
36. "Revolution Blues"
37. "Pushed It Over the End"
38. "Carry On"
39. "What Are Their Names"
40. "Chicago"

Neil Young and the Shocking Pinks
July 28, 1983
Seattle Center Coliseum
Seattle, Washington

To borrow another line, this time from the title of a much more recent release, the album *Trans* represented a true *Fork in the Road* for Neil Young.

Newly signed at the time to Geffen Records, Young's first album for the label—or at least the first one they actually accepted and released—was a bizarre and abrupt about-face, even by the artist's own often strange artistic standards. If albums like *Time Fades Away* and *On the Beach* had confused both fans and critics (at least at first) back in the seventies, *Trans* was a record that completely confounded and flabbergasted them altogether in the eighties.

Although the album did contain a few leftovers from sessions for a more traditional-sounding Neil Young album (*Island in the Sun*, which was subsequently rejected by the label), the presence of songs such as "Like an Inca" did little to lessen the initial shock of hearing strange new stuff like "Computer Cowboy," "Sample and Hold," and "Transformer Man."

With its robotic (or, depending on your viewpoint "futuristic") sounding synthesizers, vocoders, and electronically altered voices, this was an album that musically shared more with the new wave bands like Devo and Human League popular on MTV at the time, than with anything resembling an actual Neil Young record—which may have been exactly the point. Regardless, the album was not well received at the time, and is the exact point many fans say is where Young first embarked on the bizarre journey through the artistic wilderness that eventually became known as the "lost decade" of the eighties.

However, even then Young fans—perhaps hoping to hear a few of the old seventies hits—still came out to the shows. On this night in Seattle, most of them already knew going in they would be getting the whole *Trans* deal—synthesizers, electronically altered vocals, and all. What they didn't know was that was only the beginning of the surprises awaiting them, and they would in fact be getting a whole lot more than they bargained for.

For the *Trans* portion of the show, the audience was entertained by a typically weird little Neil Young touch called *Trans TV*, where a smarmy game-show host character followed all of the goings-on backstage, which were then relayed out to the crowd on one of the big screens. But there were also a whole lot more great guitar moments than perhaps many had expected, or had been otherwise led to believe were even still possible. Even the *Trans* material featured sparse but noteworthy crankage from Neil Young and the ever-trusty Old Black

But if the robotic-sounding songs of *Trans* weren't enough of a shock already, the encore would prove to be truly . . . well, "shocking" is probably the best word here.

Just like that, the synthesizers were gone, only to be replaced—completely unannounced—by the greased-back, duck-billed hair and matching pink suits of Young's newest band and latest artistic about-face, the Shocking Pinks. He and the Pinks then proceeded to play the entire, yet-to-be-released, rockabilly-influenced *Everybody's Rockin'* album for the stunned audience.

The "lost decade" was now officially underway.

SET LIST

1. "Comes a Time"
2. "Motor City"
3. "Down by the River"
4. "Soul of a Woman"
5. "Old Ways"
6. "Old Man"
7. "Helpless"
8. "Dance Dance Dance"
9. "Heart of Gold"
10. "Don't Be Denied"
11. "Sail Away"
12. "Powderfinger"
13. "Ohio"
14. "After the Gold Rush"
15. "Transformer Man"
16. "My My, Hey Hey (Out of the Blue)"
17. "Mr. Soul"
18. "Sugar Mountain"
19. "Jellyroll Man"
20. "That's All Right (Mama)"
21. "Wonderin'"
22. "Kinda Fonda Wanda"
23. "Bright Lights, Big City"
24. "Get Gone"
25. "Everybody's Rockin'"
26. "Do You Wanna Dance?"

Neil Young and Crazy Horse
April 11, 1991
Seattle Center Coliseum
Seattle, Washington

Touring after his critical and commercial early-nineties comeback behind the album *Ragged Glory,* this show may seem a little short on actual songs. However, the sheer volume of this concert more than made up for the skimpy set list. Young also chose to stretch many of the songs out past the ten-minute mark, featuring the sort of lengthy guitar solos he is known for when he goes into that trance sort of state longtime fans recognize all too well.

The Horse, as is often their part when Young decides to crank the amps up, were mostly along for the ride here. Their role was mainly one of dutifully keeping up—so much so that many songs had endings nearly as long as the songs themselves.

Every song played on this and every other date of the *Ragged Glory* tour was accompanied by some of the longest, most ear-scorching, feedback-drenched guitar solos of Young's career. At this show, the band played loud enough to blow the roof off of the poor old Seattle Coliseum, at least figuratively speaking. I'd bet that even openers Sonic Youth—no strangers to making a pretty loud racket themselves—were scrambling for the earplugs backstage.

Like the concert itself, the resulting live album from the tour, the three-disc *Arc-Weld* (the third disc consists entirely of the feedback produced as Young and Crazy Horse tried, not always altogether successfully, to bring each of the songs to a close) is something that can only fully be appreciated at maximum volume. On a side note, *Arc-Weld* also produced what may be the coolest Neil Young promotional item ever—"Arc: The Single," a four-minute-edit of random feedback from the third disc.

SET LIST
1. "Hey Hey, My My (Into the Black)"
2. "Crime in the City"
3. "Blowin' in the Wind"
4. "Love to Burn"
5. "Cinnamon Girl"
6. "Mansion on the Hill"
7. "Fuckin' Up"
8. "Cortez the Killer"
9. "Powderfinger"
10. "Love and Only Love"
11. "Rockin' in the Free World"
13. "Roll Another Number"
14. "Tonight's the Night"

Neil Young (Solo)
January 20, 1992
Paramount Theatre
Seattle, Washington

In typically unpredictable fashion, Young followed up the ear-shattering volume of *Ragged Glory* and *Arc-Weld* with the gorgeous-sounding folk-pop of 1992's *Harvest Moon*. Months before that album was released, he embarked on the first of what would be several short acoustic tours that year.

One of the earliest stops was Seattle's Paramount Theater, where he announced he would be trying out several of the new songs on the audience

Ticket stub from Neil Young's Seattle 1983 show. By this time the more ambitious *Trans* concerts, which played half-filled stadiums in Europe, had been trimmed down to a more modest solo show.   *From author's collection*

that night. Among the things that made this concert special was Young's use of the Paramount's vintage pipe organ during "After the Gold Rush." But even more so were the stories he told before many of the new songs.

For "Hank to Hendrix," he told the story of how he came to own the guitar of one of his heroes, Hank Williams, and how the guitar has remained among his most prized possessions. "Old King" was preceded by a quite humorous rap about the old dog who is the subject of the song. Many of these stories have, of course, long since become a fairly standard part of Neil Young's acoustic concerts. But on this night, it wasn't just the stories that were new, but also the songs themselves.

Regarded by many fans as the successor to his #1 best-seller *Harvest* from 1972, *Harvest Moon* is one of Young's most beautiful records and remains one of his better catalog sellers. For those at the Paramount in Seattle that night in January 1992, hearing those songs for the very first time was something special.

Set List
1. "Long May You Run"
2. "From Hank to Hendrix"
3. "Silver and Gold"
4. "You and Me"
5. "War of Man"
6. "Old King"
7. "Such a Woman"
8. "Harvest Moon"
9. "Heart of Gold"
10. "Dreamin' Man"
11. "Natural Beauty"
12. "Don't Let It Bring You Down"
13. "Down by the River"
14. "After the Gold Rush"
15. "Old Man"

Neil Young and the Restless
February 21, 1989
Paramount Theatre
Seattle, Washington

Neil Young's Seattle concert on February 21, 1989, wasn't supposed to be anything more than an evening of greatest hits played both solo-acoustic and with a small band called the Restless.

But for the lucky three thousand people at the Paramount Theatre that historic night, it proved to be much more. Which is why, even though it breaks with the chronological order of this chapter, I've placed it in this spot. I've saved the best for last.

That evening would prove to be not only the best Neil Young show I've ever seen, but one of the most amazing rock-'n'-roll performances I've ever witnessed, period.

To put this in its proper perspective, you have to understand just where Young stood as an artist in the overall picture of popular music at the time. The truth is, many, if not most fans had pretty much written him off. He was coming off of the infamous period of artistic flux most now refer to as the "lost eighties"—a decade marked by bizarre experiments like the aforementioned *Trans* and Shocking Pinks records, as well as the equally contentious battles with Geffen Records (his record label at the time) throughout this period.

There is good reason that most fans refer to the eighties as Young's lost decade. However, he had also just scored a minor commercial comeback with *This Note's for You*, the brassy blues record he made in 1988 after returning to Reprise Records (home to his greatest artistic and commercial triumphs during the sixties and seventies). Even so, many fans remained suspicious. After all, wasn't this just the latest in a decade-long line of bizarre genre-jumping experiments?

The concert started innocently enough.

As expected, Young came out with his acoustic guitar and harmonica and opened up with the friendly and familiar-sounding "Comes a Time." As the evening progressed on through such folky fare as "The Needle and the Damage Done" and "After the Gold Rush," he was soon joined by a small band for songs ranging from then-obscurities like "Silver and Gold," "The Ways of Love," and "Days That Used to Be" to more crowd-pleasing fare like "Heart of Gold."

What came next however, was one of those things that can only be described as a true "holy shit" moment.

Returning to the stage after a short intermission, Young took the stage to the unmistakable sound of feedback. But this was not just any random, ordinary-sounding hum, but rather, some of the most ungodly, loud-ass noise ever heard in the Paramount Theatre. It's one thing to crank the amps as loud as God will allow with Crazy Horse in a big-ass basketball barn like the Seattle Center

Coliseum. It's quite another to peel the paint off the ceiling in an acoustically perfect little three thousand-seat theater like the Paramount.

For the next ninety minutes or so, Young didn't so much play his trusted guitar Old Black as he did assault the living crap out of it. This was an all-out metallic frenzy. Not only was Neil Young back, he was playing with the sort of balcony-rattling intensity that much younger thrash bands like Slayer or Megadeth might well envy.

For their own part, his bandmates in the Restless—particularly bassist Rick Rosas and drummer Chad Cromwell—matched this all-out assault without skipping a beat. The Restless were as tight as a rusty old oil drum in a way that Crazy Horse—the band Young usually turns to when he wants to turn the amps up a bit—have never been.

Many of the songs he played that night were also brand spanking new.

He opened things up right out of the gate with "Heavy Love," a pounding rocker that shook that grand old building to its very foundation. This was followed in short order by "Don't Cry," a moodier song that nonetheless produced some of the loudest noise of the night. The latter would later wind up on *Freedom*, the September 1989 release that most now agree heralded the arrival of what would come to be known as Young's artistic renaissance during the nineties.

Several other new songs followed, including "Cocaine Eyes" and the title track of the now hard-to-find five-song E.P. *Eldorado*. It was these new songs that provided a taste of what was still to come on the artistic comeback that would come later that year with *Freedom*.

Ticket stub from one of two Seattle stops on the 2007–2008 *Chrome Dreams II* tour.   *From author's collection*

On his second Seattle area stop of the *Chrome Dreams II* tour, Neil Young performed at the Comcast Arena in Everett, Washington.

From author's collection

Later on that night, Young played another great new song called "Rockin' in the Free World" for the very first time. Introducing it as a song "none of us have ever heard before except me," he cautioned the crowd they might hear a few mistakes. "It's an art thing,, but by the end, you're all gonna be rocking in the free world."

Little did the crowd know at the time that the strange new lyrics about "a thousand points of light for the homeless man" and "styrofoam boxes for the ozone layer" would become one of the most recognizable rock anthems of the twentieth century. All the three thousand people at the Paramount that night knew was that this blistering rocker had one motherfucker of a riff. This was a completely brand new noise—strange, distant, and exotic, yet so instant and familiar it was as though you had known it and been waiting to hear it all of your life.

As of this night, the lost eighties were now, once and for all, a thing of the past. The line between then and now had been drawn with all the clarity and precision of a kinder, gentler machine gun hand.

SET LIST

1. "Comes a Time"
2. "Sugar Mountain"
3. "The Needle and the Damage Done"
4. "After the Gold Rush"
5. "For the Turnstiles"
6. "Silver and Gold"
7. "The Ways of Love"
8. "Days That Used to Be"
9. "Heart of Gold"
10. "Heavy Love"
11. "Don't Cry"
12. "Cocaine Eyes"
13. "Eldorado"
14. "Boxcar"
15. "Mr. Soul"
16. "Cinnamon Girl"
17. "Rockin' in the Free World" (World Premiere)
18. "Bad Fog of Loneliness"
19. "Down by the River"
20. "Hey Hey, My My (Into the Black)"
21. "On Broadway"
22. "Tonight's the Night"

(Thanks to Sugar Mountain for their invaluable assistance with the Neil Young set lists. You'll find them at http://www.sugarmtn.org/).

Why Do You Ride That Crazy Horse?

Hawks and Doves, Re-ac-tor, and a Kid Named Ben

In order to get into any serious discussion of Neil Young's music in the eighties—a period most often referred to by Neil-phytes as either the Geffen years or, perhaps more appropriately, as Neil Young's lost decade—one also has to consider the overall state of rock music at the time.

As anyone who has ever worked in the business will tell you, the music industry goes through down cycles about every ten years or so. These same precipitous periods of declining record sales almost always seem to happen like clockwork toward the end of any given decade, and are just as often accompanied by a slew of flash-in-the-pan, pop-oriented, one-hit-wonder type acts. In the seventies, it was guys like Christopher Cross and of course all the disco groups; in the eighties it was Vanilla Ice, MC Hammer, and New Kids on the Block; in the nineties it was N'Sync, the Backstreet Boys, Britney Spears, and so on.

Okay, maybe Britney has enjoyed a longer shelf life than the others, but you get the idea.

The biggest difference in these cycles as they exist now compared to previous decades, is that the industry (and the way it conducts its business) has been fundamentally changed by the emergence of the Internet. The disposable teen pop acts of today (Jonas Brothers, Miley Cyrus, Justin Bieber, and so forth) also don't seem to be going away as quickly as they did before.

Anyway, that's another story best saved for another book.

What happened in the early eighties to break this cycle was the emergence of Music Television (MTV). As a medium, MTV created an entirely new avenue for marketing music through the use of music videos. Since there was also a relative shortage of actual music videos to play (at least at first), this also opened things up for an entire new generation of artists who normally might not find themselves welcomed so warmly on the still highly formatized and strictly controlled playlists of eighties music radio.

While it could be argued convincingly that all this did was create yet another new glut of one-hit wonders (anybody remember Kajagoogoo? Missing Persons? Wall of Voodoo?), it also served to break down some of the barriers that had

Picture sleeve for the triangle-shaped single for "Southern Pacific" from the brutally abrasive *Re-ac-tor* album. Neil's perception that Reprise could have done more to market the album was one of many factors leading to his departure from the label. *Courtesy of Tom Therme collection*

gone up around the music industry like a great wall, especially during the disco and punk eras of the late seventies. In doing so, MTV opened a lot of doors for bands that might not have otherwise found a viable medium to get their music heard.

However, this refreshing new climate of musical openness only ran skin-deep.

For one thing, MTV didn't become truly color-blind until around the time Michael Jackson released *Thriller*. Music fans mostly also continued to cluster themselves around their own personal genre preferences, just as they had done in the late seventies.

At San Bernardino's US Festival in 1983, for example, each of the three days of music offered by promoter Steve Wozniak of Apple Computers were slotted according to specific genre.

"New Wave Day" featured acts like the Clash, Men at Work, and the Stray Cats, while "Heavy Metal Day" was made up entirely of hair bands like Van Halen, Judas Priest, and the Scorpions. Could you imagine such musical divisions existing at, say the 1969 Woodstock festival—where maybe one day you would get the folkies like Crosby, Stills, and Nash, Country Joe, and Joan Baez, and on the other you'd get the heavy rock of Hendrix, Jefferson Airplane, and the Who?

Not likely, but then again the late sixties were a far different time.

No matter how much you tried to hide it, the divisions of the seventies were still very much a part of the rock-'n'-roll landscape in the early eighties. They just did a much better job of sweeping them under the proverbial rug.

But for those artists who had enough foresight to see the marketing potential of music video, the eighties proved to be a goldmine. Interestingly enough, among those who were ahead of the curve in that department were a surprising number of classic rock acts from the sixties and seventies. Paul McCartney, David Bowie, and the Rolling Stones were among those who jumped on the music video bandwagon early in the game. Prog-rockers Yes and Genesis soon followed suit, as did Bruce Springsteen (who, up until the time of his 1984 blockbuster *Born in the U.S.A.*, had consciously avoided using music videos to promote his work).

Send Me a Cheeseburger and a New Rolling Stone

Neil Young on the other hand, was a bit of a Johnny-Come-Lately when it came to music video.

This is surprising on a number of levels. Young was usually first among his class to spot a new trend (like he did with punk rock) and get solidly behind it. Young also had a long, if not always completely successful, history of exploring the marriage between music and video. His experiments with rock and film already included both great successes like *Rust Never Sleeps* and some equally spectacular flops like *Journey Through the Past* and *Human Highway*. He even had his own film company in Shakey Pictures.

Even so, by the time Young finally decided to involve himself more fully in the art of music video (for his very new wavish 1982 album *Trans*), his new record company refused to give him a budget to make one. But we'll get to all of that in due course.

If music video seemed to be rather curiously off his radar as the eighties began, it was only because Young had much more weighty and personal concerns on his mind.

I Am a Child

After closing out the long, strange, and often artistically experimental trip that had been the seventies with the stunning return to critical and commercial form of *Rust Never Sleeps*, Young seemed to completely disappear off the map during the early years of the eighties—and no one (at least in the public arena) could figure out exactly why.

There continued to be records, of course.

But there were no concert tours at all in between the triumph of *Rust* and the rather strange return to a higher profile that came with 1982's *Trans*. For those who followed Neil Young's public life closely at the time, it would have been easy to just figure that after his failed relationships with Susan Acevedo and Carrie Snodgress, Neil had at long last found the mate he had so long sought in Pegi Morton (which he indeed had). Perhaps he was simply enjoying the benefits of marital bliss after so many years of being wedded first and foremost to his career.

But, as anyone who has ever been around him will almost certainly attest, this is simply not the way that Neil Young operates. There were clearly other factors at play here, even if they were unbeknownst to the general public.

In essence, he more or less quit the rigors of the "album, tour, album, tour" grind of the music business for the first few years of the eighties in order to devote time to his new son Ben, who was born in 1978. But this was no mere case of "house husbandry," along the same lines as John Lennon's final years on this earth with Yoko.

To say Ben Young was a "special needs" child would be a huge understatement.

Neil Young had already dealt with cerebral palsy once, when his first son (with Carrie Snodgress) Zeke was diagnosed with the disease. As it turned out, Neil and Pegi's son Ben had a much more severe form of the debilitating ailment, which rendered him not only physically handicapped, but verbally as well. Ben's cerebral palsy was of a much more serious nature, which was compounded by the fact that he was born both spastic and non-oral.

One can debate whether or not this crisis only strengthened the bond between then newlyweds Neil and Pegi Young, to cement that rarest of entertainment business relationships that continues to this day (which it does). But what is clear now—though it was largely unknown at the time—is that the health and welfare of their son became priority number one for the couple back then.

Still, Young did continue to work, at least as best as he could.

But there were no more marathon dusk-to-dawn recording sessions powered by tequila, honey slides, or anything else of the sort. Young's time in the recording studio had to be slotted in to fit the often eighteen hours a day he spent in a series of (at least initially) mostly failed therapy sessions in search of a communications breakthrough for Ben.

Neil and Pegi would eventually find their ultimate solution in the Bridge School, an organization that both continue to actively support to this day. Pegi sits on their board of directors, while Neil's annual benefit shows for the organization help bring home the bacon.

At the time all of this was going down, the situation with Ben was unknown to all but a very small, tight-knit circle of friends and family. Even the brass at Young's label Warner Brothers had no idea of what was happening, as he performed a juggling act between long, repetitive, and monotonous therapy for his son while squeezing in time to record. With this new

The actual triangle-shaped "Southern Pacific" vinyl single from
Re-ac-tor.   *Courtesy of Tom Therme collection*

schedule, his preferred routine of recording sessions with odd hours, often
coinciding with the full moon, were likewise put on hold.

Although the Moon Isn't Full, He Still Feels the Pull

Although the critical rub on Neil's first few post–*Rust Never Sleeps* albums made
during the eighties as being minor efforts in his overall canon is mostly justified,
what we know now about the circumstances behind them puts a lot of things
into a more proper perspective.

Hawks and Doves, released late in 1980 is rightfully considered one of the
lower points in Neil's long career. Divided equally between acoustic and more
country-flavored electric songs, the album feels more than anything else like a
collection of leftovers, similar in many ways to 1977's *American Stars and Bars*.

And in fact, many of the songs are drawn from the very same sessions (for the
unreleased *Harvest* sequel *Homegrown*) that made up *Stars and Bars*. The problem

with *Hawks and Doves* is that it lacks any of the sort of true stando ut tracks like "Will to Love" or "Like a Hurricane" that made *Stars and Bars* such a keeper.

Indeed, the most noteworthy thing one can say about *Hawks and Doves* is that it marked the beginning of Neil Young's embrace of the 1980s Reagan era, along with its accompanying right-wing Republican politics, in tracks like "Union Man." The song mostly takes it shots at the musicians union. But it was also an early hint at the newly conservative, flag-waving redneck Neil Young that would reach its full apex a few years later during his country phase with the album *Old Ways*. Listening to both albums today, one can really begin to see the stylistic bridge between the two (there is also a less obvious but still very real connection to the folk-pop of *Harvest* and *Comes a Time*).

If nothing else, *Hawks and Doves* seemed like a strange way to follow up the blockbuster that was *Rust Never Sleeps*, as well as an abrupt about-face from that album's embrace of things like the musical revolution that was punk rock at the time. But in retrospect, and especially knowing what we do now about what was happening in his personal life at the time, it almost makes sense.

Almost.

Got Mashed Potato, Ain't Got No T-Bone

Say whatever you will about Neil Young's next album, his reunion with Crazy Horse on the hard-rock, minimalist *Re-ac-tor*. As one of his loudest records, *Re-ac-tor* pales somewhat in comparison to *Rust Never Sleeps* and some of his latter-day hard-rock albums like *Mirror Ball*, or even *Living with War*. But for sheer volume and ballsy audacity, it ranks right up there with his best electric assaults with Crazy Horse.

Coming after the weird and somewhat directionless mishmash that was *Hawks and Doves*, in some respects *Re-ac-tor* couldn't have come along at a better time. If nothing else, this was evidence that Young still knew how to turn the amps to eleven and let the shit rip with Crazy Horse and the ever-trusty Old Black. The songs themselves, however, represented some of the most mind-numbingly repetitive music he had ever written, an apparent reaction to the experimental, repetitive speech therapies Neil and Pegi had been trying out at the time to treat their son Ben.

As far as traditional songs go, there really aren't any on *Re-ac-tor* to speak of. At least, there are none of the sort that you'll be humming along with in your head, after an initial listen. In some ways, *Re-ac-tor* sounds like nothing more than an excuse for Neil Young to make a lot of noise with Crazy Horse, unbridled by such mundane concerns as actual melody or songcraft. But there are at least three songs from the album that stand out.

"Southern Pacific" begins with the lonesome whistle of a locomotive train, before chugging its way into a monster riff that most definitely maintains "the spook" for the rest of the way through. As the closest thing to a perfectly con-structed actual "song" on the entire album, the chunky-sounding, rhythmic power chording is probably the nearest that Neil Young and Crazy Horse have ever gotten to actually fitting into the tight pocket of a funk groove. The song has rarely been played live since its inclusion on *Re-ac-tor*, but did become something of a standout during Young's country shows with the International Harvesters during the *Old Ways* period a few years later.

Somewhere in heaven, I suspect that Neil's old running partner in the Mynah Birds, Rick James, has this tight-ass, greasy little jam on his i-Pod. The other two most significant songs from *Re-ac-tor* are much more minimalist in nature.

"T-Bone" takes up close to ten minutes of this already very short record, and does little more than repeat the refrain of "got mashed potato, ain't got no T-Bone" over and over again, amidst walls of howling feedback and noise. These days, it's common knowledge amongst the Neil-phytes that the repetitive nature of this track represents Young's own frustration over the equally monotonous therapy his son Ben was receiving when the song was first recorded.

For "Shots," the other standout track from this record, Young first began to explore the altered sound effects he got from the synclavier—a device he would later use to much greater effect on his infamous 1982 album *Trans*. For the *Re-ac-tor* track "Shots," he uses the device to simulate the sounds of rapid machine gun fire.

But as is the case with *Hawks and Doves* and *Old Ways*, there is in fact a clear bridge from *Re-ac-tor* to *Trans* that extends far beyond Young's mere first use of electronic gadgetry.

For one thing, the influence of Ben Young is all over this record, just as he is on *Trans*—although it would take some fans a few decades to actually see the connection.

I Put in My Time, Now I'm Left to Roll, Down the Long Decline

There is an earlier chapter in this book that talks about Neil Young's biggest commercial flops, and when it came down to a coin toss between *Re-ac-tor* and *Hawks and Doves* over which album to include on that list, the latter won. But make no mistake, *Re-ac-tor* also stiffed big, climbing only three positions higher than *Hawks and Doves* to make a rather dismal #27 showing on the Billboard chart.

When *Re-ac-tor* flopped, though, it cost Young more than just a few lost record sales and the accompanying bruised artist's ego. The album's poor chart performance, combined with Young's decision to keep his family crisis with Ben a secret from nearly everyone (including, most significantly, his record company), played a key role in ending a long and successful partnership with his label, Reprise.

For more than a decade, the relationship between Young and the Warner Brothers–distributed label had been a mostly satisfying, mutually beneficial one.

A later picture sleeve for the "Southern Pacific" single from *Re-ac-tor.*
Courtesy of Tom Therme collection

By most accounts, executives like Mo Ostin also catered to Young's every whim, from last-second changes on his albums over titles and sequencing (*Comes a Time*), to pulling album releases altogether (*Homegrown*). The demands could also sometimes be as ridiculous as they were financially unwise. When Young once asked Mo to park his trailer on a western set on the Warner Brothers movie studios backlot (in order to sit out an earthquake predicted by a local psychic), for example, Ostin didn't so much as bat an eye.

But in the end, the divorce between Neil Young and Reprise came about as the result of the same sort of communication breakdown that dissolves a lot of marriages. Because of the critical situation with his son Ben, and the fact that finding an answer required so much of his time, Young was unable to tour the record or even to promote it with the usual press interviews and promotions at music retail and album rock stations.

The fact that Young kept his family situation such a closely guarded secret at the time probably didn't help matters. But the communication gap between label, management, and artist soon grew into a chasm wider than the Grand Canyon.

From Young's (and by extension, manager Elliot Roberts's) perspective, the label simply wasn't doing enough to promote *Re-ac-tor*. From the label's point of view, it was probably equally true that a certain level of frustration had to exist over trying to market a decidedly noncommercial album without the active help of the artist who made it.

There are most likely several events that contributed to Neil Young eventually leaving Warner/Reprise (a decision he would come to regret later). One of the songs on *Re-ac-tor*, "Surfer Joe and Moe the Sleaze," has even been long rumored to be a dig at Ostin and fellow Warner executive Joe Smith—which, if true, would seem to lend some credence to tensions already being there long before that album.

But by most accounts, the proverbial last straw that broke the artist's back was when the label was reluctant to bankroll a promotional, triangle-shaped single from *Re-ac-tor* matching the album's striking red and black triangle art.

After turning down a lucrative offer to defect to RCA, Young and Elliot Roberts decided to go with David Geffen, who both of them had previous dealings with. The newly launched Geffen Records was the talk of the industry at the time, signing up everyone from Donna Summer and Peter Gabriel to Elton John and John Lennon. Young was guaranteed a million dollars per album and complete creative control over everything from the music itself to budgets and promotion.

However, on the latter part of this agreement, it became apparent almost immediately that Geffen would not be keeping his word. But then again, how could anyone expect Geffen to continue to hand out a million dollars per record for an artist who seemed to have (once again) become hell-bent on committing career suicide with another series of, to put it as delicately as possible, "strange" records?

22

Sample and Hold

For Neil Young's most devoted fans, the eighties were without question a tough time, even when measured against the standards of what he had demanded of them in the past.

For those who preferred the softer sounds of *Harvest*, or even the frenzied hard rock of Crazy Horse, it was one thing to follow Young's path into the ditch on albums like *Time Fades Away, On the Beach,* and *Tonight's the Night.* The method to the artistic madness on those albums would certainly reveal itself in the years and decades to come.

But the way Young chose to tax the patience of his fans in the eighties was something else entirely. For the most part, it was just plain hard being a Neil Young fan back then.

The best way to describe his artistic output during the eighties would be to compare the albums released during this period to what you might call a series of vanity projects.

Fans of rock-'n'-roll artists ranging from Paul McCartney to Elvis Costello to Bruce Springsteen will begrudgingly recognize this term all too well. A "vanity project" is when an artist veers off of the more established artistic (and in most cases, the more commercially palatable) path of the familiar sound that the fans know, love, and indeed expect in order to indulge what often turns out to be a brief artistic whim.

Although the results of these so-called vanity projects can be successful, and in some cases even embraced (as was the case when Springsteen chose to record and tour an entire album of Pete Seeger's vintage folk songs—complete with all the accompanying fiddles and hoe-downs), they are still almost always a shock to the fans at first.

In the case of Springsteen's *The Seeger Sessions*, the initial surprise eventually gave way to something more like a reluctantly acquired taste, and then a final acceptance for many of his fans. He is Bruce Springsteen, after all. Other examples like Elvis Costello's album of classical chamber music with the Brodsky Quartet (or roughly about two-thirds of Joe Jackson's entire catalog, for that matter) wear off far less easily.

Bands like Radiohead, on the other hand, have built their entire careers on this type of artistic indulgence. Much as some Radiohead fans are actually still waiting for that follow-up to *The Bends* or *OK Computer* (neither of which are probably coming anytime soon, by the way), in this case, the more devoted followers of the group actually expect something different with every release. Many of these fans are in fact disappointed when they don't get something that radical.

To many fans, Young's so-called Geffen Years during the eighties represent something like a series of these vanity projects on steroids. For even more of them—especially those who were actually devoted enough to stick it out through all of his bizarre experimental excursions into rockabilly, country, blues, and the rest—it must have also seemed like the artist had at least temporarily lost his mind.

Never mind the wondering amongst these long-suffering fans about how long, if ever, it might take for him to actually make a "Neil Young album" again. David Geffen wondered the same thing, so much so that he eventually made it the basis of a lawsuit against the artist. Even so, you still had to wonder if there would be enough Neil Young fans left after all of the eighties weirdness to actually still care.

Young's closest peer as the greatest American songwriter rock music has ever produced, Bob Dylan, was already making his own series of less than stellar records at about the same time—albums that for the most part remain forgotten today, as they probably should be. The thing about such forgettable albums as *Empire Burlesque*, though, is that even if they may have been bad Bob Dylan albums, at least they were still somewhat recognizable as being actual Bob Dylan albums.

As for Neil Young?

Again, let's just say that it was tough being a Neil Young fan in the eighties.

A New Design

The album that most often comes to mind as signifying Young's lost decade in the eighties is 1982's *Trans*.

At the time that it was released, the computerized syntho-pop of *Trans* was such a shock to fans both of Young and of rock 'n' roll in general that a significant number of them simply refused to give it a chance. It remains one of only a handful of Neil Young albums that have never been issued in America on compact disc (it is, however, readily available as a Japanese import). Critics of the day who were normally quick to sing the praises of Young, likewise unanimously turned their noses upward in their reviews for publications like *Rolling Stone*.

Interestingly, in the decades since it was first universally panned, the album has enjoyed something of a popular and critical renaissance. In articles like "Defending the Trick of Disaster: Neil Young's 'Trans' Reconsidered " (for Pop Matters), modern-day *Trans* apologists like Zach Schonfeld have become as quick to defend the album as their eighties counterparts were to dismiss it.

In his own very well thought-out defense of *Trans*, Schonfeld writes: "Though steeped in cold, processed synths and mechanical textures, *Trans* is far from emotionless. Pay attention and you'll find some of the most personal and chilling music Young ever recorded, its emotional core endlessly belied (but never undermined) by the icy, Kraftwerk-style exterior."

A decent argument can also be made that *Trans* has had a lasting influence on subsequent generations of rock musicians. It isn't a stretch, for example, to draw a direct line between *Trans* and the cool, electronic minimalist rock of Radiohead on albums like *Kid A, Amnesiac,* and *The King of Limbs.*

In particular, there are striking similarities between the way Thom Yorke uses his high-pitched, haunting falsetto as an instrument complementing Radiohead's densely layered textures, and the way Young's electronically altered vocals on songs like "Transformer Man" convey the same sense of emotionally detached ambience.

It's probably not a coincidence that Radiohead occasionally will weave in a few lines of Young's classic "After the Gold Rush" during live performances of the *Kid A* track "Everything in Its Right Place."

We R in Control, We R in Control

Of all the genre-hopping wackiness that Neil Young became infamous for during the eighties, though, there are certainly any number of examples one could point toward as being less sincere, more misguided efforts than *Trans* (*Everybody's Rockin'*, anyone?).

But *Trans* alone remains the most visible reminder from that strangest of periods in Young's long career. Fairly or otherwise, the album that marked his brief flirtation with a Kraftwerk-influenced, synthesized brand of rock continues to be a flashpoint in the so-called eighties debate even now.

Even so, the album performed much better on the Billboard charts at the time than you might expect, peaking at a rather respectable #19. The fact that this happened despite a lack of any real support, either on radio or from the record company (even though the album represented his Geffen Records debut), has to be considered somewhat remarkable in retrospect.

The fact is, the techno-pop-flavored sounds of Young's then newly synthesized music would have fit right in with MTV's playlist at the time—heavy on videos from British syntho-pop acts like Soft Cell and Duran Duran as it was.

Still, Geffen refused to bankroll a video for *Trans*, even though Young offered to match the estimated $250,000 budget with his own money. The fact that the album still sold as well as it did was most likely due more to the curiosity factor than anything else.

Young's concept for the *Trans* video involved a hospital filled with robotic workers trying to get a baby to push a button, which of course was a metaphor for Young's own search for a communications breakthrough with Ben.

"That's what the record's about," Young told Jimmy McDonough in the biography *Shakey*. "If you listen to all the mechanized voices, if you read the lyrics, listen to the voices, it's clear that it's the beginning of my search for a way for a nonoral person, a severely physically handicapped nonoral person, to find some sort of interface for communication."

While *Trans* will never be mistaken for a classic Neil Young album on the same level as *Tonight's the Night* or *Rust Never Sleeps*, it has developed more than its fair share of fans in the years since it first shocked the music world back in 1982. As such, it holds up surprisingly well today.

Island in the Sun

Trans is an uneven album to be sure, owing mostly to its mixing of the electronically enhanced songs and all of their accompanying vocoders and synclaviers, and the much mellower-sounding leftover tracks from an aborted album recorded in Hawaii called *Island in the Sun.*

Young himself once described *Island in the Sun* as a collection of material further exploring his obsession with Indian culture ("Like an Inca") and his more mellow-sounding, tropical "water songs" ("A Little Thing Called Love"). On songs like the latter, the description mostly fits, since the leftover songs from the Hawaii sessions are also uncharacteristically watered down by the studio technology of the day.

Geffen ended up rejecting *Island in the Sun* altogether (it was supposed to be Young's debut album for the label) in favor of the far more left-of-field *Trans* project, which had by now expanded from an initially planned E.P. into a full-blown album.

In retrospect, this has to be considered somewhat ironic, since the former was probably the closest thing to the commercial album of more traditional "Neil Young" music that the label head had so publicly salivated for. Although the songs from the unreleased *Island in the Sun* (at least the ones that have been heard) are largely forgettable, they are still much closer to the more commercially palatable "Neil Young sound" cited by Geffen in his breach of contract lawsuit against the artist for refusing to make "Neil Young records."

Two of these songs, the lightweight pop of "Little Thing Called Love" and the slightly heavier-sounding "Like an Inca," bookend the otherwise electro-pop-heavy *Trans* album, making it almost seem like Young was still hedging his bets with this strange new musical direction.

By bookending *Trans* with more traditional-sounding songs, Neil Young actually seemed to be hiding the more heavily electronic-sounding tracks in the middle of this album.

Said the Condor to the Praying Mantis

Without question, *Trans* is one of the most controversial albums in the history of an artist with an already long record of making controversial albums. It is an album that even today divides Neil Young fans right down the middle.

Mostly, you either love it or you hate it. What is clear today, however, is that *Trans* was also a pivotal album in his career. The startling shift in musical direction—however briefly it lasted—and its equally stunning rejection by fans undoubtedly exercised a strong influence on Neil Young's career direction, for better or for worse, for many years to come.

The leftover songs from *Island in the Sun* remain the weakest tracks of the record. "Like an Inca" in particular becomes something of an afterthought, once it is stacked up against the much more powerful "Hitchhiker" version of the song that was eventually released on 2010's excellent *Le Noise.*

The album also has its share of goofier moments—the mechanized treatment of Young's Buffalo Springfield classic "Mr. Soul" comes most immediately to mind here. But for every misstep on the album, you'll also find more than a few keepers.

Once you can get past the barely recognizable voice of Neil Young channeled through a vocoder, "Sample and Hold"

Promotional poster for Neil Young's 1982 debut album for Geffen Records, *Trans.* The Kraftwerk-influenced synth-pop of this album divided Neil Young's fans right down the middle and signaled the beginning of his infamous, genre-hopping, "lost eighties" period.

continues to stand up as one of his better-sounding rockers from the eighties (especially on the blazing live version heard on the now hard-to-find *Live in Berlin* DVD).

The guitar parts here sound a bit more restrained than they do on more traditional, extended Neil Young barn burners like "Cowgirl in the Sand." But in their own way, they are just as powerful.

The solos here come in short, staccato bursts that stand in sharp contrast to the more drawn-out jamming of Young's better-known work with Crazy Horse. Even so, it is hard to imagine that if "Sample and Hold" were placed on a latter-day album like *Ragged Glory*, for example (with the amps turned up a notch or two), the song would not be the least bit out of place.

As one of the better, mostly undiscovered rockers in the Neil Young canon, "Sample and Hold" more than holds up today.

Power in Your Hand, Transformer Man

The other most misunderstood thing about *Trans* (at least at the time) was the way that, unbeknownst to the general public, the lyrics were so directly influenced by Neil Young's family situation and the health crisis hanging over his son, Ben.

If there is an overall lyrical theme to the album, it is certainly Young's ongoing search for a communications breakthrough for his severely handicapped son. Many of the lyrics of the songs from *Trans* serve as a metaphor for Neil Young's search, and none more so than "Transformer Man."

Listening to the lyrics of "Transformer Man" now—channeled through the vocoder treatments as they are—you can hear both the stark loneliness felt by a son trapped by the limitations of his own brain and body, and the love of a father searching desperately for that ever elusive answer.

When Neil's voice is run through the vocoder on this song, it takes on an eerily detached quality that at least one reviewer referred to as otherworldly. The description fits. On "Transformer Man," Young's voice sounds like something channeled from the furthest reaches of outer space.

Taken in the proper context that we as listeners can understand now all these years later, Ben Young was clearly the "Transformer Man" that Neil Young was referring to in lyrics like these: "Transformer man, Transformer Man . . . Every morning when I look into your eyes/I feel electrified by you. Oh yes."

Ten years later, Young would resurrect this song on a beautifully stripped-down acoustic version for MTV's then popular *Unplugged* series. This performance, which can be heard on his 1993 *Unplugged* album and DVD, reveals one of his most hauntingly beautiful songs, once removed from the admittedly distracting electronics of the *Trans* version.

"Transformer Man" may very well be one of Young's most underrated songs. It is certainly one of his loveliest.

When He Turns the Floodlights On Each Night, of Course the Herd Looks Perfect!

The release of *Trans* also coincided with Young's public reemergence as a touring artist.

On paper at least, the *Trans* tour was designed to be a massive spectacle on the same scale as similar undertakings by rock-'n'-roll legends from the classic rock era like Led Zeppelin and the Rolling Stones. In terms of execution, it proved to be anything but.

Inspired by a Rolling Stones stadium extravaganza he had witnessed on that band's 1981 *Tattoo You* tour, Young's return to the concert stage—at least in his mind—was designed not only as his coming out party, but as his own way of proving that he was in the same leagues as the big boys.

To that end, he hired Woodstock veteran Chip Monck to stage the sort of elaborate production spectacle that would blow the rest of his fellow sixties and seventies rock legends clean out of the water. Unfortunately, this ultimately proved to be a bad idea.

As an artist, Young obviously falls into the same legendary category as people like the Stones, of course. But let's face it, as a performer Neil Young is no Mick Jagger or Robert Plant. He may well be one of the greatest songwriters rock 'n' roll has ever produced, and he is certainly no slouch as a guitarist either. But when one thinks of Neil Young the artist, showmanship isn't likely to rank high on a list of his more notable attributes.

Looking back now on existing video documents of the European shows from the *Trans* tour, what one sees is an artist who is not really matched up to the big show atmosphere at all. Seeing Young all dressed up in the ridiculous eighties new wave rock attire of the day is actually quite humorous now—especially when his stylish new wave tie gets tangled up in his guitar during the solo on "Like a Hurricane." This is actually one of the funnier things that can be seen on the now hard-to-find *Live in Berlin* video.

But there were numerous other factors that doomed the *Trans* tour right from the start.

Although the set list was equally balanced to reflect all aspects of Young's career, the audiences mostly sat there stunned. The crowds responded favorably to the rockers like "Cinnamon Girl," of course, as well as the folkier, more familiar material like "Old Man."

But they also sat on their hands in silence during the much more alien-sounding new songs from the then still unreleased *Trans*.

For this biggest of Neil Young tours, the band—an all-star lineup consisting of players from all of his greatest albums like Ben Keith and Nils Lofgren—were likewise top-notch. At least they were when players like Buffalo Springfield bassist Bruce Palmer actually decided to show up sober. After an incident of heavy drinking that resulted in Young physically attacking Palmer in a hotel room after one show, Palmer was fired from the tour, only to later be rehired.

Another factor that doomed the *Trans* tour of Europe from the start was the staging.

Viewing the ramps that ran into the crowd today on existing documents like the *Live in Berlin* DVD, one can see an early precedent for the now standard multilevel staging of present-day stadium tours by superstar bands like U2.

But at the time, the logistics of transporting this equipment from city to city proved to be near impossible. These impracticalities, as well as Young somewhat overplaying his hand by booking shows in oversized venues he simply couldn't fill, only further compounded the nightmares of producing a stadium-sized show like the *Trans* tour. Once all of these factors were figured into the overall equation, it became abundantly clear that Young had a gigantic loser on his hands.

By the time the *Trans* tour made it back to the States, things became scaled back to a series of shows featuring a mostly acoustic evening with Young, along with a few leftover twists from the European shows like the big screens used for the Trans TV segments. Hosted by emcee Dan Clear (played by actor Newell Alexander), the video bits played between sets, and included live-action shots from the crowd and backstage.

But things were about to get even weirder as Young still had one surprise left up his sleeve. The world was about to meet the Shocking Pinks.

23

Computer Cowboy

The Best Neil Young Websites

N eil Young's presence on the Internet is represented by a broad range of both officially sanctioned websites and smaller, but no less worthy pages put together by the fans. These run the gamut from an official webpage (which, unlike many official artist sites, benefits greatly from Young's own ongoing involvement) to a number of unofficial fan sites. These range from Neil Young Internet radio stations (that play rare concerts and bootleg tracks!) to detailed listings of everything from his complete lyrics to the set lists of concerts dating back decades.

In nearly every instance, the sites run by the fans are labors of love (this is especially true in the case of the absolutely essential Thrasher's Wheat), that feature the painstaking, borderline nerdy sort of detail that could only be produced by the most truly devoted of Neil-phytes.

What follows is a brief list of the most essential stops in any Google search for Neil Young:

NeilYoung.com
http://www.neilyoung.com/

Although officially sanctioned, record label–supported artist websites can often suffer from a lack of actual artist involvement and a sanitizing of information from the label itself, this is most definitely not the case with Neil Young's official website.

NeilYoung.com was, for example, the first place you could stream entire prerelease tracks from such albums as *Are You Passionate?* and *Living with War.* Young also appears to have a definite input and ongoing involvement with the site, with regard to both its content and its look. His unique stamp is particularly visible on the splash page. Until recently, the site allowed visitors to click on parts of one of his cars to get to the really good stuff. A spring 2011 update (actually make that more of a do-over) introduced "Shakey's General Store," where visitors can purchase Neil Young merchandise such as albums, books, and T-shirts. The new design allows visitors to take a virtual tour, from the outside "porch" area (complete with the dog from the *Everybody Knows This Is Nowhere* sleeve—only here, he actually barks), to the rustic living room inside, the general store, and more.

Unlike many official artist sites, NeilYoung.com is updated regularly with the latest information, and you can often find news here you just won't get anywhere else (well, except for maybe Thrasher's Wheat).

As official artist sites with record label connections go, NeilYoung.com is definitely one of the better ones.

Neil Young Times

http://www.neilyoung.com/news/index.html

As an offshoot of NeilYoung.com, the Neil Young Times site is laid out like an actual newspaper, and is updated often with all of the latest-breaking NY news—including updates from the artist himself. The site also posts up-to-the-minute news and reviews of all things related to Neil Young as they happen. The NYT appears to have grown out of the original idea for a website newspaper attached to 2006's *Living with War* album.

Rare Neil Young E.P. combining tracks from several early albums and featuring the cover art from his debut.   *Courtesy of Tom Therme collection*

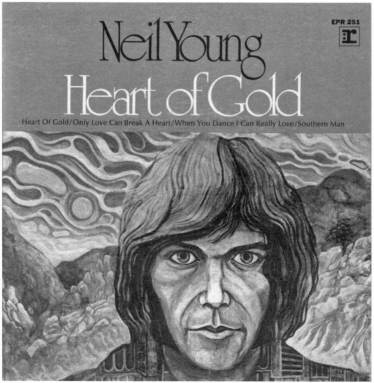

When his longtime musical foil Ben Keith died, Young's reaction to the passing of his friend and musical co-conspirator "Old Grain" was first published here, as was the artist's statement of support for Thrasher's Wheat when the future of that great unofficial Neil Young site briefly became a question mark in 2010.

Speaking of which . . .

Thrasher's Wheat/Neil Young News

http://neilyoungnews.thrasherswheat.org/

Thrasher's Wheat/Neil Young News is hands down the ultimate and unsurpassed nonofficial Neil Young fan site of the moment. It has also been the single greatest resource of information for this book. Without the direct help of the information found on this site, I couldn't possibly have completed this project.

There is simply no greater resource for breaking news and up-to-the-second information on Neil Young anywhere on the Internet, period.

But even going beyond superfan Thrasher's near daily updates on the Neil Young News splash page, where else can you find the amazingly detailed information contained in Thrasher's own Neil Young FAQ—stuff ranging from entries like "Why was "Cortez the Killer" banned in Spain?" to "What is the deal with *Greendale*?"

Thrasher's Wheat also features detailed analysis on the connections between Neil Young and artists ranging from Dylan and Springsteen to Radiohead, Eddie Vedder, and Kurt Cobain. It is also the place where you can sign the online petition for Young to release the "missing link in the Ditch Trilogy" (that would be the album *Time Fades Away*, by the way) on CD (they have gathered over twenty thousand signatures to date). Now, that's some dedication.

Finally, the site is home to the Internet's largest community of Neil Young fanatics, which has made for some spirited discussions over the years on subjects ranging from his infamous 2006 antiwar (and anti-Bush) themed *Living with War* album, to more cantankerous debates that drew words of support from none other than Neil Young himself (on his own Neil Young Times) after Thrasher briefly considered shutting it down.

On a side note, Thrasher's help in putting together this book has been an invaluable gift to this author. My hat is off to you, sir.

Rust Radio

http://www.rustradio.org/

So you say you want an Internet radio station that plays all Neil Young, all the time—including all of those rare concerts and unreleased songs? Then point your browser right here.

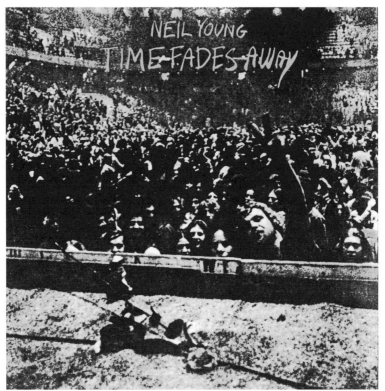

Time Fades Away, the album that kicked off the Ditch Trilogy. The website Thrasher's Wheat includes a petition for its release on CD that has drawn thousands of signatures. *Courtesy of Tom Therme collection*

Sugar Mountain—Neil Young Set Lists

http://www.sugarmtn.org/

For every single set list, from every single concert that Neil Young has ever performed, both as a solo artist and with groups like the Squires, Buffalo Springfield, and CSN&Y, your search begins and ends right here. This site came in particularly handy as I compiled my own list of the personal favorite Neil Young shows detailed in chapter 20 of this book.

Human Highway

http://human-highway.org/

For complete lyrics to every song Neil Young has ever released (and many that he hasn't) from the Squires all the way up to the *Archives* and 2009's *Fork in the Road*, Human Highway is your one-stop resource.

Each album is broken down both alphabetically and chronologically, and in many cases also includes lyrics for songs recorded for the albums that didn't make the final cut. The entire unreleased *Chrome Dreams* album, for example, even warrants its very own entry.

Human Highway also includes the latest Neil Young news (Bad News Beat) as well as sections devoted to his movies, his ongoing electronically powered car project the Linc/Volt, and is also home to a large mailing list community of Neil-phytes.

As a resource for my own research for this book, I probably couldn't have titled more than half of my chapters without these guys. We're still waiting for that update for *Le Noise* and beyond on the lyrics listings, though.

Hyperrust
http://hyperrust.org/

Once considered the gold standard of all Neil Young fan sites, this position has become largely overtaken in recent years by Thrasher's Wheat.

Even so, Hyperrust contains a treasure trove of archival information, ranging from set lists to the sorts of things that nerdier fans tend to obsess over (like how many times Young has performed certain songs in concert). Although Hyperrust is without question a great resource, the site still suffers greatly from a lack of recent updates. The fact also remains that for all of the great information contained there, the site also has a very non-user friendly interface. Because of this, it can be a rather difficult task to navigate through it all. Although the love is clearly there, the practicality of getting through it all largely is not. The bottom line here is that although Hyperrust is still up and running in name, one gets the distinct impression that its webmaster has long since left the building.

24

No Matter Where I Go, I Never Hear My Record on the Radio

The Shocking Pinks, *Old Ways,* and Farm Aid

S o how does one follow up a less than well-received album of strange computerized synth-pop?

In the case of the increasingly musical schizophrenic that was Neil Young in the eighties, you take a cue from the Stray Cats and release an album of fifties-flavored rockabilly tracks less than a year later.

Clocking in at less than a half hour of running time in an era when compact disc technology was just beginning to open up new possibilities for the long-form album, *Everybody's Rockin'* is an easy candidate (along with *Landing on Water*) for being among the worst albums of Neil Young's career. Apparently the fans thought likewise, given the album's dismal Billboard chart performance, where it peaked at #46.

With tensions between Young and Geffen Records already running high, there has been no small amount of speculation over the years that Young may have delivered this album to the label out of nothing but spite, after they rejected the early version of his country album *Old Ways.* The storyline here basically goes that when the label instead asked for the artist to make a "rock-'n'-roll album," Neil Young simply obliged by quite literally giving them one.

Although *Trans* may have been perceived as a bad idea by fans (many of whom have since reassessed that position, as detailed in chapter 22 of this book), there is still no doubt that Young's artistic aim was mostly true (if perhaps somewhat misguided) on that record. While Neil Young's sanity in releasing *Trans* may have been in question, his artistic sincerity was most definitely not.

Everybody's Rockin', on the other hand, for better or worse, comes off as mostly a rare and frankly arrogant case of pure artistic indulgence. At best, it plays like a sort of bad joke. At worst, it is quite possibly one of the most misguided vanity projects ever put to vinyl by an artist of Neil Young's stature. Either way, the album seemed like the latest, and most obvious example so far, in the ongoing eighties story of an artist intent on committing career suicide.

Even today, outside of a few bright moments like "Payola Blues," a biting commentary on the "pay for play" practices that were still secretly happening at many radio stations at the time, and the Crazy Horse leftover "Wonderin'," the album is barely listenable.

As fun in a goofy sort of way as something like "Kinda Fonda Wanda" might have seemed on paper, it just wasn't the kind of thing you expected from a "serious artist" like Neil Young. His cover of the Sun Records–period Elvis song "Mystery Train" likewise did him no favors, essentially reducing that classic to a watered-down and overproduced poor man's karaoke version of the original.

They're Rockin' in the White House All Night Long

As if Young wasn't alienating his fan base enough already with his increasingly odd shifts in artistic direction, the man who once wrote songs like "Ohio" with its "tin soldiers and Nixon coming," also seemed to be taking a hard and abrupt turn toward the political right.

In addition to a series of interviews championing President Ronald Reagan's hard-line politics (which would reach their peak during the resurrected country album *Old Ways* a short time later), Young was even invoking Reagan in the lyrics of *Everybody's Rockin's* title track. This song found Ronnie and Nancy dancing on the White House lawn to Neil Young music that could have just as easily been written for the then hit TV show "Happy Days."

The only thing missing from the new right-wing politics of born-again red-neck Neil Young was an endorsement of the fundamentalist Christian rhetoric of televangelists like the 700 Club's Pat Robertson and the Moral Majority's Jerry Falwell.

Even so, his live performances of the *Everybody's Rockin'* material with his latest band the Shocking Pinks could be a lot of fun. Dressed in matching pink outfits, and backed by a horn section (which included Ben Keith of all people) and a group of female vocalists (including his wife Pegi) dubbed the Pinkettes, Young debuted this latest musical direction during the otherwise mostly solo American leg of the *Trans* tour.

Perhaps because they were still largely shell-shocked by the synthesized vocals of the *Trans* material, when Neil brought out the Shocking Pinks for the surprise encore set, complete with their greased-back hair and pink combs being tossed into the audience, it probably seemed almost like a relief.

This novelty, however, did not translate into record sales.

If a Man Is Making Music, They Ought to Let His Record Play

Some of the material that wound up on *Everybody's Rockin'* had first been recorded for the original *Old Ways* album, recorded earlier that year in Nashville with producer Elliot Mazer once again at the helm, and with much of the original *Harvest* crew of musicians (Ben Keith, etc.) back in tow as part of the band.

Although the majority of the album was straight country, the handful of rockabilly-flavored tracks were the only parts of the album the executives at Geffen seemed interested in, once they actually heard the record.

One of these executives, Eddie Rosenblatt, went so far as to call the album "too country," which landed him a particularly special spot on Neil Young's permanent shit list. But the consensus at Geffen was for Neil Young to go back to the drawing board and expand on the fifties rock-flavored tracks.

So, while rumors persist to this day that Young gave Geffen the Shocking Pinks out of spite ("if they want a rock-'n'-roll record, I'll give them one"), it is also at least partially true that he delivered Geffen exactly the record they had asked for with *Everybody's Rockin'*. In retrospect, this makes David Geffen's decision to file a lawsuit against his most visible if frustrating artist an even stranger chapter in this already strange story.

Still, that is exactly what David Geffen did. Citing Young's "failure to deliver Neil Young albums" to the label—and using both *Trans* and *Everybody's Rockin'* as examples—the basis of the lawsuit against filed in November 1983 is one of the most curious in music history.

By essentially saying that Neil Young was guilty of making records "uncharacteristic of the artist," Geffen's suit has to be something of a first in terms of high strangeness in rock'n' roll legal history. Even when it is placed in the context of the often volatile marriage between rock 'n' roll's leftover sixties hippie values and the multimillion-dollar business of corporate commerce that governed the

T-shirt promoting *Everybody's Rockin'*, Neil Young's rockabilly album with the Shocking Pinks.   *Courtesy of Tom Therme collection*

music business even back then, the premise of this legal action is still enough to make you scratch your head in bewilderment.

It was one thing for Bruce Springsteen's former manager, after being dumped for a rock critic-turned-producer, to use the legal system to keep his one-time charge from recording (which is exactly what Mike Appel did with his suit against Springsteen and Jon Landau after *Born to Run*).

It was quite another for a record label to sue an artist for delivering albums deemed as simply not being commercial enough for radio or retail. This also coming despite Young's long history of stubbornly following his own creative muse regardless of any resulting commercial fallout, as well as Geffen's own initial promise of creative control once his company signed the artist for a million bucks an album. A decision they would later come to regret, by the way . . .

Not surprisingly, Young and Elliot Roberts filed their own countersuit, and for the next eighteen months, the war was on.

Here Comes the Night, Here Comes the Anger

Although Young would eventually return to his eighties genre-hopping ways by resurrecting his country project *Old Ways*, he first attempted to make one of those more characteristically rock-'n'-roll "Neil Young albums" desired so badly by his label.

At first, things looked promising.

Calling once again on the Horse, Young played a series of blistering concerts at the Catalyst Club in Santa Cruz that have been described by fans as producing some of the greatest racket Neil had ever made yet with his greatest rock band.

These concerts are documented on the now hard-to-find bootleg *Catalytic Reaction* (there were also copies of the shows released on a bootleg called *Touch the Night*, named for one of the new songs premiered there). Great soundboard recordings of a few of these songs, including "Barstool Blues" and "Touch the Night," can also still be found fairly easily today on the great bootleg boxed set collection *A Perfect Echo* (see chapter 19 for more on Young's bootlegs).

Recording sessions for a potential Neil Young and Crazy Horse reunion album did not go nearly as well, however.

Despite the presence of David Briggs back in the producer's chair, sessions at Broken Arrow, in Los Angeles, and later on at New York's Record Plant ultimately failed to produce a new record. By most accounts, the biggest problem with the sessions was Neil Young himself. Rather than allowing the Horse to do what they do best, laying down a loosely structured but funky foundation for Young to soar over with Old Black, he reversed his usual lackadaisical recording style and instead seemed to obsess on studio tinkering and other weird details.

The story is best told in Jimmy McDonough's *Shakey*. But in a nutshell, Young seemed to be particularly obsessed with getting a big drum sound.

During this period in the eighties, big drums were all the rage in rock music, thanks to records being produced for bands like U2, XTC, and the Police by producers such as Steve Lillywhite and Hugh Padgham. The so-called Phil Collins sound was also very much in vogue, courtesy of that particular drummer's solo albums and those with his band Genesis. Collins had even gone so far as to bring his big, bombastic drums to records he produced for outside artists such as former Abba vocalist Frida.

The novelty of big drums that overshadowed nearly everything else in their path was one that thankfully wore off once the eighties were finally over.

Young eventually got his big drum sound, recording many of the same songs intended for the original 1984 reunion album with Crazy Horse on *Landing on Water*, the underwhelming recording he made in 1986 with session musicians including veteran Eagles producer Danny Kortchmar and drummer Steve Jordan. There will be much more on that in the next chapter of this book.

Are You Ready for the Country?

Meanwhile, the musical high strangeness of Young's "lost decade" continued to grow even stranger.

Turning back to the country sounds of the thought-to-be-scrapped *Old Ways* album, he returned to the concert stage with yet another new group. The International Harvesters were comprised of a combination of Stray Gators holdovers like Ben Keith and Spooner Oldham, and a more authentically countrified breed of Nashville cats like Cajun fiddler Rufus Thibodeaux and guitarist/vocalist Anthony "Sweet Pea" Crawford.

With traditional rock promoters and fans alike understandably a little gun-shy about just what might constitute a Neil Young concert in 1984, the International Harvesters chose to take their road show out on the country circuit instead.

Playing the sort of honky-tonk joints, cowboy rodeos, and county fairs that were part and parcel of the country music touring business in those days before Garth Brooks and Kenny Chesney were filling stadiums, Young was once again reinventing himself as an artist (even if only for the time being).

In doing so, he also showed less reservation than ever before about completely alienating his traditional fan base. While his new fans in the country music community seemed to at least somewhat embrace his authenticity as a newly born-again country redneck, Young's increasingly chatty nature with the press had to be rattling some nerves with the hardcores.

In interview after interview, he railed against his former life as a hippie rock star, even going so far as to claim on at least one occasion (and probably more) that he was giving up rock 'n' roll for good. In one such interview, he somewhat humorously claimed that performing at county fairs beat "playing for a bunch of stoned hippies at the Fillmore."

Even more disconcerting to some fans was his hard turn to the political right.

In these same interviews, Young all but disowned his past as the sixties hippie who had once written songs like "Ohio." He was particularly vocal in

ie Nelson, Neil Young, and John Mellencamp relaxing backstage at Farm Aid.   *Photo by Kim Reed*

his embrace of President Ronald Reagan, calling former Democratic President Jimmy Carter a "wimp" who had given away the Panama Canal and praising Reagan's unapologetic hard-line stance on everything from foreign policy to his union-busting "trickle-down economics."

For some fans, Young particularly crossed the line when referring to AIDS with a comment about the "faggots behind the counter at the grocery store."

Although the International Harvesters initially were somewhat lacking in any musical chemistry, and some of the early shows were spotty, the band eventually seemed to come together and produce some memorable shows. Some of the better performances from the period, including countrified reworkings of songs like "Southern Pacific" as well as previously unheard material like "Grey Riders," were eventually released in 2010 as part of the *Archives Performance Series* on the album *A Treasure.*

Original fans who attended some of these concerts may have been wise to tuck their hair up under a stevedore cap. But those who did also got the occasional treat, like the reputedly quite decent versions of "Down by the River" and "Heart of Gold" from Young's new band of outlaw country pickers.

As we've already noted, Young also made a number of new friends within the country music community.

Some of these, like David Allen Coe, opened many of Young's shows on the country circuit. Others, like Waylon Jennings, scored hits recording their own versions of Neil Young songs from the period like "Are You Ready for the Country."

Of all these friendships, though, it was Young's introduction to Willie Nelson that would have the most lasting impact, eventually leading to the yearly *Farm Aid* benefit concerts that he remains a partner in to this day.

Even so, the ever dwindling base of Neil Young's original fans had to be wondering what could possibly be next? Even the possibility of an album of Gregorian chants by a converted Buddhist monk named Neil Young, or maybe a gangsta rap album, didn't seem to be too far out of left field at the time.

MC Shakey, anyone?

It's Hard to Teach a Dinosaur a New Trick

What eventually did come next was a revamped version of *Old Ways*, which in contrast to the original album's more authentic country flavor, offered a watered-down version that also suffered from overproduction (Young was still quite enamored with the new digital technology of the day at the time).

Even a duet with Willie Nelson on the song "Are There Any More Real Cowboys" suffered from a bad case of the overdubbed vocals that Young had once been so vehemently opposed to on his albums.

After Young threatened (yet again) to abandon rock 'n' roll altogether and "turn into George Jones," the contentious lawsuit with Geffen Records was also finally settled. In exchange for agreeing to release *Old Ways*, he promised to deliver one of those more commercially palatable "Neil Young" rock-'n'-roll albums the label had so desperately wanted from their most stubbornly mercurial charge.

The album that Geffen eventually got, 1986's *Landing on Water*, as well as a follow-up album with Crazy Horse (1987's *Life*) wasn't exactly the "*Harvest II*" they had probably imagined.

But the real victory for Geffen came in the deal renegotiated for the remainder of the original contract.

For Young's final two records with Geffen, his advance of a million dollars per album was cut in half (to $500,000). Neil Young also delivered his *Lucky Thirteen* collection of songs and outtakes from the Geffen years to the label for free. The album was released several years later in 1993, following Young's early nineties artistic and commercial comeback with the albums *Freedom* and *Ragged Glory*.

Where the Cattle Graze and an Old Grey Barn Still Stands

In July 1985, Young took his newest incarnation of the International Harvesters to the stage at the massive Live Aid show organized by Bob Geldof to benefit African hunger relief efforts.

The historic concert was telecast worldwide by MTV to an audience estimated at the time to be in the billions. The less-than-stellar TV production is more memorable today for its endless mid-song interruptions by babbling MTV "vee-jays" and its lecturing pleas for donations by irritating celebrities like Sally Field than it is for the music itself.

Even so, the Live Aid concert was the biggest event of its kind since Woodstock. Only this time around, it took place on two continents, with concerts in England and in America in Philadelphia. Performer Phil Collins managed to make appearances at both concerts in the same day, jumping the two continents by flying aboard the Concorde. The cause was also conceived as something far more real than the idealistic "three days of peace, love and music" of the legendary 1969 hippie fest at Woodstock.

Young's two sets that day—with the Harvesters and with a reunited for the event Crosby, Stills, Nash, and Young—were hardly memorable on a day that also included the cream of the era's superstar rock-'n'-roll talent. CSN&Y's set was particularly horrendous.

More than that, though, Young's two sets were easy to miss considering the rest of the mind-boggling lineup of talent assembled. From Madonna to Dylan, from Queen to Run-DMC, everyone who was anyone in rock and pop music played a set at Live Aid that day. There were reunions by heavy metal bands ranging from Black Sabbath to Led Zeppelin. There were once-in-a-lifetime pairings like the one between Mick Jagger and David Bowie. And there were also historic, career-making performances like the one turned in that day by an up-and-coming Irish band called U2.

But Live Aid also served as the genesis for another event, one whose seed was born out of a comment made by Bob Dylan during his performance at the mega concert. When Dylan said that it would be nice to see some of the millions generated to benefit starving Africans set aside to help the American farmers who are such a crucial part of the world's food chain, Neil Young was an artist in attendance who stood up and took notice.

Although Farm Aid is widely perceived as the brainchild of Willie Nelson—and rightfully so—Young's involvement in the annual benefit concerts for American farmers is no less significant.

It was Young who first discussed the idea of Farm Aid with Nelson—following Dylan's comments at Live Aid—and he hasn't missed an appearance at a single Farm Aid concert in the nearly thirty years since the first one was held at the University of Illinois in 1985.

Dave Matthews and Neil Young in the Farm Aid press tent.   *Photo by Mary Andrews*

Along with Nelson, John Mellencamp, and Dave Matthews, Neil Young also sits on Farm Aid's board of directors to this day. The concerts themselves occur on a mostly annual basis, with the venues ranging over the years from Ames, Iowa, to Auburn, Washington. The musical entertainment at these shows over the years has also been strictly top shelf, including a broad mix of mostly rock and country artists.

In addition to the expected annual performances from Mellencamp, Matthews, Nelson, and Neil Young, Live Aid has presented a diverse range of artists ranging from John Conlee to Jerry Lee Lewis to Wilco to Norah Jones. Dylan himself has also performed, honoring his original commitment to the cause from his original comments made at 1985's Live Aid concert.

The shows also break tradition from most major rock concerts in the form of their concession stands, which always feature organic food products grown and produced locally by farmers.

But some of the most memorable moments of the Farm Aid shows over the years have been provided by Neil Young, and they haven't always been exclusively musical ones. At the very first Farm Aid show in Illinois, he read an impassioned letter to then President Reagan from the stage—appealing to the "America first" values that he probably still believed Reagan represented at the time—by not turning a blind eye to the plight of the American farmer. The same letter was later published as a full-page ad in *USA Today*, paid for by Young himself.

A few years later at the Farm Aid concert in Ames, Iowa, he had some pointed words for the administration of then newly elected Democratic President Bill

Clinton, and in particular for Vice President Al Gore and Agriculture Secretary Mike Espy for not coming to show their support.

Not long afterwards, Willie Nelson and a group of American farmers were granted a private meeting with Espy.

One final footnote here.

When Neil Young broached the idea of releasing a five-song E.P. of new material to benefit Farm Aid to his good friends at Geffen Records, it was predictably rejected.

Strobe Lights Flashin' on the Overpass

Landing on Water, Life, Muddy Track, and the Bridge School

lthough Neil Young's next two albums for Geffen Records—1986's *Landing on Water* and 1987's *Life*—signaled a return to the more familiar, commercially viable rock sound everyone from the fans to the record label claimed to have been waiting for, both landed with the record-buying public with a resounding thud.

To put it in the vernacular of the record industry weasel, *Landing on Water*—Young's attempt at duplicating the commercially then in vogue "big drum" sound of eighties pop and rock records by using studio musicians and "modern" digital recording technology—was a big stiff.

Peaking at a dismal #58 on the Billboard charts, *Landing on Water* holds the dubious distinction of being the first "rock" record of Young's career to fail to crack the top fifty of Billboard's top 200 albums chart (although its predecessor *Old Ways* only made it to #75 on that chart, the fact that this was a country album excludes it from consideration on this list). Despite the return of Crazy Horse to active duty, the very next Neil Young album, *Life*, did even worse, stalling at #75.

When viewed in retrospect all these years later, both of these albums would have to place pretty high on an all-time "hall of shame" within the Neil Young canon. As often as the goofy *Everybody's Rockin'* has been cited as being among his worst albums ever, it often gets a pass anyway because it represents such a great punch line to an otherwise brilliant career. Today, many fans tend to view Young's fifties rockabilly album as a joke at best and an insignificant knockoff at worst.

Not so with *Landing on Water*.

A Funny Thing Happened Yesterday, I Felt the Pressure in a TV Way

For *Landing on Water*, Young ditched his usual band of cronies (David Briggs, Crazy Horse, Ben Keith, etc.), and chose instead to work with L.A. studio veterans Danny Kortchmar and Steve Jordan.

Kortchmar's studio credits at the time included hits for artists like Don Henley and Jackson Browne, both as a producer and as a studio musician. Jordan, on the other hand, was widely regarded at the time as one of the most bad-ass drummers around. His name had in fact come up several times in the past, specifically in discussions with David Briggs and others as a drummer Young might want to consider working with.

Kortchmar, on the other hand, was the sort of studio pro whose glossy approach to making records by Henley and others was about as far removed from Young's more spontaneous method of flying by the seat of your pants in the recording studio as it gets. The funny thing about this is that in retrospect, Kortchmar's slicker approach to recording may have been exactly why Young recruited him for the project.

But there was absolutely no doubt as to why he recruited Jordan.

Like many artists in the mid- to late eighties, Young had drums on the brain—or more specifically, a particular drum sound. Previous attempts to capture this sound in the studio with Crazy Horse had resulted in a dead end, but had left Young undeterred in what ultimately became a fool's quest to find it.

His continued fascination with synthesizers and electronic sounds, as well as the then just emerging new digital recording technology of the day, are among the chief factors that, when taken together, conspired to make *Landing on Water* one of his more curiously bad recordings ever.

The end result is arguably the worst album of Young's career. If nothing else, *Landing on Water* certainly stands alone as the least timeless-sounding of all his albums—including the early eighties, time-stamped techno of *Trans*. Listening to

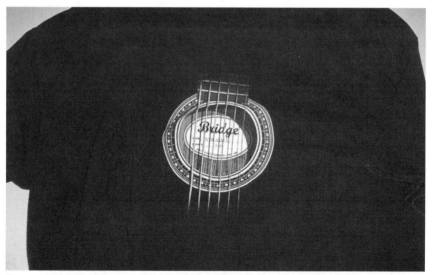

Concert T-shirt for the annual Bridge School Benefit shows in Mountain View, California. Neil Young headlines the show every year, and Pegi Young sits on the Board of Directors.
Courtesy of Tom Therme collection

this album today feels like walking through a minefield of bad eighties musical clichés. This becomes even more evident when watching the video clips from the album, but we'll get to more on that in a minute.

The songs on *Landing on Water* were mostly made with a core trio of Young on guitar, Jordan on drums, and Kortchmar playing bass parts mostly through various synthesized keyboards. With Kortchmar—a name synonymous with the often criticized, soulless L.A. sound of the eighties—credited as album producer, there has been a perhaps unfair tendency over the years to lay blame for the ultimate dud that was *Landing on Water* squarely at his doorstep.

But according to most insider accounts, it was in fact Neil Young himself who was responsible for calling the shots on this album. Those loopy-sounding synthesizers that make "People on the Street" sound like a bad outtake from a rejected Queen record? That oddly misplaced boys' choir heard on "Violent Side"? All of these were Young's ideas, according to those present, along with all of those excessive vocal overdubs. One interesting side note here is the fact that his fascination with the new digital recording technology of the day is something he would come to quite vociferously disassociate himself from in later years.

But in the end, *Landing on Water* is all about the drums.

Steve Jordan's playing on the record certainly can't be faulted here—he is as steady as a rock, even if it is in a robotic, metronomic sort of way. But the sound itself—rather than appropriating the big boom of Phil Collins, or the heavy percussive drone heard on Steve Lillywhite and Hugh Padgham's productions for early U2 and XTC—is instead an irritating, tinny sound. Basically, the drums on *Landing on Water* sound like they are being played on trash can lids.

Unfortunately, these same drums ultimately overwhelm everything else on *Landing on Water*—including the lead guitar, which should be the focal point of any rock album by Neil Young.

Many of the songs that wound up on the album, such as "Violent Side" "Hard Luck Stories," and "Touch the Night," were in fact leftovers from the blazing set of shows Young had played with Crazy Horse a few years earlier. But where the original power of those songs is on full display on bootlegs like *Catalytic Reaction* (from the legendary 1984 shows at Santa Cruz's Catalyst Club), on *Landing on Water* they simply collapse under the weight of all the excessive production. The drums in particular sound like the snap, crackle, and pop of Rice Krispies swirling in a pool of stale milk.

Capsized in Excess, if You Know What I Mean

Since this is the eighties we are talking about, Young also made a number of promotional videos for *Landing on Water*. Although you probably have to figure that given the opportunity, he might want to take some of those clips back now, they are also quite hilarious when viewed today.

The video for "Touch the Night" is in particular, a classic.

When "Touch the Night" made its debut at the 1984 shows with Crazy Horse at places like the Catalyst, the song played like a sequel to "Like a Hurricane," complete with Young's blazing guitar playing against a swirling keyboard arrangement.

In the version heard on *Landing on Water*, some of his original guitar attack remains intact, although much of it is blotted out by an arrangement typical of this album. There are more of those irritating choir vocals, and the drums are again a major point of distraction.

The funniest thing, though, is seeing him in the video—looking not unlike Clark Kent with slicked-back hair and thick, black rimmed glasses—as an obnoxious television reporter covering the aftermath of a traffic accident (the "strobe lights flashin' on the overpass" referenced in the song lyrics).

Directed by Tim Pope, who made several of Young's eighties videos including those on *Landing on Water* and earlier clips like "Wonderin'," recalled the making of "Touch the Night" in a post on his blog (misspelled and non-capitalized words are uncorrected here, in order to maintain the integrity of the original posting):

> working with neil was always fun, and he liked me to speak to him "in character," this one being "george." after the police car screeches off, my voice says two things to george—an expletive, at the speed of its departure, and then i mention a "restaurant up the road." i only decided to use the ambience of the live sound later to make things feel edgier. similarly, i shot on video and hanheld camera to make things real and edgy. considering i had not, at this time, watched too much yank t.v., not a bad parody, i'd say and perhaps even foerunner to cop reality shows you now see two-a-penny. the mustachioed cop and the other were real cops and this for me was a real eye-opener, culturally—that cops in america could "act cops" just as well as actors could. i believe we were the first people after sly stallone to close down a freeway for filming purposes whey-hey!

The video for "Weight of the World" is likewise atrocious. As if the synthesizers weren't bad enough, seeing Neil Young dancing through this mess in matching white suit and ducktails is simply hilarious. Both of these videos can be found online by doing a search for them on YouTube. Bad as they are, they also have an endearing quality to them as fairly classic eighties period pieces.

However, not everything about *Landing on Water* is overproduced drums and bad videos. One of the album's few highlights is the very underrated "Hippie Dream."

In this song, Neil takes direct aim at his friend and former CSN&Y bandmate David Crosby—who, at the time was deeply mired in a series of very public, self-destructive incidents linked to his severe addiction to crack cocaine. Young's lyrics in the song about how the "Wooden Ships were a hippie dream" and how they were "capsized in excess, if you know what I mean" may have seemed harsh at the time. But behind the scenes, he was also reaching out to his friend to clean himself up, including a promise to re-form CSN&Y once he did.

Another bright spot during the *Landing on Water* period was Young's introduction to Niko Bolas, who was a recording engineer on the album.

During the *Landing on Water* sessions, Bolas endeared himself to Young almost immediately. As a newcomer to Neil Young's world, Bolas quickly gained respect as someone who could be counted on for direct, honest opinions that were unclouded by any type of starstruck idol worship. Working together as the "Volume Dealers" (named for Bolas's tendency to shred speakers), Young and Bolas would go on to record several more albums together—a collaboration that would bear particularly significant rewards on Neil's 1989 "comeback" album, *Freedom*.

That's Why We Don't Wanna Be Good

One of the most interesting—and encouraging, at least if you are a fan—things about Young's next album (which proved to be his last for Geffen Records) is the fact that even though he had yet to completely shake the digital technology

Single release of "Weight of the World" from *Landing on Water*. This single was one of many from the mid-eighties period to be accompanied by an embarrassing video.   *Courtesy of Tom Therme collection*

bug that bit him so hard during *Landing on Water*, he did seem to be interested in making actual rock music again.

Life is an album that was made against the backdrop of the impending end of Young's often contentious relationship with Geffen Records. With the lawsuits settled, and both sides looking for a mutually acceptable way out, he closed out his commitment to the label with an album made up of live recordings of new material with Crazy Horse.

Not that there weren't any problems.

The tour was by most accounts a total disaster. With advance billing as "the third best garage band in the world," Young took Crazy Horse out on the road with a wild show that at least attempted to recapture some of the crazy vibe from *Rust Never Sleeps*.

The biggest problem by this point was that all of his musical schizophrenia the past several years had resulted in a general loss of good will between artist and audience. For a fan base whose patience had been severely tested in the eighties, many felt Young had simply used all of that up. All of the goofy props in the world (which included giant mechanized cockroaches for this tour) no longer mattered to an audience who had long since grown indifferent to Young's ever-shifting genre experiments.

Complicating matters further was Young's stubborn insistence on duplicating the studio sounds of *Landing on Water* onstage, using much of the same gadgetry he had employed in the recording studio.

As a result, Crazy Horse's normally jam-happy rhythm section Billy Talbot and Ralph Molina were forced to adapt to a new environment of drum machines and the like. The newest member of Crazy Horse, guitarist Frank "Poncho" Sampedro, fared slightly better, which probably explains how he ended up sticking around to play in bands like the Bluenotes after Young sacked the rest of Crazy Horse for the umpteenth time.

Tempers during the tour also flared frequently. Some of these incidents are captured to quite hilarious effect on *Muddy Track*, Neil Young's home movie document from the tour. *Muddy Track* has never been released, and few have seen it. But portions of the film—including some of those knock-down backstage fights and arguments—can be seen in Jim Jarmusch's Crazy Horse documentary, *Year of the Horse*, made roughly a decade later.

Live from a Rusted Out Garage

A much better, but equally hard-to-find document of the 1986 tour, however, is Larry "L.A." Johnson's excellent *Live from a Rusted Out Garage*, which many fans maintain is the best Neil Young and Crazy Horse concert film ever made.

Originally made as a special for the premium cable network Showtime, *Rusted Out Garage* captures a rare night on the tour where both Young and the rest of the Horse have recaptured the spook. His guitar shredding on "Down by the River" and "Like a Hurricane" is a particular highlight, and there are also some very funny bits with the late comedian Sam Kinnison as the stereotypical pissed-off neighbor of the "third best garage band in the world." Other highlights include the return of "Trans TV" intermission emcee Dan Clear (Newell Alexander).

It's Such a Long Walk Home

Despite all of the problems with a tour that nearly everyone agreed was a piece of shit, somehow an album was still salvaged from the mess. Like *Rust Never Sleeps* before it, 1987's *Life* was conceived as a live recording containing all new original material. But even though the album was made with what is arguably Neil Young's greatest band, and with David Briggs back in the producer's chair, the results were far less successful.

Like *Landing on Water* immediately before it, *Life* sinks under the weight of excessive studio tinkering and overproduction. It has rightfully become all but forgotten by fans. The album does, however, contain a handful of decent tracks that nonetheless stand out.

"Prisoners of Rock 'n' Roll" is a raucous little number that takes dead aim at David Geffen in lyrics like "We never listen to the record company man, They try to change us and ruin our band," not to mention the humorously honest observation "that's why we don't wanna be good." "Inca Queen" is another of Young's many Indian-themed songs, and a worthy, if less spectacular successor to songs like "Pocahontas" and "Cortez the Killer." On "Last of a Dying Breed," he continues to proudly wave the Farm Aid banner.

"Road of Plenty," another great song from the period (which inexplicably didn't make it onto the record), would eventually morph into "Eldorado" on 1989's spectacular return to artistic form with the *Freedom* album.

When a Child Is Born to Live

On October 13, 1986, Young performed the first of what has become a mostly annual tradition of concerts benefiting a cause that hits very close to home. Although he missed the next year in 1987, he has performed at the annual Bridge School concerts at Shoreline Amphitheatre in Mountain View, California, every single year since.

For that first year, Young was joined onstage by a reunited CSN&Y, as well as an all-star lineup including the likes of Bruce Springsteen, Don Henley, and Tom Petty. Over the years, the annual concerts (which have since been expanded into a two-day event) have brought together a staggering array of talent ranging from David Bowie, Patti Smith, Wilco, and Elvis Costello to repeat performers like Pearl Jam. Young has also performed at the shows with nearly all of his many bands, including CSN&Y, Crazy Horse, the Stray Gators, and in 2010, a reunited Buffalo Springfield.

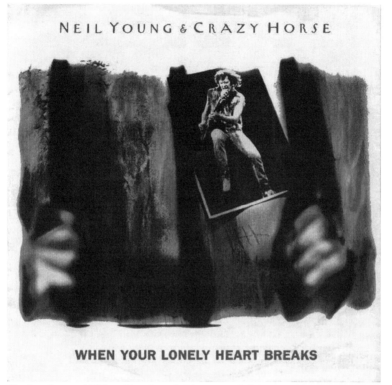

Single release of "When Your Lonely Heart Breaks" from the *Life* album.
Courtesy of Tom Therme collection

Founded in part by Pegi Young (along with Jim Forderer and Dr. Marilyn Buzolich), the Bridge School grew at least in part out of Neil and Pegi's own painful experiences finding a good therapy program for their son Ben. The Bridge School's mission, simply put, is to help children afflicted with severe disabilities like Ben to achieve their fullest potential through a combination of education and technology. Pegi Young continues to sit on the Bridge School's board of directors to this day.

We Don't Wanna Be Watered Down, Takin' Orders from Record Company Clowns

As 1987 drew to a close, the acrimonious situation between Neil Young and his record label Geffen also finally came to a merciful end. Although conventional wisdom over the years maintains that Young was simply dropped by the label once the legal problems were finally sorted out, the truth is that Elliot Roberts had been in negotiations with both Geffen and the head of Young's former label Mo Ostin for a return to Reprise Records.

Single release of "Long Walk Home" from the *Life* album.
Courtesy of Tom Therme collection

As part of the deal, Young delivered *Lucky Thirteen*, a collection of his hits, misses, and outtakes from the troubled years with Geffen to the label for free. But not before threatening—possibly out of spite or as one final, grand "f-you" gesture—to give them what Sampedro called an album of "crickets farting" called *Meadow Dusk*. The album has been alternately described as either resembling a quieter version of *Arc*—Young's album of nothing but feedback from the *Ragged Glory* tour—or as a recording of the ambient, atmospheric instrumental noodlings most often referred to as "New Age."

Geffen eventually released the *Lucky Thirteen* album several years later in 1993, after Young's star was on the rise once again following the comeback albums *Freedom* and *Ragged Glory*.

Meanwhile, the seeds of Young's next musical direction were busy being planted on the 1987 Crazy Horse tour, where he had taken to performing short sets of blues material with Sampedro on organ and guitar tech Larry Cragg on sax. Young would eventually expand this concept to become a ten-piece band, including as many as six horn players, called the Bluenotes.

Although the resulting album represented yet another eighties Neil Young genre experiment, it was also one that drew a surprisingly positive response. No one could have predicted it at the time, but 1988's *This Note's for You*, while hardly a *Harvest*-level smash, was in fact about to become a moderate hit for Neil Young.

But not before first stirring up a fresh new shitstorm of controversy.

Ain't Singin' for Pepsi

The Bluenotes, *American Dream*, Ten Men Working, and the Road Back Home

A sk any hardcore Neil-phyte what they most remember about the Bluenotes period, and they are likely to talk your ear off about the amazing live shows produced by Young's infamously short-lived but audacious ten-piece blues band with the six-piece horn section.

The Bluenotes never released an official live album (although there was briefly talk of one, with *This Shit Don't Sell* being among the funnier working titles reportedly considered). But live audience recordings from the period are among the most coveted bootleg tapes still traded today amongst hardcore fans.

While the lone studio album from Neil Young and the Bluenotes, 1988's *This Note's for You*, represented a minor commercial comeback (it peaked at #61 on Billboard, largely on the strength of the title track and its clever, controversy-generating video produced by Julien Temple), it also still suffered from the same tinny-sounding production that had plagued Young's final albums with Geffen. The horns on the album have a particularly shrill sound, as it seems the Volume Dealers (Young and his newest running buddy, co-producer Niko Bolas) hadn't quite yet exorcised the digital bug from their systems.

But by most accounts, the live shows were barn burners.

By this time, the Bluenotes had renamed themselves Ten Men Working (after a song from the *This Note's for You* album), following a legal injunction by R&B singer Harold Melvin (of certain fame with his own Bluenotes) over the name.

When Young wasn't playing his latest character creation onstage—bluesman Shakey Deal—he was otherwise busy melting faces with Old Black on new songs that could extend to twenty minutes and beyond like "Ordinary People" and "60 to 0" in concert.

What made both songs stand out as something new and noteworthy wasn't so much their length as their break in format from previous Neil Young opuses like "Down by the River" and "Cowgirl in the Sand."

Lengthy songs were certainly nothing new to his fans, especially in concert.

But where previously long songs like "Cortez" and "Cowgirl" served as showcases for electrifying guitar solos sandwiched in between short verses, on these new songs the reverse was true. The instrumental breaks were exactly that—short interludes in between new songs with as many as ten or more verses.

On the instrumental portions of "Ordinary People," Young's guitar shredding was augmented by the surprisingly tight Bluenotes horn section. But it was the lyrics—signaling a move away from the Republican politics Young had so curiously identified himself with since the *Old Ways* period, and a reacquired kinship with working-class Joes—that stood out as something new, including lines about a man with a "big fat cigar" who was "ripping off the people."

"60 to 0," on the other hand, could change radically from night to night. On one night, this new song could be an acoustic piece with as many as eleven verses, detailing a nightmare world of crooked cops and ten-year-old drug lords. On another, it became a full on electric assault, backed only by the new rhythm section of bassist Rick "the Bass Player" Rosas and drummer Chad Cromwell (both of whom had been recruited from Joe Walsh's band after Young had sacked Crazy Horse stalwarts Ralph Molina and Billy Talbot yet again). It is these early electric versions of the song that are most coveted by diehard fans, as Young's guitar soars to new heights over a rhythm section that is as razor sharp as Crazy Horse could be loose and funky.

Rosas and Cromwell would soon go on to become a cornerstone of Neil Young's full-on career resurgence a few months later, with some of his loudest music in over a decade. Among those recordings would be a curiously quieter version of "60 to 0" (retitled "Crime in the City" for the *Freedom* album).

"Ordinary People" (complete with the obligatory horns), on the other hand, wouldn't show up on an officially released Neil Young album until *Chrome Dreams II* some twenty years later.

And the Dollar's What It's All About, Hard-Workin' People

This Note's for You, Young's lone 1988 album with the Bluenotes, is not exactly one of his more remarkable works. If anything, his return to Reprise Records—home of his greatest triumphs in the seventies—probably seemed more like an extension of his genre-shifting, artistic years in the wilderness with Geffen than anything else.

But the album's title track was and is, without a doubt, a remarkable song.

At a time when rock-'n'-roll artists from Eric Clapton to the Rolling Stones to Michael Jackson were selling their artistic souls out wholesale to the highest corporate bidder, Young's initially tongue-in-cheek song took direct aim at all of them and ended up ruffling more than a few feathers in the process.

When MTV—then a crucial cog in the hit-making machinery of the record business, prior to their current incarnation as the home of reality shows like *Jersey Shore*—refused to air the video, Young instantly regained all of the outlaw cred he had lost during his disastrous years with Geffen.

"This Note's for You," with its references to heavily played MTV artists like Clapton and Jackson hawking Michelob beer and Pepsi cola, and its rallying cry of

Neil Young and Rick Rosas onstage in 1985. Rosas became a mainstay of Neil Young bands like the Restless on bass during this period, beginning an association that continues to the present day.

Photo by Kim Reed

"sponsored by nobody," became an instant cause célèbre. Young suddenly had more publicity than all of the maximum MTV and radio rotation in the world could ever hope to buy.

The standard line of MTV's dreaded standards and practices division—that they couldn't air the video due to its references to commercial products—smacked of the worst type of corporate bullshit, and everybody knew it. This was especially true given the fact that both the artist and the label had offered to edit the video in order to meet said standards and practices.

By the time the video channel was forced into issuing what amounted to a nationally televised apology, Young—an artist long since deemed as irrelevant and over the hill—was doing something he hadn't done in several years. He was actually selling records.

The end result, and the ultimate irony in all of this, was when "This Note's for You" was finally named as video of the year at MTV's Video Music Awards that year. Not surprisingly, the audio mysteriously cut out during Neil Young's televised acceptance remarks. Young's videos have rarely been played on the channel since.

Midnight, That Old Clock Keeps Ticking

Meanwhile, Young fulfilled a promise to his old friend David Crosby by participating in a CSN&Y reunion album, once Crosby had finally kicked the drug habit that very nearly killed him.

To say the resulting *American Dream* album—nearly twenty years in the making as it was, and despite the inclusion of no less than three new Neil Young songs including the title track, "This Old House," and "Name of Love"—failed to live up to expectations would to be put it politely. Although the return of the supergroup once deemed the "American Beatles" did make it to a respectable #16 on the Billboard charts, it sank just as quickly.

For his own part, Crosby, though finally clean and sober, was still in bad shape physically. Stephen Stills, who had really been the driving force behind CSN, was also mired in his own substance abuse issues.

But Young also brought his own creative issues to the table, by insisting on Niko Bolas to oversee the engineering of the much-ballyhooed reunion album. The spark between the four famously harmonizing voices was largely gone anyway, but the flat-sounding digital production that still had both Young and Bolas under its spell didn't help matters at all.

Although CSN&Y would eventually go on to several successful reunion tours, they would never make a decent record together again, despite a number of attempts. *American Dream* remains a particularly embarrassing blemish on the legacy of both CSN&Y and Neil Young.

However, and completely unbeknownst to anyone involved, Young was about to quite unexpectedly make some of the most amazing, ferocious music of his entire career.

What We Have Got Here Is a Perfect Track

Eldorado, Times Square, the Young and the Restless

Nobody knows exactly how or why the heavy rock bug once again bit Neil Young on the ass—Jimmy McDonough's *Shakey* suggests it was during a viewing of the Who's *The Kids Are Alright* documentary with Poncho. But once the Bluenotes had run their course in 1988, and it was time to move on to the next thing, there is little doubt that the rock bug bit him hard.

It was around this time that Young booked studio time at New York's Hit Factory in Times Square to record some of the most primal, aggressive—and loud—rock 'n' roll that he has ever made before or since.

Many of these songs—as well as reworked holdovers from the Bluenotes shows like "60 to 0" (now retitled "Crime in the City")—would eventually show up on the much-celebrated Neil Young "comeback" album *Freedom* in the fall of 1989. Still, the so-called *Times Square* sessions would also result in at least two false starts.

Heavy Rocks Are Falling, Heavy Love Is Coming Down

Although the songs from the Times Square sessions that eventually wound up on *Freedom*—including originals like "Don't Cry" and an over-the-top cover of the standard "On Broadway" (that is very much the antithesis of the smooth jazz version that became a hit for George Benson)—maintain some of their angry, feedback-laden snarl, subsequent studio tinkering by Young and co-producer Niko Bolas also removed some of their original bite.

What most who have heard those original recordings agree on, though, is that they were very, very loud.

Made with a core trio of Young, bassist Rick Rosas, and drummer Chad Cromwell—along with a stack of Marshall amps—new songs like "Don't Cry," "Heavy Love," and "Cocaine Eyes" displayed a newly reborn power and aggression that eclipsed even the *Rust Never Sleeps* days with Crazy Horse. Describing the all-night sessions to Jimmy McDonough in *Shakey*, guitar tech Larry Cragg summed up all the noise being made by Young and Old Black at the Hit Factory as "the biggest, most distorted sound you ever heard. It was loud in there."

The end result proved to be too extreme for many of those who heard it. Graham Nash in particular has gone on record as saying he hated the record. When record executives at Reprise likewise rolled their eyes in bewilderment upon hearing the completed masters, now an album called *Times Square*, Young returned to the studio to remix the tracks with Niko Bolas. The slightly watered-down versions of "Don't Cry" and "On Broadway" that eventually appeared on *Freedom* would be the only leftovers most fans would ever hear from the mythical sessions at New York's Hit Factory.

However, the original versions of those two songs, along with "Heavy Love," "Cocaine Eyes," and the somewhat quieter "Eldorado" (a reworking of the *Life*-era track "Road of Plenty"), did see an official, if very limited release on the five-song E.P. *Eldorado*. For American fans who were actually able to locate one of the roughly five thousand copies of *Eldorado*, they did so mainly by purchasing pricey, hard-to-find Japanese imported vinyl.

Original cover of the five-song, limited-edition Japanese import *Eldorado* CD. This now hard-to-find collector's item features rawer versions of songs that later showed up on the 1989 "comeback album" *Freedom*.   *From author's collection*

But for those who were willing to seek it out—or who even knew it existed—*Eldorado* more than lived up to all the rumors that it contained some of Young's most intense and extreme guitar playing in years.

"Don't Cry," a song he wrote about Niko Bolas splitting up with his girlfriend, begins with a lonesome-sounding (but again very loud) bass riff as Young offers the hopeful words "don't cry my sweet girl, nothing I say is written in stone." From there, any optimism for reconciliation is shattered by the most thunderous wash of feedback this side of a vintage Blue Cheer record. It's no small coincidence that grunge bands like Nirvana and Pearl Jam would later embrace Neil Young as one of their own.

The aggression in the music was equally matched by the lyrics, including some taking particular aim at the drug culture. In "Cocaine Eyes," said to be inspired by the condition Stephen Stills was in during the most recent CSN&Y reunion, Young somewhat angrily laments friends who "go for too much stuff, some to go to sleep at night, and forget to wake up." In his version of "On Broadway," Young turns the standard inside out, revealing a howling wall of feedback, punctuated by his anguished vocal portrayal of a street junkie trying to score crack. In the song, Young voice cracks even more than usual—a perfect fit for the jittery feel of his reinterpretation of the lyrics.

An ad campaign for the *Ragged Glory* CD with Crazy Horse a few years later would boast the catchphrase "feedback is back," but the moniker could have just as easily been used for the less widely distributed *Eldorado*.

Got Fuel to Burn, Got Roads to Drive

Meanwhile, Young took his new songs out on the road, with Cromwell and Rosas in tow, first calling the band Young and the Restless, and later the Lost Dogs. In a series of shows that first crisscrossed America in the fall of 1988 and then extended into 1989, the band proceeded to peel the paint off the ceilings of many small to medium-sized theatres and venues—often leaving their audiences in jaw-dropping shock in the process.

At one such show at Seattle's Paramount Theatre that I was fortunate enough to attend on February 21, 1989, I was likewise stunned by what I witnessed.

Expecting to see a fairly standard Neil Young acoustic show (particularly since it was held at the intimate, three thousand-seat Paramount), that was exactly what I got, at least for the first half. He did the usual acoustic set I'd grown accustomed to seeing over the years, including favorites like "Heart of Gold" "Sugar Mountain," and "The Needle and the Damage Done," interspersed with a few more rarely played songs like "For the Turnstiles" and "Days That Used to Be." It was a nice, somewhat nostalgic set, but nothing really special.

Nothing could have prepared me for what came next.

The last thing I ever expected to see was Neil Young blast the roof off of that grand old building the way he did. My understanding, especially given most of his output during the eighties, was that he was all but done with that sort of thing.

But that is exactly what he did, and for the next ninety or so minutes, the three thousand of us in attendance that night were treated to one of the loudest, most jaw-dropping performances I have ever witnessed before or since. Most of the songs, including the opening trio of "Heavy Love," "Don't Cry," and "Cocaine Eyes" were from a "new album" coming soon called *Eldorado,* we were told, and I made an immediate mental note to watch for it. I was going to be first line to buy that sucker, because Neil Young was back with a vengeance.

But there was also something very different about this newly energized Neil Young. He seemed as hungry again as I can ever recall for one thing. For their own part, the band (and I had absolutely no idea who they were at the time) played with the kind of tightness and punkish energy that I had never before seen in Neil's many electric shows with Crazy Horse. But Young himself was something else—he was absolutely slaughtering Old Black that night, playing with the sort of maniacal abandon and savage vengeance that would give younger noise merchants like Sonic Youth, or even a thrash-metal outfit like Slayer, a run for their money.

In addition to the new songs, he also brought out the heavy artillery with "Down by the River" and a version of "Hey, Hey, My, My" that easily bested the Crazy Horse version on *Rust Never Sleeps* for sheer volume and aggression. It was audacious stuff.

But one song in particular really stood out, and again it was a new one.

"Rockin' in the Free World," played for the very first time that night, tore the house down. I remember thinking at the time that the song's lyrics about styrofoam cups and ozone layers were kind of corny, and that the "keep on rockin' in the free world" chorus had a little too much pep-rally, "Up with People" sort of rah-rah. But there was no denying those slash-and-burn power chords, nor the anthemic, fist-pumping quality of this great new song.

I knew right then and there that Neil Young had his biggest hit since the Rust days on his hands.

On that night, I knew he was back—hell, it almost seemed like he'd never been away at that concert. It was easily one of the top five rock-'n'-roll concerts I've ever seen.

There wouldn't be an actual new Neil Young record until nearly nine months later (the *Eldorado* "album" he talked about that night never materialized—and I didn't learn about the limited-edition E.P. until over a year later).

But when it finally did arrive in October 1989, the rest of the world soon learned what those of us who had seen shows like the one in Seattle months before already knew.

Neil Young was back.

This Shit Don't Sell

A Brief History of Neil Young's Unreleased Recordings

Can you imagine anyone other than Bruce Springsteen writing and recording a song called "Born to Run"?

Well, what if we told you that Neil Young not only wrote and recorded an original song with that very title—but that he did so after Springsteen's 1975 classic with the same name had already been long committed to its iconic status in rock history?

"Born to Run"—and that would be Young's original, rather than Springsteen's—is in fact but one of a multitude of his unreleased recordings that exist in one form or another. Ranging from such curiosities as "Born to Run" to such legendarily mythical albums as *Homegrown* and *Chrome Dreams,* the pieces that make up Young's "missing catalog" would form an impressive, stand-alone body of work even by themselves.

Because of the way that he tends to work—which, when it comes to recording, is essentially nonstop—it should come as no surprise that there are any number of such recordings by the artist floating around out there in bootleg land. It should likewise come as no shock that some of these (like *Homegrown* and *Chrome Dreams*) have also been elevated to near Holy Grail status amongst his more devoted fans.

The reasons many of these albums never came out vary wildly. In some cases, the ever-mercurial Young scrapped them himself, oftentimes doing so at the very last minute. In others—most notably during the infamous Geffen years during the eighties—the albums simply fell victim to being rejected by the record label because of things like a perceived "lack of commercial potential." Imagine that, right?

Many of these unreleased recordings are far less known and celebrated than the likes of *Homegrown,* though. Did you know, for instance, that Young once recorded a New Age album? Or that he had planned to make an entire album consisting of original songs with titles made famous by other artists (including an original tune called, you guessed it, "Born to Run")?

What follows here is a brief history of Neil Young's most famous—and in some cases infamous—unreleased recordings.

It should be noted that I've left some gaps in this list, including a number of aborted projects with bands like Crosby, Stills, and Nash (which will be the

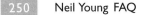

subject of another chapter), as well as things like a scrapped Farm Aid E.P. with the International Harvesters. The scrapped solo version of *Human Highway* (an album that at one point was scheduled to come out in 1974, and eventually became a very strange documentary film in the eighties featuring everyone from Dennis Hopper to Devo) has likewise been omitted (due to a lack of verifiable information).

Track listings for these albums are provided in any case we were actually able to locate them.

Untitled Live Album—1971

Planned as a double album of mostly solo acoustic performances from New York's Carnegie Hall and Washington D.C.'s Cellar Door, this also featured three performances with Crazy Horse from New York's Fillmore East, which were eventually resurrected for the *Archives* series.

"This is the album that should have come out between *After the Gold Rush* and *Harvest*," Young has been quoted as saying. "David Briggs, my producer, was adamant that this should be the record, but I was very excited about the takes we got on *Harvest*, and wanted *Harvest* out. David disagreed. As I listen to this today, I can see why."

TRACK LIST
1. "Down by the River" (with Crazy Horse)
2. "Wonderin'" (with Crazy Horse)
3. "Everybody Knows This Is Nowhere" (with Crazy Horse)
4. "I Am a Child"
5. "Expecting to Fly"
6. "Flying on the Ground Is Wrong"
7. "Nowadays Clancy Can't Even Sing"
8. "Cowgirl in the Sand"
9. "Ohio"
10. "Old Man"
11. "Dance Dance Dance"
12. "Sugar Mountain"
13. "See the Sky About to Rain"
14. "The Needle and the Damage Done"
15. "Bad Fog of Loneliness"

Homegrown—1975

Probably the most famous of Neil Young's many unreleased projects over the years, *Homegrown* was a quieter folk-rock album in the vein of *Harvest* that he famously scrapped in favor of *Tonight's the Night* after rediscovering the latter during a playback of the former that was on the same reel. Of the small group of friends present for the playback party, Rick Danko of the Band told Young that he'd be "fucking crazy" not to release the much rawer *Tonight's the Night*. Although Warner Brothers gave Young complete artistic freedom over his work, label executives hoping for a return to the million-dollar sound of *Harvest* had to be more than a little unhappy when he ultimately opted to instead release the far less commercial *Tonight's the Night*.

Explaining the choice, he says he went with *Tonight's the Night* instead because of "its overall strength in performance and feeling" and because *Homegrown* "was just a very down album." Like *Tonight's the Night* isn't, right?

Homegrown is also said to have been strongly influenced by Young's failed relationship with Carrie Snodgress, and as a result included some of his most deeply felt personal lyrics. He has indicated in more than one interview since then that the songs simply hit a little too close to home at the time.

Young has called *Homegrown* "the missing link between *Harvest, Comes a Time, Old Ways,* and *Harvest Moon*." Not surprisingly, several of the album's original songs have since shown up on subsequent albums such as *Zuma* ("Pardon My Heart"), *American Stars and Bars* ("Star of Bethlehem"), *Decade* ("Love Is a Rose" and "Deep Forbidden Lake"), and *Hawks and Doves* ("Little Wing" and "The Old Homestead"). A cover version of "Barefoot Floors" also made its way to Nicolette Larson's album *Sleep, Baby, Sleep*.

Although such things are always subject to change—particularly with Neil Young—fans who have waited decades for an official release of *Homegrown* may finally soon get their wish. Young has indicated the album may be included as part of the second volume of the *Archives* series.

TRACK LIST
1. "Homegrown"
2. "Vacancy"
3. "Homefires"
4. "Try"
5. "Star of Bethlehem"
6. "Little Wing"
7. "The Old Homestead"
8. "Hawaiian Sunrise"
9. "Pardon My Heart"
10. "Love Art Blues"
11. "Human Highway"
12. "Separate Ways"
13. "Deep Forbidden Lake"
14. "Love Is a Rose"
15. "Daughters"
16. "We Don't Smoke It No More"
17. "White Line"
18. "Give Me Strength"
19. "Long May You Run"
20. "Tie Plate Yodel" #3

Odeon/Budokan Live—1976

In 1976, Neil Young played a series of shows in Europe, Japan, and finally America with a newly revamped Crazy Horse lineup that introduced fans to new guitarist Frank "Poncho" Sampedro. In Japan, fans greeted Neil Young and Crazy Horse like rock royalty, but by most accounts the band themselves played the shows zonked clean out of their minds.

In Jimmy McDonough's *Shakey*, Sampedro recalls that both he and Billy Talbot had taken acid before the March 11 show at Nippon Budokan Hall, which was also recorded and filmed for a possible live album and documentary project. Although Crazy Horse played both sloppy and stoned according to some (and Sampedro in particular was still finding his way in the new lineup), it's also been said that Young himself played some of his most incendiary guitar solos to date during the shows in Japan.

The live *Odeon/Budokan* album was never released, but now appears to be a likely candidate for inclusion as part of the second volume of the ongoing *Archives* series of retrospective boxed sets, tentatively scheduled for release sometime in 2012. A track listing doesn't exist (at least as far we know), but versions of songs like "Cowgirl in the Sand," "Drive Back," and "The Losing End" (all featuring cranked-up solos from Young and Old Black) are likely to be included.

Oceanside, Countryside—1977

Young's 1977 album *Comes a Time* proved to be his biggest commercial hit since *Harvest* at the time of its release. But what many people don't know is that it was originally intended to be a solo acoustic album. Recorded at Florida's Triad Studios, the acoustic version of the album consisted of two sides, one titled "Oceanside" and the other "Countryside."

When Young played the original *Oceanside, Countryside* version of the album for Warner executives including Mo Ostin and Lenny Waronker, Mo indicated that he liked the record, but suggested Young try adding more musicians, and a rhythm section in particular.

Not normally one for letting the label dictate his artistic direction, Young surprisingly agreed and finished the album with a crew including Ben Keith, Tim Drummond, Karl Himmel, Spooner Oldham, and Rufus Thibodeaux. Nicolette Larson, who was also Young's girlfriend at the time, contributes backup vocals on the album, including a lovely duet with Young on Ian and Sylvia Tyson's "Four Strong Winds." Larson also had her biggest hit as a solo artist with a cover of "Lotta Love" (which also appears on the *Comes a Time* album in a version with Crazy Horse).

The original acoustic sessions have since come to be known as *Oceanside, Countryside*—making for yet another of the many "lost" Neil Young albums. It has also been mentioned as a likely candidate for inclusion on the next volume of the *Archives* series.

Chrome Dreams—1977

Chrome Dreams is another of the more legendary unreleased titles in the Neil Young canon, as evidenced by the amazingly strong track listing below. Scrapped in typical Young fashion in favor of *American Stars and Bars,* it has also been one of his more widely bootlegged unofficial his releases over the years, with copies of an original acetate of the recording in fairly wide circulation among collectors.

Several of the stronger songs included have since shown up on albums ranging from *American Stars and Bars* ("Will to Love," "Like a Hurricane") to *Rust Never Sleeps* ("Pocahontas," "Sedan Delivery," "Powderfinger") to *Freedom* ('Too Far Gone"), although in many cases the bootlegged versions found on *Chrome Dreams* are radically different. "Powderfinger," for instance, is an amazing acoustic demo, while "Hold Back the Tears" features additional lyrics.

Perhaps to pay homage to the revered status of the album among hardcore fans, Young eventually released an official "sequel" to the unreleased record with 2007's *Chrome Dreams II.* As is the case with *Homegrown,* he has indicated that the original *Chrome Dreams* album is likely to be included as part of the second round of his ongoing *Archives* project.

TRACK LIST
1. "Pocahontas"
2. "Will to Love"
3. "Star of Bethlehem"
4. "Like a Hurricane"
5. "Too Far Gone"
6. "Hold Back the Tears"
7. "Homegrown"
8. "Captain Kennedy"
9. "Stringman"
10. "Sedan Delivery"
11. "Powderfinger"
12. "Look Out for My Love"

Island in the Sun—1982

Not only was *Island in the Sun* supposed to be Neil Young's very first album for Geffen Records—his new label in the eighties—it was also the first to be subsequently turned down by the label. Much to his unending frustration in the years that followed, it wouldn't be the last. Far from it.

Often described by those who have heard it as his "water album," *Island in the Sun* was explained by Young himself as "a tropical thing all about sailing, ancient civilizations, islands and water" in an interview he did for *Mojo* magazine in 1995. Some of the songs from *Island in the Sun,* such as "Like an Inca," "Little Thing Called Love," and "Hold On to Your Love" eventually showed up on

Trans, the infamous vocoder-heavy, mostly electronic album that Geffen released instead—officially setting in motion the series of bizarre genre experiments that would lead to the eighties becoming known as Young's "lost decade."

Old Ways—1983

An earlier, and said to be rawer, version of Young's mid-eighties country album that was (rather strangely) rejected at the time by Geffen in favor of *Everybody's Rockin'*, the rockabilly album with the Shocking Pinks that followed *Trans*.

TRACK LIST
1. "Old Ways"
2. "Depression Blues"
3. "That's Alright Mama"
4. "Cry Cry Cry"
5. "Mystery Train"
6. "Wonderin'"
7. "California Sunset"
8. "My Boy"
9. "Are There Any More Real Cowboys"
10. "Silver and Gold"

Treasure—1985

It was in an interview with Young and *Le Noise* producer Daniel Lanois conducted by writer Jaan Uhelszki and first published online by *American Songwriter* in December 2010 that Young first made brief mention of yet "another album I've been listening to that I have in the can."

Of this mysterious, previously unheard of album titled *Treasure*, he doesn't reveal much in the way of details, except to say that it is "a great record" and that "I hope to release it one day." As it turns out, Young was most likely referring to an album of unreleased performances from the *Old Ways* period with his country band the International Harvesters, made during 1984-1985.

Six months after the *American Songwriter* interview, an album of these performances finally saw the light of day. Released as part of the *Archives Performance Series* on June 14, 2010, the album *A Treasure* (named for the late Ben Keith once referring to it as "a treasure") contains both previously unreleased songs like "Grey Riders" and "Amber Jean" (a song written for Young's daughter), as well as countrified reworkings of previously released Neil Young songs ranging from "Southern Pacific" to "Flying on the Ground Is Wrong."

The prerelease ramp up to *A Treasure* is also notable for a hilarious fourteen-minute promotional video that made the rounds at Neil Young sites like Thrasher's Wheat. In the video, Young rambles his way through a series of half-completed video clips in his inimitable drawl, drawing as much attention

to the flaws in the album as he does to the highlights. An off-screen voiceover
that ominously pops into the mix whenever he references the "Blu-ray" release
of *A Treasure* adds to the overall goofiness.

TRACK LIST

1. "Amber Jean" (9-20-1984, previously unreleased)
2. "Are You Ready for the Country?" (9-21-1984)
3. "It Might Have Been" (9-25-1984)
4. "Bound for Glory" (9-29-1984)
5. "Let Your Fingers Do the Walking" (10-22-1984, previously unreleased)
6. "Flying on the Ground Is Wrong" (10-26-1984)
7. "Motor City" (10-26-1984)
8. "Soul of a Woman" (10-26-1984, previously unreleased)
9. "Get Back to the Country" (10-26-1984)
10. "Southern Pacific" (9-1-1985)
11. "Nothing Is Perfect" (9-1-1985, previously unreleased)
12. "Grey Riders" (9-10-1985, previously unreleased)

Meadow Dusk—1987

Not much is known about this album, other than that its sole purpose may have
been to piss off the folks at Geffen Records. By this time, Young's nearly ten-
year-long, often difficult association with Geffen was nearing an end, and there
had been no love lost between artist and label during the often contentious
relationship

Described in Jimmy McDonough's *Shakey* by Frank "Poncho" Sampredo as
the "sounds of crickets farting," *Meadow Dusk* has also been referred to as Young's
unreleased "New Age" album.

The description found in *Shakey* goes on to describe a record that featured
synthesizers and descriptive song titles that would be either repeated or whispered over a musical backdrop of "sound concepts and industrial noise." The
same description of the album recounted in *Shakey* also says that it resembled
a softer version of the feedback sounds found on the *Arc* disc of the three-disc
version of *Arc-Weld*. To the best of our knowledge, a track list for *Meadow Dusk*
no longer exists, if in fact such a thing ever did.

1988—This Note's for You Too (a.k.a. This Shit Don't Sell)—

Buoyed by his return to Reprise Records and the mild commercial success of
This Note's for You (which won Young an MTV Video of the Year Award, despite
its none-too-veiled indictment of the crass commercialism of the music video
network), he planned, and then just as quickly scrapped, a two-disc live album
with the Bluenotes.

Although a track listing has never surfaced, one has to figure the album would have included such live standouts from the period as the eighteen-minute epic "Ordinary People" (which eventually surfaced two decades later on 2007's *Chrome Dreams II* album), and "60 to 0," a constantly evolving song that would often stretch to twenty minutes when played in concert, and later provided the template for the much shorter *Freedom* track "Crime in the City."

The unreleased Bluenotes live album was said to have been called *This Note's for You Too,* but in the *Shakey* book, it is also referred to by the title *This Shit Don't Sell.*

Times Square—1989

Recorded during sessions at New York's Hit Factory in 1988, *Times Square* is recognized by fans as the bridge between the Bluenotes period and the more complete return to artistic and commercial form that would manifest itself on 1989's "comeback" album *Freedom.* It is also generally agreed by just about everyone who has heard it (here again, the acetate was widely bootlegged) that the *Times Square* sessions represent some of the loudest shit Neil Young has ever put down on tape.

Although the album was pulled from release by Young himself because of what he felt was the lack of anything radio could play, many FM rock stations had already received their copies—something that may have played a role in the limited release of five songs from it on the Japanese import E.P. *Eldorado.*

Backed by drummer Chad Cromwell and bassist Rick Rosas (who later toured the songs with Young as a band calling themselves Young and the Restless), this is without a doubt Neil Young with Old Black cranked to eleven at his loudest, fiercest, and finest. Some of the songs from *Times Square* would eventually see release on *Freedom,* but as the available bootlegs out there and the *Eldorado* E.P. both attest, they are in nowhere near the same raw and relentlessly hard-rocking form heard here.

"Cocaine Eyes" and "Heavy Love" didn't make it to *Freedom* at all, but do show up on *Eldorado.* "Box Car" remains officially unreleased.

TRACK LIST
1. "Eldorado"
2. "Someday"
3. "Sixty to Zero (Crime in the City)"
4. "Box Car"
5. "Don't Cry"
6. "Heavy Love"
7. "Wrecking Ball"
8. "Cocaine Eyes"
9. "On Broadway"

Toast—2000

Toast * is an unreleased album recorded with Crazy Horse that as recently as 2008 was scheduled to be released as part of the *Archives* series, but has since quietly disappeared from the radar screen (even as rumors of a release continue to persist). This album, named for a defunct recording studio, is said to include reworked Crazy Horse versions of a number of songs Neil Young originally recorded with Booker T. and the MGs in the nineties. Of the songs believed to have come from these sessions, "Goin' Home," can be heard on the album *Are You Passionate?*

* In July 2010, Young announced via his official website that the albums *Homegrown, Chrome Dreams, Odeon-Budokan Oceanside-Countryside,* and *Toast* will all be released in revamped versions as part of something called the *Archives Special Release* series.

A Thousand Points of Light

Freedom and Redemption for Neil in the Nineties

T hroughout much of the eighties, David Geffen—Neil Young's boss at his record label for most of that decade—had lamented openly both in court and in public interviews about why his artist couldn't bring himself to make an album of actual "Neil Young" music. In the fall of 1989, a little more than a year after leaving that label to return to Reprise, Young finally did it.

Freedom proved to be just the beginning, too. The well that so many felt had run dry for so long suddenly began to burst forth with one amazing Neil Young record after another. Indeed, his creative juices during the nineties seemed to overflow in such a way as to prove Geffen's oft-stated claim that the artist was capable of making great records (that were also commercial hits) "at will" essentially true.

Viewing Young's nineties output today, one has to wonder if Geffen could have actually been right all along.

The floodgate first opened by the release of *Freedom* continued right up through about 1996, before slowing down (at least a little) toward the end of the decade. Along with *Freedom* (as the album that started this creative tidal wave), subsequent albums *Ragged Glory, Harvest Moon, Mirror Ball,* and *Sleeps with Angels* make up what many feel is the artist's strongest, most consistent string of great work since the mid- to late seventies period that produced the Ditch Trilogy and *Rest Never Sleeps.* Some fans argue that Young's nineties work as a whole, album for album, is even stronger than that. And in terms of overall consistency, they may have a point.

After the commercial disappointments of the eighties, *Freedom* was a renewed artistic validation for Neil Young. Although he has cranked out more than a few more clunkers in the years and decades since, his place as one of the all-time creative giants of rock 'n' roll—the same status so many had questioned during the so-called lost eighties—has to this day never again been seriously challenged.

In much the same way that Bob Dylan's late nineties creative resurgence (beginning with 1997's *Time out of Mind*) provided ample cause for a critical reassessment of his career, such has likewise been the case with Neil Young.

Like Dylan, when it comes to putting out the occasional stiff these days, Young largely gets a pass.

It goes without saying that both of these great artists have, of course, earned it.

All the Children Were Killers

But even more than Dylan, Neil Young's music has struck a particularly resonant chord with a younger generation of both his more modern artistic peers and with listeners and fans.

The modern folk-rock sound of Americana bands like Fleet Foxes, Wilco, and the Jayhawks owes more than a little to albums like *Harvest*, for example—a fact that Wilco's Jeff Tweedy and the Jayhawks' Gary Louris don't bother denying.

If anything, both artists wear these comparisons as a badge of honor. For proof of this, look no further than Wilco's letter-perfect cover of "Broken Arrow" from the 2010 concert honoring Young as MusiCares Person of the Year (the entire concert is available on the excellent 2011 *A MusiCares Tribute to Neil Young* DVD).

However, Young is just as often cited as a key influence on the alternative rock genre that rose to prominence in the nineties. "Alternative," at least by its modern definition, grew out of the ashes of seventies and eighties punk, and hit its commercial peak with the early nineties grunge sound associated with Seattle bands like Nirvana and Pearl Jam (both of whom have their own unique connections to Young).

In addition to the Seattle grunge acts, Young has also been acknowledged as a key influence by alternative bands ranging from Radiohead to Sonic Youth.

If one chooses to trace the genesis of this bridging of musical generations—an attitude that is unique in all of rock amongst younger musicians who otherwise tend to view artists from Young's generation with both suspicion and mistrust—you could probably track its beginnings back to *Rust Never Sleeps*, with its lyrical references to Johnny Rotten, and to Young's collaborations with Devo before that.

But 1989's *Freedom* album was the moment of artistic vindication, where this unlikely marriage was first fully consummated.

Send Me a Songwriter Who's Drifted Far from Home

On a first appraisal, *Freedom* seems almost like a sequel to *Rust Never Sleeps* in a lot of ways. The similarities between the two are certainly striking. Released almost exactly ten years apart, both albums were certainly perceived as a return to artistic form at the time (probably most dramatically in the case of 1989's *Freedom*).

But there are other parallel lines that can be drawn between the two albums.

Like *Rust*, the album art for *Freedom* features the title scrawled on the cover in Neil Young's own handwriting. The album is also bookended by acoustic and electric versions of a single song ("Rockin' in the Free World") that sets the tone for the entire record.

The fact that *Freedom's* "Rockin' in the Free World" is probably Neil Young's most overtly anthemic song since *Rust's* "Hey, Hey, My, My" only reinforces the similarities between the two.

Like their counterparts on *Rust Never Sleeps*, the louder songs on *Freedom* also serve to (once again) establish Young's status as a pivotal link (and perhaps the only one) between the hippie psychedelia of the sixties and the soon-to-explode post-punk and alternative rock of the nineties.

It's no accident that the tribute album *The Bridge: A Tribute to Neil Young* was also released the same year as *Freedom* in 1989. That album, which benefited the Bridge School, features covers of Young songs from a variety of alternative rockers including Sonic Youth, the Pixies, and Dinosaur Jr. (whose J. Mascis is a particularly devout student of the Neil Young school of guitar distortion).

There's Colors on the Street

However, despite *Freedom's* well-earned reputation in the years since its initial release as a weighty entry in the overall canon of Neil Young's greatest work, not everyone was initially sold. Despite receiving near universal critical acclaim as a return to artistic form, the album was only a modest hit at the time, peaking at #35 on Billboard. Neil wouldn't enjoy a return to Billboard's top twenty again until the release of *Harvest Moon*—his long-awaited sequel to *Harvest*—in 1992.

Of Young's three collaborations up to that point with co-producer Niko Bolas, there is little doubt that *Freedom* is the one where the "Volume Dealers" mostly got it right. The album has a warm, organic sound to it that stands in sharp contrast to the manufactured drum sounds heard on late eighties efforts like *Landing on Water*.

Complaints about the album most often center on Bolas decision (supported by both Frank "Poncho" Sampedro and Young himself at the time) to tone down some of the more abrasive guitar sounds heard on the leftover tracks from the *Times Square/Eldorado* sessions that eventually made the final cut on *Freedom*.

This is most often cited in the case of "Don't Cry." Listening to versions from both recordings back to back, however, the differences are largely miniscule and the wash of reverberated feedback between verses that gives the song much of its power is really barely touched.

There is also a school of thought out there amongst hardcore Neil Young fans that the abridged version of "60 to 0" (retitled "Crime in the City" for *Freedom*) barely holds a candle to the fifteen-minute-plus opus he routinely performed in concert during the Bluenotes period.

As great as those versions (mostly captured on bootlegs) were, it is the contention of this writer that the admittedly toned-down, jazzier version of the song heard on *Freedom* adds considerable mood to the seedier, inner-city ambience

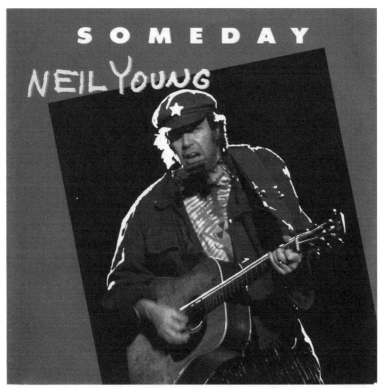

Single picture sleeve 45 of "Someday" from Neil Young's 1989 "comeback album" *Freedom.*   *Courtesy of Tom Therme collection*

that the song's lyrics about sleazy record producers and ten-year-old drug lords so vividly describe.

In other words, by tightening this cinematic lyrical opus down to a more concisely told story, the Volume Dealers largely got it right.

Got a Man of the People, Says Keep Hope Alive

Neil Young's status as an icon amongst the alternative generation wouldn't fully manifest itself until a few years after, once Seattle grunge bands like Nirvana and Pearl Jam broke that scene wide open commercially with albums like *Nevermind* and *Ten* (although the movie had already been made some years before, 1991 was really "the year that punk broke").

By that time, grunge bands from Seattle seemed to be appropriating every-thing about Young from their sound to their look (in truth, the flannel-and-ripped-jeans fashion of grunge probably owes as much to the weather in Seattle as it does to Young's more originally grungy sense of a funkier anti-style).

Even so, bands like Pearl Jam made no secret of their fandom, first by including a cover of "Rockin' in the Free World" in their own set lists, and later performing the song with Young himself at the 1993 MTV Music Awards. Eventually, Pearl Jam and Young would record an entire album together (1995's *Mirror Ball*, as well as the accompanying Pearl Jam E.P. *Merkin Ball*) and even do a joint tour of Europe. It was also Pearl Jam vocalist Eddie Vedder who made the speech inducting Young into the Rock and Roll Hall of Fame (also in 1995).

"He's taught us a lot as a band about dignity and commitment and playing in the moment and when I hear, you know, the speeches and inducting Janis Joplin and Frank Zappa, I get, uh, I'm just really glad he's still here" Vedder said in his induction remarks. "And I think I'm gonna have to say that I don't know if there's been another artist that has been inducted into the Rock 'n' Roll Hall of Fame to commemorate a career that is still as vital as he is today. Some of his best songs were on his last record."

Nirvana's Kurt Cobain also acknowledged his artistic debt to Neil Young—although he would do so most tragically in the suicide note he left behind after shooting himself in his Lake Washington home in 1994, quoting "Hey, Hey, My, My."

Single release of *Freedom*'s "Rockin' in the Free World," one of the greatest and most recognizable rock anthems of all time.   *Courtesy of Tom Therme collection*

It is widely believed that Young was first referred to as the "Godfather of Grunge" in a 1991 article for Tower Records *Pulse!* magazine (by writer Steve Martin). Ironically, there is also a very early song recorded by Nirvana from 1988 also called "Godfather of Grunge" (although there is no real indication the song is actually about Young).

Since its initial release in 1989, *Freedom* has been often cited as one of the ten most influential alternative rock albums of all time, with at least one publication (*Pagewise*) going so far as to name it number one and to call "Rockin' in the Free World" the first true alternative rock song.

The definitive performance of that song remains the incendiary, off-the-rails version Young did with a makeshift band assembled at the last minute by Bolas consisting of Young, Poncho, drummer Steve Jordan, and bassist Charley Drayton on the September 30, 1989, broadcast of NBC's *Saturday Night Live*.

It was the only recorded performance by YCS&P (short for Young, Charley, Steve, and Poncho), and would also be Niko Bolas's last stand with Shakey for nearly two decades (until 2006's *Living with War*).

With his best album in a decade now behind him, Young started the nineties a few months early. If nothing else, *Freedom* marked a clear and bold statement for the artist, that he was separating himself from the missteps that had marked so much of the previous decade. Neil Young was back.

His next move would continue this artistic revitalization, as he reconnected with two of the primary forces behind some of his greatest work. For *Ragged Glory*, Young would reunite with both producer David Briggs and his greatest band, the mighty Crazy Horse.

30

Don't Spook the Horse

Ragged Glory and Arc-Weld

As his first album released in the new decade—and his first official recording with Crazy Horse since 1987's spotty-at-best *Life*—*Ragged Glory* is the album most folks cite today as the one that solidified Neil Young's artistic resurgence in the nineties.

1989's *Freedom* had, of course, already set the table the year before (to the point where even now, some fans mistakenly insist that the album was actually released in 1990). *Freedom* also has the edge in terms of memorable songwriting—there is nothing on *Ragged Glory* that comes anywhere near the status of "Rockin' in the Free World," being a universally recognized song.

But when it comes to the sort of reckless and joyously rocking abandon that fans have come to expect from the records he sporadically makes with his greatest band, 1990's *Ragged Glory* was the best Neil Young and Crazy Horse album in many a moon. *Ragged Glory* rocks with every bit of the intensity of the loudest material on *Rust Never Sleeps*. It also recaptures the free-form, improvisational spirit of Young's very first album with the Horse—the 1969 classic *Everybody Knows This Is Nowhere*.

Like that album's two most memorable songs, "Down by the River" and "Cowgirl in the Sand," *Ragged Glory's* center lies with a pair of lengthy tracks that serve as launchpads for some of Young's most incendiary guitar playing in years. "Love and Only Love" and "Love to Burn" are noteworthy entries in the Neil Young canon not so much because of their lyrics (although the latter contains such uncommonly personal lines as "where ya taking my kid?" and "why'd ya ruin my life?"), as they are for the blazing—and long—guitar solos that take place in between them.

In retrospect, it's amazing that these ten-minute-plus guitar opuses haven't become more of a permanent fixture in those concerts where Young decides to turn the amps up to eleven with the Horse. There is little doubt they would fit right into that particular mix. The fact is, although *Ragged Glory's* two "Love" songs are somewhat lesser known, either one could fill the "Hurricane" or "Cortez" spots in a set list for a Crazy Horse show quite nicely.

Dogs That Lick and Dogs That Bite

Taking the *Everybody Knows This Is Nowhere* analogy a bit further, "Fuckin' Up" likewise fills the "Cinnamon Girl" spot as *Ragged Glory's* most perfectly constructed blast of FM ready rock (even though it never had a chance at airplay for obvious reasons).

On the two videos for the song that appear on the now rare, five-song *Ragged Glory* VHS video album, just about the only thing separating "Fuckin' Up" from a chunky slice of AC/DC-styled hard-rock stupidity is the lingering feedback at the end (something Young would devote an entire album to a short time later—but more on that in a minute).

Like the other videos on the long out-of-print *Ragged Glory* VHS, "Fuckin' Up' appears to take place in the barn where the song was recorded. In the Julien Temple–directed clip, Young is particularly animated—he screams the lyrics at everything from his reflection in the mirror to the inside of a dirty old toilet bowl. The other version of "Fuckin' Up," directed by Rusty Cundieff, concentrates more on the rest of the band, while a small crowd is served drinks in a makeshift bar below the stage. The loose video storyline centers mainly on a busty Jessica Hahn lookalike who gets a drink strategically spilled on her while a subtitle reads "this band is fucking amazing." Truly priceless.

In addition to the two clips for "Fuckin' Up," the five-song *Ragged Glory* video includes "Mansion on the Hill," "Over and Over," and Young's perfectly lascivious cover of the garage classic "Farmer John." The latter is particularly hilarious, and features a very funny cameo spot from guitar tech Larry Cragg, who gets in the faces of skirt-chasing band members as a pitchfork-wielding Farmer John.

"Fuckin' Up" is easily the most radio-friendly song on *Ragged Glory*, at least once you get past the obvious problem with actually getting it played due to the lyrics. Aside from that, "Fuckin' Up" also ranks as one of the funniest Neil Young songs ever.

But either "Mansion on the Hill" or "Farmer John" could have just as easily been radio singles on a perfect Neil Young and Crazy Horse album.

Which are just two more reasons why *Ragged Glory* qualifies as being exactly that.

In the Valley of Hearts, There's a House Full of Broken Windows

Before *Ragged Glory* could become that album, however, there were some considerable obstacles to overcome. First off, there was the none-too-easy task of getting back together with Crazy Horse, not to mention with the only man who could honestly produce such a record, David Briggs. With the bruised egos and hurt feelings that were surely felt all around since the last time he had left his former partners in crime (save for Poncho Sampedro) lying in the proverbial lurch, this had to represent quite a balancing act for Young.

As much as all the parties involved had to be chomping at the bit at the chance to work once again with the newly anointed "Godfather of Grunge," this would require the notorious control freak Young to act in the sort of diplomatic role that he was quite unaccustomed to. Diplomacy has never been one of his strong suits, or at least it hadn't been in any previous dealings up to that point.

In the beginning, he would promise Briggs and Crazy Horse everything they asked.

This most notably included a change of recording locale from the Broken Arrow Ranch, where Briggs in particular rightfully felt that Young was distracted by side interests like the *Archives* project and his growing passion (renewed from childhood) for Lionel model trains.

In the end, Young somewhat predictably reneged on most of these promises. Most significantly, *Ragged Glory* was recorded primarily live in the equipment barn at Broken Arrow after all (although Briggs won a small victory when Young agreed to have the album mixed at Indigo Ranch in Malibu).

However, Young did deliver on one crucial point—and that was his promise to Briggs, Billy Talbot, and Ralph Molina to just let the Horse be the Horse. This allowed much-maligned drummer Molina in particular to shine. Once removed from the weird drum sounds of Young's eighties productions with Niko Bolas, Molina's drumming on *Ragged Glory* turned out to be some of the most solid of his entire career.

By the time it was all over, Briggs would be gone (again), the Horse would be predictably at each other's throats, and Neil Young's hearing would be left severely damaged. Both Briggs and Crazy Horse would eventually be back, of course. Young's hearing, unfortunately, would not. As much as he was able to overcome earlier bouts with polio and epilepsy, years of cranking up the amps far beyond levels considered tolerable to the rest of us humans had finally caught up with him.

Even so, this would not stop Young from embarking on the single loudest tour of his entire career.

Try to Not Spook the Horse

One of the weirder but oddly endearing tracks to emerge from the *Ragged Glory* sessions is "Don't Spook the Horse," a seven-minute train wreck of a song that showed up as a B-side to the CD single of "Mansion on the Hill."

The song, said to be inspired when Crazy Horse "played like shit" after Briggs showed up unannounced at one of the sessions, is a glorious mess for which Young is said to have recorded his parts, quite literally, with one foot in a bucket of horse shit.

Young himself has said that "Don't Spook the Horse" is a response to critics of Crazy Horse's more notoriously looser, sloppier-sounding grooves. As such, it basically reads as a laundry list of all the reasons why it is ill advised to "Spook the Horse." Based on the song—which quite understandably has never enjoyed a wider, more commercial release—we find it hard not to disagree.

The CD single of "Mansion on the Hill" is today a bit of a collector's item, largely due to the inclusion of "Don't Spook the Horse" as its B-side.

Hounds That Howl Through the Night

For the huge tour booked to support *Ragged Glory*, Neil Young and Crazy Horse found themselves playing sold-out arenas for the first time since the seventies. For support acts, the tour also wisely chose to capitalize on Young's increasing "indie cred" within the alternative rock community by booking such respected young alt-rock noisemakers as Social Distortion and Sonic Youth (the still rising Nirvana were also approached—by Sonic Youth—for a spot on the tour, but for unknown reasons turned down the gig).

On paper at least, this mix of young cutting-edge bands with a newly cool again legend like Neil Young seemed to be a great idea, and as a PR move it was.

In execution, however, the results were decidedly mixed. Much of Young's older fan base—as thrilled as they were to see their hero back with Crazy Horse and seemingly at the top of his game again after the strangeness of the eighties—still were somewhat nonplussed by the brasher, more abrasive sounds of the youngsters.

There were also complaints about the sound from openers like Sonic Youth, whose Kim Gordon has since gone so far as to suggest that they were getting sabotaged by Young's crew—and in particular by engineer Tim Mulligan—during sound checks.

As he does every year, Neil Young headlined the 1994 Bridge School Benefit show at Shoreline Amphitheater in Mountain View, California. *Courtesy of Tom Therme collection*

The show I personally witnessed on the *Ragged Glory* tour in Seattle largely supports this allegation. As loud as Sonic Youth can be live, their noise making barely registered a whisper in the sold-out Seattle Center Coliseum. There have also been complaints over the years that the star of the show himself was conveniently inaccessible to the opening bands on the tour (although in fairness, Sonic Youth have gone on record as saying that Young did take their side over the sound check problems with Mulligan)

In spite of all this, as well as the usual infighting amongst band members that come as natural to Neil Young and Crazy Horse as feedback, the shows themselves were knockouts. Young was playing some of the loudest, fiercest-sounding guitar of his rock-'n'-roll life, and the notoriously "on" or "off" Crazy Horse were definitely in an "on" mode for more of the shows than not.

A few of the old props from the *Rust Never Sleeps* days were also brought back for the concerts—including those huge oversized Fender amp mockups (which actually hid Young's

An ad for *Weld*, the live three-CD Neil Young and Crazy Horse album from the *Ragged Glory* tour. A three-disc version of this album, *Arc-Weld*, was also released with the third disc consisting of nothing but feedback.

own customized P.A.). But the shows were largely no-frills affairs devoid of the theatrics of his previous forays into arena rock territory. For the most part, the *Ragged Glory* tour just featured Neil Young and Crazy Horse playing their asses off.

The *Ragged Glory* tour kicked off at right about the same time Young learned that his mother, the notoriously cantankerous Rassy Young, had passed away.

Feisty as ever right up until the end, Rassy's death seemed to stir something deep within Young's own sense of artistic restlessness. Along with the first Gulf War (which he vehemently opposed, breaking away from his brief eighties flirtation with right-wing Republican politics in doing so), it is these two events that seemed to most fuel the incendiary performances of the *Ragged Glory* shows.

A live album from the tour was an obvious no-brainer.

A Spirit Came to Me and Said You Gotta Move to Start

Weld, the two-disc live collection from the *Ragged Glory* tour released in October 1991 (along with its expanded three-disc companion *Arc-Weld*), certainly captures the essence—not to mention the sheer bone-rattling volume—of the *Ragged Glory* shows well enough. As an overall live document, *Weld* is a magnificent snapshot of all the sound and fury of that amazing and historic tour.

Still, the album is not without its flaws.

On the CD version, these largely come down to the sound mixing. After completing a seemingly perfect mix for the album, David Briggs famously threw up his hands and left in disgust when Young still wasn't satisfied with the results. Briggs's abrupt departure left Young and Billy Talbot to complete the task, which they proceeded to mix into the ground, resulting in the bass-heavy murk heard on the CD release.

In its final form—and despite the less-than-perfect mixing job—*Weld* still stands as a decent enough live album. If nothing else, it is certainly Young's loudest. Still, the bass heavy mix mars what could have been a perfect concert document, as do repeat appearances of concert warhorses like "Cortez" and "Hurricane" that add little to the live versions first heard on *Live Rust* a decade prior.

Fortunately, the original David Briggs mix of the tapes survived, and—if you can find it today—can be heard on the accompanying *Weld* video document. Here, the sound is much brighter, and in many ways Larry "L.A." Johnson's concert film is a much better, more uniquely organic snapshot of all the (pardon the pun) "ragged glory" of a great Neil Young and Crazy Horse concert. Johnson's minimally shot footage adds considerable impact to Young's performance of Dylan's "Blowin' in the Wind" for one thing, as the screen shots from the Gulf War hammer that song's antiwar message home.

But the real stars of this video are the members of the audience.

Where shots of fans in the crowd often tend to be irritating in concert videos (especially from this period before modern technology changed the rules of the game), here they are quite entertaining.

You've got eighties headband guy playing the air drums. Balding Chinese hippie dude flails his arms wildly. And of course there's the nerdy African American chick with the buck teeth in the front row, who knows the words to every single song. Definitely my kind of gal.

If there ever was a more perfect picture of the broad cross section of fans making up a rock concert audience in the early nineties, then by all means sign me up to see it. Sadly, the *Weld* concert film—like so many of Young's vintage videos—has long since been relegated to the out-of-print status of a now over-priced collector's item.

The *Weld* concert film is one of those items from those long-lost "Archives" that literally screams to be brought back. Are you listening, Neil?

But what makes *Weld* the most unique concert document of Neil Young's career is without a doubt the *Arc* disc that can be found on the likewise now rare three-disc edition of the album. Reportedly conceived as the result of a suggestion by Sonic Youth's Thurston Moore, *Arc* is a thirty-five-minute montage of nonstop feedback from the shows. This also made for one of the coolest promotional items ever in the form of the promo-only "Arc: The Single."

It is to this day one of the most prized possessions in my own record collection.

Arc-Weld—especially on the now rare video mix—to this day stands as perhaps the single best document of Neil Young and Crazy Horse doing what they do best, which is shaking the basketball arenas of America to their very foundation.

However, with both Crazy Horse and David Briggs gone for the time being, and with his own ears by now irreparably damaged, Young was about to embark on a very different direction for his next record. By this time, unexpectedly shifting gears had become as natural for him as the way a chameleon changes its colors.

Even so, few expected that Young was finally going to make the long-awaited sequel to his biggest hit.

Laminated all access backstage pass from Neil Young and Crazy Horse's *Ragged Glory* tour.

31

From Hank to Hendrix

The Most Noteworthy Neil Young Covers, Collaborations, Send-ups, and Tributes

G iven his vast and continuing influence as one of the greatest songwriters of the rock-'n'-roll era, it should come as no surprise that Neil Young's songs have been covered by other artists hundreds, if not thousands of times.

What is truly amazing in Young's case, however, is the staggering diversity of genre-spanning artists who have either recorded his songs or performed them live. It is a list that stretches across both generations and genres—one that ranges from Johnny Cash, Willie Nelson, Dolly Parton, and Emmylou Harris, to Rush, Radiohead, and the Flaming Lips.

Art rockers dig him too, as evidenced by David Byrne's version of "Rockin' in the Free World" as well as Peter Gabriel's "Philadelphia" and David Bowie's "I've Been Waiting for You."

As hard as it might be to fathom, even an artist as unlikely as Lady Gaga has recorded her own version of a Neil Young song ("Out on the Weekend").

When researching the musicians who have covered Young's songs, the most obvious examples, of course, are those artists who already have their own unique connections with him. So, in that respect it is no surprise that someone like Linda Ronstadt, for example, would have numerous Neil Young songs ("After the Gold Rush," "Birds," "I Believe in You," "Look Out for My Love," "Love Is a Rose," and the list goes on) included amongst her own, already considerable recorded body of work. Ronstadt's own vocal harmonies can also be heard on a number of seminal Young albums including *Harvest, American Stars and Bars,* and *Harvest Moon.*

When it comes to newer-generation artists with unique ties to Young, one could also easily point toward Pearl Jam. The Seattle grunge band has covered "Rockin' in the Free World" numerous times—perhaps most famously with Young himself at the *MTV Video Music Awards.* Pearl Jam have also been known to cover his songs like "Fuckin' Up" in concert, and they even made an entire album (1995's Billboard top five *Mirror Ball*) with him. When Young was inducted into the Rock and Roll Hall of Fame, it was none other than Pearl Jam vocalist Eddie Vedder who did the honors.

There are also those bands that have made something of a second career out of playing Young's songs. We refer here not so much to the numerous Neil Young cover bands out there playing bars in towns across America, but to those groups that have recorded so many of his songs it's difficult to keep track of them all. Bands like Uncle Tupelo and fellow Canadians the Cowboy Junkies definitely fall into this category.

Others influenced by Neil Young who have chosen to pay tribute by recording their own versions of his songs include alt-rockers Sonic Youth ("Computer Age"), country legends like Waylon Jennings ("Are You Ready for the Country?"), and, of course, Willie Nelson. In addition to co-founding Farm Aid with Young, Nelson collaborated with him on the *Old Ways* album, and has been known to cover songs like "Heart of Gold" at his own concerts.

Johnny Cash is another example where the mutual respect between the Man in Black and Neil Young cuts both ways. Cash mined Young's songbook extensively while making his final series of *American Recordings* sessions with producer Rick Rubin, ultimately settling on haunting versions of "Pocahontas" and "Heart of Gold" for those amazing final albums.

"Heart of Gold" has also been notably covered by Tori Amos and seventies disco artist Boney M.

It's Gonna Take a Lotta Love

The list of female vocalists who have uniquely interpreted Neil Young's songs—particularly those from the sensitive singer-songwriter period marked by the albums *Harvest* and *After the Gold Rush*—is likewise a very long one, and includes artists ranging from Dolly Parton, Chrissie Hynde, and Annie Lennox, to Patti Smith, Natalie Merchant, and Tori Amos.

To list all of these would take up an entire book by itself. But Nicolette Larson's recording of "Lotta Love" probably stands out as among the most memorable, by simple virtue of the fact that she is one of the handful of artists to score a Billboard hit single with a Neil Young cover (another noteworthy example would be seventies one-hit wonders Prelude and their cover of "After the Gold Rush").

St. Etienne also scored a minor alt-rock hit in the nineties with their version of 'Only Love Can Break Your Heart" (which has also been covered by the likes of Everlast, Psychic TV, Elkie Brooks, and the Mint Juleps).

But speaking of "After the Gold Rush" . . .

Look at Mother Nature on the Run

The title track of his third solo album—at least according to our research—ranks as one of the Neil Young songs most often remade by other artists. By our count, the number of artists who have either recorded or performed their own versions of this song in concert includes the aforementioned Prelude, as well as the Flaming Lips, Natalie Merchant, Linda Ronstadt, Radiohead, Dolly Parton, Michael Hedges, and others too numerous to mention here.

It is no mistake that *Mojo* magazine ranked "After the Gold Rush" #1 in its 2010 list of the 50 Greatest Neil Young songs ever. However, when it comes to the all-time champs of his songs covered by other artists, it is far from being the sole contender.

When You See Me Fly Away Without You

"Birds," the seemingly obscure track from the same *After the Gold Rush* album, has been covered by—among others—the Meters, Paul Weller, Bette Midler, Everything but the Girl, and Ronstadt (yes, her again). "The Needle and the Damage Done" boasts cover versions by no less than Duran Duran, the Pretenders, Our Lady Peace, Simple Minds, and Tori Amos (yes, her again too).

"Cinnamon Girl," which certainly ranks as one of Neil Young's greatest rockers ever, is another classic that has been reinterpreted often, most frequently by alternative rock bands like Type O Negative and the Smashing Pumpkins. There are also versions of "Cinnamon Girl" out there by Courtney Love and Hole, Dream Syndicate, Uncle Tupelo, and even Who bassist John Entwistle (on his solo album *Smash Your Head Against the Wall*).

There are also some very memorable reworkings of Neil Young songs out there by what most would refer to as "jam bands," including a lengthy live version of "Cortez the Killer" from Built to Spill and Phish's take on "Albuquerque." Another of Young's more jam-tastic songs, "Like a Hurricane," has been covered by the Mission U.K., the Walkabouts, Roxy Music, and even *Saturday Night Live* comic Adam Sandler.

Four Strong Winds

Of course, this whole cover song thing obviously goes both ways, as Young has been known to record and perform a number of songs by some of his own influences and favorites over the years.

Bob Dylan comes most immediately to mind here. Young has paid homage to his closest equal as the greatest living songwriter of his generation on numerous occasions. Among the many Dylan songs he has covered are his versions of "Blowin' in the Wind" (the incendiary performances on the *Ragged Glory* tour); "All Along the Watchtower" (his best performance of which arguably took place at the 1992 "Bobfest" Madison Square Garden Dylan tribute); and "Forever Young" (which, contrary to some, is not a song that Dylan wrote about Young).

On the mostly forgettable album *Everybody's Rockin'*, Young covers a number of blues artists including Jimmy Reed, Slim Harpo, and Albert Lee, reinventing songs like "Payola Blues" as goofball rockabilly rave-ups. The album also includes a cover of "Mystery Train," a song made famous by one of Neil Young's original idols, the King of Rock 'n' Roll himself, Elvis Presley.

Speaking of immortals, Young has also been known on rare occasions to take on Otis Redding's most famous song, "Sittin' on the Dock of the Bay" (a great version can be found on the bootleg *Archives Be Damned* box set). Young's version of John Lennon's "Imagine" was likewise one of the highlights of the 9/11 "Tribute to Heroes" broadcast that aired on American television shortly after the Twin Towers attacks in New York City.

On some of the latter shows of the *Chrome Dreams II* tour, Young also took to performing a wild version of another Lennon track, the Beatles' *Sgt. Pepper* classic "A Day in the Life." During his performance of the song at 2009's Hard Rock Calling festival in London's Hyde Park, he was joined onstage by another former Beatle, Sir Paul McCartney.

Young has also covered songs by Don Gibson (the country classic "Oh, Lonesome Me" from *After the Gold Rush*), the Drifters (the very loud, very fucked-up reworking of "On Broadway" heard on the *Freedom* album), and Don and Dewey (the lascivious version of "Farmer John" with Crazy Horse on *Ragged Glory*).

Young's most famous cover probably remains his version of Canadian folk singer Ian Tyson's "Four Strong Winds" from the *Comes a Time* album. Young has called this song his favorite of all time on more than one occasion, and has many times recounted personal stories of feeding pocketfuls of dimes into a jukebox to repeatedly hear the song during his youth in Canada.

Looking Like a Fool with Your Pants on the Ground

Out of all the versions of Neil Young songs performed by other artists (that we have attempted to keep to a brief discussion here), there are also, of course, those that stick out as some of our personal favorites.

For sheer weirdness, it's hard to beat Lady Gaga's version of "Out on the Weekend," for sure. But the seventies gay disco singer Sylvester doing a song like "Southern Man" also warrants a mention in the high strangeness department—for the sheer audacity of it alone. Speaking of seventies disco, how about trying on the Undisputed Truth's version of "Down by the River" for size? It just doesn't get much weirder than that.

While they are not exactly covers, we would also be quite remiss if we didn't mention a few of the more uncannily accurate comedic send-ups of Neil Young over the years.

The National Lampoon comedy troupe's "Southern California Brings Me Down" from the sadly out of print album *Goodbye Pop* hilariously mocks Neil Young songs from "A Man Needs a Maid" (sample lyric: "I need someone to live with me, keep my bed warm, and sew patches on my jeans") to "Alabama" and "Ohio." Both the singer and the guitarist on this "song" have got Young's vocal and guitar sound down cold.

Sheet music for Nicolette Larson's cover of Neil Young's "Lotta Love." Neil once commented that in giving Nicolette the big hit, she had gotten his "Fleetwood Mac song." *Courtesy of Tom Therme collection*

But the undisputed all-time champ of comedic Neil Young impersonations is Jimmy Fallon. No contest here, Fallon wins it hands down. On his hilarious bits of "Neil" doing *American Idol* reject General Larry Platt's "Pants on the Ground" and the "Double Rainbow" song, Fallon nails Young to the point where you could almost be fooled into thinking it was actually him. Since then, Fallon has struck again, this time in a duet with Bruce Springsteen (the real one) doing "Whip My Hair" as Neil Young and the bearded Bruce from the *Born to Run* era. Freaking hilarious.

Adam Sandler's performance of "Powderfinger" with Young at the 2009 Bridge School benefit also warrants a mention here (although Sandler actually seems to be playing it fairly straight in the video we've seen).

Okay, so that's the funny stuff. Here are some of the other Neil Young covers (the serious ones) that we really like.

Radiohead: "On the Beach"

Any musical comparisons between Neil Young and Radiohead really boil down to two things. First would be their willingness to boldly experiment regardless of any resulting commercial fallout. But secondly (and for the purposes of this discussion, perhaps most importantly), the similarities really come down to Thom Yorke and that haunting voice of his.

Remind you of anyone else we know?

Musically—on the surface anyway—these are two great acts who couldn't be further apart in terms of their approaches to creating a sound that (frequent and distracting side trips aside) remains uniquely their own.

But while both artists have repeatedly shown a bold willingness to take musical risks over the course of their careers, Radiohead's experiments with sonics and texture on albums like *Kid A, In Rainbows,* and the recent *King of Limbs* have done more to stretch the boundaries of what is possible while working within the limitations of pop music than anything Neil Young has ever done.

Young, meanwhile, while being equally eager to experiment with his own sound, has always done so while remaining within more traditional music genres. This has remained largely true even as Neil has sometimes jumped wildly between these same genres, as he did in the eighties with albums like *Trans.*

Where Neil Young and Radiohead really meet, though, is in their stubborn devotion to their art. A very convincing argument could be made that Radiohead is really the first band to consistently record noncommercial, experimental albums like *Kid A*—while still maintaining a huge level of commercial success—since Neil Young was doing the same thing in the seventies with the Ditch Trilogy.

But more than anything else, Thom Yorke's falsetto on songs like "Everything in Its Right Place" has an uncanny resemblance to the tone that Neil Young uses on his own songs like "Will to Love" or "On the Beach."

Yorke himself has said in interviews that he fell in love with Young's work after reading reviews of Radiohead albums that compared his own voice to Young's. Curious, he purchased a copy of *After the Gold Rush* and became an instant fan, or so the story goes.

Although Radiohead have never officially recorded a Neil Young cover, they have performed several of his songs in concert. Of those we have heard, we especially like the acoustic version of "On the Beach" they did for a BBC radio broadcast a few years back, which, if you can find it, can be heard on a bootleg called *Gagging Order (Acoustic Renditions).* If not, you can always do a YouTube search like we did.

For a band known to stretch musical limits, Radiohead play it very straight on this letter-perfect version of the song, and Yorke's vocal fits the melancholic feel of the lyrics like a glove—especially when his voice cracks with a rare show of emotion during the line "I went to the radio interview and ended up alone at the microphone."

That one alone is guaranteed to produce shivers.

Radiohead have also been known to cover the Neil Young songs "Tell Me Why," "Down by the River," and "After the Gold Rush" in concert (the latter often coming as an intro to their own "Everything in Its Right Place").

Buddy Miles: "Down by the River"

Although you don't hear it much anymore on the radio today, the late, great Buddy Miles's version of "Down by the River" was nearly as much of an FM staple as Young's own recording back when he originally released the song in 1970 as part of the *Them Changes* album.

Miles is today mostly remembered as Jimi Hendrix's one-time drummer in the Band of Gypsys, and for his work with guitarist Mike Bloomfield in the Electric Flag. Outside of that, Miles's own solo work has been mostly hit and miss. But he nails it here with a great version of one of Young's earliest signature extended guitar freakouts.

On Buddy Miles's version, the guitar work isn't nearly as crazy as on Young's version from *Everybody Knows This Is Nowhere*. But it does hit a particularly haunting note with its sustained tone—it's a far cry from the psychedelic histrionics of Young's recording. Miles's drums also create the effect of a wall of sound that surrounds you like a vacuum. Miles's vocal also adds a sweet touch of soul to the song, and one that contrasts nicely with Young's more detached-sounding voice on the original version.

It is definitely one of the better examples of an early period Neil Young cover song.

Wilco: "Broken Arrow"

As one of those modern-day bands that most proudly wears its Neil Young influence on its collective sleeve, we already loved Jeff Tweedy's great alt-country band Wilco anyway.

But what we like most about this great cover of Neil's Buffalo Springfield track "Broken Arrow" (from the *MusiCares Tribute to Neil Young* DVD) is the way they recreate the groundbreaking effects (at least at the time) of the original recording. The fact that Wilco accomplish this without using tapes (these guys are all incredible musicians) makes this version of the song all the more amazing.

Tweedy's vocal is also a knockout. He captures the youthful innocence and vulnerability of Young's voice from the Springfield era perfectly here, in much the same way that Thom Yorke's voice echoes Young's more emotionally detached vocal qualities when Radiohead covers Neil Young.

For their next great Neil Young cover, what we'd really like to see is Wilco's monster guitarist Nels Cline get into some of his signature shredding on something like "Cowgirl in the Sand" or "Change Your Mind."

Nils Lofgren: *The Loner—Nils Sings Neil*

Few musicians today are as eminently qualified to cover the songs of Neil Young as the present-day guitarist in Bruce Springsteen's E Street Band, Nils Lofgren. This is exactly what he does on *The Loner*, an album devoted entirely to covering the music of Neil Young.

In a previous life, Lofgren was Young's second guitarist on a variety of albums ranging from *Tonight's the Night* to *Trans*. On *The Loner*, Lofgren offers up his own unique take on songs drawing from Young's entire career—from "On the Way Home" to "Like a Hurricane" to "Harvest Moon."

Lofgren's versions mostly remain true to the spirit of the originals. But because his own vocal style is somewhat similar to Young's (and of course because he is intimately acquainted with the artist in a way few others can claim), he breathes new life into them.

We especially like his versions of "Don't Be Denied," "Don't Cry No Tears," and, of course, "The Loner."

Patti Smith: "Helpless"

Nobody in their right mind has ever denied that Patti Smith is a visionary poet, or a trailblazing figure when it comes to redefining the role of women in the misogynistic world of rock 'n' roll she was born into during the seventies. But as much as her brilliant debut album *Horses* made her a critic's darling pretty much from the get-go, there was also a considerable rub on her back then—at least when it came to her voice.

Thirty years after that landmark album, Patti Smith proved her few critics wrong by making 2007's remarkable but sadly overlooked album *Twelve*.

On this album, Patti Smith proves herself to be an amazing singer as well, covering twelve songs by some of her favorite artists including Jimi Hendrix, the Stones, and yes, Neil Young.

On her version of Young's "Helpless," Patti breaks the CSN&Y version heard on *Déjà Vu* down into a stripped-down acoustic arrangement. In doing so, she wrings out the lyrical focus of Young's wistful memoir about his childhood Ontario in a way that reveals the longing sort of ache largely missed on CSN&Y's more overproduced version. As a vocalist, Smith displays a gift for interpretation here that even some of her biggest fans may not have realized she had.

On a side note, we also love Patti's take on Kurt Cobain's "Smells Like Teen Spirit" from this album.

For a more extensive look at the artists who have covered Neil Young's music, we recommend pointing your web browsers toward the Covers Project. You'll find them at http://www.coversproject.com/artist/Neil+Young.

The always reliable Thrasher's Wheat also has a great page devoted to the subject (50 Reasons Why Neil Young Is Important). You'll find it at http://www.thrashersblog.com/2006/11/50-reasons-why-neil-young-is-important.html.

On This Harvest Moon

Thirty Years Later, the Sequel

Whether it was because of the hearing damage he suffered following the *Ragged Glory* tour, or the often heated arguments surrounding the mixing of those same shows for the live *Arc-Weld* album, Neil Young turned the amps back down and put Crazy Horse back out to pasture—at least temporarily—for his next project.

One thing is for sure.

Years of playing rock 'n' roll at deafening volume with the Horse and others—culminating in the louder-than-God shows behind *Ragged Glory*—had finally caught up to Young by 1992. The result, depending on who you talk to, was a diagnosis of at least two medical conditions related to his hearing: hyperacusis (which is described as a hyper sensitivity to noise) and tinnitus (a persistent ringing in the ears).

Whatever the reason, Young spent most of 1992 doing a series of short tours, performing solo acoustic concerts. These shows were dominated by new material like "Old King," a funny song that draws an analogy between his dog and the king of rock 'n' roll, and "From Hank to Hendrix," which was often preceded by a story of how he came to acquire the guitar of another one of his heroes, Hank Williams.

Here I Am with This Old Guitar, Doin' What I Do

These, along with several other more romantic-sounding new songs, eventually wound up on Neil Young's next album, *Harvest Moon*, released in the fall of 1992. Widely hyped as the long-awaited sequel to his multiplatinum-selling, seventies blockbuster *Harvest*, there are indeed many striking similarities between the two albums.

The most obvious parallel, of course, is the album title, which certainly suggests a connection with the best-selling album of Young's career. Much of the same supporting cast also appears on both albums—including the return of both the Stray Gators (Ben Keith, Tim Drummond, Kenny Buttrey, and relative newcomer Spooner Oldham) and backup vocalists Linda Ronstadt and James Taylor (along with Nicolette Larson and Young's sister Astrid).

As was the case with *Harvest*, the songs on *Harvest Moon* were also first tried out on audiences in solo guitar, piano, and harmonica arrangements, but are much more fleshed out in the meticulously crafted studio recordings on the final album.

Not surprisingly, *Harvest Moon* also became Young's biggest hit in years, climbing to #16 on the Billboard albums chart, going platinum quickly, and eventually going on to double-platinum status. *Harvest Moon* remains one of the strongest, most consistent sellers in his entire catalog to this day.

However, while his apparent return to the sound that brought him his biggest commercial success delighted those fans who had been waiting decades for it, others at the time groused that *Harvest Moon* represented a return to the "middle of the road" that Young had once so famously dismissed in the self-penned liner notes for his *Decade* collection.

One of These Days, and It Won't Be Long

Harvest Moon is, in fact, arguably the lushest-sounding recording of Young's career. From Ben Keith's gorgeous pedal steel accents on "From Hank to Hendrix," to the beautiful female choir vocals heard in the background of the otherwise lyrically dark "War of Man," the arrangements on the album are immaculate. In contrast to the more overblown orchestration found on parts of *Harvest*, they are also deceptively simple—with perhaps the notable exception of Jack Nitzsche's string arrangement on "Just a Woman."

But it is these simpler touches—things like Young's beautifully plucked acoustic guitar harmonics between verses on the song "Harvest Moon," and the always sublime keyboards of Spooner Oldham throughout—that give *Harvest Moon* much of its wistful flavor of romance, tempered with just the slightest tinge of regret.

The album also contains some of his most wondrously descriptive—and apparently personal—songwriting. Hearing the lyrics on "Unknown Legend" about the girl who "used to work in a diner" with "her long blonde hair flowin' in the wind," and who is now "dressin' two kids," leaves little doubt as to the object of the songwriter's quite loving affection. Pegi is one lucky gal, at least if these lyrics are to be taken literally.

Young also seems to want to make peace with those friends he's treated badly in the past with the song "One of These Days." Here, he describes the apologetic letter he apparently one day hopes to write to, among others, "that old country fiddler, and all those rough boys who play that rock 'n' roll."

But mostly, *Harvest Moon* seems to be an album that finds an older, wiser Neil Young coming to terms with both his life and his relationships.

It's not a perfect album by any means. For every gorgeously descriptive lyrical turn of phrase that describes dancing in the light under a full harvest moon (a sentiment that he positively nails), there are also those songs that drag just a bit. "You and Me," for example, is either a beautifully simple statement of romantic love or a perfectly cringe-worthy exercise in schmaltz, depending on one's point of view.

But for the most part, *Harvest Moon* holds up remarkably well all these many years and decades later. In that respect, and considering the yin and yang of Neil Young's recorded output throughout the years, *Harvest Moon* is just about the most perfect follow-up to something like *Ragged Glory* one could have hoped for in 1992.

It was not, however, the only thing he was up to that particular year.

German Neil Young concert poster from the *Harvest Moon* period.
Courtesy of ThrashersWheat.org

Roll On, Southern Pacific . . .

For anyone who had ever been associated with him up to this point, Young's fascination with model trains was simply a fact of life. Occasionally however, this same obsession—with its roots apparently dating back to his childhood in Canada—could also prove to be a distraction when it came to the business of making records.

According to those who have been inside it, one look inside of the "train barn" on Young's Broken Arrow ranch—with its elaborate labyrinth of train tracks, tunnels, and meticulously detailed landscapes (complete with their own sound system)—certainly backs up this claim.

By many of these same accounts, the "train barn" is a world unto itself, and one where Young could, and often did, find escape from the outside world.

During the heated meetings between Young, Crazy Horse, and producer David Briggs leading up to the making of the *Ragged Glory* album, for example, an early sticking point was Young's desire to record at Broken Arrow—with potential distractions like the "train barn" being a primary concern.

Although *Ragged Glory* did eventually get made there, one can see where Briggs and Crazy Horse may have had a point. For his own part, Young has claimed in a number of interviews since that his obsession with the toy trains actually helps his creative process by energizing his otherwise scattered focus.

In 1992—the same year as the release of *Harvest Moon*—Young finally made his personal model train obsession an official second professional career as well.

That year, he joined forces with Richard P. Kughn—owner of Lionel, the most recognized name in the model train industry—to form Liontech. Young's first innovation as part owner of the company (and as an inventor in his own right) was the creation of Railsounds II—a lifelike sound system for Lionel, modeled on the same principles as those he used for his own sound rig in the train barn.

Later model train innovations he either had a hand in or just invented himself (Young holds a number of patents as an inventor) include CAB-1, a handheld remote unit for Lionel, designed at least in part with the handicapped in mind.

CAB-1's big red button "technology" was in fact first tested out by Neil's own non-oral, physically handicapped son Ben.

Eventually, Young would become an owner of Lionel Trains.

Said the Joker to the Thief

In the fall of 1992, Young also participated in the all-star thirtieth anniversary tribute to Bob Dylan that took place on October 16 at New York's Madison Square Garden.

Sharing the stage with such heavyweights as Eric Clapton, George Harrison, and Johnny Cash, as well as younger stars like Eddie Vedder and Sinéad

O'Connor (who left the stage in tears after being booed—part of the backlash against her following the now infamous *Saturday Night Live* appearance, where she ripped up a picture of Pope John Paul II), Neil Young all but stole the show at the event he later dubbed "Bobfest."

Young's electrifying performance of "All Along the Watchtower" that night was also significant as his first pairing with the legendary R&B band Booker T. and the MGs.

Famous for their contributions to records by such iconic artists as Otis Redding, and later as the backup band for John Belushi and Dan Aykroyd on the *Blues Brothers* album, tour, and feature film, this great band—featuring guitarist Steve Cropper and bassist Donald "Duck" Dunn in addition to keyboardist Booker T. himself—was about to add Neil Young's name to their already impressive list of clients.

The very next year, Young toured both America and Europe with none other than Booker T. and the MGs, filling the spot usually reserved for Crazy Horse.

Another significant yet largely overlooked 1992 album project for Young was his reunion with Cajun wildman Rusty Kershaw on the latter's solo album *Now and Then*. In their first full-on collaboration since the album *On the Beach*, Kershaw, Young and Ben Keith's work on tracks like "Future Song" captures much of the same beautifully desolate feel of their work together on the classic second side of that original landmark release from Neil Young's legendary Ditch Trilogy.

Although it is a long out-of-print collector's item now, if you can find Kershaw's *Now and Then*, the album is well worth the effort—especially for fans of *On the Beach*.

Although Young had succeeded in reuniting them for *Harvest Moon*, the Stray Gators only played a handful of live shows together in support of the album. For the majority of the live shows following the release of *Harvest Moon*, he simply continued on with the string of short solo acoustic tours that he had already been doing for nearly a year leading up to the album.

A Natural Beauty Should Be Preserved Like a Monument to Nature

Among the few dates Young did play with the Stray Gators were an appearance at the now annual Bridge School benefit show and a taping—make that two tapings—for MTV's then wildly popular series of "Unplugged" broadcasts for television.

The whole *MTV Unplugged* concept had become something of a cottage industry unto itself by then, as well as a successful vehicle for classic rock artists of Young's vintage to reinvent themselves or otherwise reinvigorate their often faltering careers.

Not that Young needed either at this point, of course.

As an artist, he had already been on a creative tear ever since 1989's comeback with the *Freedom* album—and had long since reestablished the original,
aging fan base lost during the eighties, while gaining instant credibility as an
icon amongst the newer generation of younger alternative rockers.

Still, this didn't stop the executives at Warner—or Elliot Roberts, for that
matter—from pushing Young to take part in the *MTV Unplugged* series, which
had already helped revitalize the careers of fellow legacy artists Eric Clapton
and Rod Stewart.

Eventually, he agreed, if reluctantly.

Not surprisingly, what seemed like a great idea on paper at the time proved
far less successful in terms of execution. The first attempt to tape an *MTV
Unplugged* session in New York City proved to be such a disaster that Young
reportedly ate the entire cost involved in order to ensure it never aired on
TV—or even worse, saw release as an actual Neil Young album.

A second try in Los Angeles—despite his resistance right up to the actual
taping—proved more successful. This was eventually released as—you guessed
it—Neil Young's own *MTV Unplugged* album in 1993. The televised concert was
also briefly available as a VHS video, although it has long since gone out of print.

Despite the problems behind the scenes—which included Young's own
dissatisfaction with the band's performance, as well as the usual disputes over
money from certain members of the same—the final *MTV Unplugged* document
is a fairly decent one. Highlights from the varied set list include a great version
of "Like a Hurricane," with Young on the pump organ, and the always reliable

Concert shirt promoting Neil Young's 1993 tour with Booker T. and the MGs. Opening
act Pearl Jam later backed Neil themselves on the *Mirror Ball* album.

Courtesy of Tom Therme collection

guitar and backing vocals of Nils Lofgren on a surprisingly lovely, stripped-down version of "Transformer Man" from the *Trans* era.

Interestingly, Seattle grunge-rock icons Nirvana would turn in one of the best *MTV Unplugged* sets ever about a year later. The resulting album and video from that session were released at roughly the same time the world learned that Kurt Cobain had taken his own life.

The only other new Neil Young music released in 1993 was the title song from the soundtrack to Jonathan Demme's film *Philadelphia*, a legal drama about an AIDS victim's wrongful employment termination suit starring Tom Hanks and Denzel Washington. The relationship between Young and Demme continued to bear significant fruit well into the new millennium, with a trilogy of concert films including *Heart of Gold, Neil Young Trunk Show,* and *Neil Young Journeys,* a document of the 2010–2011 solo *Twisted Road* tour.

Young's song from the movie was nominated for an Academy Award, which he also performed at the Oscars telecast. It ultimately lost out to Bruce Springsteen's "Streets of Philadelphia" from the same film. Unbeknownst to the general public, Young quietly donated his portion of the royalties from the song to the Gay Men's Health Crisis Center.

Lucky Thirteen, a collection of odds and ends from the eighties years on Geffen Records, also saw release in 1993, fulfilling Neil Young's final contractual obligations to the label.

Young finished out 1993 touring America and Europe with Booker T. and the MGs, with plans to record an album with them. However, and to borrow from the title of a much later Neil Young album, destiny was about to throw a proverbial fork in that road.

Change Your Mind

Sleeps with Angels, Mirror Ball, and How the Punks Met the Godfather of Grunge

The suicide of Kurt Cobain on April 8, 1994, was an event that shook the music world in ways that the leader of Seattle grunge rock band Nirvana himself could never have possibly imagined. Although they had only released three albums up to that point—*Bleach* on the Seattle-based independent Sub Pop label, along with *Nevermind*, and *In Utero* on David Geffen's new DGC imprint—Cobain's music with Nirvana had resonated with the nineties alternative-rock generation in ways not seen since the Beatles—and their own fallen hero, John Lennon—had in the sixties.

It has been said many times over the years that in Cobain, the twenty-something generation of the nineties saw a mirror image of themselves. This was particularly true as heard in the finely tuned alienation expressed in the lyrics of so many of Cobain's darker songs (mostly inspired by an isolated childhood spent as a social outcast growing up in the small, rough-and-tumble logging town of Aberdeen, Washington).

But lying just beneath Nirvana's wall of noisy guitars, big drums, and sometimes depressing lyrics, there was little denying that Cobain also had a natural gift for good old-fashioned pop hooks. One listen to his best songs from *Nevermind*—"Come as You Are," "In Bloom," and especially the smash "Smells Like Teen Spirit"—confirms this. Like John Lennon's best work with the Beatles, the lyrics may have been the message, but the music was ultimately the messenger making its delivery possible.

As for Cobain himself, by the time he chose to end his own life with a bullet one spring day in his Lake Washington home just outside Seattle, it was clear that the latest in a long line of rock heroes touted as the new "voice of a generation" wanted no part of it.

But as shocking as the news of the suicide was, there had already been signs that he was in deep physical and psychological trouble. His heroin addiction was hardly a secret within the Seattle alternative music community. The weeks leading up to his death had already seen one brush with death as the result of an overdose in Europe. Just days before taking his own life, Cobain had checked himself out of a rehab facility. Some reports of his final days on earth indicate

Japanese promo poster for Neil Young's *Sleeps with Angels* album. Released shortly after the suicide of Nirvana's Kurt Cobain, this album has been called the sequel to *Tonight's the Night* because of its lyrical focus on issues of death, life, and mortality.

there had even been clandestine visits to a dealer in a shady apartment building in Seattle's Capitol Hill district with the intent to score.

Cobain's death wasn't exactly the first tragedy with a drug connection within the tightly knit Seattle alternative music community either. Heroin had already claimed the life of Andrew Wood—lead singer for Mother Love Bone, the early grunge pioneers who eventually morphed into Pearl Jam after Eddie Vedder took what had once been Wood's spot. A few years later, Alice in Chains lead vocalist Layne Staley became the latest fatality amongst Seattle grunge-rock musicians intent on "chasing the dragon."

Yet, even as the bodies continued to pile up, the sad fact was that heroin had become so entrenched as part of the alternative rock scene—especially in Seattle—that few were surprised by news of the latest rock casualty related to drugs. In Staley's case particularly, many insiders had in fact long expected it.

Even so, the news of Cobain's suicide hit particularly hard. But as much as his music with Nirvana had struck a chord with "Generation X" in the same way that albums like *Sgt. Pepper* had impacted their parents during the sixties, the common musical thread between the two wasn't the Beatles at all.

It was Neil Young.

It's Better to Burn Out Than to Fade Away

Perhaps nowhere is this unlikely musical, and even spiritual, connection illustrated more profoundly than in Cobain's suicide note, where he famously quoted the lines "it's better to burn out than to fade away," from Neil Young's "My, My, Hey, Hey."

Although it had been rumored at the time that Young would stop playing the song altogether as a result of Cobain's use of its key lines in that cryptic note, "My, My, Hey, Hey" was performed at the annual Bridge School benefit show later that year, appropriately coupled with "Sleeps with Angels"—a new song Young had written in direct response to the tragedy.

During subsequent performances of "My, My, Hey, Hey" in the months immediately following Cobain's death, some fans have also reported that Young seemed to place more emphasis on the lines "once you're gone, you can't come back" than he had before.

"My, My, Hey, Hey" remains a fixture of Neil Young's concerts to this day.

Are You Feeling All Right, My Friend?

Following his tours of Europe and America with Booker T. and the MGs in 1993, many expected Young to make his next record with the soul legends as well. Instead, he surprised nearly everyone by reconvening in Los Angeles with Crazy Horse and producer David Briggs to make the album that eventually became 1994's *Sleeps with Angels*.

What couldn't have been known at the time that sessions for this record began at L.A.'s Complex Studios was just how deeply the ghost of Kurt Cobain would haunt the final album.

By this time, Young's spiritual kinship with the alternative rock community—particularly in Seattle—as well as his equally iconic status amongst them was already a matter of record.

Bands like Soundgarden and Blind Melon (whose own lead singer Shannon Hoon also died as the direct result of a drug overdose in 1995) toured with him, while songs like "Rockin' in the Free World" were covered by everyone from Pearl Jam to the Melvins. Young devotees like Dinosaur Jr.'s J. Mascis paid their own unique style of homage by fashioning their entire sound around the heavy riffing associated with the beautiful noise Young made on Old Black with Crazy Horse.

You Wait Around and Get the Word

Meanwhile, the still-untitled album Neil Young had begun making with Crazy Horse was already shaping up to be far more downbeat than any of his previous efforts recorded with Briggs and the so-called second greatest garage band in the world.

The few new songs Young initially brought to the sessions included "Change Your Mind," a lengthy guitar showcase he had already been playing on tour in Europe with Booker T. and the MGs. Here, he channeled the psychedelic improvisations last heard on 1969's *Everybody Knows This Is Nowhere.* Other songs were written right there in the recording studio, marking a return to the on-the-fly style of writing and recording that had characterized the original 1973 sessions for *Tonight's the Night.*

It's no mistake that comparisons between the two albums—and the way that death permeates both—are made often, or that *Sleeps with Angels* is sometimes called the sequel to *Tonight's the Night.*

But where much of that landmark album often has the atmosphere of a boozy wake, *Sleeps with Angels* has more of a somber, elegiac feel to it. With a few notable exceptions (the violent bursts of feedback characterizing the Cobain-influenced title track and the dreamlike jamming heard on the fifteen-minute "Change Your Mind"), the songs on *Sleeps with Angels* are much quieter and more overtly bleak. It is easily Young's darkest-sounding music since *On the Beach,* making the fact that this album rose all the way to #9 on the Billboard albums chart all the more astonishing. There was no tour to support the album.

"Sleeps with Angels" was in fact one of the last songs recorded for the album, with Young deciding it would also become the title track at the last minute (the decision to recreate *Tonight's the Night's* original black label for the CD—a great touch—was also reportedly made right as copies were about to be pressed).

The song itself came to Young on the golf course as he was participating in an Eddie Van Halen celebrity tournament for charity. The song lyrics "he sleeps with angels . . . too soon" pay tribute to Cobain in a sparse arrangement, interrupted only by sharp bursts of feedback. One only hopes that the more unhinged, twenty–minute version rumored to exist will eventually see the light of day as part of the ongoing *Archives* project.

Although it was written sometime before Cobain's suicide, the epic "Change Your Mind" could have just as easily been about that very same subject, and it makes a great companion piece to "Sleeps with Angels" on the final album. The way that Young and Poncho Sampedro's guitars interweave with each other on the lengthy instrumental breaks also recalls the amazing, original chemistry between Young and Danny Whitten on songs like "Down by the River." The song represents some of the best dual guitar work heard on a Neil Young album since *Everybody Knows This Is Nowhere.*

Taken together, these two tracks make up the lyrical and musical centerpiece of the album.

"Blue Eden," which immediately follows "Change Your Mind," continues to rattle off a laundry list of those things "embracing, distorting, supporting, controlling, destroying you" before concluding "I know someday we'll meet again." Elsewhere, songs like "Prime of Life," "Driveby," and "Trans Am" fit right in with the overall lyrical theme of death and mortality heard on *Sleeps with Angels* (intentional or otherwise). The haunting, dirgelike "Safeway Cart" also remains one of the single eeriest-sounding pieces of music ever to come from the pen of Neil Young.

Only "Piece of Crap" sticks out like a sore thumb here, coming off as an amusing but ultimately out-of-place, goofy-sounding rocker more in line with something like *Ragged Glory's* "Fuckin' Up."

Going, Going, Gone and the Picture Cries

Two promotional films were made for *Sleeps with Angels.* The first of these is a thirty- minute documentary capturing Neil Young and Crazy Horse recording the actual album at Complex. This video was shot by longtime Young videographer Larry "L.A." Johnson.

Like many of Young's film projects associated with Johnson, the film is said to be quite ragged in terms of actual quality, but also an accurately raw and immediate snapshot of the odd relationship and recording process between Young, Briggs, and Crazy Horse. The film remains mostly unseen, at least outside of those within Neil Young's inner circle.

The second, more professionally filmed document from the *Sleeps with Angels* period is the *Complex Sessions* video shot by acclaimed director Jonathan Demme and released on VHS. Though long out of print, this film captures Neil Young and Crazy Horse performing four songs from *Sleeps with Angels*—"My Heart," "Prime of Life," "Piece of Crap," and an epic version of "Change Your Mind" that rivals the one on the *Sleeps with Angels* album—live in the Complex Studios, one day after that year's Bridge School benefit.

Although the *Complex Sessions* film has its critics—*Shakey* biographer Jimmy McDonough being chief among them—if you can find it today (check eBay), it is well worth owning for the stunning, twenty-minute "Change Your Mind" alone.

In the version I found (again, on eBay), the goofy video bits criticized by McDonough in *Shakey* also seem to have been largely edited out.

The Act of Love Was Slowly Pounding, Slowly Pounding, Slowly Pounding

On January 12, 1995, in a glitzy ceremony held at New York City's Waldorf Astoria Hotel, Neil Young was inducted into the Rock and Roll Hall of Fame as a solo artist. A few years later, he was inducted once again into the Hall as a member of the Buffalo Springfield—an event he famously no-showed. His apparent snub of his former Springfield bandmates prompted one of the funniest lines ever spoken during a Rock Hall ceremony, when Stephen Stills turned to Richie Furay and said, "He quit again."

Young's own 1995 Rock Hall induction (honoring his work as a solo artist) was marked by speeches from both Atlantic Records chairman Ahmet Ertegun and Pearl Jam's Eddie Vedder. Once the speeches were over, the inevitable all-star jam fest followed.

This proved to be a particularly sloppy affair that involved various members of Crazy Horse and Pearl Jam backing up Neil on songs ranging from "Fuckin' Up" to the newer "Act of Love," before devolving into an ill-conceived pairing with Led Zeppelin for an odd take on that group's "When the Levee Breaks," incorporating a few verses of Stills's "For What It's Worth."

A true WTF moment before such a thing even existed.

In his own acceptance remarks, Young thanked everyone from Rassy, Mo, and Elliot to Pegi, Crazy Horse, and Kurt Cobain. To the relief of nearly all present that night, he also refrained from going off on a rant dissing those individuals far less deserving of praise.

More significantly, and as sloppy as things often got in the jam that night, the seeds had been sown for Neil Young's next project—an album he would record over a couple of wild days two weeks later in Seattle with Pearl Jam.

"Seattle's basically over now," Young told *Shakey* biographer Jimmy McDonough of his decision to make a record with the grunge rockers on their own turf. "So it's time for me to go. Cleanup man . . ."

Where's the Feel of Body Heat?

Although the names of Neil Young and Kurt Cobain will be forever linked by virtue of the latter's suicide note, Young's closest musical allies in the alternative rock scene at the time were in fact the members of Pearl Jam.

Their musical paths had already crossed numerous times—most often when one would show up at the other's gigs. In one of the most memorable pairings from the period, Young and Pearl Jam tore the roof off the building at the 1993 MTV Video Music Awards with a blistering version of "Rockin' in the Free World."

Young was particularly energized by the way Pearl Jam had taken to his new songs like "Act of Love" during their performance together at a Washington, D.C., pro-choice benefit concert, and in the informal jams that took

Merkin Ball—Pearl Jam's companion E.P. to their album with Neil Young, *Mirror Ball.*

place in the days leading up to Young's induction into the Rock Hall. Spurred on by the endorsement of manager Elliot Roberts—who loved the idea of his elder rock statesman client collaborating with the hottest new kids on the block—the no-brainer decision to make an album together in Seattle was made official shortly after Eddie Vedder's Rock Hall speech inducting Young in New York.

Mirror Ball is an album that, even by Neil Young standards, came very quickly. Recorded over a span of just four days with Pearl Jam producer Brendan O'Brien at Seattle's Bad Animals—the studio owned by the Wilson sisters of Heart fame—the album is also notable because it represented one of those rare instances of Young making music in a strange new environment, and on terms other than his own.

This was, after all, Pearl Jam's producer recording Pearl Jam at a studio in Pearl Jam's hometown. Young's usual comfort zone of being surrounded by familiar faces like David Briggs and Crazy Horse (who had once again been left behind as Young pursued the latest of his many artistic whims) at a locale like the Broken Arrow ranch were far, far away during the whirlwind sessions in Seattle.

Even so, as anyone familiar with the stories behind the recording of such classic albums as *Tonight's the Night* and *On the Beach* already knows, this style of "capturing the moment" by writing and recording songs in the studio and on the fly suited Young just fine. Although he initially showed up at the sessions with just two songs—including one that Pearl Jam already knew ("Act of Love")—there was enough of a high-energy vibe between the two musical behemoths in the room that several other new songs quickly followed.

I Got Id

As it turned out, the sessions proved to be more prolific than anyone could have ever imagined. In just four days, they had not only a completed Neil Young album but enough leftover material for a companion E.P. from Pearl Jam.

The *Merkin Ball* E.P., as it turned out, proved to be a necessary evil.

The original plan for what became Neil Young's *Mirror Ball*, was to release the sessions as a full-on Neil Young and Pearl Jam collaborative effort, with both parties receiving equal billing on the album sleeve. Executives at Pearl Jam's label Sony, however, resisted this idea, and refused to allow their band to be credited on what they saw as a Neil Young album. The two-song *Merkin Ball* E.P. was eventually released by Sony as a Pearl Jam recording, while Reprise put out *Mirror Ball* as Neil Young's new record.

Of the two songs on PJ's *Merkin Ball*, "I Got Id" is by far the most explosive, and comes closest to capturing the frenetic energy that dominates the full-length companion album credited to Young. Eddie Vedder's passionate vocal screams on this song also serve as a perfect complement to some of the most blazing hard-rock guitar heard from Neil Young in years.

Downtown, Hear the Band Playin'

Upon a first listen, *Mirror Ball* hits you like a freight train and doesn't let up at all from there. The musical chemistry between Young and Pearl Jam is undeniable, and the result is a blast of pure hard-rock adrenaline that in some ways pulls off the trick of beating Crazy Horse albums like *Ragged Glory* at their own game. Where the Horse's specialty on those albums lies in their ability to lay down a loose and funky groove behind Young's wall of guitar, Pearl Jam more or less just let it rip here.

In that respect, *Mirror Ball* is arguably the best pure hard-rock record of Young's entire career—a sonic blast of musical Dexedrine combining the punk-rock energy of the Ramones, with the tight musical chops you'd more likely associate with a group of seasoned pros like Booker T. and the MGs.

Once you get past its amped-up, high-energy vibe, there are also some great songs on this album.

Given Pearl Jam's involvement—and the general cynicism and mistrust among alternative rockers toward their parents' generation—the way many of these songs invoke sixties nostalgia and hippie values is a bit strange. As if there were any doubt of this, one of the best songs on *Mirror Ball* sports the title "Peace and Love," and the lyrics even make direct reference to John Lennon. Elsewhere,

Promotional poster for *Mirror Ball*, Neil Young's mid-nineties album with Seattle grunge rock band Pearl Jam.

the song "Downtown" celebrates a "psychedelic dream" where "all the hippies go" and Jimi Hendrix and Led Zeppelin trade licks on the stage.

Other songs given the high-octane Pearl Jam treatment here include "Throw Your Hatred Down," one of Young's strongest antiwar songs in years (with sentiments largely shared by Pearl Jam's generation), and "I'm the Ocean," where some of Neil's most autobiographical lyrics ever become hidden deep within the glorious racket being made by the band. *Mirror Ball* also continues Neil Young's long-standing tradition of Indian-themed songs on "Big Green Country," which includes lyrics describing a great chief watching his painted braves closing in for an easy kill.

Released in June 1995, *Mirror Ball* became Young's highest-charting album in years—peaking in Billboard's top five.

Who Will You Love in a World of Constant Strangers?

The mutual admiration society between Neil Young and Pearl Jam continued with a short tour of Europe, along with a handful of shows back in the U.S. Their close relationship continues on through the present day, with PJ being a fixture at the annual Bridge School benefit concerts.

Mirror Ball is remembered today by some fans as the last of Young's amazing "comeback run" of consistently great albums made during the early to mid nineties.

Although there was still some great music to come after the new millennium, Young seemed content to ride out the remainder of the nineties more preoccupied with his newfound status as owner of the Lionel Train company. In a deal engineered by Elliot Roberts, Young fulfilled a childhood dream by purchasing the company in partnership with Martin Davis and Greg Feldman as 1995 drew to a close.

There were new Neil Young records in the nineties, of course, including reunions with both Crazy Horse and a long-awaited one with Crosby, Stills, and Nash. But *Mirror Ball* would prove to be his last real blaze of glory for several years to come.

Good to See You Again

Broken Arrow, Dead Man, and Year of the Horse

I f there is such a thing as making peace with a man like David Briggs, Neil Young can rest easy, knowing that he did so just days before the producer behind many of his greatest records died. In the days leading up to his death at age 51 on November 26, 1995, after a battle with lung cancer, Briggs and Young reconciled following the latest of their many separations over the course of a long and often volatile personal and working relationship.

The latest schism came when Young left both Briggs and Crazy Horse in the dust yet again in order to follow his latest artistic whim. This time around, he ditched his musical comrades to make *Mirror Ball* with Pearl Jam, a record Briggs reportedly threw in the trash can when Young sent him a copy. Besides recording and then touring Europe (along with a few select American dates) with Pearl Jam, Young had also been busy with a number of other projects, including buying the Lionel Train Company and making a soundtrack album for Jim Jarmusch's psychedelic western *Dead Man*, starring Johnny Depp.

Dead Man

Although many of his hardcore fans swear by it today, the music on *Dead Man* can be challenging for novice listeners even by Neil Young standards.

The album intersperses mostly short, abstract instrumental passages played by Young on electric guitar and the occasional pump organ (the 1:33 "organ solo" bears more than a slight resemblance to the intro of *Mirror Ball's* "Peace and Love"), with actual dialog from the movie.

Many of these tracks are simply labeled as numbered guitar solos. Of these, the fourteen-minute "Guitar Solo No. 5" is probably the most interesting. For all of its New Age meanderings, *Dead Man* also has a quietly desolate feel that, taken in short doses anyway, can be quite beautiful (even if in a dreamy but unsettling way). In other respects, the solo electric guitar and accompanying feedback of *Dead Man* foreshadows Young's much more focused work years later with producer Daniel Lanois on the 2010 album *Le Noise*.

Still, one has to wonder if this is what Neil Young actually had in mind for *Meadow Dusk*—the unreleased New Age album he once considered making for David Geffen as his beleaguered contractual relationship with the music mogul neared its merciful end in the late eighties.

Dead Man is also notable for being Young's lone solo release on his own Vapor Records imprint. The independent record label launched by Young and Elliot Roberts later became noteworthy as home to a variety of eclectic artists ranging from Vic Chesnutt, Tegan and Sara, and Jonathan Richman, to longtime Neil Young confidants like his wife Pegi and Ben Keith.

I'm Still Living in the Dream We Had

If any good came out of the death of David Briggs, and from Neil Young's final reconciliation with him, it was Young's subsequent rededication to working with Crazy Horse. The initial result of this rebirth was a misguided attempt to put together a Crazy Horse "solo album"—produced by Young under the pseudonym of Phil Perspective. This ultimately proved to be a dead end.

However, a short series of mostly unannounced concerts with Crazy Horse played in small venues proved to be far more successful.

Playing under assumed names like the Echos, these summer 1995 "roadhouse" shows included gigs performed at nontraditional venues like their extended residency at the Old Princeton Landing. Those fans fortunate enough to hear about it were treated to three sets a night at the tiny venue for the bargain price of twenty bucks a head. The loose set lists leaned heavily on the obscure, including a healthy dose of material from the underrated 1975 album *Zuma*. In a touch that David Briggs would have no doubt appreciated, Poncho also brought along the producer's spirit to the club gigs by keeping some of his ashes hidden inside the amps onstage.

In between these small, informal gigs, Neil Young and Crazy Horse also kept busy recording new material at his Broken Arrow Ranch. However, the album that emerged from the sessions, 1996's *Broken Arrow*, was greeted with something of a collective yawn, both by critics and the record-buying public. Where its predecessor *Mirror Ball* with Pearl Jam was a top five chart hit, *Broken Arrow* didn't even crack the top thirty, peaking at a dismal #31 on Billboard. The comeback streak Young had been riding since 1989's *Freedom* appeared to be over.

Played a Game in the Music Arcade

Despite its flaws (which are many), *Broken Arrow* may very well be one of Neil Young's most underrated records. Like many of his other albums that were dismissed at the time of their original release (the albums comprising the Ditch Trilogy and *Trans* come most immediately to mind here), this is one of those records that grows on you considerably over time.

The movie poster for Jim Jarmusch's concert film *Year of the Horse* urges fans to "Crank it up." The accompanying live album, one of several over the years featuring Neil Young and Crazy Horse, is not among their best.   *Courtesy of Noah Fleisher/Heritage Auctions*

Depending on who you talk to, *Broken Arrow* either offers a rare glimpse of Neil Young and Crazy Horse truly in their element by playing at their rawest, or it is just an uneven, sloppy mess. In truth, the album captures a little of both extremes, and probably falls somewhere in the middle. While *Broken Arrow* is far from being flat-out *Everybody's Rockin'* awful, there is also no getting around the fact that it represents a slight letdown following the streak of commercial and critical successes that Young had been consistently cranking out during the first half of the nineties.

Even so, *Broken Arrow* is certainly not without its moments.

In typical Crazy Horse fashion, four of the tracks—accounting for roughly half of the album—play out at seven minutes or longer, with varying degrees of success. With its overall loose and even sloppy feel, the album it most compares to would probably be *Time Fades Away*.

The opening "Big Time" sets the tone of *Broken Arrow* right out of the gate. This lyrical reaffirmation of purpose between Neil Young and his often abused bandmates plays out to the sort of twangy, guitar-driven country-rock groove that could fit right alongside something like *Rust Never Sleep's* "Powderfinger."

Although the playing here is unquestionably relaxed, on tracks like the meandering, nearly ten-minute jam "Loose Change," Crazy Horse also sound much more like an actual band than just Neil Young's sidemen. Even so, the seemingly endless E chord during the midsection of "Loose Change" might seem like a bit much to the uninitiated ear. And although "Slip Away" contains some truly amazing guitar passages structured around a melody so simple as to be somewhat misleading, the murky-sounding mix also manages the trick of completely burying the song's equally gorgeous lyrics.

Speaking of simple, "Music Arcade" contains the starkest arrangement of the entire record—it's basically just Neil and his acoustic guitar. It is also one of the album's most powerful songs. Here again, the lyrics seem to be about Young's reunion with Crazy Horse and the joy he experienced as he "kept winnin' while the band played." In another key metaphor, he compares this feeling to "a comet in the sky tonight, makes me feel like I'm alright" (interestingly, another of *Broken Arrow's* songs, "Scattered," also makes reference to "a comet painted on the sky"). By contrast, the stripped-down arrangement of the song—and especially Neil's more whispered than fully sung vocal—recalls the desolate musical landscape last heard on 1974's *On the Beach*.

Broken Arrow also contains the throwaway tracks "Changing Highways" and "This Town." A live version of Jimmy Reed's blues standard "Baby What You Want Me to Do," taken from the Old Princeton Landing residency, likewise comes across as a particularly ill-conceived idea—the recording is so bad it's barely listenable (although it does effectively capture the boozy, bar band ambience of Young's brief "roadhouse tour" of 1995).

The now rare vinyl-only version of *Broken Arrow* also features the even rarer track "Interstate."

Calling Me to Bring My Guitar Home

Somewhat surprisingly, and in a break from his usually clockwork prolific routine of putting out one new album every year, 1996's *Broken Arrow* turned out to be Neil Young's final solo album of studio recordings in the nineties.

In an even bigger surprise, he closed out the decade by reuniting with Crosby, Stills, and Nash for the 1999 album *Looking Forward*.

Although he continued to record off and on during this period, his next few years were primarily spent on the road. A series of tours with Crazy Horse included jaunts across Europe, as well as shows in Canada and back home in the States as part of the traveling hippie fest H.O.R.D.E., which Crazy Horse co-headlined with second-generation jam bands Big Head Todd and the Monsters, Toad the Wet Sprocket, and Squirrel Nut Zippers.

Returning the *Dead Man* soundtrack favor, director Jim Jarmusch documented a number of Crazy Horse shows from this period on film, and eventually released them as the 1997 concert rockumentary *Year of the Horse*. The resulting movie is mostly a mixed bag combining 1996–97-era concert footage of Neil

Neil Young performs live in Sedona, Arizona, during a benefit show with Jackson Browne.
Photo by Mary Andrews

and Crazy Horse, backstage interviews, and even some of the leftovers from the aborted late eighties *Muddy Track* film. It does, however, contain the now classic scene of Young responding to a heckler from the audience yelling "they all sound the same" with the deadpan line "it's all the same song."

The live soundtrack album accompanying the film is not one of his stronger concert recordings, although it is significant for having one of the more interesting set lists on a live Neil Young album. Rarities like "When Your Lonely Heart Breaks" and an even rarer full-band version of "Pocahontas" from the acoustic side of *Rust Never Sleeps* all make appearances here, as does the infrequently performed "Danger Bird" from *Zuma*.

35

Let's Roll

Silver and Gold, Looking Forward, 9/11, Are You Passionate?, and *Greendale*

W ith the dawn of the new millennium, Neil Young went on something of a creative tear with a flurry of new projects, many of which involved a revolving cast of familiar players—including CSN, various members of the Stray Gators, and the ever-reliable Crazy Horse—who had served him so well in the past.

First up was the latest CSN&Y reunion, resulting in yet another disappointing album (1999's *Looking Forward*) that once again failed to recapture the original magic of 1970's classic *Déjà Vu*.

However, for their first extended run of concerts together since 1974's Doom Tour—aside from occasional one-offs like their appearance at the 1985 Live Aid mega benefit—things went much better. If anything, the CSNY2K tour proved once and for all that the public appetite for live CSN&Y had not abated one bit. Indeed, the hunger for these shows amongst fans—including a new generation of concertgoers who were unable to experience them the first time around—remained as strong as it had ever been.

For all of its success from a musical and commercial standpoint, though, the CSNY2K tour also raised just as many questions.

Although the shows brought the expected sellout crowds—and the band also delivered the goods musically—the tour also helped set in motion a disturbing trend among touring legacy acts for charging exorbitantly high ticket prices. With the best seats for CSNY2K topping out at a then-unheard-of $200 a pop, the CSNY2K tour set a new pricing standard that was subsequently adopted by a number of other classic acts from the sixties, seventies, and eighties rock era. This included everyone from the Eagles and the Stones to U2 and the Police.

The high prices remain largely in place today, although there are a few notable exceptions to the rule. Bruce Springsteen is certainly one artist who could easily get away with charging more for his concerts, but has instead chosen to keep his reunion tours with the E Street Band priced under $100. Bob Dylan's shows have also maintained a more reasonably modest ticket price. Young, on the other hand, has continued the practice of charging the high ticket prices that he helped pioneer. This has remained true whether he is playing with a full band in an arena or doing small theatres on his solo concert tours.

But we'll get to more on that soon enough.

Neil Young performing at Willie Nelson's 2003 4th of July picnic.   *Photo by Mary Andrews*

So I Dove into the Darkness, and I Let My Missiles Fly

Young's work during the new millennium also found him reembracing various social and political concerns. These ran the gamut from the pro-environmentalist stance of albums like *Greendale* to the brasher "folk-metal-protest" of *Living with War.*

Not surprisingly, and as has always been the case with Young, many of these songs also carried mixed messages. There are few other artists in all of rock 'n' roll—and even fewer coming from his same sixties hippie era—who in just four short years could go from the patriotic rah-rah of 2002's post-9/11 "Let's Roll" to 2006's impassioned cry of "Let's Impeach the President."

It can certainly be said Neil Young was a man of many contradictions then and also that he remains one to this day.

Yet as frequently as his post-nineties work shifted lyrical gears, the changes were just as often musical ones. His status as one of the only rock-'n'-roll artists of his generation able to maintain continuing musical and social relevance for younger generations of listeners probably has as much to do with own artistic restlessness as it does with anything else. The decade about to unfold found Young about as musically all over the place as he had ever been.

But first, he would give Crosby, Stills, and Nash another try.

I Feel Like Making Up for Lost Time

In many ways, 1999's CSN&Y reunion album and subsequent tour happened as the result of a happy accident. As part of the journey of musical rediscovery that came about as the result of his own ongoing work on the *Archives* project, Young had taken an unexpected, though quite necessary side road through his sixties work with Buffalo Springfield. This ultimately resulted in a Buffalo Springfield boxed set of its own (2001's *Box Set*).

As the story goes, what began as a meeting with former Springfield bandmate Stephen Stills in order to get him to sign off on the Springfield box ended with Neil Young himself signing on for the latest Crosby, Stills, and Nash album.

At the time, he was putting the final touches on his own album—an acoustic record he had been making on and off in between Crazy Horse tours dating back to 1997. Upon hearing a new Stills song for the CSN album that his former

Picture sleeve for the "Sun Green" single from *Greendale.*
Courtesy of Tom Therme collection

bandmate was working on, Young was impressed enough with what he had heard to offer his own services on guitar. From there, he then offered up the pick of the litter of songs for his own then projected album *Silver and Gold*.

Four Neil Young songs (the most from any of CSN&Y's four members)— "Slowpoke," "Out of Control," "Queen of Them All," and "Looking Forward"— were selected for what by now was shaping up to be a full-blown Crosby, Stills, Nash, and Young reunion album. One of them, "Looking Forward," was also picked as the title track.

While the resulting *Looking Forward* album didn't exactly set the world on fire either critically or commercially, the tour did huge business, raking in $42 million and earning CSN&Y the #8 spot on that year's list of the most profitable concert attractions.

In 2000, Young also released what is arguably the quietest, most low-key record of his career. *Silver and Gold* was a record he had been attempting to complete off and on for nearly three years. At one point in the process, *Acoustica* was briefly considered as a working title.

Conceived as an acoustic album, it was eventually fleshed out with the addition of many of the same familiar names used on his previous "folkie" outings *Harvest* and *Comes a Time*, including Stray Gators Ben Keith and keyboardist Spooner Oldham as well as backup vocalists Emmylou Harris and Linda Ronstadt. They were joined by bassist Donald "Duck" Dunn and drummer Jim Keltner, both of whom had toured with Young in the nineties during his brief fling with Booker T. and the MGs after the "Bobfest" tribute to Dylan.

Where the songs on both *Harvest* and *Comes a Time* contain undeniable elements of pop craftsmanship and, in many cases, appear to be purely designed

Concert shirt for the *Greendale* tour.   *Courtesy of Tom Therme collection*

greendale tour

Vancouver, BC
Portland, OR
Sacramento, CA
Los Angeles, CA
Albuquerque, NM
Colorado Springs, CO
Milwaukee, WI
Chicago, IL
Moline, IL
Detroit, MI
Cleveland, OH
Hershey, PA
Philadelphia, PA
Wallingford, CT
New York, NY
Amherst, MA

with commercial radio play in mind, *Silver and Gold* feels like a much more personal album. It is certainly a quieter, moodier-sounding record than either of its more obviously commercial predecessors. Some of the songs are also quite old, with the title track in particular dating back several years.

What really makes *Silver and Gold* stand out, though, is the fact that Young has never sounded more, dare we say it, "contented" than he does on this album. The easy, back porch vibe of the music certainly reinforces the album's overall laid-back mood. But the lyrics of the songs also seem to reveal a far more relaxed and less restless side of Young's typically more relentless nature.

Songs like "Silver and Gold," "Good to See You Again," and especially the gorgeous "Razor Love" find him embracing simple values like love and family, even as he yearns wistfully for the opportunity of having another go with his more distant rock-'n'-roll past on "Buffalo Springfield Again." Album closer "Without Rings" also boasts one of Young's best vocal performances, with the dreamlike lyrics sung in the same beautiful lower register heard on "Ambulance Blues" from *On the Beach* (yet with nary a hint of that song's more depressing tone).

The overall result is some of the simplest and prettiest music of his entire career. Subtle is not usually a word associated with Neil Young, but the relaxed, airy sentiments heard on *Silver and Gold* are so beautifully understated, at times it's as though they are barely even there.

An acoustic concert video, also titled *Silver and Gold*, was released in 2000 on VHS format as a complement to the album. The concert features several songs from the album, along with those that ended up on CSN&Y's *Looking Forward*. There are also some interesting rarities, like a performance of "Philadelphia," the song Young wrote for the Jonathan Demme film of the same name.

For the tour to promote the *Silver and Gold* album, he hit the road with a band including Oldham, Keith, Dunn, and Keltner, along with wife Pegi and sister Astrid filling the backup singer roles of Ronstadt and Harris on the album. Yet another live album, 2000's largely forgettable *Road Rocks V1: Friends and Relatives*, was culled from the tour's stop at Colorado's Red Rocks Amphitheatre. This same show was also released in video form as *Red Rocks Live: Friends and Relatives*, and is still available on DVD.

Time Is Runnin' Out

Sometime around the year 2000, in between the barnstorming CSNY2K arena tour and the more sublime pleasures found on *Silver and Gold*, Young found time to book studio time with Crazy Horse in San Francisco for yet another rumored to be complete, but never released album called *Toast*.

The projected album title reportedly comes from the location of these sessions, as does the one song that survived and made it onto a Neil Young album. A barn burner in the tradition of "Hurricane" and *Ragged Glory's* "Love and Only Love," "Goin' Home" is the only song credited to Crazy Horse on the

2002 album *Are You Passionate?*. The recording locale is likewise simply listed as "Toast, San Francisco, CA, USA" on the CD's foldout inner sleeve. In 2002, on the second Crosby, Stills, Nash, and Young reunion tour in two years, "Goin' Home" became a highpoint of the shows night after night, as it became the vehicle for some particularly fiery guitar duels in the ongoing shootout between Young and Stills.

There are strong rumors that the rest of the *Toast* album may yet surface, as part of the second volume of *Archives*.

Another standout from the album that eventually became *Are You Passionate?* is "Let's Roll," a song Young released several months earlier as a single, just weeks following the 9/11 attacks. The title refers to the phrase Todd Beamer uttered to fellow passengers abroad United Airlines Flight 93 just before their heroic decision to fight back against the terrorists on September 11, 2011—a suicide mission that ultimately crashed their plane into a Pennsylvania field below, killing everyone onboard.

Written quickly in much the same way that "Ohio" had been some thirty years prior, the political messages of the two songs couldn't be further apart. Although "Let's Roll" wasn't initially criticized during the generally united mood of the country following 9/11, it was later thought by some to be an endorsement of George W. Bush and a return to the conservative political stance of some of Young's mid-eighties work.

Any such notions however, were put to rest a few years later with the release of 2006's *Living with War* and the strident, anti-Bush tone of songs featuring none-too-subtle titles like "Let's Impeach the President."

The remaining songs on *Are You Passionate?* feature a band comprised of Booker T. and the MGs members Donald "Duck" Dunn, and Booker T. Jones himself, along with Young mainstays like Frank "Poncho" Sampedro (all three of whom are also credited as co-producers). The album also marks the emergence of a new, more soulful, Motown-influenced sound, which drew some jeers at the time that Young had returned to his eighties genre-hopping ways.

Although the album is slightly uneven (the oddly placed sore thumb of a Crazy Horse guitar assault like "Goin' Home" in the middle of this album, great as it is, doesn't help matters much), there is little denying the tight, soulful groove of the band. Booker T.'s organ flourishes are especially sweet on "You're My Girl," "Let's Roll," and "When I Hold You in My Arms." Neil does Motown—who knew?

Generators Were Runnin', Vans Parked in the Field

Greendale, released in 2003, may be the strangest record of Neil Young's career. Part rock opera and part stream-of-consciousness political rant, *Greendale* is also perhaps the most audacious project in a body of work already characterized by such initially misunderstood albums as *Tonight's the Night*. It is certainly among his most ambitious.

Initially premiered with a series of solo shows where Neil performed the new songs in a stripped-down acoustic format, *Greendale* eventually ballooned into a full-band album with Crazy Horse, as well as an accompanying film—shot in the same grainy, surrealistic cinema verité style of previous Neil Young celluloid adventures *Journey Through the Past* and *Human Highway*.

There was also a theatrical concert presentation of *Greendale* with Crazy Horse, featuring a cheesy set composed of cardboard cutouts depicting its fictional town and what one critic described as "fifty people on stage" (they were actually actors playing the roles of *Greendale* characters like Grandpa, Carmichael, and Sun Green).

The *Greendale* tour also continued the tradition of higher ticket prices that had begun on the CSNY2K tour, a fact that Young justified in interviews by essentially saying this weeded out the riff-raff, drawing a higher caliber of concertgoer who could better appreciate this latest example of the artist chasing after his muse.

Still, perhaps as a concession to those who could afford the tickets, Young and Crazy Horse closed every show with a quick set of favorites like "Hurricane" and "Rockin' in the Free World," following the front-to-back performance of *Greendale*. He also backed the eco-friendly message of *Greendale* by transporting its larger-than-usual crew from city to city in buses powered by environmentally safe bio-diesel fuel.

Be the Rain

Where *Greendale* is concerned, the parallels to *Tonight's the Night* drawn by some longtime Neil Young observers are not without merit.

During the initial acoustic performances of the album (which were also included as a bonus disc on early pressings of the full-band CD with Crazy Horse), Young painstakingly laid out the storyline behind his new songs in some of the longest in-between song raps witnessed by audiences since the often hallucinatory breaks experienced on *Tonight's the Night's* tour of likewise previously unheard material.

For all of its lofty ambition as Young's first-ever bona fide "concept album," the music likewise most closely resembles the boozy, minimalist blues dirge of *Tonight's the Night*. Although half of the album's songs have run times of seven minutes or more (with "Grandpa's Interview" clocking in just shy of 13:00), there are no blazing solos or fiery guitar exchanges to be heard. In fact, much of the time the songs just go on in a repetitive drone that grows a little monotonous at times, with occasionally trite lyrical rhymes (see the aforementioned "Grandpa's Interview").

Critical reaction to *Greendale* at the time of its release was also predictably mixed—depending on who you talked to it was either "the most important album of 2003" or "worse than *Trans*." The album was still a modest hit,

Reprise Records green vinyl single of "Sun Green" from Neil Young's *Greendale* album.   *Courtesy of Tom Therme collection*

bought primarily by Young's hardcore fans as well as by the curious who had read about it. *Greendale* peaked at #22 on the Billboard albums chart.

John Lennon Said That

The loose story told in the lyrics of *Greendale's* songs revolves around a cast of characters including the aforementioned Grandpa, his modern-day flower child daughter Sun Green, her cop-killing brother Jed, and Carmichael (the cop he killed). With the small, rural town of Greendale as its backdrop, these characters evolve through a series of economical and ecological hardships amidst a whirlpool of small-town violence, government corruption, and environmental scandal as told through some of Young's most pointedly topical songs to date.

As has traditionally been the case when he tackles political subjects in his lyrics, there is little doubt of his sincerity, even if the messages themselves are mixed—sometimes within a single passage. On "Devil's Sidewalk," for example, he couples the lines "one thing I can tell you, is you got to be free, John Lennon said that, and I believe in love" with "I believe in action, when push comes to shove." Never let it be said that Young is one to let a simple contradiction get in the way of telling a good story.

At the end of the day, *Greendale* is exactly that, too—a very good story, told by one of the greatest musical storytellers of the twentieth century. For all of its deceptively simple, stripped-down blues, the album also contains some great songs—mostly notably the whispered, off-chord acoustic guitar standout "Bandit" and "Be the Rain," a "full cast" rock-opera closer worthy of the Who's *Tommy*.

Ambitious? Without a doubt. Overreaching? Perhaps. Uncompromising? Absolutely.

Whether you love it or hate it, 2003's *Greendale* serves as a reminder of just exactly why Neil Young still matters.

36

Falling Off the Face of the Earth

Prairie Wind and Heart of Gold

T he long shadow of death and mortality is something that has closely followed Neil Young throughout the whole of his career—from the way the departed souls of Danny Whitten and Bruce Berry permeate his dark masterpiece *Tonight's the Night*, to how Kurt Cobain's spirit—and his quoting of "My, My, Hey, Hey" in the suicide note he left behind—haunts 1994's *Sleeps with Angels*.

But never did the ominous reach of the Grim Reaper strike as close to home as it did in 2005. Shortly after losing his father, Canadian author and journalist Scott Young, to Alzheimer's disease that year, Young had his own close encounter with death.

One day after inducting his friend Chrissie Hynde and her band the Pretenders into the Rock and Roll Hall of Fame, Young was startled to find an image of what appeared to be broken glass in the mirror, clouding his field of vision while he was shaving. Except, in this case, the glass wasn't broken at all, nor did the image vanish once he looked away from it. A subsequent trip to the doctor revealed that the optic anomaly was the result of a brain aneurysm that, according to his physician, he "had probably had for a hundred years."

Even so, corrective brain surgery would prove to be necessary. So Young made an appointment to have the non-invasive *neuroradiological* procedure done at New York Presbyterian Hospital.

In the days between the initial diagnosis and the procedure needed to correct it, Young carried on as though it were business as usual. In fact, the very next day he flew out to Nashville for work on his next album, initially projected as the latest of his folk-pop successors to *Harvest*, with the by now usual cast of supporting players like Ben Keith and Spooner Oldham. *Prairie Wind* eventually proved to be much more.

In an interview with writer Richard Bienstock conducted shortly after one of the shows premiering this album at Nashville's historic Ryman Auditorium (beautifully documented in Jonathan Demme's *Heart of Gold* film), Young explained his own seemingly casual attitude toward this potentially life-threatening situation by saying that he went to the recording studio because that was where he felt the safest. A few days later, he collapsed on a New York street due to complications from his brain surgery (there was bleeding from the femoral artery). Although this setback temporarily sidelined him, he was soon back performing, most notably at Bob Geldof's worldwide Live 8 concert telecast.

Whether or not his 2005 brush with fate informs the songs of the *Prairie Wind* album has been a subject of considerable debate in the years since. Young himself has been typically coy when asked about it, saying that although the death of his father and his own recent health scare were certainly on his mind at the time, he had no specific strategy going into *Prairie Wind*.

But there is no denying that *Prairie Wind* stands out as perhaps the most deeply introspective, personal-sounding album that Young has ever made—at least up until 2010's *Le Noise*.

On songs like "Falling Off the Face of the Earth" and "When God Made Me," the normally guarded Young confronts the issues of his own faith and personal mortality in ways only offered up in glimpses over the entirety of his previously recorded work. Other songs like the starkly autobiographical "Far from

Original Reprise Records promotional ad for *Prairie Wind* touting it as "the album of the year."   *Courtesy of Robert Rodriguez*

Home" find him reminiscing back to his earliest childhood days in Canada. In between such weighty subjects, he also provides some much-needed levity with lighter tributes to his influences like Elvis ("He Was the King") and Hank Williams ("This Old Guitar").

The result is one of the finest of all Young's latter-day albums, and certainly one of his more heartfelt.

I Want to Live, I Want to Give

For the official promotional rollout of *Prairie Wind*, Young chose to play a special series of concerts at Nashville's grandest old building, the historic Ryman Auditorium.

The shows were filmed by his longtime confidant and legendary director Jonathan Demme, and released in 2006 as *Heart of Gold*. It is arguably the best of Neil Young's many official concert films, and certainly the warmest and the most sublime.

The film is beautifully shot, and finds the musicians accompanying Young— who number as many as forty for some of the songs—bathed in warm, pastel shades set against the panoramic images of heartland prairies adorning a series of gorgeous backdrops on the stage. Perhaps due to the personal nature of the songs performed and the circumstances surrounding them, or because of the historical significance of the venue, *Heart of Gold* has an uncommonly warm and

Neil Young's guitars photographed during a 2007 performance at the Keller Auditorium in Portland, Oregon.   *Photo by Anthony Stack*

even reverent sense about it. Of all the Neil Young concert documents over the years, this one just feels the most special.

The visual warmth of this film is equally matched by the performances, with songs mostly drawn from *Prairie Wind* and *Harvest*. Young comes off as particularly relaxed and unusually engaged with his audience considering his recent near meeting with his maker (who probably would get a kick out of the *Prairie Wind* song "When God Made Me"). The songs are accompanied by several anecdotal stories, including the tale of how Young came to acquire Hank Williams's guitar, and a touching moment where he reveals the pride of a father witnessing the blossoming of his daughter into a fully grown woman.

Heart of Gold also proved to be the first of a projected trilogy of Demme/Young concert film collaborations including the subsequent *Neil Young Trunk Show* (filmed in 2007 on the *Chrome Dreams II* tour and released theatrically in 2010) and *Neil Young Journeys*, which documents his return to Massey Hall during the *Twisted Road* tour.

It's a Dream, Only a Dream, and It's Fading Now

In purely musical terms, if there is a true standout player on *Prairie Wind*—an album characterized by stellar musicianship on the part of everyone involved from the subtle keyboard flourishes of Spooner Oldham to the oddly haunting backing vocals of Emmylou Harris—it is probably Ben Keith. Not coincidentally, Keith also shares a credit with Young as co-producer of the album.

Though his parts on dobro and pedal steel are often understated (wherein lies much of their beauty), Keith's accents on songs like "The Painter" often add just the right amount of color to Young's heavier-sounding guitar (even when playing acoustically, he tends to hammer the crap out of the fretboard).

Fortunately, the magic of Ben Keith's playing can be seen in a way never before experienced on a Neil Young record with the DVD accompanying *Prairie Wind* (something that Young would continue to utilize on many of his subsequent recordings). Using multiple split screens, this rather astonishing DVD reveals every layer of the songs, by drawing focus to each of the players' individual parts—whether it be Ben Keith's lonesome pedal steel on "The Painter" or his funky dobro slide on the bluesy, Elvis-influenced stomp of "He Was the King."

Another of the things revealed on this DVD is how multitextured these songs are, despite the initial, quite deceptive illusion presented on the audio CD. In contrast to Young's studio reputation as a one-take, spur-of-the-moment musician, the full complement of strings, horns, and backing voices on *Prairie Wind* reveals quite another story—especially when the DVD breaks each section down by its individual parts.

Stylistically, the songs on *Prairie Wind* are also a lot more varied than their surface appearance suggests, ranging from the prayerful gospel of "When God Made Me" (where the DVD again reveals the thought that went into its backing choir vocals) to the flat-out Cajun funk of "Far from Home."

This also reveals its fair share of warts, however. For example, as beautifully reverent as something like "Falling Off the Face of the Earth" sounds—with its understated arrangement and haunting background choir vocals—the words read with the trite sentiments of a Hallmark Greeting card. Fortunately in this case, the song is so damn pretty, the moon-and-June nature of the lyrics can be overlooked.

On *Prairie Wind's* DVD, the direction is credited to Young's cinematic alter ego Bernard Shakey. But it is the simple yet effective camera work of Larry "L.A." Johnson that brings home just how deceptively intricate a record this is. It is probably Johnson's best work as Neil Young's semiofficial videographer.

Should've Been Done Long Ago

Living with War, "Let's Impeach the President," and the *Freedom of Speech* Tour

Throughout his career, Neil Young has consistently defied convention. Where many other artists of his generation might have been content to follow the path of least commercial resistance, he has always boldly followed his artistic instincts, for better or for worse. This stubborn dedication to his muse has led him to create a body of work that is notable as much for abrupt turns of style as it is for producing so many great, timeless songs—from "Heart of Gold" to "Rockin' in the Free World."

In the seventies, this meant following up his commercial breakthrough album *Harvest* with the darkness and desolation that permeates such personal work as *On the Beach*, and the only much later to be fully appreciated *Tonight's the Night*. In the eighties, this meant releasing a series of albums so stylistically schizophrenic—from Kraftwerk-influenced syntho-pop to fifties-style rockabilly—that Geffen Records actually sued him over his failure to make a "Neil Young" album.

So it should have surprised no one when Young announced the latest of his trademark artistic curveballs in 2006—a fierce, cranked-to-eleven rock assault featuring ten new songs that could best be described as all-out antiwar anthems. The album was called *Living with War*. Less than a year after the warm-and-fuzzy, quiet reflection of *Prairie Wind*, Young shocked the world with this self described "folk metal protest" record.

In the process, he probably also made some powerful enemies.

Not Ready to Make Nice

Neil Young has often followed his louder records with quiet ones, and vice versa. *Comes a Time* was followed by *Rust Never Sleeps; Ragged Glory* by *Harvest Moon*. But there had never been anything quite like this. At a time when the country was bitterly divided over President George W. Bush's foreign adventures in Iraq (not to mention their economic repercussions at home), musicians who dared to speak out against the war and against the president were not immune from doing so at considerable risk to their own careers.

In the most famous example of this, the Dixie Chicks overnight went from country darlings to political pariahs following outspoken singer Natalie Maines's off-the-cuff, anti-Bush comments during a concert in London. "We don't want this war, this violence, and we're ashamed that the President of the United States is from Texas," Maines infamously told her foreign audience, instantly inflaming large segments of the traditionally more conservative country fan base back at home and earning Maines taunts of "traitor" and worse.

You'd have thought Hanoi Jane herself was back from Vietnam.

Fans who had once flocked to the Dixie Chicks shows, now burned their records at events organized by radio stations—with covert backing from Republican sources, according to some accusers. These same country stations were also dropping Dixie Chicks songs from their playlists faster than you could say "Disco Sucks" or "Lennon Claims Beatles Bigger Than Jesus."

After a tour marked by cancelled shows that saw their once huge audience shrink by up to fifty percent according to some estimates, the Dixie Chicks rebounded with 2007's Rick Rubin–produced *Taking the Long Way* album (and its defiant single "Not Ready to Make Nice"). The album also earned the Chicks a Grammy for Album of the Year. But the fallout over Dixie-gate still had lasting repercussions. The Dixie Chicks have remained mostly inactive as a touring and recording musical act ever since.

Neil Young fans were likewise split down the middle over his new songs like the provocatively titled "Lets Impeach the President." Although *Living with War* sold decently, peaking at #15 on Billboard's albums chart, there were still some fears that Young might be headed for the same fate of commercial death as the Dixie Chicks.

On Internet blogs like Thrasher's Wheat and *Blogcritics*, heated debates between conservative and liberal fans often turned ugly. Young himself did little to simmer the flames, dialing the rhetoric up a notch further with interviews on cable news outlets like CNN and streaming the album for free on his own website. On the same site, he also launched the *Living with War* Blog, with continuous updates from the war, along with links to various antiwar organizations and veterans' rights groups.

Déjà Vu Again

The latest reunion tour with Crosby, Stills, Nash, and Young—complete with the by-now usual practice of exorbitantly high ticket prices—focusing more on Young's Bush-bashing album than on the band's back catalog of hits only further ignited the growing firestorm. It wasn't uncommon to hear fan complaints like "I didn't pay two hundred bucks to hear this shit" during CSN&Y's 2006 *Freedom of Speech* tour, particularly when it played the southern states.

As captured on the 2008 documentary film *CSNY: Déjà Vu*, the divisions between these two equally combustible elements making up both CSNY and Young's fan bases was palpable. It also makes for a very compelling film, directed by Neil Young under his Bernard Shakey alter ego and filmed by Larry "L.A." Johnson.

From a purely musical standpoint, the film is a decent enough document of the latter-day CSN&Y in concert. You don't see much in the way of any real musical fireworks (although Stills and Young do occasionally revive their dueling guitar shootouts, proving that the old chemistry is still mostly there all these years later). The band—which is really more like a group of Neil Young all-stars like Ben Keith, Rick Rosas, Chad Cromwell, Spooner Oldham, and trumpet guy Tom Bray—is also reasonably tight. You don't really see any blown parts here.

Even though of all CSN&Y's projects, this is clearly the one where Young is the most in charge, the other guys also seem quite content to put their own famous egos aside and play second fiddle to what is essentially the Neil Young Show.

vie poster for the *Déjà Vu* film, a Shakey Pictures production capturing Crosby, Stills, Nash, and Young on : now infamous *Freedom of Speech* tour. The concerts, which focused on Neil Young's *Living with War* album, arized audiences along political lines during the controversial presidency of George W. Bush.

Courtesy of Robert Rodriguez

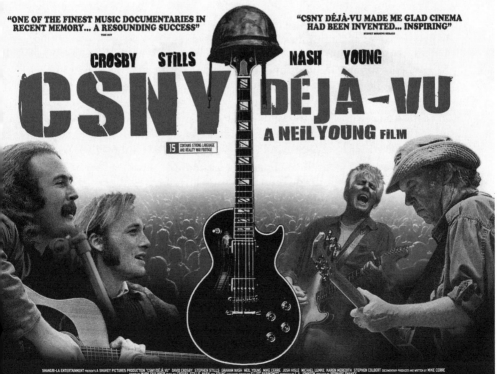

Crosby, Stills, Nash, and Young perform in Denver, Colorado, on the 2006 *Freedom of Speech* tour.
Photo by Anthony Stack

The set list is dominated by new songs from Young's *Living with War*, complemented by similarly political, antiwar songs such as Nash's "Military Madness," Crosby's "Wooden Ships," and Stills's "For What It's Worth," and if anything, Crosby, Stills, and Nash seem to be quite passionately into it. Perhaps the aging hippies saw Young's strident new antiwar songs as a golden opportunity to recapture the glory days when they were seen as writing the soundtrack for the sixties and its counterculture revolution.

Unfortunately, not everyone in the audience saw things the same way—which is what makes *CSNY: Déjà Vu* such a fascinating film. Along with the Dixie Chicks documentary *Shut Up and Sing*, *CSNY: Déjà Vu* is a unique snapshot of its time capturing just how tough the going could become for musicians who dared to speak out against the Bush administration in 2006. In fairness to the Chicks, they definitely ended up getting a rawer deal as a result of their activism than CSN&Y did. But it can also be said that CSN&Y had history on their side. Certainly anyone attending one of their shows had to know these were the same guys responsible for Neil Young's "Ohio"—or at least you'd think.

Unfortunately, not everyone attending these shows got that particular memo, and some of the fans expecting "Our House" and "Suite: Judy Blue Eyes" (at least they got "Teach Your Children") were not happy with either the song selection or the political tone. The chorus of boos during "Let's Impeach the President" is particularly telling—fans can also be seen giving the middle-finger salute during the song. But what makes this film so fascinating is that the booing redneck types are often shown side by side with fans singing the lyrics and occasionally even breaking down in tears.

As a picture of 2006 red- and blue-state middle America—complete with all of its accompanying contrasts—disguised as a rock concert, *CSNY: Déjà Vu* is one of the most compelling music documentaries of its kind made during the Bush era. The Shakey Pictures production has also been released as a DVD and Blu-ray, along with an accompanying live album/soundtrack.

Let's Impeach the President for Lyin'

Living with War is best described as antiwar, anti-Bush, and very, very loud. The album was recorded over a whirlwind three days with a core group of musicians consisting of Young himself on guitar and vocals; Rick Rosas on bass; and Chad Cromwell on drums. They are occasionally joined by Tommy Bray on trumpet (most notably on the title track and "Shock and Awe"), and a one hundred-member choir (on "Let's Impeach the President" and the beautiful, hymnlike version of "America the Beautiful" that closes the album).

"A power trio with trumpet and 100 voices—A metal version of Phil Ochs and Bob Dylan . . . folk metal protest," was how Young himself described the album in the weeks just prior to its release. For *Living with War*, Niko Bolas also returned as co-producer, reuniting the Volume Dealers for the first time since 1989's *Freedom*.

Controversy over the lyrical content aside, *Living with War* is pretty much your standard, cranked-to-eleven, grungy Neil Young album. Although the sound here harkens back to classics like *Rust Never Sleeps* and *Ragged Glory*, Crazy Horse—the band usually backing Young on these types of records—are nowhere to be found.

Living with War is not only the loudest Neil Young album since he was backed by Pearl Jam on *Mirror Ball*, it is also the tightest. The long extended jams with Crazy Horse are replaced here by ten shorter, more straightforward-sounding songs that get directly to the point. But make no mistake, the volume is cranked all the way up—and Neil's trademark guitar noise with the ever-trusty Old Black is dead front and center in the mix. On *Living with War*, feedback is definitely back.

With incendiary lyrics like "Let's impeach the President for lying," *Living with War's* best-known song rattles off a litany of reasons calling for Bush's ouster from office ranging from "lying . . . misleading our country into war" to "highjacking our religion . . . and using it to get elected." Basically a faster, more uptempo rewrite of "Powderfinger" (you can practically interchange the line "Let's Impeach the President for Lyin'" with "Shelter Me from the Powder and the Finger"), it ends with Young trading the lyrics off with a series of prerecorded sound bites from Bush.

On "Shock and Awe," his snarling guitar exchanges licks with the solemn blare of a military funeral procession trumpet as he recalls "back in the days of mission accomplished" and prior times "when we had a chance to change our mind." On "Flags of Freedom," the chorus is sung almost as a companion piece to another famous protest song with a patriotic twist—Bob Dylan's "Chimes of Freedom." He even name drops Dylan in the lyrics, right between a chorus that celebrates "these flags of freedom flying" while questioning the wisdom of sending a family's kids off to war.

Maybe It's Obama, but He Thinks That He's Too Young

On "Looking for a Leader," Young also earns his Nostradamus stripes by predicting the presidential election of a then largely unknown black senator named Barack Obama. "Maybe it's a woman, or a black man after all," Young sings. "Maybe it's Obama, but he thinks that he's too young."

The album closes with "Roger and Out," which returns Young to "that old hippie highway" repeatedly revisited throughout his career, saying "Roger and out" to a fallen comrade. This is followed appropriately enough by the choir's solemn, reverent, and gorgeous intonation of "America the Beautiful."

Young revisited the whole *Living with War* saga again some seven months after its initial May 2006 release by putting out a rawer, repackaged version of the album called *Living with War: In the Beginning* in December of that same year.

Watching the Flags of Freedom Flyin'

Living with War isn't Neil Young's greatest album, not by a long shot. But historically speaking, it may well be looked back upon as among his most courageous, and an artistic statement of purpose uniquely matched with its time.

Protest music is as uniquely rich an American art form as you'll find anywhere in our history. From the protest songs born in dust bowls and union struggles, to the negro spirituals that arose from the cotton fields of the Civil War era, to the sixties protest-rock of folks like Bob Dylan, and Neil Young himself.

It 's a little ironic that quite often the loudest voices at home in support of unpopular wars—from Vietnam in the sixties to Iraq more recently—have also been among the quickest to call for quieting voices of protest and dissent. In the often bitterly divided landscape of 2006 America, Young's *Living with War* stood as proof that those voices, which had grown somewhat quieter in recent years, were rising once again.

Sure Enough, They'll Be Selling Stuff

The Resurrection of the Archives

T he massive *Archives Volume 1 1963–1972* collection is, to any serious fan, the motherlode and the holy grail of all Neil Young recordings, all wrapped up into one enormously exhaustive—some would also say exhausting—package.

Even the most devoted fan could spend days, weeks, or even months getting through all of it, and the chances are they'd still miss something. There is just too much great stuff here to take in, and therein lies the beauty of it. Getting lost in the work of an iconic artist of Young's stature has never been so much fun, or yielded anywhere near this level of musical and historical pleasures.

The *Archives* was first conceived sometime during the eighties as a follow-up to *Decade*, the three-record anthology set released way back when vinyl was still the musical format of choice in 1977. *Decade* was considered at the time to be among the most in-depth retrospectives ever compiled by a rock-'n'-roll artist, and was often compared to the reverential treatment given the anthologies of jazz musicians on labels like Blue Note and Prestige.

Prior to the modern-day advent of CD boxed sets, and long before the current practice of remastering and repackaging thirty-year-old catalog "classics" by dressing them up as deluxe anniversary editions with "bonus tracks" (often originally rejected by the artist as not being worthy of release), *Decade* was considered so influential it was said to have prompted Bob Dylan to release his own lofty *Biograph* boxed set.

Little did anyone realize what was still coming a few decades down the pike.

Decade II

At one point during the decades-long process since its original conception, Young's *Archives* actually had the working title of *Decade II*.

But even at that early stage, his concept for the collection was so enormous in scope that some might say it could only have been the product of a massively inflated and quite possibly delusional ego. At the time, what Neil Young had in mind was a series of maybe three boxed sets containing four or five discs each. Then, as now, the idea was for each of the planned volumes to cover a specific

Promo photo by Steve Babineau for the Neil Young Archives Performance Series disc *Dreamin' Man Live '92*, which features live versions of the songs from *Harvest Moon*.   *Courtesy of Robert Rodriguez*

phase of his career. Since, when it comes to that career, Young has long been known as something of a pack rat who meticulously documents everything—including those numerous unreleased recordings and lost albums known by fans to exist—there was no doubt the archival resources were there.

Still, the plan was so audacious that some didn't take it seriously at first. As the years rolled on without the arrival of even the first of these planned volumes, many of those close to Young (who should have known better) figured he would never complete the never-ending project anyway. As recently as 2003, no less than Frank "Poncho" Sampedro told one interviewer that he thought Young might be tiring of the project. This skepticism also led some fans to release their own bootleg versions, including the surprisingly quite good, humorously titled boxed set volume *Archives Be Damned*.

By the time *Archives Volume 1 1963–1972* finally arrived in 2008, however, no one doubted Young's devotion to the decades-in-the-making project any longer. Not only was the collection more enormous than anyone could have imagined, it also turned out there had been a method to the madness of the *Archives* all along.

I've Been Waiting for You

The final arrival of the *Archives* first began in 2006 as a trickle that would soon enough grow into a flood. The first hint that the dam was about to burst came with *Live at the Fillmore East 1970*, a rare, long-sought-after Neil Young and Crazy Horse concert from the *Everybody Knows This Is Nowhere* period.

One sheet for Neil Young's *Journey Through the Past* film. Long out of print, the movie was finally made available as part of the DVD version of the massive *Archives Volume 1 1963–1972* boxed set.
Courtesy of Noah Fleisher/Heritage Auctions

Reprise Records 2004 single release of "Sugar Mountain" from the
Archive Performance Series album *Live at Canterbury House.*

Courtesy of Tom Therme collection

Released as the first installment in what soon became known as the
"Performance Series" (or "NYAPS" for short), this amazing concert features
the classic Crazy Horse lineup with original guitarist Danny Whitten doing
barn-burning versions of "Down by the River" and "Cowgirl in the Sand." Both of
these rival the studio recordings found on *Nowhere* itself. This is also the concert
where the version of Whitten's "Come On Baby Let's Go Downtown" heard on
Tonight's the Night originally comes from.

Other entries in the *Archives Performance Series* soon followed, indicating that
a ramp-up to the long-awaited main event was now well under way.

Next up in 2007 was *Live at Massey Hall 1971*, a legendary acoustic performance featuring then still-in-development versions of the songs that eventually
surfaced on *Harvest*, including a medley that melds "Heart of Gold" and "A
Man Needs a Maid" into a suite. This is the same concert that producer David
Briggs was said to have preferred over the studio recordings that were eventually
released instead as the *Harvest* album.

Sugar Mountain: Live at Canterbury Hall 1968, released in 2008, features a
very nervous Neil Young in what nonetheless turned out to be another standout
acoustic performance. Despite a pre-show case of stage fright—the promoters
reportedly had to coax him into going on—the concert is another stunner,

featuring a number of Buffalo Springfield classics, including rare acoustic versions of "Broken Arrow" and "Expecting to Fly."

Although the next volume of *Archives* is probably still a few years away, yet another entry in the *Performance Series* that has come since the 2008 release of *Volume 1 1964–1972* indicates that we may not have to wait long. *Dreamin' Man Live '92*, released in 2009, is yet another great acoustic show featuring stripped-down versions of the pastoral songs from 1992's *Harvest Moon*.

Down to the Wire

The years of waiting came to an end once and for all in 2008. Even so, nobody could have been prepared for the sheer enormity of *Archives Volume 1*.

Simultaneously released in CD, DVD, and Blu-ray formats, the volume of material found on the *Archives* is nothing short of staggering. In addition to the more than 120 songs—roughly half of them being unreleased or alternate takes—featured on the ten-disc set (eight for the CD version), there is a 236-page book.

There is also a multitude of extras, including hidden easter eggs on the DVD and Blu-ray versions, and everything from press clippings, rare photos, and even the complete (and long out of print) *Journey Through the Past* film.

But the real treat comes for those fans with Blu-ray players. As it turns out, the long road to the *Archives* release had everything to do with waiting for technology to catch up with the concepts swirling about in Neil Young's brain all along. On the Blu-ray version, fans can experience the songs while scrolling through menus featuring biographical information and other assorted goodies like the original lyric sheets and more.

As for the actual music, it is everything fans could have hoped for and more.

On *Archives Volume 1 1963–1972*, you get previously unheard gems like the original recordings from Young's first band the Squires. The BD-live technology on the Blu-ray set also allows for the *Archives* to be a continuously evolving project, made possible by providing ongoing free downloads of newly unearthed material as it is discovered.

So the story of the *Archives* becomes one that is never-ending. This is apparently exactly how Young first envisioned the project way back in the eighties.

Here We Are in the Years

Perhaps even more alluring to those fans who waited patiently for that first installment of the *Archives* is what Young reportedly has planned for future volumes of the series.

Among the things that have been reported on his own website and in subsequent interviews, Young has teased out such mythically unreleased albums as *Homegrown, Chrome Dreams, Toast,* and *Oceanside/Countryside.* Yet another new entry in the *Performance Series*, comprised of live recordings made with

MUSTANG b/w AURORA

SWINGING NEIL YOUNG
and THE SQUIRES

Enjoy the swinging music of Neil Young and The Squires, just recently returned from an Eastern Tour. Recording stars under the "Vee" label.

Original art for "Swinging" Neil Young and the Squires single "Mustang" b/w "Aurora." Both songs can be found on *Archives Volume 1*.

Courtesy of Tom Therme collection

the International Harvesters during the country-flavored *Old Ways* period was released in June 2011, as an album titled *A Treasure*.

Even more exciting are hints of a possible *Time Fades Away II* (Young remains noncommittal about rereleasing the original album, the legendarily ragged live 1973 recording long coveted as a collector's item by fans).

In an interview with writer Richard Bienstock, Young spoke of the "sequel" by saying "I switched drummers halfway through the tour, Kenny Buttrey was in there for the first half, and Johnny Barbata came in for the second. It's a completely different thing, with completely different songs."

There are at least three more future volumes of *Archives* planned. We can't wait.

No Hidden Path

Chrome Dreams II, Linc/Volt, and Fork in the Road

In addition to the release of the monumental *Archives Volume 1 1963–1972*, the first decade of the new century ended with a flurry of other new activity from Neil Young. The fall of 2007 brought the release of *Chrome Dreams II* and yet another round of touring that continued well into the following year.

With the *Archives* prompting Young's personal journey into the past, much of that same spirit carried over to the "new" album as well. The title *Chrome Dreams II* is itself a reference to one of his mythical, unreleased lost albums, and certainly seems to position itself as a sequel.

Beyond its title, however, an actual and direct connection to that famously missing album from the mid-seventies isn't made entirely clear. A number of the songs from the original *Chrome Dreams* eventually made their way to other seventies Neil Young albums, including "Will to Love" and "Like a Hurricane" (*American Stars and Bars*) as well as "Pocahontas" and "Powderfinger" (*Rust Never Sleeps*).

Some Are Saints, and Some Are Jerks, Everyday People

But while some of the songs on 2007's *Chrome Dreams II* are drawn from past sources, many of them appear to be of a relatively more recent vintage. The blazing, eighteen-minute guitar-driven track "Ordinary People," for example, was already well known to fans as a high point from Young's concerts with the Bluenotes during the late eighties. Along with the equally lengthy "Sixty to Zero" from the same period, "Ordinary People" had become somewhat legendary among tape traders and bootleggers as a lost Neil Young classic, prior to showing up years later in 2007 on his then new album.

As was the case then, his blistering guitar work is supported by the Bluenotes horn section in the version heard on *Chrome Dreams II*, and is reportedly taken from a source recorded at one of those eighties shows. Like its soul mate "Sixty to Zero," the lyrics of "Ordinary People" go on for nearly as long as the guitar solos do, telling a sordid tale set in a seedy world populated by drug lords, gun runners and other "ordinary people." As Young himself says in the lyrics, "some are saints and some are jerks."

Together, "Ordinary People" and another extended guitar freakout, the fourteen-minute "No Hidden Path," form the centerpieces of the album. Both of these proved themselves to be crowd-pleasers on the 2007–08 *Chrome Dreams II* tour as well.

These two more guitar-driven pieces are balanced out by a solid collection of tunes that draw equally from Young's fresh mining of the vaults and more recently written songs. The result is a satisfying album, even if it seems a bit all over the place at times.

In the Great Spirit I Place My Trust

"Dirty Old Man" is one of those goofy-ass songs in the tradition of *Ragged Glory's* "Fuckin' Up" or "Piece of Crap" from *Sleeps with Angels* that Neil comes up with from time to time. This one is about a "Dirty Old Man" who likes to get hammered and fool around with the boss's wife. This track is actually a lot of fun, and hearkens back to the loving, sloppily executed rock sound that fans of Crazy Horse swear by.

"Boxcar" starts out with a banjo sound that would have been right at home on *Prairie Wind*, and maintains a lovely sort of country vibe as the lyrics weave a plaintive tale of a vagabond on a freight train.

Meanwhile, other tracks explore spiritual themes, or what some observers have labeled as Young's "eco-spirituality." The borderline gospel of "Shining Light" never makes it quite clear whether the "shining light" that he has found here comes in the form of carnal desire or something more divine. Either way, the song is one of his prettiest. "The Believer" is likewise another song that hints at a nebulous spirituality divined from sources that are never made quite clear, and features a quiet, simple arrangement of piano, guitar, and drums.

"Spirit Road" mines similar lyrical territory, but this time with a full-band arrangement where Young once again straps on the electric guitar. This track finds him "headed out on the long highway in your mind" in search of the "spirit road you had to find" where "getting home to peace again" await the traveler at road's end.

On *Chrome Dreams II*, there are pieces of every ingredient that make up the so-called Neil Young sound—from grungy Crazy Horse–styled rock to the softer, more introspective stuff. Unlike some of his past work, here he doesn't stick to any one of these stylistic elements, making *Chrome Dreams II* one of his more stylistically varied (and some would say all over the place) releases.

In the end, what makes this one a keeper, though, are the two extended showcases for his blazing guitar, "Ordinary People" and "No Hidden Path." The album, which once again reunites the production team of the Volume Dealers (Neil Young and Niko Bolas), made a very decent showing of #11 on Billboard's Album Chart.

Neil Young captured live during the *Chrome Dreams II* tour at Hop Farm, Kent, UK, on July 6, 2008.   *Photo by Chris Greenwood*

Neil Young performing in Europe during the *Chrome Dreams II* tour.

Photo by Constanze Metzner

Spirit Road

For what was initially billed as the *Chrome Dreams Continental* tour, Neil Young assembled a band made up of familiar faces like Ralph "Crazy Horse" Molina, Ben "Long Grain" Keith, Rick "the Bass Player" Rosas, and Pegi "the Wife" Young.

When the jaunt began in the fall of 2007, a mere seven weeks' worth of shows were booked. But the tour eventually wound up continuing on for a year, encompassing dates across North America, Europe, and beyond. Support acts for the shows included Young disciples like Wilco in a number of cities, while Pegi Young (who had just released her own solo album) appeared in the opening slot for nearly all of the shows.

For the concerts, Young performed both solo acoustic and with the full band each night, on a stage adorned with props like Christmas tree lights and the obligatory wooden Indian. Each new song was also announced on a painted placard with original art illustrating its title, carnival style. Although the set lists changed little from night to night, they did include a number of rarely played songs, including a stunning acoustic rendition of *On the Beach's* "Ambulance Blues" that proved to be a nightly standout.

Two particularly great shows from Philadelphia are captured as the second of director Jonathan Demme's trilogy of Neil Young concert documentary films,

Neil Young Trunk Show. Like its predecessor *Heart of Gold, Trunk Show* is a great documentary that puts you right in the front row of an equally great Neil Young show. But it is especially notable for including a performance of "The Sultan" (Young's very first single as part of the Squires), as well as other rarities like "Mellow My Mind," "Mexico" and "Kansas."

Following its brief theatrical run, *Trunk Show* seems to have disappeared completely, promting more than one fan to ask: "Where is the DVD and Blu-ray release, Neil?"

Get Behind the Wheel

In a scene that could have been taken from the comedy film *Planes Trains and Automobiles,* Young's next move was a nonmusical one, more closely resembling his work with Lionel Trains than with Crazy Horse or the Stray Gators. But unlike John Candy's movie, Young was dead serious about the Linc/Volt.

As with his obsession with the model trains, Young has always had a thing for big cars, dating clear back to the days of his beloved hearse Mortimer in Canada. But besides being a gear head, he is also a tech head—an environmentally conscious tech head. Understanding the need for a fuel-efficient, low-emissions vehicle, while also sharing the love affair that most Americans have for their cars, he came up with the idea of converting a classic gas-guzzling 1959 Lincoln Continental into an energy- efficient vehicle powered by alternative fuel sources.

Working with people like Jonathan Goodwin of Wichita's H-Line Conversions and Uli Kruger of Australia's Alternative Energy Technologies, Young unveiled his Linc/Volt in 2008, bringing it to the South by Southwest music conference in Austin, Texas, and to Sun Microsystems in California, among other events.

The Linc/Volt was also entered to win the $10 million Progressive Insurance Automotive X PRIZE, given to new automobiles able to reach the 100 miles per gallon standard. Unfortunately, it had to subsequently withdraw from the competition due to a conflict with Progressive over the lack of a more commercially oriented business plan for the car.

On November 9, 2010, the Linc/Volt caught fire in a garage at Young's Broken Arrow ranch, where he also had been storing valuable memorabilia related to his music career. Both the car and much of the historically priceless collection—valued at $850,000—were damaged. Young, however, still stands by his Linc/Volt.

"The wall charging system was not completely tested and had never been left unattended. A mistake was made. It was not the fault of the car," he said after the fire. The Linc/Volt is in the process of being restored.

Fuel Line

Many of the songs on 2009's *Fork in the Road* are either directly about, or influenced by, Young's work on the Linc/Volt project, including titles like "Johnny

Magic" (written in tribute to Linc/Volt designer Jonathan Goodwin), "Fuel Line," "Get Behind the Wheel," "Hit the Road," and "Off the Road." You'd be quite correct in thinking there are a lot of road songs on *Fork in the Road*.

While this is not one of the more memorable entries in Neil Young's vast catalog, it does contain at least one great song in "Just Singin' a Song (Won't Change the World)." Like *Fork in the Road's* other songs, the lyrics on this one also veer off into stuff about cars and roads, but ties them in with a call for environmental activism, reflecting Young's renewed commitment to eco-friendly causes. Besides, "Just Singin' a Song (Won't Change the World)" also boasts a killer Neil Young guitar riff.

Other songs on the album could best be described as falling into the goofball category of songs like "Fuckin' Up," "Piece of Crap" and "Dirty Old Man." "Get Behind the Wheel" even dredges up the long-thought-buried rockabilly corpse of 1983's positively dreadful *Everybody's Rockin'* album.

Even so, *Fork in the Road* joined other new millennium Neil Young albums in the top twenty spot that Billboard seems to have reserved just for him.

It peaked at #19.

Baseball cap promoting the eco-friendly, energy-efficient Linc-Volt automobile, signed "with love" by Neil Young.

Photo by Elisabeth Piontek

I Said Solo, They Said Acoustic

Neil Young Brings *Le Noise* to the Twisted Road

eil Young spent much of 2010 giving concert audiences a preview of the new album he was recording in Los Angeles at the time with producer Daniel Lanois. As a renowned producer (and occasional solo artist), Lanois is best known for his work with a wide array of artists including Bob Dylan, U2, Peter Gabriel and Coldplay, and for occasionally collaborating with fellow avant musical deconstructionist Brian Eno.

But more than that, he is known for his electronic treatments on the albums he has produced for those artists and others, using the sort of effects like tape loops and echo that the producer simply refers to as "sonics." The year 2010 proved to be one where Young fans would be learning a lot more about Daniel Lanois and his sonics.

For *Le Noise*, the album that was eventually released on September 28, 2010, these sonics are applied to his mostly electric guitar to produce a wall of feedback-laden sound the likes of which had never been heard on a Neil Young album before. The songs were mostly recorded at Lanois's home in the Silver Lake neighborhood of Los Angeles during a series of full moons (recording during a full moon has become a custom of Young's over the years).

The album was originally going to be titled "Twisted Road," but was finally released as *Le Noise* as an apparent nod to Lanois. Whether or not the album title is a clever tribute to the producer or not (Lanois equals *Le Noise*, get it?), in this case, the shoe certainly fits.

Twisted Road

As has become his standard operating procedure over the years, Young previewed many of the songs on the *Twisted Road* tour. With this tour, billed as a series of solo concerts, Neil Young fans once again probably expected an evening of acoustic music, heavy on favorites from albums like *Harvest* and *Harvest Moon*. While they did get some of that, the bulk of the shows were comprised of the new

Neil Young performs at Bonnaroo 2011.   *Photo by Mary Andrews*

songs that ended up on *Le Noise* (as well as a few that didn't make the final cut like "Leah").

Here again, the *Twisted Road* tour found Young stretching boundaries by trying something new—which in this case meant playing the songs solo on a suitably cranked electric guitar, rather than on an acoustic.

However, his audiences—who had perhaps by now become more accustomed to expecting the unexpected at his concerts—responded much more favorably to the new songs than on past tours like the infamous 1973 *Tonight's the Night* shows, and for good reason.

The new songs represented some of Young's best songwriting in years, and indeed were a highlight of the shows (at least according to the mostly rave notices the shows received from critics). As word got out about his latest new artistic direction, concert posters and T-shirts sporting the catchphrase "I Said Solo, They Said Acoustic" began cropping up.

Not that all of the new songs were played with the amps cranked up, though. For two of the songs, "Love and War" and "Peaceful Valley Boulevard," he strapped on an acoustic guitar. But this wasn't your "Heart of Gold" folkie-sounding Young either. Both songs mirror the dark tone of the louder, feedback-heavy electric songs like "Walk with Me," and also feature the signature Lanois sonic treatments.

But what is most striking about these songs is the simple, more direct approach of the lyrics, which again represent some of Young's best songwriting in years, if not decades.

On "Walk with Me" he acknowledges the still fresh loss of friends in 2010 like Ben Keith and Larry "L.A." Johnson with lines like "I lost some friends I was traveling with, I miss the soul and the old friendship," while expressing both gratitude and a promise that "I'll never let you down no matter what we do, if you'll just walk with me" to those loved ones who remain.

"Love and War" is an antiwar song as the title suggests, but also has a more subtle and mournful tone than Young's previous stabs at protest music like "Ohio" or the songs on 2006's controversial *Living with War* album. Most interestingly, he occasionally seems to even acknowledge this with lines like "I sang for justice, but I hit a bad chord."

On the almost shockingly confessional "The Hitchhiker," Young takes this new lyrical forthrightness even further. In a rare moment of lyrical candor, he runs through much of his history—from the drugs to the failed relationships—in what has to rank as one of the most bluntly honest and personal songs he has ever written. It's a stunning piece of work coming from an artist not known for such personal candor, and who has historically been notoriously reluctant to reveal his hand.

There is in fact a feel of creeping mortality in many of these songs, as well as a sense that Young may be trying to get his house in order.

When I Was a Hitchhiker on the Road, I Had to Count on You

If *Sleeps with Angels*—Young's 1994 reaction to the death of Kurt Cobain—has been called the sequel to his dark masterpiece *Tonight's the Night*, you could just as easily label *Le Noise* an extension of past work ranging from 1983's *Trans* to 2005's *Prairie Wind*.

To do so, however, would also be to sell it way too short. *Le Noise* is in fact the boldest-sounding, most artistically challenging record Young has made in a decade or more. It is also easily his best album in at least that long. As is so often the case with this artist, time will probably tell. But on an initial listen, *Le Noise* has the feel of a classic.

This is also an album that is best played very loud on a stereo system with a pair of speakers that can take it (and preferably somewhere where you won't piss off the neighbors). Forget the iPod and the earbuds. There is simply no other way to properly experience how producer Lanois has added multiple sonic dimensions to Young's guitar the way he does on *Le Noise* than playing it at maximum volume. This sucker needs to be turned up way loud.

Comparisons to the infamous syntho-pop of *Trans* are probably inevitable, though. Lanois's electronic treatments of Young's massively cranked, white electric Gretsch guitar manifest themselves nearly as often in the whirring and clicking noises heard at the end of "Walk with Me" as they do in the deep-humming, speaker-rattling feedback of "The Hitchhiker." On the latter, Young even manages to sneak in a line from "Like an Inca"—a song from, you guessed it, *Trans.*

As it turns out, the connection between "Like an Inca" and "The Hitchhiker" is no coincidence. Although some fans may recognize "The Hitchhiker" as a song Young often played live during the *Harvest Moon* era, it actually dates back much further.

Originally recorded as "Like an Inca (Hitchhiker)" during a full moon on August 11, 1976, at Indigo Studios in Malibu Canyon, the original acoustic version was part of a particularly fertile session that also produced gems like "Will to Love" and the original solo acoustic masters for songs like "Pocahontas," "Powderfinger," "Captain Kennedy," "Ride My Llama," "Campaigner," and others. Many of these original recordings can be heard on bootleg copies of the unreleased album *Chrome Dreams*, but nearly all of them eventually made their way to officially released albums like *American Stars and Bars* and *Rust Never Sleeps.*

As for the original "Like an Inca (Hitchhiker)," this would eventually end up splitting into two songs: "Like an Inca," which was released on 1983's *Trans,* and "The Hitchhiker," which makes its official debut on *Le Noise.*

Then Came Paranoia and It Ran Away with Me

The eight songs on *Le Noise* also find Young at his most lyrically personal and introspective since *Prairie Wind.*

On the aforementioned "Walk with Me" and "Hitchhiker," as well as on "Sign of Love" and "Love and War," he reflects back on his life—and even questions some of his past decisions and behavior—before seeming to finally find a tentative sort of peace within himself.

The most obvious and fascinating example of this, again, is "The Hitchhiker." Set against a howling backdrop of fuzzed-out power chords and feedback, the song finds Young reciting a personal history that reads like the darkest, most forbidden entries from a personal diary.

In this remarkable song, he lists every drug he's ever taken, name checks both Toronto and California, and even briefly revisits his relationship with Carrie

Snodgress ("then we had a kid and we split apart, and I was living on the road, and a little cocaine went a long, long way to ease that heavy load").

Young even confronts his early stardom in a way those most familiar with his history will instantly recognize ("then came paranoia and it ran away with me, I would not sign an autograph or appear on TV"). Following this five minutes of confession time, he ends by simply stating, "I don't know how I'm standing here, living my life, I'm thankful for my children and my faithful wife."

It's probably not a coincidence that when Young performed "The Hitchhiker" at the 25th Anniversary of Farm Aid on October 4, 2010, he told the crowd of 35,000, "now you know my secrets" at the song's conclusion.

Promotional poster for the 2010/2011 *Twisted Road* tour, where "I Said Solo, They Said Acoustic" became a mantra for lucky fans witnessing Neil Young perform new, mostly electric material without a band.

Courtesy of Robert Rodriguez

Neil Young on the *Twisted Road* tour in Clearwater, Florida.   *Photo by Donald Gibson*

I Hit a Bad Chord, but I Still Try to Sing About Love and War

"Sign of Love" is another song where Young expresses his feelings for Pegi ("when we're just walking and holding hands, you can take it as a sign of love"). He also sneaks in a rather sweet nod to "Cinnamon Girl" here. During the line "when the music played, I watched you dance," you'll probably find yourself anticipating the power chords of that particular classic just as much I did.

In the same way that Lanois's sonic treatments of Young's blasting electric power chords add stunning new dimensions to that side of his sound (even without Crazy Horse or any eighteen-minute guitar solos), the two acoustic songs here serve as a reminder of just how good Young can be with the amps turned back down.

On both "Love and War" and "Peaceful Valley Boulevard," Lanois's recording brings out the deeper, darker bass tones as well as the lighter, more finessed flamenco tones of Young's acoustic guitar playing in a way you've never quite heard before.

Even so, Lanois's electronic "treatments" on the acoustic songs are another reason this album needs to be played extremely loud. On my own first listen, I found myself being jerked out of my seat wondering just what those odd noises I was hearing were. At one point, I even thought one of the neighbor cats was scratching on my window. The closest thing I could compare it to is the crackling fire heard on "Will to Love" from the *American Stars and Bars* album. Needless to say, these sonic treatments are about as organically real-sounding as it gets.

Of the two acoustic songs, "Love and War" is the more politically themed— although the antiwar sentiments expressed here are much lighter in tone than the bludgeoning over the head of Young's 2006 firecracker *Living with War*. As with "The Hitchhiker," he also waxes both autobiographical ("I sang songs about war since the backstreets of Toronto") and even regretful ("I sang about justice and I hit a bad chord, but I still try to sing about love and war").

"Peaceful Valley Boulevard," on the other hand, is much broader in its subject matter. In the same way "The Hitchhiker" plays like a glimpse into his personal journal, "Peaceful Valley Boulevard" is filled with the sort of cinematic, historically minded imagery Young is simply unmatched at.

From scenes where "shots rang out" and "the bullets hit the bison from the train" in a Wild West Kansas City, to more modern images where an "electro cruiser coasted toward the exit, and turned on Peaceful Valley Boulevard," the common thread between mining for gold and oil is God's tears thundering down like rain.

Just when you least expected it, Young has delivered yet another masterpiece with 2010's *Le Noise*. Even at this late stage of his career, his ability to create yet another game-changing record never ceases to astonish.

In that regard, he stands mostly alone amongst his musical peers of the sixties generation. Dylan and Springsteen are really the only other guys who even come close.

41

Buffalo Springfield Again

Holding Our Breath with Our Eyes Closed

On September 23, 2010, one of the most anticipated reunions in rock-'n'-roll history took place at the 24th annual Bridge School concert, held at Mountain View, California's Shoreline Amphitheatre.

Rock 'n' roll's most famous split ever, of course, remains that of the Beatles. The music history books have long since rewritten that story many times over, recasting it with as many villains—it seems that everyone from Yoko Ono to Allen Klein owns a piece of the blame there—as there are conspiracy theories as to what actually happened way back in 1970.

But from the moment the Beatles' breakup actually happened, the release of Paul McCartney's solo album has been most often identified as the singular event that really signaled the end of the greatest musical phenomenon of the twentieth century. As a result—rightly or otherwise—McCartney is also historically looked back upon as the Beatle with the black hat who actually broke up the band.

In the case of Buffalo Springfield, there were certainly just as many factors—and villains—that contributed to that group's premature demise in 1968. But in the same way that McCartney has become—perhaps somewhat unfairly—regarded as the man who broke up the Beatles, Neil Young has just as often been singled out as the key, combustible element in the ultimate implosion of the Buffalo Springfield.

In Young's case, unlike that of McCartney, much of the blame is probably justified. Before leaving Buffalo Springfield for good and releasing his own first solo album, Young had already walked out on the group more times than one could possibly count—most famously on the eve of the band's potentially star-making appearance at the 1967 Monterey Pop Festival (where his spot was hastily filled by the Byrds' David Crosby).

Many of Young's most notable contributions to Buffalo Springfield— "Expecting to Fly," "Broken Arrow," and "I Am a Child" among them—are also essentially solo recordings.

But where any hopes for a Beatles reunion were forever dashed by the deaths of John Lennon and George Harrison, Neil Young, Stephen Stills, and Richie Furay have all survived long enough—and quite inexplicably in many ways—to escape the trick of disaster and fulfill the dreams of Buffalo Springfield fans with a reunion. Those dreams became reality at 2010's Bridge School show.

Richie Furay and Neil Young onstage at Bonnaroo 2011 during the short-lived Buffalo Springfield reunion tour.   *Photo by Mary Andrews*

Amazingly, it's been even longer since original Buffalo Springfield members Young, Stills and Furay have shared a public stage or recording studio together than the Beatles—forty-two years to be exact. To put this in perspective, Lyndon Baines Johnson was President when Buffalo Springfield released their final album.

Not that there haven't been rumors along the way.

When Young recorded the song "Buffalo Springfield Again" on his 2000 album *Silver and Gold*, for example, speculation about a Springfield tour ran high (Young reunited with Crosby, Stills, and Nash instead, although rumors of a private Buffalo Springfield jam also taking place persist to this day).

When Buffalo Springfield were inducted into the Rock and Roll Hall of Fame in 1997, there was talk about a surprise reunion jam for the ceremony. This was put to rest when Young famously no-showed the ceremony (prompting Stills's equally famous onstage comment "he quit again").

On the Way Home

Buffalo Springfield nostalgia had already been running quite high when surviving members Young, Stills, and Furay (joined by bassist Rick Rosas and drummer Joe Vitale, filling in for departed band members Bruce Palmer and Dewey Martin respectively) reunited for the 2010 Bridge benefit show. Earlier that year, at the MusiCares ceremony honoring Neil Young as its Person of the Year, the musical highlight of the evening was Wilco's dead-on version of "Broken Arrow," the early solo Young recording that made its debut appearance on a Buffalo Springfield album.

For their historic reunion, Buffalo Springfield took to the Shoreline Amphitheatre stage with a letter-perfect "On the Way Home." The early Neil Young original was beautifully sung by Richie Furay, just as it had been on Buffalo Springfield's groundbreaking original single.

From there, time seemed to come to a standstill as the set continued on with letter-perfect renderings of original Springfield hits "Mr. Soul," "Burned," "For What It's Worth," and a stunning version of Young's "Nowadays Clancy Can't Even Sing."

Fortunately for fans, the good vibes of the Bridge School reunion did not end there.

2011 found Neil Young continuing to promote the *Le Noise* album by extending the solo *Twisted Road* shows from the prior year, and preparing for the release of the lost International Harvesters album *A Treasure*.

Meanwhile, plans for more Buffalo Springfield concerts were soon announced, including an appearance at the annual Tennessee Bonnaroo festival, with a more extended run of American dates in the fall of 2011 expected to follow. Assuming the loose threads holding together the reunion many never expected to see remain in place, fans who missed them the first time around should be seeing "Buffalo Springfield Again" in 2011 after all.

Footnote: Plans for a more extended run of Buffalo Springfield tour dates were, as of this writing, put on hold as Neil Young announced plans to write his autobiography, which is expected to be published in the fall of 2012.

Stephen Stills, Richie Furay, Neil Young, and Rick "the Bass Player" Rosas locked into a groove with Buffalo Springfield at Bonnaroo 2011.   *Photo by Mary Andrews*

42

Words (Between the Lines of Age)

What Other Artists Have to Say About Neil Young

As one of the most influential musical artists of the twentieth century, Neil Young's work has obviously drawn a broad range of comments from his artistic peers, particularly in the rock-'n'-roll community.

These range from the artists he has played with (CSN&Y, Buffalo Springfield, etc.) to those he shares an iconic connection with as a legend (Dylan, McCartney, Joni Mitchell, etc.).

Of course, there are also those younger-generation musicians—particularly in the punk and alternative-rock arenas—upon whom Neil Young has had a profound influence (Radiohead, Wilco, Pearl Jam, the Jayhawks, Sonic Youth, and even Metallica, being not the least of them).

And the list goes on.

Obviously, not all of these great quotes could be reproduced here. But what follows is a short collection of some of our favorite quotes by his peers in the rock-'n'-roll community describing their feelings about the ultimately enduring enigma that is Neil Young.

Most are complimentary, although we simply couldn't resist injecting a few of the more humorous ones as well (see Glenn Frey's analogy between art and a dog on Neil Young's porch, below). We also got a chuckle from Bob Dylan's simple two-word response upon hearing that Young was doing a rockabilly album ("That figures"). That one remains our personal favorite, so we'll get it out of the way right here.

In the meantime, enjoy the rest of these—some of our favorite comments from Neil Young's peers regarding his continuing influence. At this point, it is also prudent that we acknowledge (once again) the Internet site Thrasher's Wheat as an invaluable resource in pulling this collection together.

"He's taught us a lot as a band about dignity and commitment and playing in the moment and when I hear, you know, the speeches and inducting Janis Joplin and Frank Zappa, I get, uh, I'm just really glad he's still here. And I think I'm gonna have to say that I don't know if there's been another artist that has been inducted into the Rock 'n' Roll Hall of Fame to commemorate a career that is still as vital as he is today. Some of his best songs were on his last record."

—Eddie Vedder (Pearl Jam)
1995 Speech Inducting Neil Young into the Rock and Roll Hall of Fame

"Art is just a dog on Neil Young's porch."

—Glenn Frey (the Eagles)
Rolling Stone interview

"I always liked Neil Young, but it bothered me every time I listened to 'Heart of Gold.' I think it was up at number one for a long time, and I'd say, 'Shit, that's me. If it sounds like me, it should as well be me.' I used to hate it when it came on the radio."

—Bob Dylan
Uncut magazine interview

"I saw Neil Young live a few years ago (for €105) playing a solo acoustic gig and it was amazing, he just rolled along swallowing up drunk clapping hecklers and ignoring Bono who sat over there and tapping his feet and bobbing his neck and explaining the songs and Greendale and Grandpa and then he played this song ('After the Gold Rush') but he changed the lyrics to 'Look at Mother Nature on the run/in the twenty-first century' and still wow."

—Thom Yorke (Radiohead)
Thrasher's Wheat/Neil Young News

"He's right up there in terms of a constant in my musical life as an influence and as a mentor. He's kind of just a force of nature. And I take him for granted sometimes like I take the sun for granted . . . I'm really happy the sun comes up every day and I'm happy Neil Young keeps making records."

—Jeff Tweedy (Wilco)
The Canadian Press on Neil Young being honored as
2010 MusiCares Person of the Year

"I've seen a lot of people win Grammys that have gone on to really disappoint after that and then I have seen a lot of people that have not won any Grammys, and I guess Neil's a perfect example, who continue to have honesty and integrity and strive to connect with the world in a totally unique way, and I am excited that they are finally honoring him tonight then."

—Josh Groban
AP Wire story on Neil Young being named 2010 MusiCares Person of the Year

"He seemed to marry folk music and country music and for me, where I was from in Missouri, it really sort of set me on course as far as a songwriter goes, and he also managed to interject really socially, politically, moving lyrics into rock songs and he still is for me the template that I hold up and hope to eventually accomplish the things that he's done."

—Sheryl Crow
AP Wire story on Neil Young being named 2010 MusiCares Person of the Year

"He's a huge influence on me. His music is heartfelt. He's always exploring and pushing the envelope."

—Booker T. Jones (Booker T. and the MGs)
Vancouver Sun

"His songwriting is the stuff. You hear his music and you know that's the stuff."

—James Taylor
Vancouver Sun

"Neil Young's singular use of language is what amazes me. It really raises the bar. Nobody but Neil would say, 'When you dance, I can really love.' He's got this powerful way of carving language in very simple blocks of meaning that go right to the core of you."

—Jackson Browne
Vancouver Sun

"Playing with Neil is very intense, and very exciting. He leans forward into what's possible, all the time. He's powerful. He's got a lot of juice."

—David Crosby
UK magazine *Record Collector* (September 2001)

"There's a rare contradiction in Neil Young's work. He works so hard as a songwriter, and he's written a phenomenal number of perfect songs. And, at the same time, he doesn't give a fuck. That comes from caring about essence. There can be things out of tune and all wild-sounding and not recorded meticulously. And he doesn't care. He's made whole albums that aren't great, and instead of going back to a formula that he knows works, he would rather represent where he is at the time. That's what's so awesome: watching his career wax and wane according to the truth of his character at the moment. It's never phony. It's always real. The truth is not always perfect."

—Flea (Red Hot Chili Peppers)
Rolling Stone article "The Immortals: 50 Greatest Artists of All Time"

"There's youthful redemption in everything he does, a joyfulness about being an independent thinker in America."

—David Bowie
Thrasher's Wheat/Powell's Books

"It's not about chops (technique) with Neil, even though he's a great guitar player. The guy just inhabits the damn music. It doesn't matter if he looks like Ebenezer Scrooge, the truth is he still kicks arse. When some 12-year-old kid sees that, he's going to remember and one day he's going to play like Neil Young, not like some wuss."

—Bonnie Raitt
The Australian

"Neil's a great musician, he's very eccentric, eclectic and has a beautiful, haunting voice. But you know what? All of those things are a distant second to being an amazing, amazing songwriter. The same thing could be said about Bruce Springsteen. When you combine the words with the melody and the music, it's a power that everything emanates from. They happen to be amazing singers and musicians, but if they weren't, they couldn't ruin those songs. They would still be part of our emotional landscape and be just as powerful. You can't hurt songs that good."

—Nils Lofgren
Thrasher's Wheat/Shine Silently

"Here's an artist that is one of the great voices, both literally and figuratively, of rock 'n' roll, of American music, of world music, who has never stopped, as he says, following the muse. Everything goes into the music. And he gets an idea and he trusts that idea and he follows it. And he has had the success and made the money to be able to do it, but everything has gone back into the well."

—Emmylou Harris
Blogcritics magazine

"Most people did their best work when they were younger. Neil Young is as good as he ever was, which is quite an accomplishment . . . It seems like there's no tricks to him. I don't know if you could name anybody better who came out of rock and roll."
—Randy Newman
Powell's Books

"Pegi and Neil are amazing people, and I'm honored to be presenting this award, and I just wanna say how important [Neil's] music is and the world that he's created. It's made a big impact on myself and a lot of people I know."
—Beck
MTV News on an award he presented to Neil and Pegi Young for their charitable work on causes like Farm Aid and the Bridge School at Rock the Vote's Sixth Annual Patrick Lippert Awards

"What's cool about Neil is that he never hesitates to try whatever it takes to get his point across musically. Whether it's just him on acoustic guitar, him solo on the piano, or with Crazy Horse, it seems that he will find the best way to play the song, whether its grungy or doo-wop . . . he always finds the best way to serve his music."
—Kirk Hammett (Metallica)
Mojo magazine article, February 2011 "The 50 Greatest Neil Young Songs"

Selected Bibliography

Although the source material used in this book was drawn from a wide variety of both printed and Internet resources, there are a few that need to be singled out for specific thanks, as it could not have been completed without them.

As a historical resource, Jimmy McDonough's semiofficial Neil Young biography *Shakey* is simply unmatched in terms of little-known, often obscure details. It also served as an essential fact checker over the course of compiling the information here. Daniel Durchholz and Gary Graff's *Long May You Run: The Illustrated History* also proved invaluable, particularly when it came to obtaining Billboard peak chart positions for Young's many albums and checking release dates.

As for Internet resources, Human Highway.com was my go-to place to check lyrical references. Thrasher's Wheat/Neil Young News was likewise a daily must-visit in keeping up with all the latest developments in the ever-changing Neil Young universe (causing me to rewrite entire chapters more than once). Thrasher himself also proved to be a very supportive partner in this process, feeding me lots of information and playing a pivotal role in helping me to obtain some of the amazing images in this book by posting the need for them on his site. Without his partnership and counsel, the book you now hold in your hands simply would not have been possible.

What follows is a very select list of those resources used for *Neil Young FAQ*.

Books

Browne, David. *Fire and Rain: The Beatles, Simon & Garfunkel, James Taylor, CSNY and the Lost Story of 1970*. Cambridge, MA: Da Capo Press, 2011.

Durchholz, Daniel, and Gary Graff. *Long May You Run: The Illustrated Biography*. Minneapolis: Voyageur Press, 2010.

Goodman, Fred. *The Mansion on the Hill: Dylan, Young, Geffen, Springsteen, and the Head-On Collision of Rock and Commerce*. New York: Vintage Books, 1997.

Hoskyns, Barney. *Waiting for the Sun: A Rock 'n' Roll History of Los Angeles*. Milwaukee, WI: Backbeat Books, 2009.

Hoskyns, Barney. *Hotel California: The True-Life Adventures of Crosby, Stills, Nash, Young, Mitchell, Taylor, Browne, Ronstadt, Geffen, the Eagles, and Their Many Friends*. Hoboken, NJ: Wiley, 2007.

McDonough, Jimmy. *Shakey*. New York: Random House, 2002.

Young, Astrid. *Being Young*. London, Canada: Insomniac Press, 2008.

Young, Scott. *Neil and Me*. Toronto: McCelland & Stewart, 2006.

Zimmer, Dave. *Crosby, Stills & Nash: The Biography*. Cambridge, MA: Da Capo Press, 2008.

Magazines

Rolling Stone

Musician

Guitar Player

Guitar World

Guitar World Acoustic

Billboard

American Songwriter: Jaan Uhelszki Interview with Neil Young and Daniel Lanois (December 2010, Nashville, TN).
http://www.americansongwriter.com/2010/12/neil-young-with-daniel-lanois-love-and-war/

Uncut: The Fifty Greatest Lost Albums (May 2010, U.K.).
http://www.uncut.com

Mojo: Neil Young Tribute Issue (February 2011, U.K.).
http://www.mojo4music.com/

Guitar Legends: Neil Young Tribute Issue #118 (2011, New York)

Websites

Neil Young's Official Site
http://www.neilyoung.com/

Neil Young Times
http://www.neilyoung.com/news/index.html

Thrasher's Wheat/Neil Young News
http://neilyoungnews.thrasherswheat.org/

Blogcritics magazine
http://blogcritics.org/music/

Human Highway
http://human-highway.com/lyrics/albums.html

Hyperrust
http://hyperrust.org/

Rust Radio
http://www.rustradio.org/

Sugar Mountain—Neil Young Set lists
http://www.sugarmtn.org/

Cameron Crowe's Neil Young Articles
http://www.theuncool.com/journalism/articles/crowe_jrl_eagles_chip.html

The Covers Project
http://www.coversproject.com/artist/Neil+Young

Purple Words on a Grey Background
http://purplewordsonagreybackground.blogspot.com/

Broken Arrow/Neil Young Appreciation Society
http://www.nyas.org.uk/

Index